Frontier Calgary

Town, City, and Region
1875-1914

Edited by Anthony W. Rasporich
and Henry C. Klassen

University of Calgary
McClelland and Stewart West

Copyright © 1975 by University of Calgary

All rights reserved

ISBN 0-7712-1017-5

McClelland and Stewart West
Calgary, Alberta

Printed and bound in Canada

EDITORS' PREFACE

This collection of essays on early Calgary history began as a question posed by the executive officers of the Chinook Country Chapter of the Historical Society of Alberta. How might the Society, in conjunction with the Department of History at The University of Calgary, best celebrate Calgary's forthcoming centennial in 1975? Various projects were discussed, and the most promising seemed to be a jointly sponsored conference on the history of frontier Calgary. The History Department had long experience in organizing the annual Western Canadian Studies Conference, and the executive of the Historical Society could pledge the support of its membership to the project. There was little doubt that many citizens of Calgary would be interested in the early history of their community and would come to the conference or read its printed proceedings. The next and most crucial question was—were there enough people with something new and interesting to contribute? The program committee, which consisted of David Coutts and Grant Weber of the Chinook Country Chapter and Henry Klassen and Anthony Rasporich of the Department of History, concluded that there were.

Calgary may in fact be unique among Canadian cities today for the number of those involved in the writing of history and the quality of its historical enterprise. For years, Grant MacEwan, James Gray, and Hugh Dempsey have written prolific, indeed prodigious, amounts on aspects of the regional history of Western Canada and on topics touching the history of Calgary. And in recent years, the University has sent faculty and students in increasing numbers to use the excellent documentary collection at the Glenbow Archives as source material for these and other essays on the urban history of Calgary. In addition, there were a larger number of local citizens who, perhaps inspired by Canada's centennial in 1967, had resolved to celebrate their own community's hundredth birthday by exploring some aspect of her history. In short, there were enough writers and educators, archivists and librarians, professors and graduate students, upon whom the committee could draw for material.

The resulting conference on the history of frontier Calgary, held in May of this year, was a gratifying tribute to the city's centennial. The speakers were prompt and to the point. The record for brevity probably belonged to the keynote speaker, Grant Mac-Ewan, who bolted from the stage when reminded that his time was up and left his audience delightfully suspended with a friendly wave and terse farewell rejoinder, "That's it!" Others were even courageous, as was George Stanley during his banquet address which was challenged by a vigorous rock band in an adjoining room. He coolly held his ground and his audience with the more sedate subject of Viscount Richard Bedford Bennett's early Calgary years. Yet other moments were pure Hollywood entertainment, such as the film of the *Calgary Stampede* of 1925 starring Hoot Gibson, which was so ably introduced by Georgeen Barrass of the Glenbow Archives.

For whatever successes the conference could claim, the program committee must accept collective credit, and, of course, responsibility for its flaws as well. But there are a number of individuals whom it must thank for their support—first and foremost the membership of the Historical Society which supported the enterprise with its numerous registrations. Secondly, we are indebted to those who assisted in its organization: to Liesbeth von Wolzogen and her staff at the Department of History who handled the pre-registration and hospitality arrangements so well; to conference helpers from the Historical Society, Bonnie Lemay and Diane Keats; and to Grace Turner, Treasurer, for her prompt care of financial arrangements. Our thanks must also be extended to John Charyk of Hanna, Alberta, who had consented to deliver a paper at the conference, but was prevented from delivering it because of illness. Thanks are due as well to the Public Relations staff at The University of Calgary for their help in advertising the conference, particularly to Maura Kadutski and Beverley Foy.

Thanks are also due to those who were involved in the second stage of this project, which resulted in the appearance of this volume. This book of proceedings would not have been possible without the generous financial support of The University of Calgary, part of the Office of Research Grants which expedited the request. The generous publications grant which it bestowed upon the manuscript allowed the entire proceedings to appear at a reasonable price to readers and subscribers from the Historical Society. To others involved in the technical production of the book we are also indebted. To Doreen Nordquist, who typed a flawless manuscript, with such prompt regard for editorial deadlines, our foremost gratitude is extended. Credit must also be extended to the Graphics section of Com-Media at the University for the initial conference poster upon which the cover design is based, and to the Glenbow Archives photographic section and Miss Alison Jackson for the original illustrations which adorn this book and its cover. Finally, our thanks are due to David and Rose Scollard of McClelland and Stewart West for their prescient editorial advice and guidance.

In lieu of a formal dedication of this volume, the editors would like to thank directly their co-producers in this enterprise, David Coutts, President of the Chinook Country Chapter of the Historical Society of Alberta, and Grant Weber, the President of the Historical Society of Alberta. We shared many good hours in the planning of this centennial project.

Anthony W. Rasporich
Henry C. Klassen

Calgary, 1975

INTRODUCTION

A.W. Rasporich

The picture of frontier Calgary which follows pretends neither to completeness nor to a single perspective. It is a multi-faceted approach to the development of a small frontier ranching town into a cosmopolitan urban environment in the short space of a generation. It is also dedicated to the proposition that professionals and amateurs share equal place in the same craft of local history. The former lend the breadth of generalization to urban development and its relation to metropolitan and frontier influences, and the latter develop the particular context of community life, with its manners and institutions. Both the broader and the closer weave of larger theme and local colour attempt to give a multi-dimensional view of a town and city in transition.

Physically, the community had moved from a small shack-town at the confluence of two rivers to a proud sandstone city of nearly sixty thousand people on the eve of the Great War. While the spatial and structural features of growth were startling, the psychological and cultural transformation was equally profound. In the eighteen seventies and eighties, Calgary was a frontier garrison town peering through the chinks of its wooden armour at hostile forces without—at Indians stealing cattle; at its ranching competitor, Fort Macleod; at the outside world of territorial and national government in Regina and Ottawa; and at the alien forces of immigration and settlement. It had a small-town garrison mentality which resulted in such public explosions against Ottawa as occurred against Stipendiary Magistrate Travis in 1885 for his sentencing of a town councillor who allegedly assaulted a mounted policeman. And it would finally explode in 1892 with racial violence against the local Chinese, who were suspected of a nefarious plot to exterminate Calgary's white population.

Yet by 1914 Calgary was a mature cosmopolitan community,

incapable of certain identification from other North American and European cities at its central core. It exuded a sense of Edwardian optimism, as one glance at the cover photograph of "Handsome Dan" Finlayson and the plumed Victorian matron visually attests. It was only the second city in western Canada to have a Planning Commission and a vision of its future, however grandiose, in the Mawson Plan. Calgary was no longer the closed quasi-rural community of thirty years past, but an open city of commerce, speculation, and rugged free enterprise.

It was also a scene of highly conflicting styles. On the one hand, it could contain, if not satisfy, the nascent economic ambitions of a young R.B. Bennett, yet endure the urbane and occasionally savage satire of a Bob Edwards. Other social contrasts are suggested in the feminist vision and prohibitionist crusade of Nellie McClung and the social pretensions she saw about her on the slopes of Mount Royal. There are others as well: Chief Cuddy's zealous vice raids on the newly relocated Chinatown; the working-class suburbs of Ogden, Germantown, and East Calgary, and the projected middle-class suburbia of Tuxedo Gardens, North Bronx, and Lakeview Park; and finally, the integration of Calgary into the North American economy, which began to suggest itself in the Stampede of 1912, the Dingman well in Turner Valley, and the Board of Trade's advertisement of Calgary as the "Denver of the North." Such images and symbols contrasted visibly with the older Anglo-Canadian Calgary, which identified so strongly with imperial loyalties, institutions, and traditions.

What had happened to produce such a transformation within the short space of a generation? The chapters of this book attempt an explanation in part by exploring the dimensions of physical and social growth of early Calgary. They address themselves variously to the institutions and personalities which were most characteristic of this transition, and to the underlying economic forces which predetermined Calgary's evolution from military outpost to commercial centre of south central Alberta.

The chapters may be divided into several themes: Calgary's early founding; the ranching community surrounding Calgary; social history and minorities; the churches and education; real estate and early building; and economic development and political life. The following is a summary of the topics and a brief introduction to the authors.

The first two chapters are intended as an overview of Calgary's early history. The first by Grant MacEwan, former Lieutenant-Governor and currently Adjunct Professor of History at The University of Calgary, treats the keynote theme of town and country relationships which typified the unique character of frontier Calgary. The second is by Janice Dickin McGinnis, a doctoral student in history at the University of Alberta and formerly a researcher for the historical buildings inventory conducted by the federal branch of Parks Canada. Its theme, "Birth to Boom to Bust", traces the physical development of Calgary's buildings over the forty years from 1875 to 1914. Both papers address themselves to key aspects of Calgary's fundamental character, both as a town with blurred lines of demarcation between rural and urban people, and as a slowly developing urban organism which suddenly became a mature city in the first decade of the twentieth century. The reader's visual sense of Calgary's architectural growth during the frontier period is assisted by illustrations of early domestic and public buildings provided by Alison Jackson. Formerly of the Calgary Public Library, Miss Jackson has selected a few of the representative pieces of Calgary's architecture from the many others in her extensive private collection which formed the basis of her illuminating conference lecture.

The next pair of chapters deal with two important themes in the founding of Calgary. The first, by Brian Reeves of the Department of Archaeology at The University of Calgary, treats the subject of prehistoric uses of the Calgary vicinity to the plains Indians who occupied the Bow and Elbow valleys. The second, by Hugh Dempsey, the Director of History at Glenbow-Alberta Institute, addresses itself to the subject of Inspector Ephrem Brisebois of the NWMP and his place in the early struggle for the naming of the fort which occupied the junction of the two rivers.

The following cluster of four chapters deals with the ranching community, a subject integral to any history of frontier Calgary. The first, by Simon Evans, a doctoral candidate in the Department of Geography at The University of Calgary, deals with the establishment of the range cattle industry in the period 1882-92 by the Macdonald government, and Calgary's development as the central place of the industry in southern Alberta. The following chapter by Sheilagh Jameson, Archivist at Glenbow-Alberta Institute, delightfully traces the unique social character of the small ranching community to the west of Calgary. It is supplemented in the following treatment of the literature of the ranching community by Ermeline Ference, Chief Archivist with the Provincial Archives of the Province of Alberta. A somewhat neglected theme by John Jennings, a doctoral student in history at the University of Toronto, rounds out this section. It traces the inter-relationship between the ranchers, the Mounted Police, and the Indians, particularly on the thorny question of cattle stealing, which was a constant temptation after the disappearance of the buffalo from the range.

The next three chapters, all by graduate students at The University of Calgary, bring to light neglected aspects in the social history of early Calgary. The first, by Tom Thorner, a graduate student in the Department of History, treats somewhat differently than the previous chapter the question of law and order in the frontier society in and around Calgary, seeing as it does the troubled waters of social discontent and inequities within a primitive legal system. The second, by Catherine Philip, a freelance journalist and student with the Committee for Resources and the Environment, examines the day-to-day social life of women in the frontier city. The third chapter in this section was added after the conference had taken place, since its research was still in process while the original proceedings transpired. Written by Brian Dawson, also a graduate student in the Department of History, it treats the neglected subject of the Chinese, a much maligned and often violently treated minority.

Following these are two further chapters in the social history of education, by Douglas Coats and Robert Stamp. Douglas Coats, a former honours student in history and currently a teacher with the Calgary Board of Education, offers a thorough discussion of six private schools in the city and their substantial impact on early education before their decline during and after the First World War. A reflection of the suddenly acquired wealth of an emergent business elite, the private schools imparted a formative and unique character to the upper stratum of Calgary society. The middle and lower end of the social spectrum is discussed by Robert Stamp, a professor in the Department of Educational Foundations and author of a forthcoming study of public education in Calgary. He identifies five phases in the education of public school children, beginning with voluntary and private approaches to education in the eighteen seventies and eighties. Gradually, public schooling evolved into a complex urban school system by 1914, thereby compressing a century of eastern growth into a few short decades.

The churches of south-central Alberta and Calgary are the subject of the next three chapters. Without a doubt, they wielded great influence in the nineteenth century when church and state were closely intertwined, and the churches were the foremost pioneer institutions in their missionary function of converting the native peoples. Three churches, the Catholic, the Methodist, and the Anglican, and their maturation from missionary to urban churches, are the concern of this section. The Roman Catholic Church's story is told by Mrs. M.B. Byrne, author of the full-length book *From the Buffalo to the Cross*, which examines a century of development in the Diocese of Calgary. The Methodist Central Church congregation is the subject of Fraser Perry's chapter on the evolution of this "inner city" church which counted among its early lay leaders men like Bennett, Cushing and Lougheed. A public relations consultant in Calgary, Mr. Perry is currently involved as well in the writing of a full-length history of Central United Church over the past century. Calgary's early Anglicans are next discussed by the Very Reverend David Carter of the Cathedral Church of the Redeemer in central Calgary, who is the author of numerous publications on the history of the Anglican Church in southern Alberta.

The following pair of chapters deal with the neglected subject of Calgary's economic development. Max Foran, a Principal with the Calgary Board of Education and author of a forthcoming book for the National Museum on the history of Calgary, closely analyzes the intricacies of real estate speculation in Calgary before World War One. Its companion piece by Paul Voisey, a doctoral student at the University of Toronto, examines the early Calgary business elite as a corporate group on the model of other studies of larger Canadian business circles during the late nineteenth century. His study focusses upon forty of Calgary's most prominent businessmen, who were largely of humble eastern Canadian origins and who found great opportunity for economic and social advancement on the urban frontier of western Canada. Together, the two chapters provide fresh insights into the ascendancy of a propertied elite in the boom years of the early twentieth century.

The final essay, on Richard Bedford Bennett, is a summation, through the biographical approach, of Calgary's transition to a dynamic business community by 1914. Essentially a personal reminiscence of Bennett by George Stanley, Director of Canadian Studies at Mount Allison University, it distills a sense of the past as only biography can. Dr. Stanley's perspective as a native Calgarian puts flesh and blood and emotion, as Carlyle once said, onto the bare bones of history.

As a political biography the chapter also provides a counterpoint to the earlier essay by Hugh Dempsey on Ephrem Brisebois. French Canadian Conservatives had an important place to play in the early society of frontier Calgary, in the church, the Mounted Police, and among the official appointees of the Macdonald government in Ottawa. Times had indeed changed. For Bennett was a symbol of the Anglo-Canadian West and of imperial attitudes and loyalties which transcended eastern Canada and certainly Quebec. The Calgary of which he was the optimistic Edwardian expression would also pass into oblivion with the disillusionment of the war and profound democratization of politics in Alberta during the nineteen twenties and thirties.

The concluding essay by my co-editor, Henry Klassen, addresses itself to a noticeable gap in the conference proceedings. Where were the working men of frontier Calgary and what were their thoughts, feelings, and aspirations? The perspective of labour is thus added to round out the social history of the city. The development of a sense of class-consciousness marked a further dimension in the maturation of Calgary as a city by the early twentieth century.

CONTENTS

THE TOWN-COUNTRY BACKGROUND AT CALGARY

Grant MacEwan

I like the Town-Country theme, suggesting interdependence in the community. To an unfortunate extent we have segregated Canadians. It was easy to do it. Geography contributed to it. The Maritimes were like occupants of an apartment suite with a front entrance only, Ontario and Quebec with a side entrance, British Columbia with a back entrance, the Midwest with its only entrance through another suite and the Yukon and Northwest Territories in an attic suite with a fire-escape entrance. Great distances contributed to isolations and misunderstandings, and immigrants tended to segregate in ethnic groups.

Nor was that all. There was division, real and obvious, between farming and non-farming communities. The homesteader was a farmer, generally nothing else. The merchant was an urbanite and commonly nothing else. They lived miles apart and failed to know each other very well. I grew up with it. The MacEwans were farmers until they retired to live in the city and then they were city people pure and simple, until they moved back to the land when the change of status was again complete—no half measures. It was that way in most western Canadian communities, perhaps especially at Winnipeg where the civic image seemed to be determined by the Winnipeg Grain Exchange.

The point to be argued is that Calgary managed to escape the divisive force more than most cities. Perhaps it was the aura of the ranching country or of the Foothills, but in any case there was a distinctiveness about the pioneers who came to the Calgary area, and among other things they tended to erase the line of demarcation between the men of the street and the men of the soil. Many of the urban people held homesteads and many of the rural people retained business interests in the town. They were difficult to classify.

The earliest permanent residents in the area were farmers who were as much at home on Stephen Avenue as in their own fields—Sam Livingston and John Glenn for example—and the pattern persisted. But to start at the beginning, we see Inspector Ephrem Brisebois and his fifty mounted men of "F" Troop, NWMP, riding in on the north side of the Bow late in August, 1875, and pausing on a level site east of present-day Center Street Bridge, to consider a location for a night camp. The cross-river view was magnificent and the officer instructed Constable George Clift King to cross the Bow and determine if the attractive spot beside the mouth of the Elbow—or Swift as it was then known—would be suitable for a campground for the night. King crossed and replied with a signal to follow. The place was unoccupied except for a priest squatting in a tent, and Brisebois was impressed. He resolved almost at once to recommend this location for the new fort to be built. He was soon to discover that Livingston and Glenn were settling down nearby, and to his delight he found the ruins of a log structure which he chose to believe was the fabled Fort La Jonquière, built in 1751 by La Verendrye's people, three hundred leagues above the present site of The Pas, Manitoba. The exact location was long in doubt. Brisebois' wishful thinking is understandable but it seems appropriate at this point to explode the myth. The builders of La Jonquière, within the time schedule recorded in the French journals, could not have paddled against the current all the way from The Pas to the mouth of the Elbow and built the post; and besides, the local logs cut in 1751 would have rotted down long before 124 years had passed. It is now fairly clear from the researches of the late Professor A.S. Morton that La Jonquière was indeed the most westerly of all trading forts when built, but only by a few yards; cellars found two hundred yards west of the Fort La Corne site, north of Kinistino, Saskatchewan, are believed to be those of the mysterious La Jonquière.

Had Brisebois followed a mile or two up the Elbow he might have encountered the remains of a recent structure, the Fred Kanouse post built just four years earlier in 1871, an ill-fated fort which was not used very long. It was the setting for the so-called Battle of Elbow Park.

But Livingston and Glenn were very real, both Irishmen and both seasoned goldminers. Livingston, who was found squatting on the west side of the Elbow, was from the Vale of Avoka in Ireland. After sailing to New York he joined a wagon train crossing the continent to the gold diggings in California in 1849, and was thus a forty-niner. Later he was in gold rushes elsewhere, including the one to the Fraser River; from there he travelled over mountain passes to Fort Edmonton where he panned for gold, raised pigs, and acquired a wife. In 1873, thinking to settle down, he moved to the Elbow River, first to trade and then to decide upon farming. He was just starting to build a house when the Police found him and heard him magnanimously offer to move across the river, leaving the west side for the Police.

Sam Livingston was a colourful fellow and it would be wrong to try to identify him as either rural or urban; he was both and he was enterprising. He had fourteen children and had to build bigger houses. He ran the first cattle on the local grass and grew the first wheat and other grains. He furnished the cows for the first milk delivery and he planted the first fruit trees to be set out in the soil of southern Alberta. The Calgary *Tribune* of April 1, 1887, notes that "all the fruit trees he set out last year show signs of life so far." At the same time, Livingston was one of the founding fathers in the Calgary Agricultural Society which conducted the first fairs. He was one of Calgary's boosters.

Sam's friend and neighbour, John Glenn, experienced the same gold rushes and came into Alberta territory in company with the celebrated Kamoose Taylor, later proprietor of the Macleod Hotel. Settling beside Fish Creek, Glenn was named the first postmaster there and managed well enough, notwithstanding the fact that he couldn't read or write. Shorter and plumper than Livingston, Glenn was no less enterprising, and should be remembered as the first to conduct irrigation in what is now Alberta. It was in 1878 that he conducted water from Fish Creek to irrigate twenty acres of flat land on the east side of today's Number Two Highway at Midnapore. And making him urban as much as rural, there he was buying the first town lots in Calgary. When the first sale was held in December, 1883, John Glenn was one of the bigger purchasers, and obtained the lots at the corner of present-day Centre Street and Ninth Avenue, where the new Four Seasons hotel now stands.

Rev. John McDougall was one who was prominent in the seventies, and in addition to building a church in Calgary, he shared in bringing the first cattle to southern Alberta in 1873: twelve cows and a bull driven from Edmonton to Morley, marking McDougall as a man of wide interests. A.P. Patrick, surveyor, discoverer of oil at Pincher Creek in 1889, and homesteader outside of Calgary, was another who helped to break that barrier between urban and rural interests.

With the eighties, the trend continued. Senator Cochrane who was at home at the higher levels of government, is the one whose three thousand head of cattle—the first big herd to be brought to the area—were driven across the Elbow and Bow at Calgary in 1881, then on to graze at Big Hill beside today's Cochrane. Three years later, making the frontier town of Calgary look more and more like a ranchland crossroads, eight thousand Cochrane sheep were driven from Montana—six miles per day—to cross the rivers at Calgary.

Major James Walker, who had retired from the Mounted Police to become the Cochrane Ranch Manager, in 1883 resigned again to live in Calgary and be a builder in the broadest sense. He was the one chosen to head the first administrative committee before Calgary was incorporated; he was the president of the Agricultural Society when it conducted its first fair; and he was the person who "rescued" a visiting Deputy Minister of the Interior, A.M. Burgess, when the latter was rudely bucked from a horse while inspecting dominion lands at Fish Creek, then took advantage of the situation to extract an assurance from the recuperating official that the ninety-four acres Walker wanted from Section Ten would be made available for a Fair Ground at $2.50 per acre. It was the land which became Victoria Park and the home of the Calgary Stampede. And Walker, like so many others thereabout, filed on a homestead beside the Bow River and built handsomely and lived on it.

At the first election after the town was incorporated, New Brunswicker George Murdoch, who drove from Maple Creek ahead of the rails in 1883, was elected to be Mayor. Then he too homesteaded outside the City and lived on the homestead. Of course, he might have said. Why not?

Even Father Lacombe and Father Leduc—whatever their motives—homesteaded two quarters of the west half of Section Ten, embracing what became known as the Mission District. It was in 1883 that Father Lacombe travelled to Ottawa to confirm the homestead arrangements and, becoming impatient with Capital red tape, refused to leave the Minister's office until he received confirmation, cheerfully proclaiming his intention of simply camping in the office for as long as it would take to get a decision. Needless to say the decision was not long in coming.

There was General T.B. Strange, retired Imperial Army officer, who was ranching downstream on the Bow and was pressed into service to command the Southern Alberta Field Force in rebellion year, 1885, whose versatile interests and talents appeared rather typical for the area, just like the Big Four cattlemen—Burns, Lane, Cross, and MacLean. And just like Calgarian Augustus Carney who homesteaded and whose homestead land became Union Cemetery. It might have been claimed that Calgary was a community of homesteaders, a community of citizens who refused to be confined to either rural or urban category.

If more examples were required, there was Samuel Shaw and family from London, England, driving all the way from the end of the steel at Swift Current in 1883. Along with father and mother there were nine children. But instead of coming with their belongings in a Red River cart of buckboard, they had breeding cattle, sheep, hens, and ten tons of freight hauled by five pairs of oxen. Granted, they were not typical homesteaders or typical of any particular category. They were simply going to the frontier to make a new life to suit themselves, which happened to be Calgary style. Their goods at arrival included photographic equipment, sixteen guns, medical supplies, food for two years, equipment for telegraphic participation, and machinery with which to start a woollen mill. The Shaws built a mill as planned, started a school, and did everything good citizens might be expected to do.

They stood straddling that imaginary boundary separating town and farm people. And Calgary's leading lady—in point of notoriety—Mother Fulham, kept pigs. It is supposed to support the point that Calgary in its beginning had something distinctive in personality.

BIRTH TO BOOM TO BUST: BUILDING IN CALGARY 1875–1914

J.P. Dickin McGinnis

Canadians have, in recent years, been accused of being too modest about their architecture. Before that they were charged with being downright apathetic.[1] Inhabitants of Calgary around the turn of the century would never have understood this. Catapulting headlong from primitive forms of architecture such as tents and huts through frame construction and finally to stone mansions and skyscrapers,[2] Calgary went from birth to boom to bust in the building industry within forty years. Throughout the entire time, Calgarians were ecstatic with the buildings appearing on their skyline, the more and bigger the better. Some of these still stand and it is hoped that Calgarians can again work up a sufficient amount of ecstasy for them to save a few from the newer building boom the city is undergoing.

The original dwellings erected in the vicinity of present-day Calgary were tents, made largely of buffalo skins, belonging to Blackfoot Indians who favored the Douglas fir standing in groves along the river for the construction of their weapons (hence Bow River)[3] and who also appreciated the protection from winter winds afforded by the high banks of the river valley.[4] Their tee-pees could hardly be termed permanent structures. Neither could the camp erected by David Thompson, who wintered at the confluence of the Bow and Elbow rivers in 1787, nor that of Captain John Palliser, who passed through in 1858. A more substantial effort was made by Fred Kanouse, a whisky trader on leave from his position as Deputy Sheriff (later Sheriff) of Chouteau County, Montana, who set up a fort on the banks of the Elbow in 1871. However, his residence turned out to be rather short-lived.

A gunpowder explosion blew out one wall of his log cabin in 1872 and Kanouse decided to abandon his whisky trade and return south.[5] Within three years, settlers of an entirely different type again made an attempt at settlement. In the spring of 1875, Fathers Lacombe, Remus, and Scollen built an eight-foot by ten-foot log cabin on the banks of the Elbow River. The roof was of spruce bark and the doors and windows of buffalo skin. In the fall of 1875, when the NWMP arrived to establish the fort around which Calgary would eventually grow, a French-Canadian missionary, Father Léon Doucet, and an Indian boy were there, living in the tiny cabin, to greet them.[6]

Sent north from Fort Macleod on August 18, 1875 to establish order in the area, Inspector Brisebois and fifty Mounties probably followed the Old North or Whoop-Up Trail and finally gazed upon the future site of the settlement from the glacial moraine of the North Hill.[7] According to an account written thirty-four years later, the police were presented with a fairy-tale scene:[8]

Far to the west of them were innumerable foothills and to the east the open prairies while before them was a spacious valley through which two good sized rivers wound their way; the Bow coming from the west, the Swift from the southwest. The site of the present city of Calgary was covered with long grass and the numerous small lakes were literally swarming with wild fowl. The river banks were heavily timbered on the south side, the present Victoria Park was covered with large cottonwood trees as was a large island in the Swift which was washed away by the floods of 1885. A colony of beavers had built a large dam across the Swift and it had flooded much of the land south of the present Canadian Pacific Railway.

Two things should be noted about this passage. First of all, the Elbow River was interchangeably called the Swift during the early period. Secondly, the description is obviously embroidered. But even though it may not show what the mounties saw in 1875, it does express what Calgarians in 1909 wanted to believe they saw.

It was late in the season when "F" Troop arrived and their first concern was shelter. On the trek north, they had found tents insufficient and had dug trenches and built brush shelters to ward off the cold. Now they built huts to house six to eight men. Each encompassed a crude fireplace, but still they were cold. Nevertheless, these had to serve until the fort was constructed.[9]

The site chosen was on a piece of high ground at the forks of the rivers which provided natural protection on two sides. The building was not to be done by the Police but had been contracted to the famous I.G. Baker company from Fort Benton, Montana, which until the arrival of track, was the settlement's main link with civilization, albeit that of the United States.

The Baker men arrived in a few days and set off about six miles up the Elbow to cut dry pine logs. After the boom was floated down, fourteen-foot logs were placed upright in three-foot trenches to form the outer walls of the buildings, facing inward and forming a square of about one hundred and fifty to two hundred feet on the side. The men's quarters were on the east side, storerooms and shops on the west, stables for fifty horses to the north, and the officers' quarters and guardroom opposite. The walls were chinked with clay and roofs built of poles and earth. Métis, camped in the area, cut lumber for the doors and floors by whipsaw and the fireplaces were built by homesteader John Glenn of building stone taken from the river. The ten-foot palisade was not finished until later but the buildings were habitable by Christmas.[10]

Having brought the police in out of the cold, the Baker men next put up two cabins and a substantial hundred-foot-long log store, complete with billiard table, just south of the barracks, for their own use.[11] Shortly thereafter, the Hudson's Bay Company moved its Ghost River post further up the Bow and by Christmas, 1875, Calgary consisted of the fort, the two trading posts, and Doucet's mission.[12]

Within two months, the settlement was the most prosperous between Fort Macleod and Fort Edmonton. That may have amounted to something at the time but for five years Calgary grew at a painfully slow rate. Aside from the Police and the traders, the only settlers were the Métis brought in to work on the fort, who afterwards built log cabins on both sides of the Elbow and supported themselves by hauling freight in their Red River carts.[13] During this period, the affairs of the Mounted Police and of the trading companies dominated the life of the community. The latter traded for skins with the Indians while the former tried to settle them peacefully on reserves. This was pretty well accomplished by 1880, and the way was left open for white immigration.

The Dominion Lands Act had provided for free homesteads in the West in 1872[14] but it was not until 1881, when the federal government began to offer leases on up to one hundred thousand acres for one cent per acre per year for the purposes of cattle ranching,[15] that settlers began to pour into Calgary. The Baker company drove in the first big herd that year for Major James Walker, who had ordered three thousand head for the Cochrane Ranch on behalf of several eastern lessees. The first two years were fraught with problems, but these were mostly due to inexperience, and soon other ranchers followed suit.[16]

Early in 1881, one inhabitant, Frank White, noted in his diary that he had stood atop the North Hill and counted sixteen log shacks, nine teepees, and the fort.[17] The trappings of civilization began to move in that summer. George E. Jacques established himself as the first watchmaker west of Winnipeg and located his log cabin jewellery store near the barracks. The next year he brought out his wife, the first white woman in the settlement, for whom he bought the log cabin of the surveyor, McVittie. It was twelve by sixteen feet and had a dirt floor, a mud roof, a leather-hinged door and one window. It was furnished with a homemade bed complete with hay-stuffed mattress, a three-legged stool, two homemade benches and a trunk for a table. All cooking was done over an open fire.[18]

In the spring of 1883, a British traveller who later wrote a book called *Life and Labour in the Far, Far West* stayed at the Royal Hotel, a tent thirty feet by eighteen feet. He recorded forty to sixty tents and frame houses.[19] In May, George Murdoch, harness-maker and future mayor, arrived and soon put up the first sign in the settlement. S. Costello opened a furniture store and James C. Linton, the stationer, carried wallpaper. The photographer Cornelius J. Saule, also advertised himself as an architect and building superintendent. Walker, who had given up the managership of the Cochrane Ranch to set up a small sawmill, tried to stock timbers, doors, windows and builders' supplies, but he had a difficult time keeping ahead of his orders. There was even a firm entitled the "Plain and Artistic Sign and Showcard Writers". Obviously, building and its sidelines were beginning to become profitable businesses—the settlement was already beginning to live on its own growth. By November of that year, Calgary had a core of about twenty-four businesses housed in tents, log cabins, and frame houses on the east side of the Elbow, plus the fort and some other concerns on the west.[20]

None of the buildings were particularly substantial or permanent, which no doubt explains why it was so easy for the Canadian Pacific Railway to persuade Calgarians to abandon the original townsite. Track had reached the settlement in mid-August. Calgary had so far been situated on Section Fourteen, belonging to Captain Denny of the Police. However, the CPR owned Section Fifteen, and that was where it built its station, a twelve-foot by sixty-foot one-storey building with a large platform and freight and coal sheds. This was obviously not just a move for mere economy but one to pressure resettlement on CPR land, thereby bringing in money in addition to savings. Captain Denny complained but to no avail. There was as yet no traffic bridge across the Elbow. Crossing in winter was easy enough and in summer the river could be forded about one hundred yards up from the railway bridge. However, the periods between absolute thaw and absolute freeze-up presented more of a problem. The ice would hold the horse and vehicle so far and then plunge all in violently, causing considerable discomfort to the driver.[21] For concerns receiving goods by rail, frequent trips to the station presented a rather nasty prospect. If that were not persuasion enough, the CPR offered to donate land on its own section for a town hall and fire station.[22] Clearly, it would be a disadvantage to have these separated from the bulk of the community by a bridgeless river. Fate was sealed when someone tied a rope around the new post office and towed it across the frozen Elbow in the dark of night.[23] When the railway offered lots for sale at 450 dollars for corner lots and 350 dollars for all others on its new townsite (complete with such proper CPR street names as Stephen, Smith, and Van Horne[24]) in December, it had little trouble making sales. Shacks were towed over the ice and the first structure on the new townsite was a log cabin put up by Felix McHugh in what is now the heart of the downtown.[25] The Hudson's Bay Company built a new frame structure, one-storey, thirty-five by one hundred feet that was considered the finest store west of Winnipeg.[26] On 26 March 1884, the Calgary *Herald* (which had started printing as soon as its press was delivered by the railway near the end of August 1883) listed the major buildings in town. It considered thirty worth mentioning by name and hinted at the existence of "many others".[27]

By the end of that year the population had passed the one thousand mark, up from four hundred at the beginning. The area between McIntyre (Seventh) Avenue and Atlantic (Ninth) Avenue, facing the railway track and extending a few blocks east and west, was pretty well built up. The buildings were usually of frame construction, some painted but most simply tarpapered. They were usually one storey with straight fronts topped by large signs. Some were built right up to the street lines, others set back a few feet with hitching posts in front. Inside, they usually consisted of two rooms—one a shop, the other living quarters. As the buildings went up, the streets were graded and wooden sidewalks laid. The most imposing building was the Royal Hotel, considered to be the finest hotel west of Winnipeg, although, like most frontier hotels, its rooms were separated by factory cotton rather than walls. Calgarians were pretty proud of their little town. (In fact, rumour had it that the population figure had been padded to allow its incorporation as a town that year.) And even the fact that a visiting English traveller had referred to some of the edifices as huts[28] did not squelch the general fervor. Then the dream almost went up in smoke.

Fire had long been a topic of concern in Calgary. Not only were most of the buildings made of wood, the building boom meant that wood chips and sawdust were scattered around everywhere. On 12 March 1884, the question was brought up in Council and it was decided to engage a man to plough furrows around all the buildings. In an election in early July, one of the main platforms was the restriction of prairie fires, which were blamed on the CPR.[29] The first by-law, passed December 17, 1884, provided for the purchase of fire equipment and the erection of a fire hall as soon as finances permitted.[30] The first serious warning came on 18 January 1885 when the house of J.L. Bowen, valued at 575 dollars and located on Ninth Avenue, caught fire. Attempts by the crowd to extinguish the blaze with snowballs proved, not surprisingly, to be of no avail.[31] That August, the town finally abandoned the volunteer bucket brigade system and set up a hook and ladder company, a proper bucket corps, and ordered a chemical engine.[32] However, when the engine arrived, the town council was, as usual, chronically short of funds and it remained in the customs warehouse subject to unpaid duties. After all, it was not needed—at least not until the night of November 4, 1886, when fire broke out in S. Parrish's flour and feed store. Within minutes flames covered the entire block on the southwest corner of McTavish (Centre) Street and Atlantic Avenue. Matters grew more serious when the wind whipped them across the street to engulf the Union Hotel. By this time someone had had the presence of mind to break into the customs warehouse and free the new chemical engine, but, of course, no one had as yet learned how to operate it effectively. Soon the flames had reached the Grand Central hotel and were proceeding north towards the main business section, Stephen (Eighth) Avenue. An attempt was made to dynamite Murdoch's harness shop to form a fire break but that failed. Then, as a last resort, all attention was turned to saving the Royal Hotel, the largest building and most eminent hostelry in town. Wet blankets were spread on the roof and hung from the windows. The precautions were effective. The blaze failed to jump the alley and late on the morning of November 5, the danger was past. The community had suffered heavy losses. Gone were sixteen of its best buildings, including four stores, three warehouses, three hotels, one tinsmithy, and a saloon. The total damage was 100,200 dollars, less than one third of which was covered by insurance.[33] Calgary experienced more costly fires in later years but never again one that would threaten the entire settlement.

As a result of the fire, the fire department suggested an ordinance be passed stipulating that all large downtown buildings be built of sandstone.[34] This appealed to the populace, not only because of the fear of fire, but because it would make the town appear a little more substantial, bringing it a little closer into line with their dreams. They had great plans for their town, as is witnessed by the promotional literature they began to put out. The first business directory had appeared in 1885.[35] When a "delegation of practical farmers" came out from Arthabaska, Québec, a pamphlet celebrated their experiences.[36] Enumerations were made of the town's possibilities,[37] Colonel Walker wrote promotional pieces to a British newspaper,[38] the CPR sent out immigration material complete with testimonial letters,[39] and, even though the overland route was known to be dangerous, Calgary was touted as a major stop on the way to the Klondike.[40] Between 1888 and 1895, the population approximately tripled and construction averaged three hundred thousand dollars a year. In 1889, three large stone structures—the Alberta Hotel, the Bank of Montreal, and the Alexander Block—all went up on Stephen Avenue, and accounted alone for a quarter million dollars in building permits.[41] Building in Calgary was big business and soon the town was liberally serviced with architects, construction companies, stone quarries, brickworks, and other trappings which Calgarians gladly welcomed.

Up until the arrival of the railway, the only source of building materials, other than logs and animal skins, had been

Walker's mill established in 1881. He was a reasonable man and if a customer could not pay in full, Walker allowed him to work off the balance at the mill.[42] But by the spring of 1883, due to the boom preceding the arrival of the railway, Walker could not keep up. In October that year, he advertised for twenty carpenters at three dollars to three fifty per day to help fill orders that brought in fifty dollars for a thousand board feet.[43] When the move was made to the new townsite that winter, the demand became impossible. The CPR had promised a fifty percent rebate on the price of all lots which had inhabited buildings on them by April 1, 1884. Naturally everyone wanted the rebate and, naturally, the CPR was now there to deliver the lumber. But weeks went by and no lumber came and the company was accused of holding it up to avoid paying the rebates. Finally the lumber came through but it was still so expensive that many chose to establish themselves in less substantial quarters until the price came down.[44] Supply and price both improved somewhat when the Eau Claire Lumber Company came in from Wisconsin in 1886. The manager, Peter Prince, set up the mill across from what is now Prince's Island, blasted through the neck of connecting land, making the little peninsula truly an island, to give him a separate and controllable stream with which to run his mill, obtained leave to proceed up the Bow for timber and soon set into motion one of Calgary's most prosperous companies.[45]

At about the same time, other types of building material became available. The Catholic diocese of Calgary leased fifteen acres in what is now the Roxboro district just south of the Elbow to J.F. Peel and his partner, a Mr. Sparrow, on April 5, 1885, for the purposes of a brickyard. The clay in the area was claimed to be superior to any other in Canada except possibly for that found along the Ottawa River. At its height the yard employed fifteen men and ten horses and had a weekly payroll of three hundred dollars.[46] In 1893, two more small brickyards were set up and "Gravity" Watson established a brick and terra cotta works just outside the town limits.[47] He advertised his wares in his own lovely brick house that still stands on Ninth Street S.W. between Seventeenth and Cameron Avenues. The largest brick works was the Crandell Pressed Brick and Sandstone Co. By 1914 the plant was worth two hundred thousand dollars and produced 45,000 to 80,000 bricks per day. During the summer, seventy-five workers were employed and accommodation provided for them on the company's land. The only traces now remaining of this little

community are some rubble and the sign ""
CPR tracks.[48]

But by far the most prestigious building
stone, which was easily obtainable from the b
ing the town. It was in abundant supply, fai
"a very solid and substantial appearance" to
ture. In fact, these were the very words use
pamphlet which was willing to use anythin
stone, to convince the federal government to b
rium in Calgary.[49] The stone sold for twenty
the rubble for six. The blocks could be smooth
according to taste and the rubble used for fo
first quarry, which belonged to Wesley F. Or
town on the Bow in the year of the fire. Four
lished in short order, including John MacC
Freestone Quarry, a sample from which won
Chicago World's Fair in 1896. Over the yea
the Great War, at least six other quarries wer
gary area, the most important being the Gl
Cochrane, which at one time was surrounde
a population of five to six hundred people; t
blanc in the Shaganappi area, which provid
Calgary's finest buildings; and the Oliver
what is now the intersection of the Crowchi
teenth Avenue S.W. which employed four
prime.[50]

Most of the major buildings constructed
sandstone. Some are even still standing, alth
appeared in recent years. If one walks do
Eighth Avenue Mall and looks above the
marble fronts to the second and third storey
the very stone laid over seventy-five years a
whole block of these was torn out to make
vention Centre.[51] Among those still standing
Bank on the northeast corner of Eighth
Street, built in 1892 to house the first bank i
Calgary, now vacant; the 1891 Hudson's Ba
Street from the Imperial and which since 19
of the Royal Bank of Canada; and, rather a
Calgary's old buildings, the legendary Al
from its completion in 1889 for its one hun
foot bar, reduced by prohibition to an offic

government began to offer leases on up to one hundred thousand acres for one cent per acre per year for the purposes of cattle ranching,[15] that settlers began to pour into Calgary. The Baker company drove in the first big herd that year for Major James Walker, who had ordered three thousand head for the Cochrane Ranch on behalf of several eastern lessees. The first two years were fraught with problems, but these were mostly due to inexperience, and soon other ranchers followed suit.[16]

Early in 1881, one inhabitant, Frank White, noted in his diary that he had stood atop the North Hill and counted sixteen log shacks, nine teepees, and the fort.[17] The trappings of civilization began to move in that summer. George E. Jacques established himself as the first watchmaker west of Winnipeg and located his log cabin jewellery store near the barracks. The next year he brought out his wife, the first white woman in the settlement, for whom he bought the log cabin of the surveyor, McVittie. It was twelve by sixteen feet and had a dirt floor, a mud roof, a leather-hinged door and one window. It was furnished with a homemade bed complete with hay-stuffed mattress, a three-legged stool, two homemade benches and a trunk for a table. All cooking was done over an open fire.[18]

In the spring of 1883, a British traveller who later wrote a book called *Life and Labour in the Far, Far West* stayed at the Royal Hotel, a tent thirty feet by eighteen feet. He recorded forty to sixty tents and frame houses.[19] In May, George Murdoch, harness-maker and future mayor, arrived and soon put up the first sign in the settlement. S. Costello opened a furniture store and James C. Linton, the stationer, carried wallpaper. The photographer Cornelius J. Saule, also advertised himself as an architect and building superintendent. Walker, who had given up the managership of the Cochrane Ranch to set up a small sawmill, tried to stock timbers, doors, windows and builders' supplies, but he had a difficult time keeping ahead of his orders. There was even a firm entitled the "Plain and Artistic Sign and Showcard Writers". Obviously, building and its sidelines were beginning to become profitable businesses—the settlement was already beginning to live on its own growth. By November of that year, Calgary had a core of about twenty-four businesses housed in tents, log cabins, and frame houses on the east side of the Elbow, plus the fort and some other concerns on the west.[20]

None of the buildings were particularly substantial or permanent, which no doubt explains why it was so easy for the Canadian Pacific Railway to persuade Calgarians to abandon the original townsite. Track had reached the settlement in mid-August. Calgary had so far been situated on Section Fourteen, belonging to Captain Denny of the Police. However, the CPR owned Section Fifteen, and that was where it built its station, a twelve-foot by sixty-foot one-storey building with a large platform and freight and coal sheds. This was obviously not just a move for mere economy but one to pressure resettlement on CPR land, thereby bringing in money in addition to savings. Captain Denny complained but to no avail. There was as yet no traffic bridge across the Elbow. Crossing in winter was easy enough and in summer the river could be forded about one hundred yards up from the railway bridge. However, the periods between absolute thaw and absolute freeze-up presented more of a problem. The ice would hold the horse and vehicle so far and then plunge all in violently, causing considerable discomfort to the driver.[21] For concerns receiving goods by rail, frequent trips to the station presented a rather nasty prospect. If that were not persuasion enough, the CPR offered to donate land on its own section for a town hall and fire station.[22] Clearly, it would be a disadvantage to have these separated from the bulk of the community by a bridgeless river. Fate was sealed when someone tied a rope around the new post office and towed it across the frozen Elbow in the dark of night.[23] When the railway offered lots for sale at 450 dollars for corner lots and 350 dollars for all others on its new townsite (complete with such proper CPR street names as Stephen, Smith, and Van Horne[24]) in December, it had little trouble making sales. Shacks were towed over the ice and the first structure on the new townsite was a log cabin put up by Felix McHugh in what is now the heart of the downtown.[25] The Hudson's Bay Company built a new frame structure, one-storey, thirty-five by one hundred feet that was considered the finest store west of Winnipeg.[26] On 26 March 1884, the Calgary *Herald* (which had started printing as soon as its press was delivered by the railway near the end of August 1883) listed the major buildings in town. It considered thirty worth mentioning by name and hinted at the existence of "many others".[27]

By the end of that year the population had passed the one thousand mark, up from four hundred at the beginning. The area between McIntyre (Seventh) Avenue and Atlantic (Ninth) Avenue, facing the railway track and extending a few blocks east and west, was pretty well built up. The buildings were usually of frame construction, some painted but most simply tarpapered. They were usually one storey with straight fronts topped by large signs. Some were built right up to the street lines, others set back a few feet with hitching posts in front. Inside, they usually consisted of two rooms—one a shop, the other living quarters. As the buildings went up, the streets were graded and wooden sidewalks laid. The most imposing building was the Royal Hotel, considered to be the finest hotel west of Winnipeg, although, like most frontier hotels, its rooms were separated by factory cotton rather than walls. Calgarians were pretty proud of their little town. (In fact, rumour had it that the population figure had been padded to allow its incorporation as a town that year.) And even the fact that a visiting English traveller had referred to some of the edifices as huts[28] did not squelch the general fervor. Then the dream almost went up in smoke.

Fire had long been a topic of concern in Calgary. Not only were most of the buildings made of wood, the building boom meant that wood chips and sawdust were scattered around everywhere. On 12 March 1884, the question was brought up in Council and it was decided to engage a man to plough furrows around all the buildings. In an election in early July, one of the main platforms was the restriction of prairie fires, which were blamed on the CPR.[29] The first by-law, passed December 17, 1884, provided for the purchase of fire equipment and the erection of a fire hall as soon as finances permitted.[30] The first serious warning came on 18 January 1885 when the house of J.L. Bowen, valued at 575 dollars and located on Ninth Avenue, caught fire. Attempts by the crowd to extinguish the blaze with snowballs proved, not surprisingly, to be of no avail.[31] That August, the town finally abandoned the volunteer bucket brigade system and set up a hook and ladder company, a proper bucket corps, and ordered a chemical engine.[32] However, when the engine arrived, the town council was, as usual, chronically short of funds and it remained in the customs warehouse subject to unpaid duties. After all, it was not needed—at least not until the night of November 4, 1886, when fire broke out in S. Parrish's flour and feed store. Within minutes flames covered the entire block on the southwest corner of McTavish (Centre) Street and Atlantic Avenue. Matters grew more serious when the wind whipped them across the street to engulf the Union Hotel. By this time someone had had the presence of mind to break into the customs warehouse and free the new chemical engine, but, of course, no one had as yet learned how to operate it effectively. Soon the flames had reached the Grand Central hotel and were proceeding north towards the main business section, Stephen (Eighth) Avenue. An attempt was made to dynamite Murdoch's harness shop to form a fire break but that failed. Then, as a last resort, all attention was turned to saving the Royal Hotel, the largest building and most eminent hostelry in town. Wet blankets were spread on the roof and hung from the windows. The precautions were effective. The blaze failed to jump the alley and late on the morning of November 5, the danger was past. The community had suffered heavy losses. Gone were sixteen of its best buildings, including four stores, three warehouses, three hotels, one tinsmithy, and a saloon. The total damage was 100,200 dollars, less than one third of which was covered by insurance.[33] Calgary experienced more costly fires in later years but never again one that would threaten the entire settlement.

As a result of the fire, the fire department suggested an ordinance be passed stipulating that all large downtown buildings be built of sandstone.[34] This appealed to the populace, not only because of the fear of fire, but because it would make the town appear a little more substantial, bringing it a little closer into line with their dreams. They had great plans for their town, as is witnessed by the promotional literature they began to put out. The first business directory had appeared in 1885.[35] When a "delegation of practical farmers" came out from Arthabaska, Québec, a pamphlet celebrated their experiences.[36] Enumerations were made of the town's possibilities,[37] Colonel Walker wrote promotional pieces to a British newspaper,[38] the CPR sent out immigration material complete with testimonial letters,[39] and, even though the overland route was known to be dangerous, Calgary was touted as a major stop on the way to the Klondike.[40] Between 1888 and 1895, the population approximately tripled and construction averaged three hundred thousand dollars a year. In 1889, three large stone structures—the Alberta Hotel, the Bank of Montreal, and the Alexander Block—all went up on Stephen Avenue, and accounted alone for a quarter million dollars in building permits.[41] Building in Calgary was big business and soon the town was liberally serviced with architects, construction companies, stone quarries, brickworks, and other trappings which Calgarians gladly welcomed.

Up until the arrival of the railway, the only source of building materials, other than logs and animal skins, had been

Walker's mill established in 1881. He was a reasonable man and if a customer could not pay in full, Walker allowed him to work off the balance at the mill.[42] But by the spring of 1883, due to the boom preceding the arrival of the railway, Walker could not keep up. In October that year, he advertised for twenty carpenters at three dollars to three fifty per day to help fill orders that brought in fifty dollars for a thousand board feet.[43] When the move was made to the new townsite that winter, the demand became impossible. The CPR had promised a fifty percent rebate on the price of all lots which had inhabited buildings on them by April 1, 1884. Naturally everyone wanted the rebate and, naturally, the CPR was now there to deliver the lumber. But weeks went by and no lumber came and the company was accused of holding it up to avoid paying the rebates. Finally the lumber came through but it was still so expensive that many chose to establish themselves in less substantial quarters until the price came down.[44] Supply and price both improved somewhat when the Eau Claire Lumber Company came in from Wisconsin in 1886. The manager, Peter Prince, set up the mill across from what is now Prince's Island, blasted through the neck of connecting land, making the little peninsula truly an island, to give him a separate and controllable stream with which to run his mill, obtained leave to proceed up the Bow for timber and soon set into motion one of Calgary's most prosperous companies.[45]

At about the same time, other types of building material became available. The Catholic diocese of Calgary leased fifteen acres in what is now the Roxboro district just south of the Elbow to J.F. Peel and his partner, a Mr. Sparrow, on April 5, 1885, for the purposes of a brickyard. The clay in the area was claimed to be superior to any other in Canada except possibly for that found along the Ottawa River. At its height the yard employed fifteen men and ten horses and had a weekly payroll of three hundred dollars.[46] In 1893, two more small brickyards were set up and "Gravity" Watson established a brick and terra cotta works just outside the town limits.[47] He advertised his wares in his own lovely brick house that still stands on Ninth Street S.W. between Seventeenth and Cameron Avenues. The largest brick works was the Crandell Pressed Brick and Sandstone Co. By 1914 the plant was worth two hundred thousand dollars and produced 45,000 to 80,000 bricks per day. During the summer, seventy-five workers were employed and accommodation provided for them on the company's land. The only traces now remaining of this little community are some rubble and the sign "Brickburn" on the CPR tracks.[48]

But by far the most prestigious building material was sandstone, which was easily obtainable from the benchland surrounding the town. It was in abundant supply, fairly cheap, and lent "a very solid and substantial appearance" to Calgary architecture. In fact, these were the very words used in a promotional pamphlet which was willing to use anything, including sandstone, to convince the federal government to build its new sanatorium in Calgary.[49] The stone sold for twenty dollars a cord and the rubble for six. The blocks could be smooth-faced or rough-cut according to taste and the rubble used for foundation walls. The first quarry, which belonged to Wesley F. Orr, appeared west of town on the Bow in the year of the fire. Four more were established in short order, including John MacCallum's Sunny Side Freestone Quarry, a sample from which won a medallion at the Chicago World's Fair in 1896. Over the years until the start of the Great War, at least six other quarries were set up in the Calgary area, the most important being the Glenbow quarry near Cochrane, which at one time was surrounded by a townsite with a population of five to six hundred people; that of Bone and Leblanc in the Shaganappi area, which provided stone for some of Calgary's finest buildings; and the Oliver quarry, situated at what is now the intersection of the Crowchild Trail and Seventeenth Avenue S.W. which employed four hundred men in its prime.[50]

Most of the major buildings constructed at the time were of sandstone. Some are even still standing, although many have disappeared in recent years. If one walks down the centre of the Eighth Avenue Mall and looks above the neon signs and false marble fronts to the second and third storeys, it is possible to see the very stone laid over seventy-five years ago. Only recently, a whole block of these was torn out to make way for the new Convention Centre.[51] Among those still standing are the old Imperial Bank on the northeast corner of Eighth Avenue and Centre Street, built in 1892 to house the first banking house to come to Calgary, now vacant; the 1891 Hudson's Bay store across Centre Street from the Imperial and which since 1913 has been a branch of the Royal Bank of Canada; and, rather a success story among Calgary's old buildings, the legendary Alberta Hotel, famous from its completion in 1889 for its one hundred and twenty-five foot bar, reduced by prohibition to an office building, buried for years by neon and neglect and just recently refurbished for a good deal of money by a local firm to serve as a picturesque location for small shops.

Neither was civic architecture ignored during this period. In 1886, the school inspector finally declared the rented facilities used for a school to be utterly unfit[52] and the city began to build small ward schools in the residential areas. The South Ward School, now generally called the Haultain School, was built in 1893–94 and still stands in Victoria Park. And, of course, people who were getting rich off all the building were building fine mansions. Of all of these, the most famous was Beaulieu, the grandiose domicile James Lougheed built for himself off in the midst of the prairie southwest of town and funded by the fortune he had made in early land speculation. The house and its furnishings were shamefully luxurious and, luckily for Calgarians, are still recognizably so, even though the house has lost its grounds, has a modern addition to one side, and is now used as offices and clinic by the Red Cross Society. Everyone in Calgary must have known the mansion during its heyday. The governor general and the Prince of Wales stayed there.[53] Even such an unimportant entertainment as a ball featuring only local celebrities was duly reported in the newspapers.[54] By 1895, Calgary had all the needs of a small western city plus many frills. According to an article in the *Herald* that year it offered "in short. . .innumerable attractions to the immigrant, the capitalist, or the invalid."[55]

But this was all really only a foretaste of the real boom. In the first twenty years on the new townsite the population had multiplied twenty times. In the next ten years, it again multiplied more than five times. The population of eight thousand in 1903 became over forty thousand by 1914. The building trades had never done so well before, and for a long time afterwards, they did not do half so well again. In 1904, building permits had been issued to the amount of almost nine hundred thousand dollars. The next year they fell slightly but in 1906 they topped one million dollars, the next year two million dollars, then fell again to half in 1908. But they regained their former amount in 1909, more than doubled in 1910, more than redoubled in 1911, and hit a euphoric 20,394,220 dollars in 1912. The next year they fell to just over 8.5 million dollars, a depressing drop but still respectable.[56] But that was the last respectable showing as far as builders were concerned. In 1914, the bottom washed right out of the building boom.

During the years of steady growth, wages were good in the construction industry. At the quarries, steam drillers were paid 45 cents per hour, quarrymen 40 cents, stone cutters 65 cents and laborers between 32 and 35 cents.[57] Carpenters received 30 to 37.5 cents per hour, bricklayers 60 to 65 cents, stonemasons 55 to 65 cents, painters 30 to 35 cents and laborers 20 to 30 cents. Work days were between eight and nine hours. Considering that board could be had for 4.50 to 5.50 per week, a five-room house rented for 16 to 20 dollars a month or built for 1,400 to 1,500 dollars, and a seven-room one rented for 30 per month or built for 2,400 to 2,600 dollars,[58] these wages provided a decent standard of living.[59]

To employ these men there were at least nineteen major building concerns in the city during the pre-war era.[60] In addition, building supervisors occasionally came in to oversee the construction of a building that had been contracted to builders as far away as Winnipeg.[61] There were probably also several smaller builders. Plans for these were drawn up by at least forty-eight architects,[62] of shorter or longer term residence. Again, some buildings were designed by out-of-town architects: the Imperial Bank plans came from Toronto, those of the Anglican cathedral built in 1904 on its present site from a Scotsman resident in Victoria,[63] the Customs Building was drawn up by the Department of Public Works in Ottawa,[64] the Carnegie Library plans came from Boston.[65] Central High School was said to have been designed by an Australian[66] and the plans for Peter Prince's house now standing in Heritage Park to have come from the November 1893 edition of the *Scientific American*.[67]

The promotional literature started to flow again. In 1907, the city was touted to be the "commercial metropolis of Western Canada;"[68] in 1908, it was extolled for its climate;[69] and the next year, its various merits were crammed, with difficulty, into one thousand basic facts.[70] The growth, indeed, had been phenomenal. In the 1911 census, Calgary was listed as the tenth largest city in Canada, with a population increase of 893.72 percent since the previous federal count in 1900.[71] Family houses had increased in number by 9,661, not far behind the increase in the number of families at 10,172.[72] Among those listed as employed in the building trades were 218 bricklayers, 343 builders and contractors, 1,430 carpenters, 27 concrete builders, 218 masons and stone cutters, 87 metal workers and roofers, 391 painters and decorators, 243 plasterers, 288 plumbers and steam fitters, and 451 building labourers.[73]

In 1910, building permits worth a total of 5,589,594 dollars were issued for fourteen business blocks, sixteen warehouses, eight hotels and additions, four oil warehouses, five schools, two hospitals and additions, and for several other projects, including Mount Royal College and the Carnegie Library. Contracts being prepared for the next year included "several" eight-storey buildings, as well as one of six storeys, five of five storeys, a five-storey wholesale warehouse, a five-storey hotel for 100,000 dollars and a six-storey hotel for 200,000 dollars. Every architect's and contractor's office in town was said to be swamped with work and the city expected the value of building permits to soar the next year to ten million dollars.[74]

The city was too modest. Its wildest dreams were surpassed by nearly three million dollars. In 1911, the city alone spent over one million dollars on civic building, and an additional three million went into the street railway, waterworks, sewers, schools, electric lighting, paving, and parks.[75] The CPR built the largest repair shops in western Canada and the working man's communities of Ogden and Ceepeear sprang up around them.[76] The CPR also gave impetus to warehouses which followed the line of the tracks and again were surrounded by blue collar housing.[77] New sub-divisions spread out in all directions, including what were to be the garden cities of Forest Lawn and Bowness.[78] The next year, things were even more frenetic. The building permits topped twenty million dollars.

Calgarians were absolutely wild about the heady progress of their little city. William Roper Hull's Grain Exchange Building, which still stands kitty-corner from the Palliser and is now dwarfed on the Calgary skyline, was reputed to be "the Finest Business Block in the Province."[79] The new Dominion Bank (still in use as the Toronto Dominion Bank in the 200-block of Eight Avenue S.E.), a true temple of commerce if ever there was one, Parthenon pillars and all, was declared "a very complete, artistic and beautiful structure,"[80] and captioned a "Typical Calgary Bank".[81] As if life were not wonderful enough, Rupert Brooke, the poet, came through town and declared to the readers of the Westminster *Gazette* back home that Calgary's new Carnegie Library was the pleasantest in all of Canada.[82] The city officials got so caught up in the euphoria that the already disgracefully over-budget City Hall was pushed even further into the red by the purchase of 210 palm trees to facilitate its opening ceremonies.[83] In November 1911, the planning commission also hired the English town planner, Thomas Mawson, to map out blueprints to eradicate the old grid system of streets and to impose the circular and elliptical spoke design[84]—a common architectural vulgarism adopted by many North American cities in pursuit of Parisian and Viennese elegance. The city entered into some practical projects too: in October 1912, it finally passed its first really solid comprehensive set of building codes.[85]

But it was all a little too late. In 1913, the city which had been heralded only two years before as "the commercial capital of sunny Alberta"[86] and "the industrial prodigy of the great West,"[87] went bust. It took the inhabitants a little while to catch on. After all, Calgary's manufacturing development had increased by 2,893 percent between 1890 and 1910[88] and that was a little hard to forget. Why should not things continue as they ought? The promotional literature still went out[89] and there was still active lobbying for government building contracts.[90] The school board even made a policy decision to build all future schools with sandstone blocks because "this material lends itself to an imposing and reserved architecture."[91] And Mawson presented his finished report. But nothing could change the fact that building permits had fallen to less than nine million dollars that year, a not unrespectable figure except that the next year they fell again. By 1915, there was not one stone quarry operating in the area.[92] Calgary had entered a recession. It would be followed by war, another recession, a slight expansion, a depression and another war before the city would escape from the river valley and move up the bluffs into the sub-divisions mapped out during the boom. Never a city to give up without a fight, Calgary was still issuing promotional material as late as 1918,[93] perhaps hoping that the men returning from the war would give the economy a boost. The great building fortunes were really and truly gone, but Calgary was not left without hope altogether. On May 14, 1914, the Dingman well came in at Turner Valley. Overnight, impoverished real estate salesmen stampeded into the oil business.[94] Their rush was premature by about forty years but if they have lived long enough, they by now have had the moral satisfaction of knowing that they had early foreseen the source of the city's next great boom.

As of 1973, there were still standing at least one hundred and ten major business blocks and apartments built before 1915.[95] In addition there are several schools, churches and houses. Doubtless some of these have disappeared in the past two years. But generally, interest in our architectural heritage is on the upswing

ABOVE: Archibald McVittie's cabin, built 1882. BELOW: Sam Livingston's log house, built 1883.

ABOVE: St. Paul's Anglican Church, built 1885. BELOW: A.E. Cross's house, built 1891.

ABOVE: Sir James Lougheed's home, built 1891. BELOW: C.D. Rickard's house, built about 1897.

ABOVE: James Short School, built 1904. BELOW: R.B. Bennett's house, built about 1909.

City commissioners and a local Chinese delegation discussing relocation of Chinatown, 1910.

Group at Fort Macleod, photographed in 1886.

PREVIOUS PAGE ABOVE: Coyote hunt near Calgary, 1914. PREVIOUS PAGE BELOW: Bow River Horse Ranch near Cochrane.

ABOVE: Hunters and dogs at the Rawlinson Ranch near Calgary, in the early 1900's. RIGHT: Inspector Ephrem Brisebois.

in Canada. In 1970, the Canadian Inventory of Historic Buildings was set up to do a comprehensive survey of all buildings built in the East before 1880 and in the West before 1914. The goal of this organization is not so much to preserve old architecture as to compile data on it before it disappears and perhaps to generally encourage preservation of a few. A similar project is the Canadian Engineering Heritage Record which specializes in such items as lighthouses and bridges. Both are funded by the federal government and are administered by the Parks Canada division of the Department of Indian and Northern Affairs. Locally, concerned Calgarians are attempting to save some of the city's old landmarks. The Anglican diocese has in recent years put considerable money into preserving the old neo-Gothic cathedral. An active decision was made to keep City Hall when in 1962 an extension was built onto it rather than demolish the old sandstone building and start from scratch. Recently, relatively long-term plans have been proposed for both the little Haultain School and the Glenbow Archives diagonally opposite. However, the buildings that are really in trouble are single family dwellings. As soon as these are past their prime, they are sold to real estate developers and are slated for demolition. Even mildly important structures such as Aberhart's first Calgary home have met this fate.[96] Victoria Park is a newsworthy example of this type of activity, while Mount Royal, no doubt due to its prestige and pleasant setting, seems to be exempt and Elbow Park has experienced an upswing in recent years.

This chapter started out by emphasizing that early Calgarians were fantastically pleased with the new buildings springing up on their streets. This is true but, unfortunately, the introduction also carried a hint, very probably untrue, that they would not be so pleased with them now. When the time came for them to rebuild at the turn of the century, they had absolutely no qualms about destroying what had stood before. Perhaps destroy is too value-laden a word. Modern society lives for tomorrow and must continually revamp to keep up with that dream. It is petty to chide those who must demolish out-dated structures to make way for new ones. After all, who would patronize a log cabin store, except of course as a curiosity, today? All that can be asked is a little thought and hopefully, the preservation of enough of the old landmarks to remind us of what things used to be like in cities like Calgary.

"KOOTSISAW": CALGARY BEFORE THE CANADIANS

B.O.K. Reeves

Kootsisaw, "meeting of the waters" in Sarcee, was to historic and prehistoric peoples an important place of settlement, located between the Highwood and Elbow River junctions along the Bow. Native People (Blackfoot, Sarcee, Stony) were often seen encamped here in historic times by early explorers and fur traders. Both Peter Fidler, in 1792, and Sir James Hector of the Palliser Expedition, in 1859, make reference to these encampments.[1]

These nomadic peoples and their prehistoric ancestors lived basically by hunting, frequenting the Calgary area at various seasons of the year in search of game. Evidence of their existence—stone tools, butchered animal remains, and cracked rocks from their fires—is found today in differing types of archaeological sites in the area, some of which are 12,000 or more years old. These sites and their location and use in the seasonal round of activities are the prime focus of this paper.

Past Archaeological Research

Serious archaeological study began in Alberta some twenty years ago when the Glenbow Foundation undertook the first research in the province.[2] Most of the Glenbow's work, and studies by staff and students from the University of Calgary after 1965, largely concentrated on the more southerly regions of the province. It is only in recent years, after the establishment of the Department of Archaeology at the University, that archaeological research has concentrated in the area immediate to Calgary. It provides a natural outdoor laboratory for student education in field archaeology, and most programs have been oriented towards these goals.

Archaeological inventories designed to locate sites in endangered areas have been done in the once-proposed Bow-Highwood Reservoir;[3] downstream on the Bow; inside the City itself;[4] along the Elbow west towards Pirmez Creek; on the Bow west of Cochrane; and on Fish and Jumping Pound Creeks. Excavations have been carried out on Fish Creek, in downtown Calgary under the Mona Lisa art salon,[5] on Jumping Pound Creek at Happy Valley, and on the FM Ranch downstream on the Bow.[6] These studies done by students are mostly unpublished. They provide the data on which the following discussion is based.

Past Peoples

Man has been in the New World for more than 20,000 years. He crossed from Asia, sometime prior to the last ice age, via the Bering Strait, which at that time was part of a vast land bridge known as Beringia. Once in Alaska he moved south, probably along the eastern slopes of the Rocky Mountains. Remains of these earliest peoples are few, and all are controversial. The nearest find to Calgary comes from Taber, where a child's skull was found, some fifteen years ago, exposed some sixty feet below the surface, in the banks of the Oldman River. Lying under glacial sediments, deposited by the last glacial advance from the Canadian Shield to reach western Alberta, the child is estimated to be over forty thousand years old.[7] Few archaeologists accept its validity, as the find was not properly documented when discovered.

Remains of these first immigrants, if present, were probably destroyed by the last ice age. Around twenty thousand years ago, glaciers from the Canadian Shield advanced westward, stopping at Calgary. They destroyed what lay beneath them, and formed a large glacial lake at their front, known as Glacial Lake Calgary. The lake lay in the Bow valley and extended west of Morley. The surrounding lands, a cold treeless steppe, could have been occupied by man. Perhaps some day evidence of these peoples will be found.

The earliest finds in the Calgary area are some 12,000 years old. They consist of spear points found in ploughed fields east of town, which in excavated sites elsewhere occur in association with the remains of ice age mammals—mammoth, horse, camel, and giant bison—dating to the close of the last ice age. Skeletal remains of these animals have been found in southern Alberta, some close to Calgary, but none in association with evidence of man.

The prehistoric record of the following 12,000 years is one of a succession of nomadic cultures, oriented primarily to hunting bison. The earliest date site of these bison-hunting peoples in Calgary was located under the previously mentioned art salon. Here some eight thousand years ago bison were driven down from the hills of present-day Mount Royal and trapped in the backwaters of the Bow River. The bison, probably killed in the fall, were dispatched with spears and the carcasses butchered.

These early peoples lived here for some three thousand years and had a distinctive culture. They were replaced some 7,500 years ago by peoples of another culture, who moved into the Northern Plains from the Eastern Woodlands around 5,500 B.C. These new inhabitants quickly adapted to the rich grassland environment then extant, and occupied the area for another three thousand years. During this time the climate was quite different from that of today, being characterized by milder, warmer winters with more frequent chinooks, and made an ideal winter habitat for man and bison.

Around five thousand years ago, the climate changed to conditions similar to those of today. Two more cultures appeared in the area; the first around three thousand B.C. and the second about the time of Christ. The latter influx of people probably represents the movement of the ancestral Blackfoot from the Eastern Woodlands onto the Saskatchewan Plains.

Later peoples to move into the Calgary area include a group of Middle Missouri village farming Indians, found at the Cluny Site on the Blackfoot Reserve.[8] They remained only a few years. Historic occupants, along with the Blackfoot, were the Sarcee, who came from the northern woods in the late 1700's; and the Stony, who accompanied the fur trade from Manitoba where their homeland lay.

Prehistoric Subsistence

The livelihood of the prehistoric foot nomads in the Calgary area changed little after the introduction of the bow and arrow some 1,500 years ago. Prior to this they used the spear and spear thrower. While capable of greater penetration, it lacked the rapid reload capability of the bow, which was more advantageous in hunting. With the introduction of the bow and arrow minor changes occurred in hunting methods and settlement. These have yet to be delineated.

The Calgary area, lying in the Chinook belt, was part of the foothills bison range. Bison were hunted by various techniques, the most common and effective being the strategic employment of various types of traps—corrals, spring heads, snowdrifts, cliffs, banks, lakes and rivers—into or over which a herd of bison could be driven and killed.

The most spectacular bison kill sites are the buffalo jumps, where the bison were driven over a cliff, or a very steep slope. The fall and tumble would maim or kill the animals. To be effective, jumps require a particular combination of topography and grazing range, including a natural amphitheatre behind, "the gathering basin", from which the bison could be driven in converging fashion towards a jump off. Those which have the best combination of these features are relatively rare, and tended to be used repeatedly for thousands of years. Jumps in the Calgary area include the Madden Jump north on McPherson Coulee, and the FM Jump on the Bow south of the city. Smaller and less frequently used jumps are those along Spruce Cliff and east of Centre Street on the north banks of the Bow.

The historical literature indicates that pounds, which utilized artificial corrals to trap the animals, were the most frequently used type of kill site. As they do not require the combination of topography needed for a successful jump, they are more common and are usually found below hills or bluffs which served to shield the corrals from the view of the approaching bison herds. Pounds are known to have existed at Jumping Pound and Fish Creeks, and some are more than two thousand years old.

Natural traps, another common type of kill site, can be found in the muddy wetland areas of river and stream backwaters, and around spring heads. In Calgary, the Mona Lisa site and spring head kills in the Silver Springs area are examples of natural-trap kills. But, in contrast to large jumps, pounds and natural traps are smaller in size and do not have long histories of use, and, in most cases they are used only once.

The native peoples' subsistence was based almost entirely on bison. Other ungulates—deer, elk, antelope—are rarely found. Furbearers—coyote, wolf, fox, rabbit, beaver—were taken in sea-

son, and on occasion eaten, as were domestic dogs. Migratory
and upland game birds were also hunted. No evidence of fishing
has been found. Plants were primarily used as diet supplements
for minerals and vitamins, and as medicines, rather than for their
nutrient value. Little evidence has been found of tools for grind-
ing and preparing wild food plants.

Prehistoric Sites

Prehistoric settlement in the Calgary area is represented by a
well defined series of sites reflecting various uses of the area by
native peoples during the year. The previously mentioned bison
kills were a major component, and campsites were another.
These sites, where the people carried out their daily domestic activities, were found in a wide variety of locales and vary greatly
in size and content. They may represent a brief family encamp-
ment, or a major campsite of seventy or more tents.

Processing camps are a specialized type found adjacent to
large bison jumps and pounds. These were used during the jump
to process the bison carcasses into various products—dried and
smoked meat, pemmican, and by-products such as hides, robes,
and horn and bone implements. These sites would be abandoned
after the bison driving was completed. Terrace campsites are
common, and found in sheltered locales along river and stream
terraces. These sites, probably used during the fall to spring
months, are situated adjacent to water and firewood, sheltered
from the westerlies, and in locales which received considerable
winter sunlight. Fireplaces, storage pits, and considerable
amounts of cultural refuse are found. Known sites date within
the last two thousand years.

Tipi ring sites, consisting of one or more stone rings used to
hold down the tipi, were also common. Usually found on higher
more exposed terraces, or along the edge of the bluffs on the prairie level, they probably represent spring-to-fall campsites. Such
sites are often some distance from wood and water. The primary
concern in their selection, probably was to catch the prevailing
winds, which would help relieve the insect problem. Extant and
intact tipi ring sites date back over two thousand years, and
range in size from groups of one to five rings to encampments of
over two hundred. Seasonal encampments lacking rings are often
found along the prairie bluffs, and back in the hinterland around

the small pothole lakes or on knolls and high points. These, which have yet to be investigated, presumably represent small hunting camps occupied during the summer months.

Sites reflecting the native peoples' various religious and ceremonial practices are rare. Occasionally human burials are unearthed along the Elbow and other streams, and on the top of high hills. A recently discovered burial in the Arrowood Hills consisted of a female, who had died from a blow to the head. A group of bison skulls was found in her grave. Also a boy was found buried on a hill near Okotoks. A grizzly bear skull and bird bones were found in his grave.

Field-stone medicine wheels, cairns, and effigies are found in the area. Pictograph panels occur at McPherson Coulee, in the Bearspaw Reservoir area, and to the south on the Big Rock at Okotoks. These sites of religious significance are usually found on the tops of prominent hills and provide some insight into the native peoples' ceremonial and religious life.

Prehistoric Settlement

Locations of campsites and bison kills in the Calgary area reflect the preferential use of the several river and stream valleys by native peoples. These patterns reflect various environmental factors, which influenced the location of preferred settlement and subsistence areas.

Campsites and kills on the Bow above Calgary are widely scattered, and mainly located on terraces along the southern side. Terraces on the north side usually have small tipi ring sites, often situated in the downstream curve of a river bend. The terraces are very windswept, and perhaps this is the reason there are fewer sites here in comparison to the Bow below the Elbow. Above Calgary, settlement seems to concentrate in the side valleys—at Big Hill Spring Creek and Coal Creeks on the north, and Jumping Pound Creek on the south. In these valleys there are many small campsites and kills, some of which were utilized during the winter months. Kills tend to be on the western valley sides, and camps on the east.

Below the junction of the Elbow and Bow, the settlement pattern changes dramatically. Terrace campsites and kills are common on both valley sides. Large kills are usually along the western edge, reflecting a preference for driving bison downwind.

Tipi ring sites are also common, occurring both on terraces and along the prairie bluffs above. Sites also seem to increase in number downstream towards the Highwood, and are particularly common in the Highwood River Valley below the Sheep River junction. The Highwood Valley is by contrast narrow with a series of well developed sheltered terraces. A similar pattern characterizes the Elbow below Glenmore Dam. Both valleys contain a higher density of sites than the Bow, reflecting the more sheltered conditions afforded by these deep, narrow valleys.

The Elbow above Glenmore Dam has very few camp or kill sites, and tipi rings have not been found. In this section, terraces are poorly developed, and when present are usually low, wet, and heavily forested. These are poor habitats for native peoples, suggesting at least one reason why they were little used.

Patterns also vary between the Fish Creek and Nose/Beddington Creek valleys. Prehistoric camps and kills are relatively common along Fish Creek, presently within the confines of the city limits. However, the common type of site on the northern valley terraces are tipi rings. These valleys are broad and much more exposed to the winds than the Fish Creek valley, and the floodplains are poorly developed.

Conclusions

The prehistoric native peoples' subsistence, site and settlement pattern for the Calgary area was controlled by many environmental, and some cultural variables. The size, behaviour, and seasonal movement of bison in the Calgary area was the principal control. This area was part of the bison wintering range. Winter conditions combined with the rangeland carrying capacities and topography would structure the location and success of bison kills, jumps, pounds, and traps, which in turn would control both size and location of the processing and winter camps.

Native occupation in the Calgary area is part of the larger prehistoric settlement pattern of the southern Alberta-northern Montana foothills and adjacent plains. Geographic and environmental factors resulted in a common basic culture and settlement pattern throughout the area. The ebb and flow of native peoples, which historically took place in the winter (as recorded by Fidler in 1792), was probably characteristic of the Chinook Belt in prehistoric times as well. No doubt in some years, particularly during severe winters, neither bison nor man wintered in the Calgary area, while at other times it was an area of preferred and considerable settlement.

The matrix for settlement was the mild winter and frequent Chinooks which laid bare the prime winter rangelands in Alberta. Bison range in the past, and cattle range today, the foothills first attracted the native peoples many thousands of years ago, and in the recent past brought the whisky traders and the North-West Mounted Police. Ranchers and settlers followed soon after, maintaining in essence the historical rationale for settlement of the city of Calgary and area, which began some ten thousand or more years ago.

BRISEBOIS: CALGARY'S FORGOTTEN FOUNDER

Hugh A. Dempsey

Early in 1876, Assistant Commissioner A.G. Irvine wrote to Ottawa saying that without his authority the North-West Mounted Police post on the Bow River had been named Fort Brisebois. He stated that the people in the area did not want this name, and Colonel J.F. Macleod had suggested "Fort Calgary" instead.

With this incident, the man who had named the fort after himself, Inspector Ephrem A. Brisebois, stepped briefly into the pages of Calgary's history and then disappeared. He was remembered only because he had, in a negative way, helped the great Stampede City receive its name.

But Brisebois was a real person, not just a name in a government report. Surrounded as he was by controversy, both his achievements and transgressions were forgotten for an entire century even by the city which he helped to found.

Ephrem Brisebois (or BriseBois, as he usually signed himself) was born on March 7, 1850, in the village of South Durham, Quebec, the son of Joseph Brisebois and Henriette Piette. His father was a successful hotel keeper, a justice of the peace, and an influential member of the Conservative party. A Catholic family, the Briseboises were deeply religious, bilingual, and well educated. Besides Ephrem, there were at least two girls and a boy in the family; in later years the brother and a sister moved to the United States.

Nothing is known of Ephrem's childhood years, except that he received a good education. By the time he was in his teens he was ready for adventure. The opportunity came when, near the age of fifteen, he crossed the border into the United States and joined the Union Army during the dying days of the Civil War.[1]

Because of his age, his service must have been short and does not appear in existing official records.

Military life agreed with young Brisebois, and when the opportunity arose he left Canada again, this time to fight with the army of Pope Pius IX. Even as a boy he had heard about the problems in the Vatican, and, as a devout Catholic, he had shared the concern of fellow Quebecers.

In 1860 the Pope had organized several regiments to resist the invasion of Piedmontese troops who were attempting to unify the Italian kingdom. In its first battle, the small papal army was almost annihilated, but a swift reaction from Catholics brought volunteers from many parts of Europe. In the following year they were reorganized as the Battalion of Pontifical Zouaves, named after Algerian and Tunisian regiments of the French army.

The war continued for several years, and in 1867 the Pope sent an appeal for help to the church in Quebec. This created great excitement, and within a few months a total of 507 volunteers had embarked for Rome. Among them was Ephrem Brisebois, who was a member of the Second Detachment which reached Rome in the spring of 1868.

When hostilities ended in September, 1870, with the capitulation of Rome, the Canadian Zouaves were seasoned veterans; and although they had missed the actual fighting, they had served as guards or helped in suppressing the activities of local bandits. The unit became known as the "Devils of the Good Lord".

While some of the Canadians went on to enlist with the French in the Franco-Prussian War, Brisebois returned to Quebec, and two years later, in June, 1872, his father's political connections resulted in Ephrem's appointment as compiling clerk with Canada's first dominion census in Ottawa (the minister in charge of the project, Hon. Christopher Dunkin, was the sitting Member of Parliament for Brisebois' home constituency). Yet even by this time events were occurring in Ottawa and Red River which were to affect young Brisebois' career. In 1870 western Canada, which had been under the control of the Hudson's Bay Company, was transferred to the newly formed Dominion of Canada. From the first, the Prime Minister, John A. Macdonald, recognized the need for law enforcement in the North-West, but was satisfied to have a small military force stationed at Fort Garry.

Within a short time, however, reports filtered back about

Americans building whisky forts on Canadian soil, and of warlike Blackfoot Indians stealing horses and selling them to British traders. There was no law between Fort Garry and the Rocky Mountains, and unscrupulous traders were flooding the land with whisky and repeating rifles. Indians were fighting with each other and dying from the poisonous effects of the rotgut liquor.

Although the prime minister procrastinated as long as he could, in 1873 he finally introduced an Act to establish a police force in western Canada. And on September 25, the day after it became law, the first nine appointments were made: Charles F. Young, W.O. Smith, W.D. Jarvis, William Winder, James A. Walsh, E.D. Clark, J. Carvell, James F. Macleod, and Ephrem Brisebois. While some of the men may have been selected solely because of their military experience, Brisebois' appointment to Sub-Inspector at the rather tender age of twenty-three came through the political influence of Sir Hector Langevin, leader of the French Canadian wing of the Conservative party, and of Louis Masson, later Lieutenant-Governor of Quebec.[2]

Although a number of officers and men were sent to the Red River Settlement for the winter of 1873–74, Brisebois became a recruiting officer in the Maritime provinces, where he interviewed prospective candidates for the new Force. The successful recruits were brought to Toronto for training, and in June, 1874, the entire contingent was sent west via Chicago to the end of steel at Moorhead, Minnesota. From there the men marched overland 160 miles to join the rest of the Force at Dufferin, Manitoba.

Initially, Brisebois was appointed second in command of "B" Division under Inspector Young, but when the latter officer disputed the Commissioner's orders, he was dismissed from the Force. Sub-Inspector Brisebois was then placed in charge of "B" Division, with Sub-Inspector Edwin Allen as his junior officer.

On July 8, the Mounted Police expedition set out for the West, ignoring established trails and following a route a few miles north of the International Boundary. The summer of 1874 proved to be one of the driest on record, and as one weary day followed another, the heat, dust, and lack of water took their toll of men and horses. During this time, Brisebois' conduct was apparently exemplary, for on July 28, while encamped at Roche Percée, he was promoted to the rank of full Inspector. Later in the March, when the Force reached Sweetgrass Hills, he was also chosen to accompany Colonel Macleod to Fort Benton, Montana, to seek help and supplies.

Upon arrival at the Oldman River in September, the police set to work to build a fort for the winter. By this time, the initial favourable impression made by Brisebois had been replaced with strong doubts that he could control his men. Accordingly, he was transferred from the command of "B" Division to "F" Division, and then ordered to take his fifty men to the whisky post of Fort Kipp, fifteen miles away, for the winter.

"This officer was in command of "B" Division," Colonel Macleod wrote in a confidential report, "but there was so much crime and misconduct that I had to remove him therefrom. He is now in command of "F" Division. He is inclined to be insubordinate and to make difficulties about trifles."[3]

As few of the records have survived from that period, little is known of Brisebois' activities during the winter of 1874–75. Yet he must have had his troubles, for in March a fellow officer wrote, "Yesterday I heard that Brisebois at Fort Kipp had threatened to bombard the Indian camp for sending some impertinent message to him." The next day, a letter from Brisebois confirmed the rumour but added that all was quiet and he had had more protestations of lasting friendship than ever before.[4] Considering that relations between the Indians and Mounted Police were cordial elsewhere, one can only speculate about the cause of the dispute. Cecil Denny, who was second in command of "F" Division, remarked that during the first winter the Indians "were hospitable in the extreme, and if on our journeys we came upon an Indian camp, we were welcome to their tents, and any food they had."[5]

In the spring, "F" Division returned to Fort Macleod where Brisebois was informed that his troop would establish an outpost on the Bow River. Just as they left headquarters early in August, word was received that the commander of the Canadian Militia, Sir E. Selby-Smyth, might be in danger. The officer was making a tour of police posts when information was received that a delegation of Métis intended to stop him, by force if necessary, from crossing the South Saskatchewan.

Although not convinced of the accuracy of the rumour, the police decided to send "F" Division to the Red Deer River, where it would be within a three-day ride of Battleford in case hostilities did occur. Later, when the story proved false, the troop marched south to the Bow to resume its task of building a fort.

Within a few days of the Force's arrival, bull trains of I.G. Baker & Co. appeared, bringing with them the glass, nails, tools, and other equipment for construction. According to an agreement, the American company would erect the buildings while the Police were responsible for the palisades. As soon as the Baker people arrived, however, a dispute erupted over the fact that Brisebois had selected a site a mile from the one originally chosen. I.G. Baker's estimate of 2,476 dollars had been based on the old location on the Elbow River which was close to a large stand of pine. When Brisebois insisted on his location, I.G. Baker later tried, unsuccessfully, to add another 1,000 dollars to their invoice.[6]

The winter of 1875–76 proved to be bitterly cold and stormy. By this time, many of the men had not been paid in over a year, new clothing was not available, and the isolation left the Police under primitive frontier conditions. They lived in tents until December, digging trenches for palisades in ground which was frozen solid. The fort itself wasn't much warmer, for the vertical log construction left many gaps for wind and frost to creep in. There was but a single iron stove in the whole fort to provide respite from the cold, and besides, the stone chimneys built by John Glenn were smoky and ineffective.

Conditions at that time required an officer who was a stern disciplinarian to control his men under these adverse conditions. Brisebois, judging by his later experiences, was a courtly gentleman, good humoured but lacking in fundamental concern for the larger problems which confronted him. He concerned himself during the winter with such matters as the preservation of the buffalo, the welfare of the nearby Métis camp, and above all his own well being. Accordingly, during the course of the winter, he lost his men's respect and then his control over them.

The first incident occurred in December, when Brisebois ordered three men to build log cabins for his Métis interpreters Piscan Munro and E. Berard. When the policemen refused, they were ordered to be placed under arrest, but the other men would not take them into custody. The whole division then mutinied and drafted a list of charges against Brisebois.[7] To make doubly sure that official action would be taken, the Rev. George McDougall, a Methodist missionary, agreed to send a copy of the list to Sir Selby-Smyth[8] while Constable Griffiths sent a copy to his father asking him to give it to their Member of Parliament.[9]

In the meantime, when the post was finished its commander christened it Fort Brisebois, just as Fort Macleod and Fort Walsh had been named after their founders. The officers at headquarters, however, still referred to it as Bow River Post.

The harsh winter continued unabated. Brisebois showed considerable sympathy for his men, but his actions were usually seen as signs of weakness. For example, he handed out only light punishment to three men who had disobeyed orders because of the extreme weather conditions. One man, Constable Shead, had committed the grave military offence of leaving his sentry duty to warm himself. Another man, Constable James Pell, had disobeyed his NCO by going into the stable to warm his bare hands when he had been told not to do so. A third policeman, Constable J.S. Perault, was accused of leaving the stables before being dismissed from duty, and then refusing to go back when ordered.

Later, Brisebois defended his actions, but there can be little doubt that discipline was lax and that the authority of officers and NCO's was being undermined by the commander's weakness. In fact, Brisebois' second-in-command, Cecil Denny, had so little respect for his superior officer that in later years he barely acknowledged his existence. Although Denny became the author of two books and numerous articles on the Mounted Police, he gave little indication that Brisebois had been his fellow officer for almost two years. For example, he passed off his commander's role in an offhand way when he reminisced simply that "The men were under an officer named Brisbois [*sic*] who was in command of F Troop."[10] It is obvious from his writings that Denny had neither love nor respect for his superior officer.

Brisebois, on the other hand, became interested in problems of the country, rather than the dissension within his own ranks. He became convinced that the disappearance of the buffalo would mean the destitution of the Indians, so he took quick action to enforce hunting regulations. His two Métis interpreters were sent to nearby Blackfoot camps where they instructed the Indians to kill only enough buffalo for food.

"This will come hard on the Indians," commented a local fur trader, ". . .and this will be a drawback to our Trade."[11]

Brisebois also drafted a series of proposed regulations which he submitted directly to the Minister of the Interior, David Mills. He recommended that anyone killing a buffalo cow or calf in the spring be fined five dollars and that the same fine be levied in winter against anyone killing more than their own needs. He also planned to outlaw the use of buffalo empoundments and recommended a hundred dollar fine against white traders who employed Indians to hunt buffalo for their skins. "Unless this is done," wrote Brisebois, "the Buffalo will disappear *in less* than *ten years*. Those Indians will then be in a starving condition and entirely dependent upon the Canadian Government for subsistence."[12]

Of course, Brisebois was perfectly correct. His prediction came true in five years, not ten, and the government had to take on the expensive task of feeding the Indians.

But, right or wrong, Brisebois was ignoring the serious problems right in his own fort. The breaking point finally came with trouble over a woman. According to his NCO, James Stanford, Brisebois took to his quarters a Métis woman from the nearby camp. Apparently unsatisfied with the heat from the stone fireplace, he also appropriated the only iron stove, which the men had been using for cooking purposes.

In all likelihood, Brisebois had an eye for attractive girls, if one is to judge from a comment made by Bishop Vital Grandin. After the policeman had left the country and wanted to return, the bishop commented that Brisebois "has shown himself to be little enough of a Christian while in this country and I would have doubts about him if he came back to us unmarried."[13]

The trouble over the woman and the stove erupted into further demonstrations. "The men, half-frozen," said Stanford, "rebelled & three of them—one Corporal and two privates—were sent as messengers to Fort Macleod, in mid-winter, and were immediately put under arrest. The whole of "F" Troop then mutinied."[14]

On January 1, 1876, Colonel A.G. Irvine assumed the title of Assistant Commissioner, replacing Colonel Macleod who was retiring to become a stipendiary magistrate. As Irvine was still new to the position, he responded to the report of mutiny by asking Macleod to accompany him to the Bow River. After their return, Irvine penned his famous—but not altogether honest—letter to the Minister of Justice in Ottawa.

"As we now have a post or fort at the Bow River," he began, "it would be well if it was known by some name. I visited the post about a fortnight ago with Colonel Macleod and when we were there Inspector Brisebois, who is in command of that station, issued an order without consulting either Colonel Macleod or myself, stating that all public documents sent out from this fort were to be headed 'Fort Brisebois'." This probably wasn't true. Brisebois likely had been issuing such documents for some time before the visit, and by early January the word had even filtered down to local traders, one of whom used the title "Fort Brisebois" as early as January 13th.[15]

"I, of course, cancelled the order at once," Irvine continued, "as in the first place, Inspector Brisebois had no authority to issue such an order, and in the second place, the fort was not built by Inspector Brisebois' troop, and neither the troop or the people about there wish the place to be called Brisebois."

At this point, the Assistant Commissioner was splitting hairs. It is true that "F" Division had not erected the buildings at the fort, as this had been done by I.G. Baker & Co., but the whole project had been under Brisebois' control.

"Colonel Macleod," the letter concluded, "has suggested the name Calgary, which I believe, in Scotch means 'clear running water', a very appropriate name, I think. Should the Minister be pleased to approve of this name, I will issue an order to that effect."[16]

Again Irvine was wrong. "Clear running water" in Gaelic is *an t-sruthrain shoilleir* or *uisge shoilleir*. Calgary probably had its origin in the word *Cala-ghearridh*, meaning "bay pasture" or "bay farm".[17] Yet the purpose of Irvine's letter is clear. Brisebois had lost control of his men; he had lost the respect of his officers; and he would soon be eased out of the Force. They could not bear the embarrassment of having a fort named after an officer who, in their view, had failed in his duty.

While they were at the fort, Irvine and Macleod interviewed the mutineers and settled their grievances. No records exist to show what transpired, but the Assistant Commissioner was emphatic in his opinion of the commanding officer.

"I consider Inspector Brisebois utterly unfit to command them," he reported. "It is to be regretted that such a fine Troop should be commanded by one who is perfectly ignorant of the duties of commanding. I consider Inspector Brisebois unfit for the position he holds."[18]

Aware of the hostility of his superior officers, Brisebois applied for four months leave of absence "for the purpose of transacting private business in the Province of Quebec,"[19] but more likely to seek political support for his tenuous position. The request was denied.

In March, Irvine returned to Bow River to pay the men. This time he found them to be "a fine body of men, ready and willing to do anything they were ordered, their behaviour excellent, their arms, accoutrements and horses well cared for, and they had not a single complaint to make."[20] They were still under Brisebois' command, but no explanation was offered to show how a troop of mutineers with a list of grievances against their superior officer were now a fine body of men with no complaints—even though they were under the same commander. Of course, the arrival of spring had alleviated the problems of cold, inadequate clothing, and isolation. And perhaps too, everyone knew their commander would soon be leaving.

In April, Brisebois travelled to Fort Macleod to discuss his situation, but ended up in another dispute with Irvine over the failure to take appropriate action against men who had committed a number of gross offences. Brisebois replied that the regulations covering such offences had never been forwarded to him. In the following month, Irvine issued an order that all documents from the Bow River were to be headed "Fort Calgary", but the stubborn commander continued to use the title Fort Brisebois until June 5, the day before he posted the official order. And even when he finally complied, he must have taken some perverse delight in misspelling the name "Fort Calgarry".

By this time, Ottawa had reconsidered Brisebois' request for leave, and on July 3 Irvine informed the now thoroughly discredited officer that he could go as soon as another officer returned to replace him. When his successor arrived early in August, Brisebois had become so completely alienated from the Force that he cancelled his plans for a leave of absence and submitted his resignation. Then, ignoring the easy route to eastern Canada through Fort Macleod and Montana Territory, he chose to avoid all contact with Irvine by taking the more circuitous overland route via Fort Edmonton and Winnipeg.

In the meantime, he had informed his father about the sequence of events, and even though Joseph Brisebois started the political wheels turning, he was unable to halt the action. Not only was a Liberal government now in office, but even the senior Brisebois' approaches through the Minister of Militia were too late; the Order-in-Council accepting his son's resignation had already been passed.

And so ended Ephrem Brisebois' career in the North-West Mounted Police. Upon arrival in Ottawa, he tried unsuccessfully to withdraw his resignation, and a few months later he sought the appointment of Commissioner of Indian Affairs. But he was now a true-blue Conservative in a Liberal stronghold.

Brisebois returned to South Durham to lick his wounds. But being a political animal in a political milieu, he soon turned his attention to Conservative problems in Quebec. When a federal by-election was being held in his home constituency of Drummond-Arthabaska in 1877 he put all his efforts to defeating the Liberal member, a rising young cabinet minister named Wilfrid Laurier. When the by-election was held, Laurier lost by 22 votes!

That Brisebois had played an important role in the upset, even Sir John A. Macdonald could not ignore. "He has perhaps more than any man," Louis Masson told the prime minister, "contributed to the defeat of Laurier in Arthabaska when he came out as a minister."[21]

Brisebois himself believed his role in the election had been significant. "I threw myself into the battle," he wrote. "Beginning with Drummond-Arthabaska I took part in the fight in 18 different parishes. . .and for this I received a pittance from the candidate or some committee, regardless of what my personal or other expenses may have been."[22]

Brisebois expected a government appointment as soon as the Conservatives swept back into power in 1878, but a year later, when he was still unemployed, he let the Prime Minister know through a Member of Parliament that he was very unhappy. "He felt discouraged on account of the nominations recently made for North West," Macdonald was informed. "He fears that no French Canadian need apply; although he did not say much, he was sorry. . . .His nomination would be well seen by our friends and specially the French population, and would prove once more that you are protecting them."[23]

By 1880, Brisebois was in a desperate situation. "For four years I have fought the party's battles," he complained, "sparing neither my time, my honour, nor my money, and often paying for others. The three elections of Drummond & Arthabaska have cost me $650.00 without including the time of my own horse and carriage. . . .Finally, I have spent my savings for the party and I have waited in vain for the promised compensation. I am not speaking of the services I rendered in the North-West; you are aware of them. . .It is true that I have heard of the existence of confidential reports against me. However, these same men who have made these secret reports publicly recommended me for promotion."[24]

At last the political lobbying paid off in December, 1880, when Ephrem Brisebois was appointed registrar of land titles for the federal district of Little Saskatchewan. Just before he left for the West, twenty-two French-Canadian senators and members of parliament gathered in the House of Commons to present him with a gold watch. After the ceremonies, Brisebois paid his political debts by taking them all to dinner at the House of Commons restaurant.

And so Brisebois was back in the West and back in the government service. A year later, when Little Saskatchewan was taken into the province of Manitoba, he became an employee of John Norquay's Conservative provincial government.

With headquarters in Minnedosa, Brisebois was the only French-Canadian in the community until J.F. Dumouchel was appointed as assistant. Yet both Brisebois and his aide, nicknamed McDuff, were popular in the town. Brisebois was a member of the snowshoe club, a noted singer, and an avid gardener. By this time he had taken a wife, Adele, although they had no children.

Comments in the Minnedosa *Tribune* over the next few years reflected Brisebois' popularity and importance in the community. "Capt. Gagnon, a superintendent of the North-West Mounted Police, passed west on Saturday to inspect the detachment at Langenburg. . .He was much pleased to meet here his old companion in arms, Major Brisebois."[25] "On the return home [from a concert] the passengers on the train were determined to have a pleasant time, and did so, the "Marseillaise' being well sung by Major Brisebois. . ."[26] "The people of Minnedosa hold the Major in high esteem. . ."[27]

The only real interruption in Brisebois' routine in Minnedosa occurred during the Riel Rebellion of 1885. At that time he organized an effective home guard and then recruited a company of men for active service in the Winnipeg Light Infantry.

Brisebois was anxious for service himself, so he wired Joseph Ouimet, an old friend who was now commander of the 65th Mount Royal Rifles. On the way west to join the regiment, Brisebois met some of the Minnedosa recruits guarding the rail lines at Gleichen and Crowfoot. "I saw Capt. BriseBois," one of them wrote home proudly. "He called to see the boys."[28]

For the first time since 1876, Brisebois visited Calgary, now a substantial town on the main line of the Canadian Pacific. By then, the name of Brisebois had been forgotten, and no-one associated the visiting militia officer with the founding of the town.

Brisebois continued on to Edmonton, where he was appointed

Brigade Major in charge of the military district. Still a stickler for petty details, he then became involved in a dispute with the Edmonton Home Guard, who demanded guns for guard duty. Brisebois refused to act unless the required number of men turned out on parade. When they failed to appear, the guns were kept in storage, in spite of violent protests from the townspeople. A complaint to Colonel Ouimet provided the Edmontonians with a second chance, but when only a handful of men turned out, the home guard was disbanded.

At the end of the rebellion, Brisebois returned to Minnedosa to receive a hero's welcome. "He was met at the station by a detachment of the Home Guard and many of his friends," commented the *Tribune*, "who welcomed him and escorted him from the depot, and on passing up Main Street, he was saluted by the shrill notes of the mill whistles. At the armory he addressed a few words to the men of the Home Guard who gave three hearty cheers for the gallant major."[29]

During the next few years, Brisebois more and more took on the role of a leading citizen of the town. His land titles records were said to be among the best kept in the province and his work brought him into touch with almost everyone in the community.

In 1888, however, a cloud loomed on the horizon when the Conservatives lost the provincial election to Thomas Greenway's Liberals. At first, Brisebois was not affected, perhaps because of his influential role in the community. Then the bombshell struck. Instead of firing Brisebois, the government decided that in October, 1889, the land titles office would be closed and the registrar's position abolished.

"Numerous letters have been received by Major BriseBois, ex-registrar of this county," said the *Tribune* a few days later, "from parties who have transacted business with him, expressing very much regret at the loss of his services, he being, as is well known to Minnedosans, a most courteous and pains-taking official."[30]

Realizing that he had no future in Minnedosa, Brisebois made tentative plans to leave for Winnipeg early in 1890, perhaps to seek a posting with the still-Conservative federal government. On New Year's Day he entertained a large gathering of friends at his home, commenting on the kindly feeling that had always existed between him and the community.

The purpose of the evening was to say farewell. And it was his final farewell, for six weeks later, on February 13th, Ephrem Brisebois died of a heart attack. He was thirty-nine years old.

As the Montreal *Gazette* stated: "He was a most sincere and devoted Conservative. . . .Personally he was of polished and courtly manner; was dignified without appearing to condescend. He was loyal to a degree towards his Queen, and to all who needed his assistance his purse was as open as his heart was full of sympathy for those of all nations or religions or politics."[31]

His passing was noted in the Manitoba and eastern press, but nothing appeared in the newspapers of Alberta. Who was Brisebois? A forgotten incident in Calgary's history.

SPATIAL ASPECTS OF THE CATTLE KINGDOM: THE FIRST DECADE, 1882–1892

Simon Evans

The decade from 1882 to 1892 may claim pride of place as the most exciting and revolutionary period in the history of southern Alberta. The government, in pursuit of its National Policy, established lease legislation which propelled the range cattle industry to take off from small scale local beginnings to become a major industry contributing to international trade. The completion of the railway to Calgary completely altered the pattern of circulation within the area. The great ox-trains which had laboured up the Whoop-Up Trail maintained their function during the early years of the decade, but Fort Benton, which had boosted itself as the "Chicago of the Plains" in the early 1880's, had become a sleepy village by 1890.[1] It became possible to use Canadian stamps on letters, and to draw Canadian money from Canadian banks. The police could now communicate directly with Winnipeg and Ottawa. Calgary replaced Fort Macleod as the capital of the cattle kingdom, and became the dominant central place in an emerging network of supply centres.

The aim of this chapter is: (1) to describe the growth of the range cattle industry during the decade, (2) to point out some of the significant changes that occurred within this time period, and (3) to relate the changes observed to variables operating on regional, continental and global scales.

Establishment and Growth of The Range Cattle Industry, 1882–86

In 1881 there were some nine thousand head of cattle in the whole of the North-West Territories.[2] Small herds were being grazed around Fort Macleod, Pincher Creek, High River, and Calgary. Indigenous settlers like John Glenn and Joseph Macfarlane had been joined by officers and men from the North-West Mounted Police.[3] In addition large herds were moved north by I.G. Baker & Company to meet the requirements of contracts to feed the Indians.[4] Experienced frontiersmen were drawn into the Canadian west and were joined by eastern adventurers from the ranks of the police. They proved that stock could thrive on the northern range, and together they began to establish a distinctive ranching community in the grand dimensions of the "Great Lone Land".

Regulations under which tracts of the North-West Territories could be leased for grazing purposes were promulgated in 1881.[5] The terms were generous in the extreme. Leases of up to one hundred thousand acres were made available for a period of twenty-one years at a rental of one cent per acre per annum.

The response was overwhelming. During 1882, 154 applications for leases were received, and seventy-five leases were authorized covering an area of more than four million acres.[6] The uncertainties of 1885 resulted in some dampening of interest, but 1886 saw another boom.[7] The leased acreage authorized by Order-in-Council reached almost ten million acres in 1887 (FIG. ONE).

The leases issued in 1882 form a compact block of townships reaching from the international border northwards to the Bow River (MAP ONE). The line of the Whoop-Up Trail ran through the middle of this block, and there was little penetration of the plains grasslands for more than twenty miles eastward from this axis.

The area of foothills country so described had certain marked physical advantages for the range-cattle industry. It was most frequently influenced by Chinook winds,[8] its varied topography offered shelter, and the area had a higher and more reliable rainfall than the short grass prairie further east.[9]

Some of these advantages were recognized by those who took out the original leases. Macoun and Begg had eulogised the Bow Valley,[10] and this influenced Cochrane when he came west to select his lease in 1881. Duncan McEachran too was well aware of the advantages of the foothills, and he published a report on the area in the eastern press in 1881.[11] Men like Winder and Stewart, who had been ranching in the area for some years, advised their eastern friends. The remainder of those who took out leases fol-

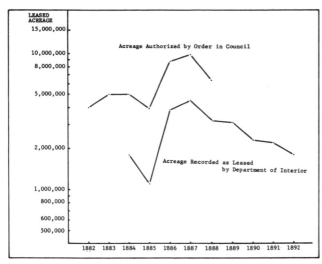

Figure 1.1   THE EXTENT OF THE LEASED ACREAGE

Sources:- Canada, <u>Sessional Papers</u>, Department of Interior Reports;
and Orders in Council, Department of Interior, 1882-92.

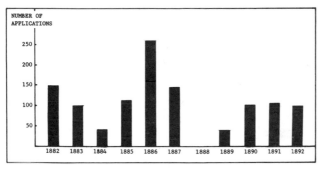

Figure 1.2   APPLICATIONS FOR LEASES

Source:- Canada, <u>Sessional Papers</u>, Department of Interior,
1883-1893.

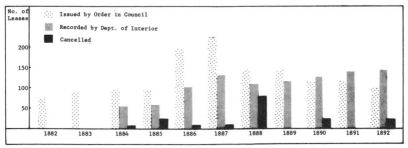

Figure 1.3   LEASES AUTHORIZED, IN FORCE, AND CANCELLED, 1882-1892

Source:- As above.

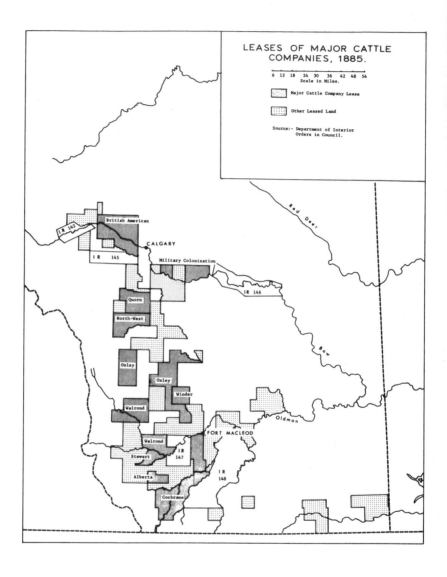

LEASES OF MAJOR CATTLE
COMPANIES, 1885.

6 12 18   24 30   36   42 48 54
Scale in Miles.

Major Cattle Company Lease

Other Leased Land

Source:- Department of Interior
         Orders in Council.

British American

I R 142

CALGARY

I R 145

Military Colonization

I R 146

Quorn

North-West

Bow

Oxley

Oxley

Winder

Walrond

Oldman

Walrond

FORT MACLEOD

Stewart

I R
147

Alberta

I R
148

Cochrane

Red Deer

lowed their lead, for many had neither visited the West nor could discriminate between good and poor range. Some of the later comers applied for blocks of land adjacent to land already leased, only to find that their lands were entirely made up of steep, forested mountain slopes.[12]

The massive extension of the leased acreage in 1886 involved expansion into new areas. Leases were taken out along the international border as far east as Wood Mountain, and northeastward from Calgary along the Rosebud River as far as the Red Deer River. The Deputy Minister of the Interior greeted this expansion with enthusiasm, remarking, "The area within which this industry may be successfully prosecuted is daily proving to be more extensive than had ever been anticipated."[13]

The period immediately after 1882 witnessed a flow of cattle onto the grasslands of Alberta and Assiniboia which dwarfed the small-scale trading which had preceded it (FIG. TWO). Estimated number of stock on the range rose from nine thousand head in 1881 to more than one hundred thousand head in 1886.[14] During this period the border with Montana was, to all intents and purposes, an open one. The legislation which established the leases also empowered leaseholders to import herds free of duty. This privilege was extended first until 1885, and then until September, 1886.[15] Quarantine inspection was instigated in 1884, but it was impossible to implement such regulations thoroughly until 1886. By that time an Inspector of Ranches was established on the St. Mary's River south of Fort Macleod,[16] quarantine reserves had been assigned,[17] and Commissioner Herchmer had begun his crusade to make the border a reality, by establishing regular police patrols.[18]

Evidence suggests that these incoming herds were carefully selected from among the best range cattle in Montana. The great Canadian cattle companies purchased stock from the most progressive cattlemen in the Territory, who had been engaged in "breeding up" their herds for more than a decade. The genetic base of these cattle was a Durham-Shorthorn cross. They were "westerns" from the Oregon country, and far removed from the Longhorns which were moving in large numbers up the Texas Trail into eastern Montana.

What were some of the characteristics of this industry which had sprung into being so quickly? First, the Canadian range-cattle industry in the early 1880's was a "big man's frontier". It was dominated by large corporate concerns, and was thus an ex-

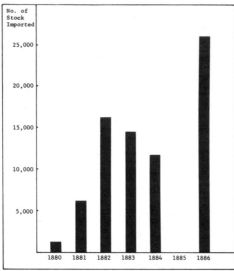

Fig. 2.1   CATTLE IMPORTS INTO ALBERTA, 1880-1886.

Source:- Department of Interior, "Statement showing the
number of horses, cattle, and sheep...entering
the District of Alberta."

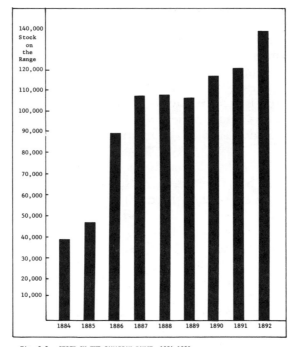

Fig. 2.2   STOCK ON THE CANADIAN RANGE, 1884-1892.

Sources:- Canada, Sessional Papers, Annual Reports of
Departments of Agriculture and Interior.

pression of metropolitan capital and entrepreneurial skill. In 1882 more than sixty percent of the leased acreage was held in units of more than 75,000 acres. By 1885 four leading companies had engrossed a number of speculative leases and together they controlled thirteen leases amounting to 883,500 acres or forty-two percent of the leased acreage. There were a number of other well established companies active in the area which were large concerns in their own right. They are only classified as second class because of the massive holdings of the "big four". The Stewart Ranche Company, the Military Colonization Company, the Quorn, and the Alberta Ranche Company are representative of these major concerns.

The importance of these large companies is further illustrated by the size of their herds. A few large herds accounted for a great proportion of the cattle on the range, while the number of small herds shows that the smaller rancher, who had gained a foothold in the area prior to the arrival of the great companies, was engulfed but not dislodged (FIG. THREE).

The second characteristic is the degree to which the spectacular developments in Alberta and Assiniboia were underwritten by Canadian capital. It can be argued that the instantaneous success achieved by the cattle industry was manipulated by the Canadian government for the "purposes of the Dominion", but their efforts would have been to no avail if they had not received the support of the investment community, represented by the twenty-three cattle and ranching companies incorporated in Canada between 1882 and 1886.

The British contribution to the range-cattle industry was dominated by the activities of three major companies, the Oxley, the Waldron, and the Quorn. These three companies maintained a continuous presence in Alberta until the twentieth century, although they were subject to periodic reorganization. In 1886 British interests held about twenty-two percent of the total leased acreage. Compared with the flood of investment which flowed from Great Britain to the Great Plains of the United States, this Imperial contribution seems undercapitalized. The total flow of capital from Britain to the ranges of the United States has been estimated at forty million dollars, and ten British companies were organized in 1882 alone.[19] Moreover, while representatives of Scottish and English joint stock companies toured the western states appraising likely investment opportunities, both the Oxley and the Waldron companies resulted from the initiative of Cana-

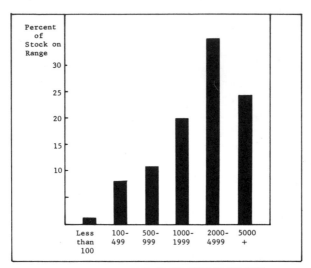

Fig. 3.1   PERCENTAGE OF STOCK ON THE RANGE IN SIX SIZE
            CATEGORIES, 1884.

            Source:- <u>Calgary Herald</u>, March 14, 1884.

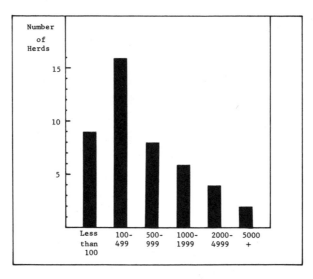

Fig. 3.2   NUMBER OF HERDS ON THE RANGE IN SIX SIZE
            CATEGORIES, 1884.

            Source:- As above

dians who went to London in search of financial backing.

Only one American cattle company operated in Canada from 1882 to 1885. This was I.G. Baker & Co., or the "Circle Outfit", which secured and held onto vital supply contracts. In addition, Orrin Main traded cattle across the line from a base in Montana until 1884, when he moved to a lease on Willow Creek, while R.S. Ford, one of the original Montana cattle kings, entered into a partnership with Captain John Stewart to fulfill government contracts.[20]

Changing conditions in both Canada and the United States combined to promote an American "invasion" of the Canadian range in 1886. In Canada the border patrols started during the rebellion were maintained and extended. Quarantine regulations were rigorously implemented. The possibility of a tariff on imported range stock, which was merely a nagging threat in 1883, became inevitable in 1885, and only the timing of its introduction was subject to negotiation.[21] If American concerns wanted to take advantage of the under-stocked grasslands north of the line, they had to act quickly.

South of the border, the cattle boom was ending. A drop in prices and drought conditions in the south were compounded by the actions of a reform administration under President Cleveland.[22] Illegal fences were torn down, and hundreds of thousands of head of cattle were forcibly turned off Indian lands. A feeling of unease permeated the plains. It was summed up by the foreman of the Powder River Cattle Company. Morton Frewen quotes him as saying, "Boss, can we get clear out of Wyoming before the fall and save ourselves in Alberta? You will have these southern cattle here in five months, thick as grasshoppers, and this being so, if you lose those five months you had better advertise for skinning outfits; your money will be in green hides the next two winters here, unless I mistake."[23] The company followed Murphy's advice, and their herds were pushed north of the border to leases along Mosquito Creek before the tariff became operative.[24]

American interests finalized nine leases during 1886, covering about nineteen percent of the total leased acreage. A further sixteen leases covering 1,200,000 acres were authorized by Order-in-Council but were never taken out.[25] Conrad Kohrs, who had started as a butcher's assistant in Virginia City and had risen to become a cattle king, visited Ottawa and obtained a lease of 187,000 acres for his Pioneer Cattle Company, as well as a substantial acreage for his friend Dan Floweree.[26] Authorities in Montana estimated that thirty thousand head of American stock had moved across the line during the summer of 1886. In Alberta, William Pearce reported a total of 28,000 head.[27] If this wholesale expansion of the American range frontier had materialized the whole character of the industry in Canada might have been changed (MAP TWO).

The catastrophic impact of the killing winter of 1886–87 curbed the thrust of American cattlemen onto the Canadian range. In the foothills Canadian herds survived without abnormally high losses,[28] but to the east the newly arrived American herds were decimated.[29] Several of the larger herds were particularly vulnerable since they were made up of "pilgrim" cattle from the mid-western states. Floweree's herd was made up of "she-stock", and few calving heifers survived the winter's onslaught.[30] Other herds had been grazing the parched and overcrowded ranges of the Judith and Tongue Rivers, and reached the unfamiliar Canadian ranges late in the fall in no condition to face the rigours of even an average winter. The Home Land and Cattle Company lost four of the six thousand cattle which were running on their Wood Mountain lease.[31] The Niobrara Cattle Company, which had also taken out a Canadian lease, went bankrupt.[32] The survivors retreated to their familiar home ranges during the summer of 1887. The deaths of thousands of head of cattle in Montana, and increased shipments to meet debts, meant that there was once more room for expansion within the Territory. In 1888, the massive Indian reservation which reached northward from the Missouri to the Canadian border was severely reduced in size, and some twenty million acres of grazing land were made available to stockmen.[33] The invasion of the Canadian range was thus put off for almost a decade.

Transition, 1887–92

The year 1887 marked an important turning point in the development of the Canadian cattle industry. The leased acreage decreased from that date. By 1892 it stood at 1,800,000 acres, or at much the same total as had been recorded in 1884. The planned expansion northward and eastward of Calgary, and around the Cypress Hills, came to nothing. Large numbers of leases were cancelled in 1888 and 1890.

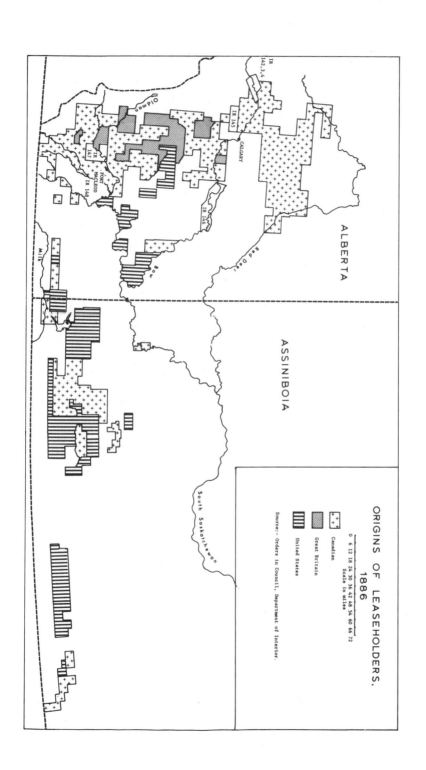

ORIGINS OF LEASEHOLDERS,
1886

0 6 12 18 24 30 36 42 48 54 60 66 72
Scale in miles

	Canadian
	Great Britain
	United States

Source:- Orders in Council, Department of Interior.

In Canada, as on the Great Plains in general, the cattle boom was at an end, and grandiose dreams were swept away. J.I. Evans had leased three large tracts along the Rosebud River for the Hand in Hand Cattle Company and the Union Ranche Company. He assured Prime Minister Macdonald that these ranch enterprises were to be followed up by the opening of a coal mine, and the building of a railway to tie the mine to the market.[34] In fact the whole enterprise rested on tenuous promises of financial support from Britain. The devastating winter of 1886–87 had graphically exposed the risks of investment in cattle and caused the interested parties to withdraw. D.C. Plumb's alliance with American interests which sought to control the whole of the Milk River area, was another victim of deflated optimism.[35]

Marked alteration occurred in the structure of the leases held. Almost all the leases issued after 1887 were for less than four sections. By 1892, three-quarters of the leaseholders held less than fifteen thousand acres each. The percentage of land held in units of more than 75,000 acres was halved. There was a rapid growth in the number of small herds run both by leaseholders and by stockholders without leases (FIG. FOUR). The great corporate concerns continued to maintain their pre-eminent position, and the day of the open range was far from past. However, smaller more intensive operations run by farmer-ranchers were emerging as an important element in the cattle industry. These far-reaching changes were provoked both by alterations in political and administrative decisions external to the industry, and by a process of technological change which was taking place within the industry.

The lease legislation of 1882 involved a radical departure from the ideal of the settler and the family farm. This was justified both by the urgent "purposes of the Dominion" and by the belief that the grazing country was unsuitable for agriculture. By the late 1880's a flourishing industry had been established which was capable of self-sustained growth; and the development of flourishing farms made it less and less easy to treat southern Alberta and Assiniboia as a special case. The Conservative government was faced with increasingly vocal and intensive criticism of its policy from 1885 until 1892, when notice of cancellation was given to those who still held closed leases.[36] An attempt was made to outflank this opposition by instigating amendments to the conditions under which new leases were issued. All new leases were open to homestead and pre-emption entry.[37] Large leases

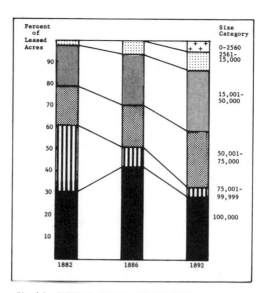

Fig. 4.1   PROPORTION OF LEASED LAND HELD IN SIX SIZE
            CATEGORIES, 1882, 1886, AND 1892.

            Sources:- Canada, <u>Sessional Papers</u>, Department
            of Interior Lease Lists, and Department of
            Interior Orders in Council.

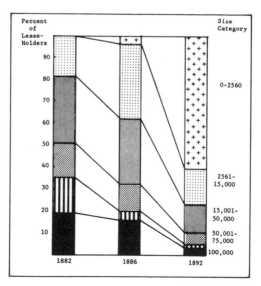

Fig. 4.2   PROPORTION OF LEASEHOLDERS FOUND IN SIX SIZE CATEGORIES,
            1882, 1886, AND 1892.

            Sources:- As above
            Note:- Each lease is regarded as a unit, Companies
            holding several leases are therefore over represented.

were only granted after public competition.[38] Rental rates were doubled,[39] and incoming settlers were encouraged to apply for leases of up to four sections in the vicinity of their homestead[40] Thus the emergence of a new class of farmer-ranchers was facilitated.

Technological changes also encouraged small-scale more intensive operations. The winter of 1886–87 demonstrated the wastefulness of the open range system. The influx of more and more small herds served by scrub bulls frustrated every attempt to maintain or to improve the quality of stock.[41] In succeeding years greater amounts of hay were put up, the time of calving was carefully regulated, and calves were weaned before the onset of winter. These innovations meant increased labour costs, and the optimum size of production units declined. The rancher-farmer could close herd his stock during the winter and feed them both natural hay and pasture crops. At the same time he could do something to protect his she-stock from the attentions of lower-class swains. He was rewarded by consistently higher rates of natural increase, and improved herd quality.[42]

The Broader Context

One of the tasks geographers set themselves is to study "the evolution of space content on the earth's surface."[43] Between 1882 and 1892 a radically new geography was created in the southern part of the Canadian West. A system of commercial production replaced the indigenous ecology of the plains Indians and the buffalo. As a result, eco-systems were profoundly modified. New patterns of circulation and exchange were created which tied the region to metropolitan centres in eastern Canada, and to world markets.

Five inter-related variables seem to have contributed to this transformation:

1. The Dominion government played a vital role in encouraging risk capital to invest in an under-developed area. This was an early and successful attempt at pump-priming to promote regional development.

2. In a wider context, the growth of ranching along the foothills of the Rockies was a response to increased world demand for pastoral products. In Britain, a rising population

meant that the country became increasingly dependent on imported foodstuffs. Domestic agriculture suffered a period of "distress or even ruination", which was compounded by a series of infectious diseases which reduced the livestock population substantially.[44] During the 1870's an important movement of livestock from eastern Canada to lairages at Liverpool, Glasgow, and London was established. The value of this trade jumped from 823,522 dollars in 1875 to 2,800,000 dollars in 1880. To some extent at least the lease legislation must be regarded as an attempt to capitalize on the prospects of this expanding staple.[45] Successful attempts were made to establish and then to protect a "special relationship" with Britain as far as trade in livestock was concerned.

3. At every stage in the establishment and development of the range cattle industry, perceptions and realities of the physical environment played their part. In 1881 the government's view of the grazing area was coloured by the reports of Palliser and Hind, both of whom stressed the division of the North-West into a fertile belt, and a region of arid plains.[46] Thus a departure from the norm of the 160 acre homestead could be justified. The initial settlement pattern, and the location of the early leases, reflected the spatial variations of environmental possibilities. The impact of the cataclysmic winter of 1886–87 has already been mentioned. The winter of 1906–07 precipitated a further series of structural changes. Thus environmental factors provided both a continuing backdrop to the process of adaption, and an occasional intrusive element which encouraged change.

4. Local technological adaption within ranching has received brief mention. In a broader context developments in the Canadian West reflect movements of W.P. Webb's world frontier.[47] The range industry was dependent upon the extension of the railway system. The advances made in refrigeration subjected the Canadian export trade to additional competition.[48] Closer to home, the dominance of the cattleman was threatened by the adoption of drought-resistant seed, by new machinery, and by the development of new techniques for handling the problems posed by a semi-arid area.[49]

5. It is the response, within this framework, of a wonderfully heterogeneous collection of people to the opportunities offered by a beautiful and richly endowed corner of the earth's surface, which makes the history of ranching in the Canadian west such a fascinating and colourful story. The cast is drawn from every segment of society, and each group pursued their interest on the range to fulfill different goals.

To some eastern investors the ranch was merely one facet of an investment portfolio which included interest in land companies, mines, and railways. To men like Cochrane, Stimpson, and McEachran, the ranches were both a business and the extension of their eastern farms and estates. The care with which herds were selected and bred reflects aesthetic as well as commercial dictates. To others like F.W. Godsal or the Garnett brothers, ranching was a way of life as well as a means of making a living. The contribution made by these men, with their educational advantages and social connections, to community development was very striking. Cowboys, drawn to the Canadian West with the herds they tended, stayed, first to work and then to establish themselves as independent stockmen. Farm settlers, some of whom had established residence prior to the lease legislation, maintained a continuous presence throughout the period.

These groups interacted with each other, constantly adapting their strategies to the opportunities offered by changing governmental policies, developing technology, the march of the seasons, and the vagaries of demand for the products which they produced.

THE SOCIAL ELITE OF THE RANCH COMMUNITY AND CALGARY

Sheilagh S. Jameson

The ranch community to the south and west of Calgary has, from its inception, had certain unique qualities. Because of the city's close association with, and dependence upon, this hinterland, the flavour of its distinctiveness has become a part of Calgary's character. It is proposed in this chapter to explore some aspects of the particular social pattern of a part of the ranch society.

During the year 1881, the sixth in Calgary's existence, several events occurred which profoundly influenced the future of both the city and the adjacent ranch country. That spring the decision was made by the executive committee of the CPR to run the rails across the southern part of the prairies and through the Kicking Horse Pass, thus establishing Calgary's position on the main line and ensuring for southern Alberta a direct link with eastern Canada. The Governor General of Canada, the Marquis of Lorne, who made his famed Western tour during that summer, was particularly impressed by the attractiveness and potentiality of the Fort Calgary site, and he, his friends, and the correspondents who accompanied the expedition did much to publicize the charm of the area and the inviting ranching possibilities of southern Alberta.[1] Doubtless the impact of their statements was further strengthened by the fact that a number of them shortly became personally involved in the establishment of ranches in Alberta.[2] Also, in September, 1881, some seven thousand head of cattle bound for the famed Cochrane Ranch crossed the site of the future city of Calgary. Earlier that year, Senator M.H. Cochrane, cognizant of favourable lease regulations shortly to be passed by Sir John A. Macdonald's government,[3] had founded the Cochrane Ranch Company and selected a site for ranch headquarters some twenty-five miles west of Fort Calgary, a location where a settlement bearing the Cochrane name was soon to develop.

These events heralded the reign of the cattle kings in southern Alberta. Beef prices were rising and the Western range lands lay empty and beckoning. Following the lead of the Cochrane Ranch came the Oxley, the North-West Cattle Company or Bar U, and the Walrond, in quick succession, all financed by wealthy British or eastern Canadian shareholders. Other ranch companies followed and by the mid-1880's a dozen or so big ranches had commenced operations in Southern Alberta, the founding capital in each case being provided by eastern Canadian or British financiers and entrepreneurs.

The operators of these spreads and of a number of less ambitious ranches taken up during this period and earlier, many of them by former members of the North-West Mounted Police, set the tone of the first settlement in the area. It developed from an attitude of respect for law and an interest in things cultural; it was far removed from that which is generally associated with settlement of an agricultural frontier and it bore little resemblance to the popular picture of the Wild West. This society, the ranch élite, influential and pervasive in nature, had a significant effect on the emergent settlement of Calgary.

In actual fact the ranch society consisted of two component parts. The managers, or occasionally shareholder managers, of the huge company-owned outfits, and the owner-operators of the small ranches formed the respective cores of these two groups. They were largely homogeneous in character, their members being mainly of similar educational and cultural backgrounds. It is reasonable to suggest that in general it was the larger companies, greater in monetary power as well as in lease holdings, with their strategic bases in London or Montreal and their reliable Conservative connections with Ottawa, which exerted the stronger political influence. Their economic dominance was without question. Unchallenged too was the social standing of the cattle barons of Alberta in the Ranchmen's Club of Calgary, St. James Club of Montreal, and the drawing rooms in cities across the English-speaking world.[4] However, as indicated at the beginning of this chapter, a ranch life style, community based, evolved in Alberta, notably in the Foothills region, which was essentially unique. It would seem that the special nature of this social pattern of life, which existed as a prevailing influence close to Calgary's environs, was mainly determined by the more cohesive and more permanent smaller ranch group.

The area to be considered extends from the Cochrane district south to the lands west of Pincher Creek. It is undeniably beautiful country. Its rolling broken hills, wide ravines and verdant open valleys, entrancing in themselves, are in a sense but prelude to the majesty of the mountains beyond. Early artists tried to portray these scenes; many writers produced eloquent descriptions and others attempted to probe more deeply into the heart-stirring appeal of the Foothills country. One of the latter, after living for a time on the North Fork Ranch west and north of Pincher Creek, wrote:

. . .it is the spirit of the West that charms one and I can't convey it to you, try as I may. It is a shy wild spirit and will not leave its native mountains and rolling prairies. . .but I must warn you that if it once charms you it becomes an obsession and one grows very lonely away from it. No Westerner who has felt its fascination ever is really content again in the conventional East. . . .[5]

What type of people settled in this country? Obviously they were individuals to whom beauty of surroundings had meaning. Their practice of building homes on sites commanding the most attractive views indicated this interest.[6] Doubtless, too, coming from regions of great trees and lush greenness in Britain and Eastern Canada, as the majority of them did, they found that the Foothills area, despite its ruggedness, offered less of a contrast than the harsh barrenness of the open prairie. Certainly these Foothills settlers were not of farming stock. The barrenness of the prairie invited the true farmer to sink his ploughshare into that unencumbered sod, but rocky hillsides and treed slopes presented obvious difficulties—even the open valleys of the region were too small, too rolling and too prone to frost to appeal to farmers. It had an attraction as ranch land—and yet in this regard the productivity of the region was modified by the very diversity from which stemmed much of its charm. True, the country west of Nanton and Claresholm, the valleys and slopes of the Porcupine Hills, which one old-timer referred to as "the finest cattle country in the world,"[7]indeed, the outer fringes of the whole range of the southern hills, constituted excellent range land. Prairie wool[8] grew on these hillsides and the famed Chinook winds bared this sun-cured grass for winter grazing. This area was included in the original leases of the first four major ranches, the Cochrane, the Bar U, the Oxley and the Walrond, the ranch headquarters in each case being located within the fringe. No doubt the encroachment of leases influenced some of the smaller ranchers who settled in the rougher country further back in the hills, where the advantages of good natural shelter, plenty of water and greater rainfall were offset by the difficulties in gathering cattle, putting up hay, breaking land; however, whatever the reasons that governed their choice of land, the reactions and subsequent history of a number of these settlers indicated a supreme impracticality and surprising indifference to the remunerative qualities of their holdings.

The majority of the early ranchers in the Foothills area were members of the British middle and upper middle class. As early as 1881 a reporter on Lord Lorne's expedition recorded that at Pincher Creek:

. . .*Quite a little colony had been attracted by the beauty and fertility of the country, and among them men of high English family, who have taken kindly to the rough free life of the pioneer settler.* . .[9]

Another writer, herself Irish, noted the adaptability of people of her race:

. . .*There is perhaps a good deal of sympathy between Ireland and the North-West.* . . . *we are accustomed to disregard appearances, to make all kinds of shifts and laugh at them, to neglect superfluities, mind our manners, follow after sport, and love horses. All that is good training for the North-West.*[10]

In fact there was some concentration of Irish in the Foothills, notably in the Millarville district; included also were a few Frenchmen, some eastern Canadians, a comparatively small number of Americans and a sprinkling of British aristocracy. The Scots seemed to predominate in the Cochrane area. For the most part there appeared to be a happy congeniality of backgrounds and interests.[11] A considerable number were British and Canadian military men, and certainly landed families were well represented. For young men in Britain around the turn of the century it was "the thing. . .to go to the Colonies,"[12] and southern Alberta seemed specially favoured; in fact the Foothills country has been referred to as "a land of the Younger Son".[13] Economic conditions in the home lands were a factor and the promise of adventure lured them on. A surprising proportion of the Foothills ranchers were former members of the North-West Mounted Police. In 1893 a total of fifty-eight ex-Mounted Policemen were engaged in ranching, including four who were listed as cowhands.[14]

In many cases the young prospective rancher worked for a time for one of the larger ranches, such as the Bar U, the Quorn or others, before going into the business for himself. This practice contributed to the general homogeneity of the whole ranching group and to the elevation of the status of the Canadian cowboy. A writer in Calgary compares the local cowboy with his American counterpart. He says:

Calgary is a western town, but not. . .in the ancient sense of the word. It is peopled by native Canadians and Englishmen. . .who own religion and respect law. The rough and festive cowboy of Texas and Oregon has no counterpart here. [There are] two or three beardless lads who wear jingling spurs and walk with a slouch. . .The genuine Alberta cowboy is a gentleman.[15]

The majority of the Foothills ranchers had sufficient capital to establish their spreads and to maintain a way of life that was reminiscent of that which they had enjoyed before emigrating. There were however certain essential differences—some of which will emerge in this chapter. Initially the main income of many came in the form of remittances from "home", received either sporadically as special needs arose or regularly. The provision of such financial help was accepted practice; a visitor in the Cochrane area expressed the general attitude when she spoke of two ranchers who were true types of "western men" and added on a disapproving note, "their father in England is a rich man, but he seems to do little for his two sons."[16] However, this is not to suggest that men receiving remittances were necessarily the degenerate, dissolute profligates that fill the popular conception of remittance men. Some, doubtless, through alcoholic tendencies and irresponsibility of attitude bore resemblance to the remittance men of Western Canadian folklore,[17] but the majority of them were quite soon operating their ranches with at least some degree of success and the cheques had ceased to arrive.[18]

Nevertheless an examination of the activities of the ranchers in the Foothills region leads one to believe that, for the most part, greater emphasis was placed on living, or the art of living, one might say, than the process of making a living. The main work they performed in the Foothills proper consisted of riding after cattle, breaking horses to ride or drive, building corrals, fencing, breaking and cultivating small acreages, putting up hay or feeding cattle as the season dictated. Their life was quite dissimilar from the overwhelming work ethic of farm families described in the prairie literature of a later decade. In the Foothills, life seemed to revolve largely around sport and the church—it would seem, in that order. Nevertheless it was evidently important to the settlers of this area to establish a church and in some instances services were held in homes before a building was erected. The church was definitely a community project; for example, Christ Church, Millarville, was built of logs which the surrounding ranchers cut, hauled and helped to erect;[19] with the possible exception of one helper, only the builder received payment.

The number of Anglican churches located within the Foothills indicate the religious persuasion of the majority of the ranchers. The towns that were strung along the Calgary and Edmonton railway line to the east each supported churches of various denominations, including Church of England, but nestled within the hills themselves were St. Martin's in the Livingstone area on the North Fork of the Oldman River; St. Aidan's, Pekisko, west of High River; Christ Church, Millarville; and St. James', Priddis. An Anglican church was also erected at Mitford, a few miles west of Cochrane, but a large number of the early settlers in this general area were Catholic, so Cochrane's first church was St. Mary's Catholic Church.[20]

The propensity of the Foothills people for social life and entertainment is evidenced strongly in the histories of their churches. Members of the congregation often gathered at some convenient home after services for tea,[21] a practice that continued, at Millarville at least, well into the 1940's—indeed, it was customary for church supporters living in the vicinity of the Christ Church to make extra dinner preparations also on church Sundays in anticipation of the guests expected to extend their visit well into the evening.

More formal entertainments and events such as "dinner concerts" or "theatricals" were staged to raise money to assist in church upkeep or to finance special projects such as the building of a vicarage.[22] In some areas gymkhanas and garden parties and whist drives were held to augment church coffers, and there is one instance that may be unique in the history of church financing. At one time the roof of Christ Church, Millarville, was badly in need of paint but money was short, so a group of church people who enjoyed their weekly game of poker put their winnings into a container appropriately labelled "The Paint Pot", and when a sufficiently large sum had accumulated, the roof was painted.

Another need in the Foothills area was met through the construction of halls in which dances, theatrical productions, meetings and, at times, church services were held: two such halls which might be mentioned are the Spring Creek Hall in the North Fork country and the Rancher's Hall, Millarville. Here and at other points, among the main functions were formal balls, featuring printed invitations and dance programmes with those in attendance suitably attired in evening dress. Participants travelled by team in buggies, California carts,[23] cutters, sleighs, or by saddle horse with their dress suits or evening gowns tied on their saddles.[24] The balls were conducted with dignity, decorum and due recognition of proprieties. It was proper for young ladies to be suitably chaperoned; indeed, invitations might be regretfully declined on these grounds.[25] Usually once in a season a group of unmarried men in a district or town would collaborate in holding a Bachelor's Ball. The main purpose was to provide some return for the hospitality which had been extended to them in the homes of their married friends[26]—and of course to offer suitable entertainment to the unmarried young ladies in the district.

The air of Victorian gentility of these events was tempered perhaps by certain typically Western touches. For example, when a number of young gentlemen found themselves without evening gloves and, temporarily at least, short of funds, cheap cotton gardening gloves were found to answer the required purpose of preventing warm hands from soiling the ladies' dresses and were deemed perfectly acceptable.[27] Also, at the Ranchers' Hall at Millarville, when a certain titled English gentleman's predilection to strong drink resulted in unbecoming behaviour, his friends quietly removed him and tried immersing his head in a handy barrel of water, or if beyond this treatment he was surreptitiously tucked away under a bench in the outer room to sleep it off.

Then there were dances to which everyone went. One lady in the North Fork area wrote of being invited into a town to a ball at the Police barracks and of arrangements made for her accommodation for the night; one senses a note of disapproval in her statement, "My maid also had an invitation to the same place and to the same ball. (I have since had to dismiss her as she got so discontented with her position.)"[28]

Stories of children being taken to dances from babyhood on are common in Western frontier lore and this happened, too, in the Foothills communities at less formal parties in homes and in public places. Surprise parties were popular[29] and on at least one occasion in the Millarville area when approaching teams and jingling sleigh bells signalled the arrival of merrymakers, the greatest surprise lay in the fact that a piano, loaned for the evening, had been loaded onto one of the sleighs—the host home was the largest in the area but lacked this necessary source of music.

During the first decades of its existence, and indeed, until the advent of the First World War, sport was an integral part of life in the Foothills ranch community and in the towns which it supported. The types of sports indulged in indicated the racial background of the ranchers. There appears to be no record of baseball being played in the Foothills during this early period;[30] cricket, rugby, polo, hockey and tennis were the games in vogue. Tennis was widely supported and many ranch homes boasted a court of some type. This was a sport in which it was quite proper for women to participate. Also, there was at least one occasion when a ladies' cricket match was held. It was at Millarville and the ladies played the men who, with the gallantry characteristic of the period, "used sticks about the thickness of broom handles for bats and were allowed to bowl and catch with left hand only—the ladies won."[31] As a matter of fact, cricket was particularly popular during this period, rival teams from various points competed and local newspapers reported fully. The Millarville Cricket Club, a branch of the Millarville Athletic Association, supported a noted team which in playing Calgary in 1900 won with a record score for the North-West Territories, 309 runs.[32]

In the Foothills country the horse was king; a man was judged largely on the quality and condition of the horses he rode or drove and on his degree of expertise in handling them. Well bred horses, animals whose proud pedigrees included at least one well known aristocratic thoroughbred sire or dam, were plentiful.[33] A high-stepping, well-matched team was a must; saddle horses, like their owners, were inclined to be very well-mannered, or conversely, noted for some wild eccentricity. As horses were such an important part of the activity, the conversation and the life of the ranch community, very naturally they dominated its sport. Probably the first sport indulged in through the Foothills area was horse racing. Matched races were common but during the 1890's and early 1900's racing was well organized with tracks laid out at convenient points from Pincher Creek to Cochrane, and of course, at Calgary. The series of race meetings held at these points each summer were gala affairs and very well attended. Most of the ranchers brought horses, so many spectators were in the position of being personally acquainted with owners, riders, horses and, indeed, each other—a most happy situation. At times liquid refreshment no doubt added to the enjoyment; this might take the form of strong punch served with sandwiches in Lady Adela Cochrane's gaily coloured tent at Mitford,[34] or brew from a "blind pig" located behind a six-foot board fence at the High River track.[35] Quite possibly the same people patronized both.

Calgarians' identification with the ranch community is evidenced by the wide support given to races at Foothills tracks as well as those held within the city. During the early 1900's a special train took the crowd from Calgary to the Cochrane races. Also, for many years, attendance at the Millarville races was an annual ritual for numerous Calgarians as well as Foothills residents; indeed as one writer noted, ". . .to have missed the Millarville races is considered a major social error."[36]

During the early years races at Millarville as at other meets in the Foothills had certain distinctive features. For a few years a steeple chase over a difficult two-mile course was held; at times the race cards included Hurdle, Polo Pony, Cowboy, Indian, Ladies and District races. Betting was brisk. Many participants might have obtained even greater enjoyment from the exercise had they known it was illegal—the honourable, upright officials of the Club were innocently conducting an unregistered parimutuel operation.

Predictably the ranchers with their predominantly British middle class background introduced hunting into the Foothills. The primary idea seemed to have been sport, the secondary to kill coyotes. Moira O'Neill writes of the fun of coyote hunting as a part of Christmas festivities.[37] Quite a number of Foothills ranches had packs of hounds; the Quorn, for example, imported Scottish deer and fox hounds and paws of the coyotes caught were used to form the number of each stallion above his loose box in the large stud-stable.[38]

It was inevitable that the Foothills ranchers with their love of horses, their superb horsemanship and a propensity for recklessness should play polo. This game they made essentially their own. The Pincher Creek polo team is said to have been the first in North America,[39] and during the 1890's and early 1900's polo was the thing in the Foothills country. Numerous clubs had been formed and every point up the length of the hills boasted a team, Pincher Creek, North Fork, Beaver Creek, Fort Macleod, Pekisko, High River, Millarville, Pine Creek, Fish Creek, Calgary, Springbank, Cochrane. The life of some of the teams was a comparatively brief flash; others endured for many years. Invitations were issued to teams from adjoining points to play matches on a fairly informal basis; refreshment for thirsty players, including teas served by ladies of the hosting district, were an important feature of these gatherings—indeed, in the Foothills any game or competition seemed to be an excuse for an evening party such as a "smoker" or a dance.[40] However the tournaments were the big events of the polo season, the largest being held in Calgary. As many teams as possible competed and there were play-offs for cups, as well as for the honor and glory. The keynote was good sportsmanship; if a team was short a player, an extra man from another team would fill in. After the regular games some special matches would be arranged, for example, for quite a number of years the Irish players issued a general challenge and Irish vs. the World games were played.[41] The calibre of the Foothills polo teams may be attested to by the fact that they competed, very often successfully, at points across the continent, playing teams from Toronto, Rochester, Buffalo, Winnipeg, Spokane, Vancouver and other cities.

There were those who criticized the Foothills ranchers' preoccupation with sport. One woman from the eastern part of the Millarville district writing to a friend who had left the area said:

. . .*so glad to hear you are having so pleasant a life and can see new and pretty things for you can appreciate them and it must be a comfort not to be bringing up your children in the roughness of the North West. To be sure there is now polo and cricket and hockey and tennis—these seem to embrace about all the capabilities of most of the Sheep Creek people—of course there are exceptions and I am a great advocate for these things in their place. . .*[42]

True, the writer was comparatively elderly and rather crippled, in a country where nearly everyone was young and active; also she was an accomplished musician and seldom had a chance to attend concerts, certainly she did add to the enjoyment of evening gatherings in the neighborhood.[43] Musical evenings were not uncommon. One Pincher Creek rancher's wife, herself an organist and a lover of music, in speaking of the early years said that there were "many musicians among the cowboys. . .Nearly all had good voices and sang well."[44] At times there were opportunities to take advantage of musical and theatrical events in Calgary.[45] Millarville people, for example, could drive in, such an excursion occupying at least three days. The trip would include a visit with friends en route, a stay of a day or several days in town, probably registered at the Alberta Hotel, where time would be occupied in shopping, meeting friends for dinner or tea—and of course going to the theatre. The return journey would require another day.

Having easy access to opera and performances of concert artists was one of the highlights of the winter sojourns in which a number of the more wealthy Foothills ranchers indulged. One Pincher Creek resident wrote of plans to go away for the winter, preferably to Southern California, and added, "If we get to any civilized place this winter I hope we shall hear some good music. . ."[46]

Trips were made to the coast or to the East, and most Britishers went "Home" periodically, sometimes with the avowed intention of staying forever only to appear again in the spring.[47]

Winters abroad when possible must have been extremely welcome, particularly for the women. The Foothills settlement like most frontiers was a man's country—it would seem that transition to life on a Western ranch required greater adjustment on the part of women. Theirs was the major responsibility for producing those special touches, that atmosphere of graciousness, which characterized these homes. A traveller riding through the country south and west of the Quorn Ranch in 1886 commented on the different feeling in those homes in which a woman lived.[48] Most of the women coming onto Foothills ranches were quite unaccustomed to household work. Some brought their servants or maids with them but this precaution did not serve as planned, as indicated in the following letter:

The Fews are having an awful time with their servants, those they brought out left in a very short time and then Mrs. Scobie brought what was thought to be a splendid woman for them from Toronto. She very soon kicked up her heels, married Perry and they have both left. . .[49]

The term "servant" did not endure either—its connotation was not in keeping with the spirit of the West. Some of the girls who came were in a sense counterparts of the "younger sons". They, too, were imbued with a love of adventure and either from choice or necessity they were prepared to make their own way in this new country. Some were referred to as "lady helps," others were governesses, some undertook dressmaking. However, the hills were abounding with bachelors, marriageable, in some cases moneyed, and certainly eager, so the young ladies became ranchers' wives and few had assistance, other than that given possibly by relatives, in their work of homemaking.

Some of the homes were very fine structures, others, initially at least, were quite rough. Walls might be of fine spruce logs, or wood nicely panelled, or of rough boards. Some of the latter were improved by a coat of whitewash; on others cotton was used to cover rough or unsightly walls.[50] Pictures were also used profusely, prints from magazines might adorn walls, at times completely covering them—hunting scenes from British publications being particularly favoured. In other homes were fine works of art, portraits, landscapes, seascapes, hunting scenes. The inclination for clutter of ornaments and ornamentation characteristic of the Victorian era was evidenced in the ranchers' homes. There were books, too, with perhaps emphasis on the classics—these filled a need in the lives of the Foothills people.

The preparation of meals was a most demanding job on the early ranches. In addition to the family and regular ranch hands there were frequently extra people at the dinner table; these might be visitors from "home" staying for short or extended periods, and constantly there were neighbours, friends or strangers stopping in for a meal and often staying the night. "Put your horse in [the stable] and come on in for dinner," was the usual greeting.

However, coping with this situation obviously presented problems. True, on the larger ranches it was customary to have a cook, often Chinese, and on many of the smaller ones attempts were made to obtain at least some help in the kitchen. Such assistance might well be spasmodic, at times inadequate, or again non-existent. Given these conditions, the efforts of many of the

Foothills ranch families to retain their custom of dining, as opposed to merely consuming food, surely exemplifies their determination to retain their traditions. In some of these homes fine china and monogrammed silver might receive general use; usually the snowy linen tablecloths and the most prized family heirlooms were used for particular occasions or special guests.

Certain specific instances might be mentioned as reflections of individual attitudes. One rancher's wife records insisting that the cowboys wear coats instead of coming to the dinner table in shirt sleeves.[51] Another story tells of casual visitors at a fine ranch house situated near the entrance to the Crow's Nest Pass being rather surprised to find the family appearing for dinner in evening dress. The host apologetically explained that:

this was not a display of swank or "side" but a custom to which they had rigidly adhered since their arrival in the West and designed to keep them from reverting to savagery. We accepted this explanation, but Brooke was greatly annoyed; later on he described it as nothing less than snobbery, adjectives omitted.[52]

This might be seen as a case of rather delightful unconscious irony as the man expressing criticism, a neighbouring rancher, himself always appeared as the epitome of an English country gentleman with riding breeches, white stockcollar and monocle—except for his fringed buckskin jacket.[53]

Despite the varieties and affectations of dress in the Foothills country there was a tendency to overlook eccentricities and to accept people as they were. Recognition was given to ability and true worth. Illustrative of this fact was the appointment for several years of the negro rancher John Ware as captain of the cattle roundup in the Sheep Creek area. He was recognized as the best man for the job so the ranchers were ready to accept his authority.[54]

In this chapter some of the elements of the society of the Foothills ranch community have been examined. It had qualities as varied as the Foothills themselves and perhaps its spirit is as difficult to capture. Determined in part by customs and traditions brought from a different land, it was shaped and tempered by the values, the colour of the West and by its own distinctive environment. It contained contradictions and incongruities. A feeling of closeness to reality underlay its entertainment-oriented, funloving character; at its core was a sense of the importance of people. Therein perhaps lay its strength. Essentially it was from the pervading influence of this society, the social elite of the Foothills ranch community, unique in itself, that Calgary derived some essence of the uniqueness of its own individuality.

ALBERTA RANCHING IN LITERATURE

Ermeline Ference

Marc Bloch regarded literature as an expression of the life and spirit of the people.[1] An expression of the life of ranching people in southern Alberta in the late nineteenth and early twentieth centuries can be found in a variety of literary sources: contemporary accounts, newspaper articles, memoirs, and the verse and fiction associated with ranching. These sources reveal: (1) the influence of the natural environment upon the ranching industry and its literature, (2) the distinctive nature of the ranching community, and (3) the refutation of the idea that the American myth also pertains to the Canadian West.

The Influence Of The Natural Environment Upon The Literature Of Southern Alberta

Southern Alberta was a rancher's paradise, "God's country", as the Marquis of Lorne called it when he paid it a visit in 1881. It abounded in rivers, creeks, water-holes, excellent springs, and natural shelters.[2] In the summertime this territory was one vast pasture. "The buffalo grass, blue-joint, timothy, oat, and other natural grasses that carpeted it were not only rich and nutritious in themselves but possessed the peculiar property of curing as they stood in the sun and winds of autumn."[3] Even in winter the country was one massive hayfield; for the prevalent warm dry Chinook winds generally left the country free of deep snow, enabling the cattle to muzzle through to the grass.

Moira O'Neill, an Irish poetess who married Walter Skrine and spent more than six years on a ranch near High River, expressed the beauties of the ranchlands of southern Alberta not only in her vivid prose but also in her verse. She writes:

> *O would ye hear, and would ye hear*
> *Of the windy, wide North-West?*
> *Faith! 'tis a land as green as the sea,*
> *That rolls as far and rolls as free,*
> *With drifts of flowers, so many there be,*
> *Where the cattle roam and rest.*
>
> *Oh could ye see, and could ye see*
> *The great gold skies so clear,*
> *The rivers that race through the pine-shade dark,*
> *The mountainous snows that take no mark*
> *Sun-lit and high on the Rockies stark,*
> *So far they seem so near.*
>
> . . . .
>
> *But could ye know, and for ever know*
> *The word of the young North-West!*
> *A word she breathes to the true and bold,*
> *A word misknown to the false and cold,*
> *A word that never was spoken or sold,*
> *But the one that knows is blest.*[4]

It is not surprising that the unique and picturesque environment of the foothills region would also seem to be pervaded with a peculiar spirit, a spirit that captured the hearts of ranchers and writers alike. Mrs. Inderwick of East Ranch tried to convey this spirit in a letter she wrote on May 13, 1884:

It is the spirit of the West that charms one, and I can't convey it to you, try as I may. It is a shy wild spirit and will not leave its native mountains and rolling prairies, and although I try to get it in my letters I fail, but I must warn you that if it once charms you it becomes an obsession, and one grows very lonely away from it. No Westerner who has felt its fascination ever is really content again in the conventional East.[5]

This peculiar spirit, described by another writer as the "*joie de vivre*",[6] was the product of the environment, a sense of freedom, security, and peace. At other times, however, the environment blanketed the heart and soul with melancholy loneliness. Its particular victims were the women pioneers. "The moaning of the prairie winds in the dead grasses and about the buildings, or in the still cold night, the lugubrious yelp of the coyotes all added the last touch to their loneliness and desolation."[7] Such a feeling was depressing enough in summer when everyone was busy, but it was worse still in winter when the sense of timelessness was much more acute. Mrs. Inderwick recorded in her diary on January 5, 1884:

Another very cold day—woke up with such a desolate feeling that I just turned over and cried myself into a headache then I could not get up I was so miserable however turned out at eleven—Put in the day. . .but it was an awful day—went to sleep on lounge at six. Took no tea—woke up at seven to find the fire black. So went to bed in disgust. . .I am sick of the N.W.!![8]

Nevertheless, there was something soul-restoring in the foothills atmosphere of Alberta, as many writers testify; and perhaps this mystical, rejuvenating spirit within the ranching environment can be attributed to a peculiar phenomenon that excited universal interest and admiration, the Chinook wind. Because this thirsty west wind was of the utmost importance to the ranching industry, it made an overwhelming thematic appeal to many writers. The frequent periods of gloom and hardship, when cattle perished by the hundreds, were attributable to its absence. Consequently, when the Chinook made its appearance, joy reigned throughout the foothills. Moira O'Neill describes its coming:

All the months of winter are months of conflict between the north and west winds. We watch the powers of the air fighting over us, and feel as if we lived in the heart of a myth of the winds. . .While the north wind blows, every breathing thing shrinks and cowers. The mere holding on to life is a struggle for poor unsheltered animals, and the longer it lasts the harder is the struggle, and the less their strength for it. But there comes a change in the air. Some night on looking out we see the clouds have rolled upwards, as if a curtain were lifted in the west, leaving a well-defined arch of clear sky with stars shining in it. That arch means that the west wind, the preserver, is on his way; and sometime we hear his voice beforehand in a long, distant roar among the mountains. When next morning breaks, the north wind had fled, overcome. You may go to the house door in a dressing-gown to look out on the snow prairie, and the chinook blowing over you feels like a warm bath. It seems miraculous. All living things are revived and gladdened.[9]

Without the Chinook, the ranching industry could not survive. The severe winters of 1886–87 and 1906–07 witnessed the catastrophic results of its absence. The winter of 1886–87 was hard, cold, and steady; and the "cowmen spent most of it in the saddle, turning back their cattle from ranging too far and digging them out of snow drifts—all for nothing; there was not enough feed to give them and they died by thousands."[10] The winter weather began on November 14, 1906 and the temperature remained below zero until February 24, 1907.[11] Even after that date intermittent cold continued. In May a temperature of fifteen degrees below zero was registered.[12] Rhonda Sivell, a former Medicine Hat district resident, aptly depicts the experiences of that winter in her lengthy poem entitled "The Hard Winter."

> *We knew we were up against it,*
> *For the snow on the hills lay deep;*
> *It drifted into the coulees,*
> *And most of the drifts ten feet.*
>
> *'Twas a poor lay out for the range stock*
> *And most of them looked a sight;*
> *For four long months they had fought it,*
> *And put up a desp'rate fight.*
>
> . . . .
>
> *They went staggering out at daybreak,*
> *All starving and weak and cold,*
> *Big steers gaunt and wild-eyed,*
> *And calves looking sick and old.*
>
> *They were all straying on together,*
> *With dumb despair in their eye,*
> *God! how it hurt to see them—*
> *To see them suffer and die!*
>
> . . . .
>
> *We had waited long for the Chinook*
> *But she'd forgotten the way*
> *Over the old range hilltops,*
> *Where the pups of the grey wolf play.*

Four long months she'd forgot us
    And she blew in some other land.
The snow lay deep on the ranges.
    It was more than the stock could stand.

Their legs were sore and bleeding
    With crust from the frozen snow,
For the South Wind had forgot us
    God! why didn't she blow?
. . . .

The riders down in the bunk-house,
    They tried to forget the sight
Of seeing the starving range stock
    Pass by on a winter's night.

Pass by on a winter's evening;
    They moaned like a man in pain
Hundreds strung out together,
    Like cars on a long freight train.

Now and again one would fall
    Down in the snow beaten track;
Desp'rate and wary the others moved on.
    They never stopped to look back.
. . . .

The struggle that each day brought them,
    And the dead stock lying around,
The hay that was short for the sick ones,
    The crust on the frozen ground.

And the ranchers they banked that winter
    Their stock in the coulees deep,
And their notes in the local banks in town
    And ten percent, which is steep—

And their riders fought to save them,
    But when the winter was done,
Was a poor show-down for the rancher,
    And mighty little fun.[13]

The Daily Life Of A Distinctive Ranching Community

Dr. David H. Breen, in his analysis of ranching in southern Alberta, has drawn attention to the political, economic, and institutional bias of the "cattle compact", an elite group composed of middle and upper-class Britons and Canadians who had a "definite propensity for gentlemanly equestrian sport, for propriety of dress and manner, and for the amenities of a leisure class."[14] This group dictated the peculiar and distinctive nature of the ranching community in southern Alberta. English customs were in vogue, and during the winter, concerts, dramatic presentation, formal balls, and neighbourhood parties broke the monotony of the season. John W. Hugill gives a glimpse of the social customs of the Calgary district in his poem "The Rose Ball":

> *Auspicious eve—arrived at last*
> *The worries of five hundred passed*
> *Six debutantes in evening dress*
> *Will read descriptions in the press,*
> *Old timers having seen things grow*
> *Just turned their thoughts to long ago.*[15]

Polo was *the* sport of the ranching community, second in popularity only to horse racing. A frequent contributor to the Macleod *Gazette*, who wrote under the pseudonym "Hermit", testifies to the popularity of the sport in his ballad-like poem, appropriately and simply entitled "Polo":

> *Chorus*
>
> *Then fill up and drink to the galloping game*
> *Here's to pony and rider whatever his name,*
> *And cursed be who won't drink to the same,*
> *Three cheers and a tiger for polo!*
>
> *When you ride a swingy pony, hell for leather on the grass,*
> *While the sticks are clicking sharply on the ball,*
> *There is something very pleasant in the scientific "pass"*
> *Quick delivered, right directed, on the call;*
> *In the melee, or the ride off, or the boundary skirting run*

With a racing pony after you at score,
When you hear the thud behind you, and the goal is nearly
won,
You are living as you never lived before.[16]

Horse racing also greatly appealed to those of British background; and it is not surprising, therefore, that such a popular sport attracted the attention of poets. A Lineham resident, Richard B. Spackman, described in doggerel the proceedings of "The Creamery Handicap" at the Black Diamond Races in 1912. This piece is significant in that it mentions real places and names and gives a colourful insight into the nature of the society of southern Alberta and the importance it attached to horse racing.

Now you all remember, the 14th September.
For you all were feeling gay, in your very best array,
The night before you had us sleep, 't rise up sharp at
    day-lights peep.
The Races—Yes, and weather grand and coyote yells
    made up the band.

The crowd that came from Okotoks, wealthy men and
    Stony Brokes—
And quite a few from Millarville, the sort that races
    always thrill
Some of course came down from Lineham, either selling
    broncs or buying 'em
And lots to see the scenery, the Rockies and the
    Creamery.[17]

Although the social life of the ranching community of Southern Alberta was moulded by the interests of a peculiar community, that of British origin, such a society was not a mere transplanting from the British Isles. It was rather a society which, while making a conscientious effort to preserve the way of life to which it was accustomed, was in turn shaped by the ranching environment to make it distinctively "Canadian". Such a community was a unique mixture of elements found both in the British and American ways of life. The practical side of ranching was dictated by American techniques and the social and cultural life of the community by British modes and customs.

There was a certain type of English immigrant, known as a

"remittance man", whose principal function seemed to be to bring the ambitious, hard-working English rancher into disrepute. Such an individual, according to F.G. Roe, had "no desire to learn anything that couldn't be acquired in the bar-room on Main Street."[18] But, the misconception has come to prevail that the only Englishman found in Southern Alberta was the remittance man of caricature. This notion has largely been the result of its appeal to writers of folk-lore and popular mythology. Writers like Robert E. Gard and "Eye-Opener" Bob Edwards "have dwelt lovingly but uncharitably upon their picturesque follies, their wild extravagances, [and] their epic drinking."[19]

Although those of British and eastern Canadian heritage were most prominent in directing the social affairs of southern Alberta's ranching community, those of American background constituted the nucleus who directed the cowpuncher's practical life on the range. This was largely due to the fact that Canadians modelled the operations of their ranching enterprises on the American experience. When the American rangelands reached their full extent, a considerable number of stockmen trailed herds into Alberta and brought with them the techniques of their occupation. One experienced American cowpuncher tells why he chose to stay in Alberta:

> Let them sing of the hills down in Oklahoma
>   Of the grass in Wyoming where I used to ride
> I'd settle for some of that prairie wooled range
>   Spreading north from the boundary on Canada's
>   side.
>
> If God had a country as good as this was
>   I'd go there to-morrow and never more roam
> But I reckon the only one left is above
>   And some say I ain't fit for that heavenly
>   home.[20]

It is not surprising, therefore, that there is a comparatively large body of literature dealing with the practising life of the cowboy which such an environment fostered. In fact the literature dealing with such a theme stresses the life of the cowboy in such a way as to make it appear that the cowpunchers were a distinctive class in themselves. Thus there has been infused into the history of ranching in southern Alberta the romantic image of cowboys

riding the range and of cowpunchers singing melancholy songs of
last roundups, rodeos, and night stampedes.[21]

The horses and the men who could handle them were the
symbol of the rangeland. Grant MacEwan, for example, preserved the memory of the mighty Negro horseman John Ware;[22]
Robert E. Gard wrote a book on the unconquerable rodeo champion horse, "Midnight";[23] and Dick Imes, an old-time cowboy
who turned to the writing of the rangelands of early days and of
the men whose lives he knew so well, wrote a poem in honour of
one of the greatest riders of the foothills, Slim Parker.[24]

The picturesque figures of experienced cowhands provided an
inexhaustible source of inspiration for many poets. Representative of most of those poems dealing with the round-up is that of
the one-time range rider, Bill Wilde:

> *A round-up wasn't for glamour, by any manner of means,*
> *It wasn't too tough to sleep on the ground, or to eat baking*
> *powder and beans.*
> *The first job was to gather the cattle, as you rode in circles*
> *wide,*
> *Then hold them all together after you had them inside.*
>
> *Each bunch that you gathered were strange—you worked*
> *hard to get them to mix,*
> *They would fight to get back on their range, using all*
> *kinds of tricks,*
> *Day trailing was easy, you could rest as you strung them*
> *along,*
> *But at night the picture was changed, as you sang their*
> *bedding down song.*
>
> . . . .
>
> *If you have heard a thousand cattle feed, just as the sun*
> *goes down,*
> *You know how the click of their razor-teeth sounds, as*
> *they feed quickly over the ground,*
> *Then when they have had their fill, and the herd seems to*
> *gather in,*
> *You watch for signs of them bedding down, as everything*
> *seems deadly still.*
>
> . . . .

*Stampedes were looked on as bad handling, the cowboys
    and the boss got the blame,
But it was much more dangerous to have a stampede, than
    it was to have a bad name.
It might be that your pony would stumble, then they would
    be on their feet lightning fast,
You kept singing above the rumble, hoping the worst has
    passed.*

*But if they really got moving, you kept well back on the
    wing,
Trying to turn back the leaders, at the same time trying to
    sing.
You might calm them down very easily, or it might be they
    would run all night,
For it was the fear of the darkness that drove them, and
    they wouldn't settle down till daylight.*

*The boys who rode on the night guard, and sang or
    hummed a tune,
They kept the herd a-sleeping, when there wasn't any
    moon,
Have a place in prairie history that Caruso couldn't fill,
For they had to keep on singing, or a thousand cuds were
    still.*[25]

The nostalgia that many ranchers felt when the days of the open range were obviously beginning to be numbered is evident in their writing. Although the immediate effect of the coming of the Canadian Pacific Railway was to stimulate greatly the ranching industry by opening up wider markets, it really marked the beginning of the end. The railway as an "ardent champion of immigration"[26] opened up the way for settlement on a large scale. This meant the fencing of the range. Rather than expressing bitterness towards the CPR for ultimately lowering the curtain on an era in Southern Alberta's history, the literature indicates that the ranchers continued to remember the days in which the railway brought prosperity with new and wider markets. One anonymous poet writes:

The Railroad Corral

. . . .

Oh, come take up your cinches, come shake out your reins;
Come wake up your old bronco and break for the plains,
Come roust out your steers for the long chaparral
For the outfit is off to the C.P. corral.

. . . .

But the longest of days must reach evening at last,
The hills all climbed, the creeks all past;
The tired herd droops in the yellowing light;
Let them loaf if they will, for the railroad's in sight.

So flap up your holster and snap up your belt
And strap up your saddle whose lap you have felt;
Goodbye to the steers from the long chaparral,
For there's a town that's a trunk by the C.P. corral.[27]

When studying the verse honouring the CPR, however, one must take into consideration that most of it was written for the annual Old-time Range Men's Dinners given by the CPR at the Palliser Hotel in Calgary. Not only was most of the poetry written especially for these occasions, but the passage of time may also have dimmed any prejudices which the ranchers felt against the railway.

Gradually stock-raising gave way to mixed farming. The roundup which took place after the disastrous winter of 1906–07 marked the end of the era of large-scale ranching, but the spirit of those days continued to live on through the recollections of the old-timers and through the prose and verse which those days inspired. Not even barbed wire could comb out the charm of the past. Those like A.L. Freebairn and C.B. Dick, who knew ranching during its early period, always looked back on it with fond nostalgia:

The Walrond Range

. . . .

I'm tired of the sights and the city's bright lights,
I long for the peace of the range,

The spell of the mountains; majestic and grand,
  The nights that are awesome and strange;
The men who will smile as they cuss you the while
  In a language no preacher employs—
You can take it from me, that I'd sure like to be
  On the range with the old Waldron boys.

I sit here and dream of that faraway scene,
  And live it all over again;
The round-up, the branding, the heat and the dust,
  The free open life on the plain;
The lure of the past that forever will last,
  For distance ne'er dims or destroys—
You can take it from me, it's worth while to be
  On the range with the old Waldron boys.[28]

The American Myth In The Literature Of Southern Alberta

The historic era of the open range with its cattlemen, cowboys, trail herds, chuckwagons, roundups, bronco busters and top cutting and roping horses has been a subject upon which fiction writers, motion picture producers, stampede and rodeo managements, singers and dude ranches have thrived.[29] Never, however, has such an era been more misunderstood or misrepresented.

There are a few novelists who portrayed the life of the cowboy of southern Alberta in terms of the myth of the "wild and woolly" American West. John Mackie's titles, *The Devil's Playground, Sinners Twain*, and *The Prodigal's Brother*, are indicative of his highly romantic style. Like American novelists such as Zane Grey, he tends to play up the exciting incidents at the expense of atmosphere and characterization.[30] In his novel *The Heart of the Prairie*,[31] for example, Mackie gives a highly fictionalized account of the experiences of an English boy on a ranch in the Cypress Hills. Mackie dwells lovingly on mysterious escapades revolving about the Lake of the Lost Spirits and on encounters with "bad men" and blood-thirsty Indians. This concentration on the thrilling and breath-taking was probably the result of Mackie's awareness of what the reading public desired in a novel. By importing the American myth into his writings of southern Alberta, Mackie hoped his novels would sell.

Amy Lucy, who adopted the pseudonym Luke Allan, is perhaps the most successful in attempting to portray the composite picture drawn from the mythical pattern of life in the American West and the actual way of life in southern Alberta. A British author, said by his publisher to be a dangerous rival to Zane Grey, Luke Allan wrote a series of novels focused upon his popular character, Blue Pete, the half-breed. Setting his novels in the rangelands around Medicine Hat, Allan concentrates upon the roundups, cattle rustling, the construction of the transcontinental railway, and the North-West Mounted Police. Although he too at times gives way in this series to the colour and excitement of the imaginary life propagated by the American myth, his novel *Lone Trail*,[32] in which Blue Pete does not appear, describes the actual life on the range country in which his other novels are set. The ranch here is owned and directed by an Englishman but managed by the experienced and capable hands of an American cowboy. Mention is made of shipping cattle by rail for market in England. One also learns that "out there on the prairie no house is locked. There, where the nearest neighbour may be hours of hard riding distant, no decent woman need be afraid."[33] Cowboys "carried rifles only on special work on the prairie."[34] In his western Canada a man could "lift a latch on any ranch in the country, any day, and time;"[35] there was "a plate and a bed for you as long as you wish[ed] to remain."[36] Allan also gives a glimpse of table manners on the Alberta range:

In the dining-room they [the ranchers and cowboys and their families] became more formal than the freshest "remittance-man" from "back home." They might hanker to seize their soup plates and gulp the contents into impatient throats, but they genteelly spooned it up, titling it daintily to the last drop.[37]

Allan relates this setting to the American myth by having cowboys in his plot expose an eastern journalist to their artificial creation of a "wild and woolly" West because they knew that such an impression of the Canadian West was held by the tenderfoot. In so doing they were able to negate the myth and portray actuality. Thus it is in this novel that Allan is most successful in creating a composite plot drawn upon two polarities, that of the mythical life in the American West and that of the range life in southern Alberta.

Among the fiction writers are several whose works support

the view that southern Alberta ranching had a distinctive quality. Ralph Connor, Robert Stead, Bessie Merchant, Onoto Wa-
tanna, Carter Goodloe, and Louise Riley tried to convey to their
readers a sense of fidelity to the Alberta scene.

Charles Gordon, who wrote under the pseudonym of Ralph
Connor, was so impressed by the beauty of the Alberta rangelands that he placed his novel *The Sky Pilot* in the foothill setting.
Familiar with the Foothills, Connor was able to base his ficti-
tious characters on real personages, most of whom were of Eastern Canadian or British heritage. His descriptions of the southern Alberta society support the view that the nature of the
ranching community was indeed different from that portrayed by
the American myth. Like others who visited the Canadian West
for the first time, Connor expressed surprise in his novel "at the
grace of the bows made me" when he was introduced to the
Company of the Noble Seven, a group of "roughly-dressed wild-
looking fellows."[38] Learning their background, Connor realised
why he might have been deceived into thinking he was in a London drawing-room[39] when the introductions were made:

*Well born and delicately bred in that atmosphere of culture mingled with a
sturdy common sense and a certain high chivalry which surrounds the stately
homes of Britain, these young lads, freed from the restraints of custom and
surrounding, soon shed all that was superficial in their make-up and stood
forth in the naked simplicity of their native manhood. The West discovered
and revealed the man in them, sometimes to their honor, often to their
shame.[40]*

Unlike many other writers, Connor has not capitalized on the
remittance man of caricature. Like historian C.M. MacInnes,
Connor emphasizes the British character of the ranching society:

*At the Ashley Ranch the traditions of Ashley Court were preserved as far as
possible. The Hon. Fred appeared at the wolf-hunts in riding-breeches and
top boots, with hunting crop and English saddle, while in all the appointments of the house the customs of the English home were observed. It was
characteristic, however, of western life that his two cowboys, Hi Kendal and
Bronco Bill, felt themselves quite his social equals, though in the presence of
his beautiful stately wife, they confessed that they "rather weakened."[41]*

That "beautiful stately wife", Lady Charlotte, is reputed to have
been in actual life Lady Adela Charlotte Cochrane, daughter of

the Earl of Stradbroke, who married T.B.H. Cochrane, son of Admiral Sir Thomas Cochrane of England.[42]

Although most of the literature on ranching in southern Alberta refutes the conception that the American myth applies to the Canadian West, the myth has become naturalized into the Canadian environment insofar as the modern rodeos, and particularly the Calgary Stampede, have capitalized on the picturesque events of the life and spirit of the ranchers and cowboys of past decades. Poems like the following give unmistakable evidence of the way in which the American myth has become naturalized into the Canadian setting.

Calgary Stampede

With the jingle of bit and toss of the rein
We're hittin' the trail for Calgary again!
The Stampede's comin' our horses are keen,
The prizes? Good as they ever have been.

. . . .

So dig out your Stetson, and throw out your chest,
We'll show you a glimpse of the old, real West,
When the men were men and could ride and rope,
And I'll bet you'll yell and say, "That's the dope!"[43]

W.J. Wilde, also an old-time cowpuncher, communicates in verse that the stampedes of today, particularly the Calgary Stampede, are exaggerations of reality. He is particularly irate at Calgary for adopting the White Stetson as their symbol of the past, a representation of their ranching heritage and a token of the warm hospitality of former eras.

The Big White Hat

Today we try to live the past,
The West's romantic days,
The dress, the habits of the ranch
In many different ways.

The Stampede breathes the spirit
That was out upon the range,
The cowboys and their outfits
All show the greatest change.

The boots are a good deal splashier now,
We all go along with these,
The shirts are gaudier than we knew,
As they blow out in the breeze.

The one thing that a cowboy didn't do
In the days of long ago,
Was to wear a big ten-gallon hat,
The colour of the snow.

It is good to see the town's folk,
Dressed up in ranch attire,
With shirts of blue—and overalls,
And handkerchiefs red as fire.

But let's get back to cowboy hats,
Small, and the colour of dobie dirt,
We can string along with the shiny boots,
And the multi-coloured shirt.

But to the big white hat,
Every cowboy should say "no,"
It's too much like a gopher-hole mound,
That's all covered over with snow.[44]

The majority of those writing about Southern Alberta did recognize the distinctiveness of the ranching community there and appear to have made it their prime concern to portray it realistically. It is their reminiscences, memoirs and articles that, in the aggregate, give an accurate picture of the Alberta cowhand of the past.

POLICEMEN AND POACHERS: INDIAN RELATIONS ON THE RANCHING FRONTIER

John Jennings

The calm of the Canadian West has become a cliché. There are no major horrors to be exposed by revisionists or gross injustices to Indians which might surface. The white settlement of southern Alberta, and the Canadian West in general, was peaceful and comparatively enlightened. The relations between the Indians and the ranchers, who pre-empted their hunting grounds, were surprisingly benign. There seemed to be little of the racial friction between Indians and ranchers which had erupted into major Indian wars south of the border.

The obvious explanation for this difference is the presence of the Mounted Police. But perhaps there were fundamental differences in frontier attitudes which resulted in greater racial harmony. The Macleod *Gazette*, the early journal of the ranching community of southern Alberta, demonstrated its journalistic sagacity in an editorial in 1883:

It has just come to this, these Indians must be kept on their reserves, else the indignant stockmen will some day catch the red rascals and make such an example of them that the noble red man will think h-ll's a poppin, besides a probable attack of kink in the back of the neck [hanging] and we can't say that we should greatly blame them either. That a lot of dirty, thieving, lazy ruffians should be allowed to go where they will, carrying the latest improved weapons, when there is no game in the country, seems absurd.[1]

A footnote was added two months later when the *Gazette* stated, "If we are obliged to fight these Indians to stop their depredations, let the entertainment commence. . . ."[2]

The Calgary *Herald*, by 1887, had become even more violent than the *Gazette* in its attitude toward Indians. Several editorials, one entitled the "Indian Pest", advocated a policy of removing the Indians from the path of white settlement. The implications of these editorials are chilling, for in both language and sentiment they echoed the American Indian removal policy of the 1830's, one of the worst blights on that country's history.[3]

It could easily be concluded from the vitriolic tone in southern Alberta's early newspapers and the continual barrage of letters from ranchers both to the newspapers and to the Mounted Police complaining about Indians, that the Indians were causing much friction. The sad fact is that western Canada's much-lauded history of peaceful and enlightened Indian relations did not rest on the tolerance and understanding of early settlers. In the newspapers and in the complaints from ranchers to the Mounted Police were all the ingredients for trouble which were also found in the American West. If it had not been for the influence of the Mounted Police it is hard to avoid the conclusion that Indian wars would have broken out in the Canadian West.

In fairness to these early ranchers it must be pointed out that most of the violently anti-Indian attitudes were found in towns like Calgary and not in the ranching community. Many of the ranchers had very good relations with the Indians and defended them against those who accused them of tampering with most of the livestock in the country. It is difficult to prove that these good relations existed because, for the most part, proof is found in chance remarks in diaries and other reminiscences, while proof to the contrary is all too obvious in newspapers and letters of complaint to the Mounted Police.

F.W. Stimson, manager of the North-West Cattle Company, and Captain Stewart, of the Stewart Ranche Company, two of the largest ranches in the territory, both expressed deep sympathy and understanding for their Indian neighbours. In an article in the Calgary *Herald* in 1885 they accused the government of starving the Stonies and stated that, although they had not heard of the Stonies killing cattle, they would not blame them if they did.[4]

Fred Ings, owner of the Rio Alto ranch in the Highwood, described the Stonies in his part of the country as "decent, well-behaved and fairly friendly," but added that the Blackfoot and Bloods were "a constant source of annoyance."[5] On the other hand, Harold Mayne Daly, writing about the Bar U ranch, recalled that the Blackfoot had the run of the house and were perfectly honest, but when the Stonies arrived all the doors were locked.[6]

There were many ranchers who lived in genuine harmony with their Indian neighbours. For instance, E.H. Maunsell was made an honorary chief by the Peigan Indians, the same Indians who had earlier forced him to leave the country with the remnants of his herd in the starvation years at the end of the 1870's.[7] He did not hold it against the Indians that they had killed half his herd to survive, and returned to the Canadian range as soon as the Indians were on reserves and provided for by the government.

H.M. Hatfield was a close neighbour of both the Blood reserve and the Cochrane ranch, whose owner was continually complaining of Indians killing cattle. In a very detailed diary during the 1890's Hatfield complains constantly of wolves, gophers, and cutworms, but not about Indians.[8]

The conclusion which can be drawn from numerous ranching diaries and reminiscences is that relations with the Indians were often friendly, but usually distant and condescending. Many ranchers make no mention whatever of Indians in their diaries, while others refer to them in a most casual way.[9] A picture emerges of two cultures widely separated by custom and development, but more fundamentally by government policy. The regulations of the Mounted Police and the Indian Affairs Department produced a gulf between rancher and Indian which resulted in some lack of understanding, but on the other hand led also to a lack of friction.

A tentative conclusion can be drawn from these diaries concerning Indian poachers. Those who spoke well of the Indian did not refer to cattle killing. A few, who were continually complaining of Indian depredations, such as General Thomas Bland Strange of the Military Colonization Company, had some rather harsh things to say about Indians. Either those in Strange's category developed a hardened view toward Indians because the Indians were killing their cattle or, perhaps more likely, the Indians picked on those who treated them with disdain.

Among ranchers who were not bothered by cattle losses to Indians there is much evidence of real friendship. The wife of one rancher was given the name White Angel by the Blackfoot because she drove many miles to the Blackfoot reserve to nurse an Indian girl.[10] Joe Fisher, a rancher near Millarville, often had Indians camped near his ranch, and his children were asked by the Indians to stay for dinner. They took one horrified look at Indian cooking and fled home. When their father discovered what had happened he promptly sent them back to the Indian camp to apologize. The Fishers were often visited by Indians, particularly in later years when they acquired a phonograph.[11]

Another Millarville pioneer, Jack Stagg, remembered seeing a group of Stony Indians swimming the Sheep River and hanging onto their horses by the tails in order to join the ranchers for the church service.[12] It is perhaps significant that these ranchers who accepted the Indians as friends and knelt with them on Sunday morning did not complain of cattle killing.

The two ranchers who complained most loudly about Indians killing cattle were General Strange and W.F. Cochrane. In both their cases there were possible reasons why they were singled out for special attention by the Indians. General Strange often had Chief Crowfoot as a guest in his house and had a great admiration for the chief, comparing him on one occasion to the Duke of Wellington. But the rank and file of Indians, as he called them, were not invited into his house.[13] This would obviously offend the Indian sense of democracy. Strange blamed the Mounted Police and the courts for being too soft with the Indians and added, "with all savages, leniency has no meaning but cowardice, and is followed by contempt."[14]

In the case of the Cochrane Ranch, there was a steady pressure on the Mounted Police to give them better protection because of cattle losses to Indians. However the Cochrane Ranch letterbook shows clearly that many of the Cochrane cattle had strayed on to the Blood reserve and were devouring Indian pasture. There were no more complaints from W.F. Cochrane after he paid the Blood chiefs to winter his cattle on the reserve.[15]

There is clear evidence of cattle killing by Indians in the writings of early ranchers, but in hardly any of them is found the frenzied attitudes of the newspapers toward the Indians. Ranchers expected to lose some stock to Indians, but at the same time realized that their losses would have been far greater except for the Mounted Police. Actually, the ranchers seemed more concerned about white horse stealing which required a sophistication with a branding iron which Indians did not possess.

It would be unfair to accuse most ranchers of antagonism toward their Indian neighbours or of a desire to possess their land, but this, to a degree, was also an unfair accusation of the rancher in the American West. It took only a small minority in the American West to guarantee turmoil. That same turmoil could easily have been created in the Canadian West if there had not been a different concept of law.

Armed with the steady flow of newspaper accounts of Indian depredations, one would expect to find stout files in the Mounted Police records concerned with Indian horse-stealing and cattle-killing. These are conspicuously lacking. The Mounted Police records show that in the early stages of relations between the Police and the Indians, the Indians showed an incredible restraint toward cattle.

Even during the worst years at the end of the 1870's, when the buffalo officially disappeared from the Canadian plains and many Indians were hovering on starvation, the Mounted Police reports express both admiration and surprise at Indian behaviour.[16] Some ranchers in 1878 and 1879 took their herds back to Montana, claiming that Indian cattle-killing forced them to do so.[17] Certainly there was some truth to this but there were many extenuating circumstances. In the first place the Indian Affairs Department only began to function systematically in the West in 1879. Until the early 1880's there were large numbers of Indians who were totally dislocated and without food in the face of the buffalo's extinction.

Cattle looked similar to buffalo and tasted much the same. Undoubtedly many Indians minimized the difference and began to hunt this new source of meat which, through providence, had been left largely unattended. But the striking fact of this period is not that cattle, left to roam at will, were occasionally killed, but that thousands of Indians, literally dying of starvation, existed on their own horses and dogs and even whatever gophers could be snared, rather than touch the white man's cattle.[18]

A surprising aspect of Indian history during the period of the cattle frontier from the late 1870's to the mid-1890's is the very low rate of Indian crime. Mounted Police crime statistics show unequivocally that the Indian population had a much lower crime rate than did the white.[19] The Police expressed astonishment at the fact that the Indians, faced with starvation, were showing extraordinary restraint toward cattle. It is also evident that in this early period the Mounted Police were more lenient toward the Indians than they were toward whites. During the 1880's the Indians, with a much larger population than the whites, had fewer total convictions than did whites for liquor offences alone.[20] However, the two offences that Indians were most frequently arrested for were horse-stealing and cattle-killing. The early cattlemen, whose stock largely wandered an open range, had a very real cause for anxiety.

Fortunately there was little thought on the part of the ranchers of taking the law into their own hands. Occasionally their complaints to the Mounted Police became rather strident, but the great majority of them realized how fortunate they were, in contrast to their American counterparts, in having strong protection. The vitriolic tone of the newspapers probably did not accurately represent the attitudes of ranchers, for whom the newspapers professed to be speaking.

In several instances, an informal vigilance committee of ranchers would pay a visit to someone strongly suspected of putting his brand on other men's cattle, and he would be escorted across the border. But there was never any real threat of violence or lynching, nor was this type of informal justice extended to the Indians.[21]

Throughout the period of the ranching frontier there is only one recorded incident of a rancher shooting an Indian, and that was done in self-defence. A man named Thompson followed a party of three Blackfoot who had broken into his house and stolen a few articles. When he found their camp he and a friend were attacked, and in the shoot-out that followed one of the Indians was wounded. This incident is significant because the wounded Indian, Trembling Man, later died, and for a time his band was in a great state of excitement. There was much talk among the Indians of killing Thompson, and the Mounted Police had great difficulty in soothing these passions.[22] The importance of this incident is clear to anyone who has read American Indian history. It was exactly this sort of situation south of the border which, in the absence of effective police action, so often escalated into a major Indian war.

Undoubtedly there would have been far more friction between ranchers and Indians than there was, except for two main factors of police control. The Mounted Police, through very tough liquor laws, were able to eliminate almost entirely the liquor trade to the Indians. The other main contribution to orderly development was a very thorough patrol system which reached its maximum effectiveness after Lawrence W. Herchmer became commissioner in 1886. This patrol system included a network of rather primitive posts, and it is significant that each of the four largest ranches in the Canadian West had a Police post situated within a few miles of the home buildings. It is doubtful that any other ranching community has ever had the sort of protection that the Mounted Police gave to Alberta ranchers.[23]

This was an enthusiastic protection, partly because there were very strong links between the Police and the ranchers. The ranch owners and the Mounted Police, particularly the officers, shared much the same social values and had a mutual respect for each other. The bonds went very deep, for ex-Mounted Police formed the core of the ranching industry after 1877 and were a dominant element in ranching society. Many Mounted Police had originally been attracted to the Force by the promise of free land after three years' service. The Mounted Police files for 1893 give a list of the occupations of former policemen in which fifty-four are listed as ranchers in southern Alberta and many more are associated with the ranching community.[24] Their influence in ranching society undoubtedly had a large influence on attitudes toward law generally and toward Indians specifically.

All of these early Mounted Policemen who became ranchers had been fortunate enough to fall under the influence of Colonel Macleod, who was commissioner at one of the most crucial moments in Mounted Police history. There have been few to equal his influence in Mounted Police history; certainly none have surpassed it. Perhaps his most important legacy was the establishment of precedents in dealing with Indians which, though eroded in later years, formed the core of successful control of the Canadian frontier. Under Colonel Macleod's tutelage the Indians were given time to understand white laws and came to look on the Mounted Police as their protectors, not their persecutors.

One of Colonel Macleod's most important accomplishments was his ability to gain the friendship and confidence of Indian chiefs, particularly Crowfoot. This confidence to some extent sifted down through Indian ranks, and even led in many cases to Indians turning themselves in to the police and quite cheerfully admitting their crimes, confident that they would be treated fairly.[25] The friendship of chiefs was crucial to effective law enforcement because in most cases it was virtually impossible for the Police to capture Indians without Indian help.[26] There were many instances in which an Indian gave himself up to the Police for horse-stealing or cattle-killing because a chief convinced him that he should do so.[27] But, as the influence of the chiefs waned, due to the policy of the Indian Affairs Department, the Mounted

Police found it increasingly difficult to make Indian arrests.

In convincing the Indians that it was better not to steal horses, the Police were tackling a major tenet of their cultural values. The horse formed the basis of their entire monetary and social system. Before the arrival of the white man it was the ultimate goal to borrow as many horses as possible from enemies. This was the road to social prominence and to acquiring an attractive and useful wife.[28]

The Mounted Police found it impossible to control horse stealing in southern Alberta due to the proximity of the border. Horses belonging to Alberta ranchers were hardly touched by Canadian Indians, but a fair number were stolen by American Indians who were basically after the Canadian Indians' horses. Many horses belonging to American ranchers were also lost in the same way. Indians on both sides of the border soon learned that the "medicine line" gave them a large degree of immunity from the law. But they also learned very quickly that it was foolish to steal branded stock.

Alberta ranchers were largely immune from Indian horse-stealing because brands could be very quickly traced. American sheriffs were notoriously unhelpful to Canadian authorities in tracing stolen horses, but the American army and the Mounted Police had extremely good relations with each other and with the advent of the telegraph it was not uncommon for Indians to be apprehended in their raids across the border before they reached their reserves. The Indian departments in both countries aided this procedure by notifying the authorities if a number of Indians did not turn up for their rations. In this way the Police were often able to apprehend potential horse-stealing parties shortly after they left their reserve.[29]

The dwindling of horse-stealing among the Plains tribes poignantly marked inevitable acceptance of their new condition as total dependents of the Canadian government. When, with considerable government prodding, they gave in to the policy of trading their horses for equal numbers of government cows, their nomadic heritage was flickering on the point of extinction.

Many of them lashed out against the inevitability of reservation life by continuing to steal horses, though by the 1890's the odds were against them and many ended behind bars.[30] But cattle-killing was a different matter. With ranchers' cattle scattered over a vast range it was relatively easy for Indians to kill individual animals without being caught. It was pure luck when these

Indians were detected either by the Mounted Police or by cowboys. Even if detected, it was usually quite simple to outrun the pursuers and evaporate into the foothills. There was a steady stream of complaints to the Police about cattle-killing, but the Police could do little.

By the early 1880's the Indians were beginning to realize the fatal impact of the reserve system. The threat of starvation was replaced by a new blow. Within an incredibly short time, a decade or less, the entire way of life of the Plains Indians was revolutionized and disoriented, leaving the Indians in a state of anxiety, and ultimately, torpor.

In essence, the Indians became Canada's first welfare recipients. The extinction of the buffalo forced the Canadian government to take over completely the feeding of the Indians after 1880. This, of course, erased the momentary problem of starvation, but introduced one that was more serious. There was now nothing to compel the Indians to do anything. There was not even enough work to be done on the reserves to justify a policy of food in return for work. Thus the Indians began in the early 1880's to accept and even demand that the government would take care of them completely. Herein lay one of the most fundamental reasons for the disintegration of Indian society.

At the same time, partly through the pressure of cattlemen, the government introduced a policy of not allowing Indians to leave their reserves without a pass signed by the Indian Agent.[31] The purpose of this policy was to prevent Indians loitering around towns like Calgary for immoral purposes, and also to control the parties of Indians who were wandering over the cattle ranges. These Indians were allegedly on hunting trips, but there was virtually nothing left to hunt except cattle. This pass system was not really necessary to control Indians in towns because the vagrancy laws were adequate for this. Its primary purpose was to prevent Indian horse-stealing raids into the U.S. and to keep Indians off ranch land. It was also designed to ensure that Indians were weaned of their roving habits so that they could become good farmers.

The pass system represented, in fact, a total reversal of the early philosophy of the federal government and the Mounted Police toward the Indians. It had no validity in law and ran directly counter to the promises made to the Indians in Treaty Seven that they would still be free to roam the plains. It came dangerously close to a policy of apartheid.

It became the duty of the Mounted Police to uphold this system. This law put them in a rather awkward position since the system was not legal and they felt they would lose much of their credibility with the Indians if they enforced it too strictly and the Indians refused to comply. Indians could not be prosecuted for being off reserves without passes but there were still very compelling reasons for obeying the regulation. Indian agents had the power, and often used it, of cutting off annuities and rations to Indians who refused to comply.[32]

The Mounted Police took an equivocal attitude toward passes. Some officers complained of their inequity and injustice, while others like Sam Steele were much in favour of them.[33] Generally the officers saw the pass system as a necessity to avoid friction between Indians and ranchers. But at the same time they were all too aware of the potential for violence in its enforcement. Although most ranchers had sense enough not to take the law into their own hands, it took only a small minority to start a major conflict. The pass system did at least have the virtue of enforcing tranquility and, by separating the races, ensuring that Indians would be insulated from some of the worst aspects of white society. To those who accused the Indians of an assortment of depredations, the Mounted Police and the Indian Affairs Department could answer that the great majority of Indians were quietly working on their reserves and bothering no one.

The situation was, however, not so simple. By taking over the feeding of the Indians, the government was now faced with the problem of trying to make them self-supporting. Quite naturally the Indians saw no virtue in working if they could be supported in leisure. Furthermore, the Indians of Treaty Seven made reluctant farmers, partly because their land was generally unsuited for crops. The success of the government's farming policy on reserves in Treaty Four and Treaty Six was conspicuously lacking in Treaty Seven.[34] This meant that the government policy of cutting back rations on reserves in an effort to make the Indians industrious and self-supporting was not a success in Treaty Seven. The Indians complained that they were not given enough to eat, and the ranchers complained that starving Indians were killing their cattle.

The situation came to a head in the mid 1890's. A group of Blood Indians finally went to the Mounted Police of Fort Macleod, admitted that they were killing cattle, but stressed the necessity of their doing so because rations had been cut by the Indian Department, leaving them in their present half-starving state. They admitted that the Bloods alone were killing from twenty-five to thirty head per month and that the killing was done at night on the same day as beef rations were issued so that they could not be detected.[35]

Sam Steele, who commanded the Mounted Police post at Fort Macleod, initiated night patrols, but at the same time wrote to the commissioner that three times the number of police would have no effect on the cattle-killing. He also felt that the Indian scouts, who in many cases had been very effective, were useless in this situation because their sympathies were totally with their people.

The situation became intense at the time of the annual roundup and branding. During this period most of the cattle on the range were closely bunched and guarded, making it almost impossible for Indians to kill them. The Mounted Police now feared serious trouble because the Indians' safety valve of cattle-killing was closed.[36]

The commissioner of the Mounted Police immediately wired the Indian Affairs Department warning of serious trouble if rations in Treaty Seven were not increased.[37] This Mounted Police interference in Indian Affairs policy set off a minor explosion in relations between the Police and the Indian Department which had been simmering below the surface for years. The Blood agent accused the Police of listening to the "groundless complaints of unreliable Indians," even though the chief of the Bloods, Red Crow, and a number of other Blood chiefs had led the delegation to the Police. The official investigation by the Indian Department concluded that the Indians were killing cattle out of "pure devilment" and were better fed than the Mounted Police.[38] At the same time the commissioner of the Mounted Police was directed by the commissioner of Indian Affairs to see to it that the Police "be no longer permitted to interfere in matters which properly belong to the Indian Department."

The attitude of the Indian Department prompted the commissioner of the Mounted Police to send a plea to the Lieutenant-Governor:

You are aware, Sir, that outside the rations actually issued by the Government to the Bloods, they have absolutely no lawful means of support; there is positively no game in the district, and unless the Government rations are sufficient to sustain life, the Indians must resort to cattle-killing for subsist-

ence, as, even if they would work, there is very little available. The tempta-
tion to kill cattle grazing on the Reserve for which the Indians receive no
compensation from the owners thereof, is very great. . . .the peace and safety
of these Territories have been placed in my charge, and as these hinge in a
very great measure on the Indian question, I think it is my duty to report
whenever in my opinion the Indians have been badly treated.[39]

Despite the assertions of the Indian Department, it is clear from the annual reports of the Department that rations in the 1890's were being cut back as a conscious policy of forcing Indians to become self-supporting. Indian Department officials were very concerned that reserve policy would foster laziness and lack of purpose unless the Indians were goaded into supporting themselves.[40]

The Indians of Treaty Seven were caught between the policy of the Indian Department, whose philosophy it was to force them to alter drastically their way of life; and the policy of the Mounted Police and ranchers who wanted the Indians to be well fed and contented on their reserves, insulated by a full stomach from thoughts of roaming the plains and shooting their dinner. The Indians of Treaty Seven became little more than pawns in the policies of the government agencies which saw to their well-being.

For the Indian both policies meant enforced compliance and even pure compulsion. They were compelled by the Police to stay away from cattle ranges; they were compelled by Indian agents, through the threat of the loss of their rations, to work at the occupation of farming for which both they and the land were not suited; they were compelled to send their children to schools which they did not like; they were compelled to remain on their reserves unless given a pass by the agent.

This was the price of harmony in the Canadian West. The ranchers of Alberta were almost completely insulated by these policies and by the effectiveness of the Mounted Police from negative contact with the Indians. There was enough cattle-killing by Indians to create a frontier atmosphere, but not enough to cause serious friction.

The rights of the Indians guaranteed by Treaty Seven were sacrificed for peace. Because of this the relations between the Indians and the ranchers were, on the whole, very good. The majority of the ranchers showed the Indians both sympathy and understanding. But they could afford to have these attitudes, for rebellious elements in Indian society had been defused and the ranchers dealt with Indians completely on white terms. Beneath this surface calm there were still the threats of the newspapers to remind one that bigotry could easily rise to the surface to destroy the harmony with the Indians which had been so carefully nurtured by the Mounted Police.

THE NOT-SO-PEACEABLE KINGDOM: CRIME AND CRIMINAL JUSTICE IN FRONTIER CALGARY

T. Thorner

The Western Canadian frontier has been traditionally regarded as relatively free of crime and violence. Prominent western historian George F. Stanley has claimed that:

The Canadian frontier was peopled by peaceful, law-abiding ranchers, families, and government encouraged colonists. Here the settler looked to organized justice and the Mounted Police for his protection, and not the rifle over his door. . . .in this instance it does appear that the inherent British respect for legal authority and desire to perpetuate the tradition, survived its period of exposure to the destructive influence of the frontier.[1]

Another historian, David Breen, has referred to the southern Alberta region as containing "essentially educated, well-to-do migrants from central Canada and Great Britain," who emulated Victorian England with an "ingrained respect for the rule of law and the maintenance of order."[2] The *Herald* of 1884 viewed Calgary as "not a western town in the ancient use of the word. It is peopled by native Canadians and English citizens who own religion and respect for law. The rough and festive cowboy of Texas and Oregon has no counterpart here. . .the genuine Alberta cowboy is a gentleman."[3]

The purpose of this paper is to examine the legal institutions, the attitudes towards crime, and the amount of lawlessness which occurred in the Calgary district during the closing decades of the nineteenth century. Between 1875 and 1900 Calgary grew slowly from a small post of the Mounted Police into a city with a population in excess of four thousand. Since the Calgary area passed through a period of establishment and adjustment, which involved a measure of instability, the term "frontier" seems an appropriate description of these early years. Problems developed with the local Indians changing their life-style from one of nomadic buffalo hunters to that of sedentary agriculturalists, white settlers creating a large ranching industry and Calgary residents attempting to establish municipal institutions.

Crimes against property, particularly horse-stealing and cattle-killing, occurred on a large scale. Organized theft by whites began in the early 1890's and peaked just after the turn of the century. However, in previous years the chief culprits involved with these offences were Indians.[4] According to cases heard before the courts, as recorded in the Sessional Papers and local newspapers, these offences accounted for a small percentage of all crimes. The Sessional Papers and the newspaper reports of convictions, however, do not provide a very accurate picture of crime; they reveal neither the number of unsolved cases nor the number that were subsequently acquitted on appeals.[5] In the area of stock theft, such records are particularly deficient since they do not substantiate what remained a persistent problem. In 1889 the *Herald* itself commented, "There is scarcely an owner of stock in Alberta who has not suffered more or less from horse and cattle thieves during the past twelve months, and some of the larger ranchers have been very heavy losers."[6]

Other common crimes, both before the courts and in the public mind, were those of petty theft and vagrancy. Rural settlers and town citizens alike complained of repeated, unsolved petty thievery.[7] Vagrancy offences, meanwhile, seem to have violated a law whose purpose was to remove any undesirable persons from the area. Indians were repeatedly charged under this statute. The *Herald*, regarding the Indians as a nuisance, depicted them as persons "loitering around private premises and stealing noiselessly into apartments where they were not expected, frightening small children and women in delicate health."[8] But under their treaties the Indians had every right to visit the towns. If they had no "visible means of support" it was the fault of their guardians, the Canadian government, rather than themselves.

Crimes of extreme violence against persons, on the other hand, were few. According to the Sessional Papers, less than ten murders were committed in the district before 1900. These isolated incidents included an event in 1892 when a substantial portion of the local male population destroyed the property of Chinese residents and threatened them with lynching.[9] Other incidents involving threats of personal violence occurred in 1885 when local homesteaders threatened to confront the larger ranchers over their right to evict squatters, and when ranchers issued repeated warnings to the Indian population which they suspected of thievery.[10] But while these offences were either very few or merely took the form of threats, there were numerous cases of assault.

Moral crimes such as gambling and prostitution steadily increased during the period under discussion. The type of offences included in this category expanded at a rate greater than that of the increase of population. It seems that once Calgary reached a moderate size, the standards of moral behaviour became a community concern. Whereas prostitution and gambling were generally not prosecuted because they were regarded as individual vices before 1890, after that date conditions changed dramatically. Not only were these offences vigorously enforced, but cases such as violation of the Lord's Day and profanation filled the arrest records and the pages of the local press. The public concern for morality seems to have been paramount in determining the prosecution and the scope of these types of crime.[11]

It seems that the largest number of crimes in the Calgary area involved liquor; either possessing liquor in contravention of the territorial prohibition laws, or being drunk. These offences accounted for more than one half of all cases heard before the courts, and usually involved about ten percent of the population per year.[12] But, as in the case of stock thefts, the available records of these offences are not a reliable index of criminal behaviour. Evidence presented before the Royal Commission of Liquor Traffic of 1892 revealed that liquor had been sold openly, both by day and night during these years of prohibition.[13] Large quantities of alcohol had been smuggled into Calgary "packed in pianos and organ cases, also in barrels of apples, sugar and rice."[14]

The attitudes of the local residents towards crime varied with different infractions. Prohibition, for example, existed throughout the North-West Territories from 1873 to 1891. The majority of the population viewed the liquor laws as infringing upon their rights as Canadian citizens. Westerners felt persecuted since they had no representation in this matter, whereas eastern Canadians determined prohibition by local plebiscite. The reaction to such a state of affairs was an open disregard of prohibition throughout the West. Even the most respectable citizens in Calgary broke this law without the slightest qualm.[15]

Crimes involving substantial amounts of property or extreme violence against persons were viewed quite differently. One can almost detect a certain paranoia in these matters. Citizens were outraged by a single murder in 1884 when it occurred in broad daylight.[16] Similarly, when Calgary's only major rural holdup took place in 1886, the *Herald* warned "that revolvers must be the order of the day when citizens travel through the country."[17] It was in response to these types of offences that threats of extra-legal action resulted. The first suspected murderer in the town, a Negro named Jess Williams, faced a mob ready to lynch him.[18] The Chinese riot occurred after three whites had died of small-pox allegedly carried into the town by the Chinese and subsequently concealed from the local authorities. Gentleman rancher T.B. Strange called for vigilante action when Indians repeatedly killed his cattle and escaped conviction.[19] Racial differences also seem to have played a part in these responses since neither white murderers nor white cattle rustlers were ever threatened with vigilante action.

Despite public threats and harsh sentences, however, crimes against property continued. One reason was that during the early years it was the local Indian population that was responsible for many of these actions. In discussing the western population's Victorian respect for the law, some accounts have neglected the attitudes of a large part of that population. Unlike the whites who committed crimes fully cognizant of the laws, the Indians were motivated by necessity, custom, and ignorance. Their attitudes toward crime had as much of an influence on offences committed as did that of the whites.

The culture of the Plains Indians had long regarded horse theft as a sport and a symbol of virility, rather than an act against society. This custom was slow to die especially among the young men of the tribes. The extermination of the buffalo caused cattle killing for the simple reason that the Indians had difficulty in understanding why they should not be allowed to hunt the so-called "white man's buffalo" or cattle, when white hunters had enjoyed open season on the buffalo and consequently threatened the basis of Indian existence.[20]

The Stony Indians on the reserve south of Calgary were perhaps the best agriculturalists among the Plains tribes. Yet, in the winter of 1885 they were "wandering through the hills from below Pincher Creek to the main line of the CPR, begging for food from ranchers, picking the flesh from the bones of dead horses and cattle, even eating coyotes when they could get them."[21] Zealous Indian agents had reported that the Stonies were self-sufficient and hence all rations had been stopped. Similar conditions existed on the Blackfoot reserve. To make matters worse, the type of agricultural tool which the government had supplied were "ploughs [that] would not cut the sod" and "spades [that] buckled and broke when a man's weight was thrown on the handle."[22] When their meagre crops or ranching efforts failed, they were subject to small quantities of poor-quality government rations. It is not surprising that they killed the "white man's buffalo" on the open range. Thus life on the reserves often made the white man's notion of crime irrelevant.

The laws themselves were often another factor which promoted crime. Frequently the law was unsuited to the prairie environment or ill-adapted to the unique nature of western enterprise. The livestock industry was a case in point. Although branding laws had been called for as early as 1884, they were not instituted until 1897. The result was sporadic branding and uncertainty of ownership before that date. This was particularly unsettling for the small farmer who never branded his own few head, and then had trouble claiming them from the unbranded offspring of the larger ranchers.[23] Another prominent example of the law being unsuited to western conditions was the mining legislation. Claim jumping was common because of the amount of red tape and distance between claims and government officials. The *Herald* complained:

Let us suppose Calgary to be his starting point, he travels to the mountains, a distance of 150 or 200 miles, makes his location, he then has to return to procure a Dominion land surveyor. . .get his claim surveyed, return again to Calgary, hunt up a justice of the peace. . .before him sign an affidavit and deposit the sum of $50. . ."[24]

The inappropriateness of much of the law to the western frontier community was often a function of this wider problem of space. Calgary began as an outpost of justice in 1875 when fifty members of the North-West Mounted Police built a fort at the junction of the Bow and Elbow rivers in order to supervise the Indian population. Their jurisdiction spread over 150 square miles, and they doubled as customs agents, mail clerks, undertakers, health inspectors, and weather-bureau officials. And until the white population of the region reached nearly a thousand, the Mounted Police were the only local enforcement agency.

When John Ingram was appointed the town's first chief constable in 1885, his duties, like those of the Mounted Police, were numerous and varied. His responsibilities included inspecting buildings; fire-regulation supervision; inspection of roads, markets, and weights and measures; issuing licenses; and maintaining the local animal pound.[25] He was both dog and cat catcher. In 1885 the Town Council had rejected an offer to employ constables of the Mounted Police for town duty since a police force was seen as a money-making proposition. "Being under salary," the *Herald* noted, "the council calculated to pocket his [Ingram's] share of the liquor fines in town, as informant, which is thought will more than pay his salary of $60 per month as well as pay the expense of having a town lock-up."[26] Usually informants received half the fines from liquor cases, and from this source the town police were not only expected to balance their own budget but add to the small tax bases upon which the town operated.

During the early years of western settlement the Calgary police force was not large. When Ingram was employed he acted as a one-man force. In 1886 two men were added, and later a fourth. The town council seems to have always felt that, should the need arise, a large local contingent of the Mounted Police was always nearby. Calgary's incorporation as a town restricted the Mounted Police jurisdiction to violations outside of the town limits unless the mayor requested their aid. As police costs increased the town council repeatedly tried to have the Mounted Police take over all town duties, but to no avail.[27] The Mounted Police had no desire to enforce the law within towns since that would include by-laws and in effect leave them acting under the order of both the federal government and the town council, a situation they wished to avoid.

There were usually numerous applications for the few positions on the town police force. Yet the occupation seems to have been held in low esteem. The basic requirements were those of size and strength. No evidence has been found to indicate that policemen were ever expected to be familiar with the town by-laws or the criminal code, except that the chief constable usually had experience in that position before arriving in Calgary. Like their town counterpart, the Mounted Police generally lacked training and the respect of the local population.

A low standard of training was only one of the factors that limited the efficiency of the two enforcement agencies. Both suffered from internal corruption. Concerning the town policy, the *Herald* noted, "That on account of the so-called liquor laws of the country, the private members of the force can and do extort contraband wares from the town people by various threats."[28] In 1890 the chief of police was charged with neglect of duty since he refused to collect evidence against liquor dealers and employed Indian women for "immoral purposes".[29] Scandals involving the local police occurred in several other instances to the chagrin of the local population.

The detachment of the NWMP stationed in Calgary was also involved in corrupt practices. Evidence given before the Royal Commission on Liquor Traffic of 1892 revealed that local constables earned thirty or forty dollars per month in so-called "tips" for ignoring liquor offences.[30] Calgarians also felt that they misused their authority under the prohibition laws to search without warrant, since under this ruse, "Whenever a man had a private vengeance against anyone, and he was on the force, he exercised it."[31]

Between the two police forces there existed a failure to cooperate, and a confusion over jurisdiction within the town. Theoretically, once a town was incorporated the Mounted Police were to be no longer responsible for police duties. In practice they did make arrests in Calgary since the town council continually debated whether they should involve the town police with territorial ordinances or merely enforce municipal by-laws.[32] Amid the confusion it was often the case that the territorial ordinances were not enforced. When things did get out of hand, as in the riot of 1892, the town police proved to be powerless, and the municipal authorities were slow to assume any responsibility to call in the Mounties.[33]

There were numerous complaints regarding the efficiency of the Mounted Police. John Glenn, ranching near Calgary in 1881, stated "We have no protection from the police. The Indians may steal our cattle, as they often do, but we can get no redress. In that we would be better off if there were no police in the country at all."[34] Many of the original ranchers in the area returned to Montana because of the lack of protection, while others paid the Indians to return stock. The *Herald*, meanwhile, complained bitterly:

Indians are playing sad havoc among the calves. One gentleman says that out of 70 of last year's calves he has only seven left and a neighbour who last year had a 100 cattle can count 25. . . . .It is a pity that so near to a town Calgary's size, where there is stationed a force of one hundred police such depredations should be allowed to continue with impunity.[35]

These complaints continued throughout the "frontier" era of Calgary's development.

The lack of police protection had an effect on the disclosure of crimes. Long after law and order had "marched west" in 1874, to use Cecil Denny's phrase, it was alleged that "settlers do not always report when they lose stock in this way, as many of them have the idea that if they lay information against an Indian and get him punished, other Indians will kill more cattle by way of retaliation."[36] This fear of Indian reprisals made its way into the police reports even as late as 1902.

The blame for stock losses was usually placed on the NWMP. They were accused of being overly cautious, requiring eyewitnesses, and not accepting the identification of stock as proof of theft. The *Herald* suggested that extra-legal means should be employed. "A well organized stock association would be the best agency for prosecuting those guilty," together with a clever stock detective since, "the Mounted Police as detectives do not fill the bill, their uniform, their manner and their horses are all against successful detective work."[37] Thus in 1892 most of the influential cattlemen did unite to hire stock detectives and establish a five hundred dollar reward for the conviction of anyone caught illegally handling cattle.[38]

The loss of stock, however, was not caused simply by deficiencies in Mounted Police surveillance but by the prairie environment and the manner of stock grazing. As Superintendent McIllree stated, "The country is so large that unless a case is reported at once and you have a hot scent to go on, it is hard to trace a horse."[39] Often cattle and horses strayed for hundreds of miles, or sometimes died in blizzards only to become statistics on the lists of stolen property.

Police efficiency also suffered from a lack of public cooperation, especially in offences involving the unpopular prohibition law. McIllree stated:

It is no use trying to deny the fact that all sentiments of the greater part of the country is distinctly adverse to the statute on this subject; we get no sympathy with our efforts to put a stop to the traffic, and it is the most disagreeable of many duties we have to perform.[40]

Without public support, evidence was particularly difficult to obtain since most convictions had to be based on complaints by informants. The local police were too easily recognized and proved inept in penetrating the local whisky trade. Informants were willing to supply evidence since they received half the fine imposed on those they helped to convict. But when the technicalities of the liquor law upheld increasing appeals, few informants were any longer willing to help the police. Those who continued were often beaten.[41] It seems that the popular consensus which supported the violation of the liquor laws also influenced the incentive of the constables to carry out this duty, for they often seem to have overlooked these offences. But public resentment of the liquor laws continued to grow particularly over the police powers to search without badge or warrant under the liquor statute. Complaints culminated in 1886 when two men posing as police officers in search of whisky robbed two cattlemen of seven hundred dollars, thereby increasing public indignation and further reducing the number of informants willing to help the police.[42]

Judicial process and institutions were not free from complaints, and their contribution to western development was certainly not as clear cut as George Stanley has suggested. A common grievance concerned the qualifications of the men who administered justice. When asked the cause of lawlessness in Calgary, A.L. Sifton, the town solicitor in 1892, censured the local Justices of the Peace.[43] But even the town solicitor was not without his critics. The Calgary *Tribune* referred to him as poorly educated and incompetent, because of his inability to frame adequate by-laws.[44] Sifton's views on the Justices of the Peace were often substantiated. An editorial of 1895 states:

If anything were wanting to destroy the last vestige of confidence that the Calgary public may have had in its magistracy, the disgraceful occurrences of the last few days have done so. While there may be worthy exception, the Herald *has no hesitation in saying that as a rule the peace commissioners of this country, and this city in particular, are in the hands of third class men, whether judged by their morals, their probity or their ability. Some years ago an heroic effort was made to purify the inferior courts by cancelling the whole commission, but on the reappointments the worst kind of favoritism crept in and Governor Royal very soon found himself in as bad a predicament as ever. The ridiculous scenes of the past few days, disgusting as they are to the respectable public and bringing as they do the whole city into disrepute should leave no shadow of doubt in any man's mind as to what should now be done.*

Nothing short of wholesale and immediate cancellation of commissions of the Justices of the Peace will purify the air; nothing less will satisfy the public.

It is a matter of common notoriety that that little police court has been the scenes of the most unblushing scandals; that Justices of the Peace have sat on the bench while in a state of intoxication, not once but repeatedly; that fines paid in have never been accounted for and this not merely in isolated cases; that prisoners under sentence of the court have paid their fines by putting in accounts against the presiding Justice of the Peace; and other crimes and scandals enacted, the mere mention of which should arouse any self-respecting community to arise in its might and shake itself clear of the foul encumbrance.[45]

The *Herald* was also highly critical of the dual role of the officers of the Mounted Police who were ex-officio Justices of the Peace. In their place the *Herald* desired men "with brain enough to act as magistrates."[46]

The distance between population centres and the sparse density of the prairie had its own peculiar effects on judicial institutions. Calgary was always part of a very extensive judicial circuit, and even when the circuit radiated from Calgary the local magistrate's time in town was very limited. By 1890 this resulted in a backlog of cases, some of which went back over two years.[47] The most significant effect of such a system was the high number of cases which were dismissed because of unforeseen travelling conditions or longer court sittings in some localities, which made it impossible to schedule definite court dates. Since many witnesses often came from miles around, it was not unusual to find that they could not afford the expenses of long delays and thus would return home. Under such circumstances not only were some guilty parties allowed to escape, but persons held in custody often served longer periods of time in detention before trial than their actual offences could bring them from conviction.[48]

Calgary residents repeatedly petitioned for a magistrate to handle the large amount of legal business in the district which extended 150 miles north and south, and 300 miles east and west.[49] The district court met only four times a year at irregular intervals but Calgary could have supported a resident magistrate. Magistrates on the Calgary circuit throughout this era were often refused leaves of absence and holidays due to the amount of business. The responsibility for this situation lay with the Macdonald administration in Ottawa, which stood on a policy of economy. It advised that judicial expenses in the North-

West should be held to a minimum unless "life and property were in direct danger."[50]

Federal policy created other legal institutions detrimental to western development. The jury of the North-West Territories was one such factor. It was composed of six members, unlike twelve in other parts of Canada, and it was appointed by the Lieutenant-Governor whereas it was chosen by lot in the rest of the Dominion. Calgarians saw these practices as consistent with their inferior territorial status. Other irregularities sustained such a point of view. Writs of *habeus corpus, certiorari,* and *mandamus,* and injunctions were regarded as safeguards of liberty by the local population, but they were absent until 1887 due to the circumscribed nature of the judicial system.[51] Before 1887 appeals from local magistrates were largely absent because the only court with appellate jurisdiction was in Manitoba, a distance of eight hundred miles from Calgary

Within this system magistrates not only executed the laws, but helped to frame them. All judges spent a month or six weeks of each year in the Territorial Legislative Assembly as legal experts. "It is a well known fact," reported the *Herald,* "that lawmakers have a general dislike to prove themselves to have been stupid and that, for this reason, bad ordinances have been upheld on the bench contrary to constitutional convictions."[52]

Similar feelings of indignation and loss of rights were expressed over the dual function of the officers of the Mounted Police. Calgary's first mayor blessed the incorporation of the town since it freed its citizens from the jurisdiction of the Mounted Police:

. . .*who besides being policemen have from force of circumstances and a lack of magistrates when required, been appointed justices with full powers to try and convict the very men they have arrested, and act as jailors upon them. . . . The police have trampled upon our rights as citizens.*[53]

There seems to have been some genuine concern over the loss of legal guarantees and aberrant legal procedure. However, other motives were at work in the criticism of judicial administration in frontier Calgary. What the mayor was referring to when he objected to the Mounted Police acting as Justices of the Peace was the town's financial position. All fines collected by the Police justices and those paid to the magistrate's court passed to the territorial government in Regina. With the creation of a local police court, the town hoped to share this apparently lucrative aspect of providing justice. "That thriving institution the town police court will make the fortune of the corporation yet. . . .The fines are averaging some forty or fifty dollars a week regularly," stated the *Herald* in 1885.[54]

The quality of justice rendered by the local police court seems indeed to have been largely determined by its financial objectives. Public complaints censured the bending of laws, since after the territorial government reasserted its right to certain fines the Calgary Chief of Police made careful efforts to charge offenders only under the town by-laws, even if their crimes were of a more substantial nature.[55] The town also seems to have played a game of cat and mouse with local saloons and houses of ill-fame, since the town licensed them and later sent the police to raid them, thus pocketing both license fees and fines.[56]

The business of fining had to be closely controlled in a financially strained economy such as the one that existed in early Calgary. In 1884, before the creation of the local police court, this relationship between justice and economics was made clear by Justice of the Peace George Murdoch:

In cases that have come before me of contravention of the Liquor Act I have acted in the only way that I could possibly do as a fixture in this town, and having the welfare of the place at heart, I have not imposed the heaviest fines on residents of this place as that would be suicidal, the proceeds of the fine having to be sent out of this place. We would therefore be deprived of just so much working capital. In cases of outsiders coming in to sell the stuff and pack the proceeds off I acted more severely.[57]

In some cases fines seem to have been important to individual justices. A member of the early town police force recalled that the force was often admonished for lack of arrests, the reason being that the justices collected the costs of the case, usually about two dollars and fifty cents. Apparently some justices came to blows in their struggles to preside before newly arrested criminals.[58]

Punishments in liquor and prostitution cases were slight deterrents. Profits from the sale of illicit liquor were said to be so high that smugglers once convicted were quite ready to pay the standard two hundred dollar fine. Likewise, prostitutes viewed their fines as "license fees". If they were unable to pay their fine, the sentence usually did not come into effect until after the departure of the next train.[59]

The popularity of employing fines and allowing women offenders to escape jail terms seems to have been related to the quality of the local jail system. Police Magistrate Van Wart would not sentence prisoners to terms in the local police cells because of the filth, stench, and lack of ventilation.[60] Numerous escapes, the absence of separate facilities for women, and rising costs of upkeep seem to have deterred its usage. More often prisoners seem to have been fined or warned than incarcerated. If necessary, dangerous prisoners were housed in the Mounted Police guardroom. But that structure suffered from the same problems as the city jail. Sentences over two years in length were served at Manitoba's Stony Mountain Penitentiary. There, prisoners were crowded together in damp, cold cells, and, hence, typhoid and pneumonia were a common ailment. Lunatics were housed with other prisoners and the conditions must have been appalling to say the least.[61]

While it certainly seems to have been the exception rather than the rule, some verdicts did reflect an informal or "sage-brush" character of justice. In 1892 this verdict was rendered by Supreme Court Judge C.B. Rouleau:

Prisoner, the evidence is conflicting, but I find you guilty and sentence you to three months in the guard-room. The evidence, as I say, is very conflicting but if I was sure, if I was quite sure, that you stole that horse I would give you two years in the Manitoba Penitentiary.[62]

A similar verdict, "Not guilty, but don't do it again," was passed on two Indians caught killing cattle near Gleichen.[63] In 1895 Justices Creagh and Boswell of Calgary refused to sit on the bench together. Two years earlier while sitting together on a case they had each arrived at a different verdict and settled the matter by wrestling in the courtroom.[64]

The attitudes toward the judicial system were two-sided. On the one hand the local population resented the loss of legal formalities, and on the other they accepted informal justice. The best illustration of this dichotomy concerns the career of Judge Jeremiah Travis in Calgary. In 1885 when Travis arrived the citizens lauded his coming. However, when Travis upheld the conviction of a leading resident, charged a local editor with contempt of court, and ousted a town council, threats were made on his life and, public meetings were instigated to protest the "Judicial Tyranny". Local pressure on the federal government finally secured the removal of Travis.[65] The local population seems to have had their own ideas about what "justice" meant.

The local Indians, while at first impressed by the honesty and impartiality of the courts and the police, grew increasingly discontented. Whisky seems to have always found its way to the reserves, as did the cattle of many whites seeking virgin pasture lands. With the arbitrary use of vagrancy charges many chiefs lost their respect for white justice as increasing numbers of Indians were forcibly arrested only to be released or given stiff sentences on the grounds of circumstantial evidence.[66] Once sentenced to jail or prison, regardless of the term, Indians were under a death sentence, since many of them contracted tuberculosis and subsequently died.[67]

In conclusion, it seems that if the fragment of population that settled the Calgary area did have notions of legal respect and formal justice, they soon lost them in the face of frontier conditions. They openly broke liquor laws, attacked the local Chinese, armed themselves as homesteaders and ranchers to defend their interests, and threatened the local Indians and at least one judge who failed to conform to their standards. The legal institutions which supposedly maintained law and order appear to have been maladjusted. Backlogs, delays, insecure jails, ill-adapted laws, and short-handed police forces made crime a simple matter on the prairie landscape where detection alone was often impossible.

There is no more persistent myth in Canada than the myth that Canada is or has been a society free of crime and violence. Many influences have entered into the creation of this myth in Western Canadian history, but three factors seem to have been chiefly responsible for its general acceptance. One has been the standard of comparison. When Canada pushed westward so did the United States, followed by vigilance, outlaws, range wars, and campaigns of Indian extermination to which western Canada has compared itself. Secondly, the gulf between moral ideas and the actual facts of behaviour in Calgary suggests that a "Chamber of Commerce" attitude existed which contemporaries accepted in order to promote immigration to the Canadian West rather than the American. Finally, it seems that a peculiar vision of "law and order" has seemed necessary to a Canadian identity and has coloured our view of the western past.

THE FAIR, FRAIL FLOWERS OF WESTERN WOMANHOOD

Catherine Philip

Any consideration of the women of the western frontier must take into account the fact that they could not vote. They were permitted to vote in 1917 (three years beyond the period of this study) in provincial elections, and in 1918 in federal elections.[1] They had to wait until 1929 when, through the efforts of five Alberta women, they were legally recognized as persons, thus qualifying them for appointment to the Canadian Senate.[2] So this discussion is concerned with non-persons.

Although women could not vote, according to the North-West Territories Act of 1880 they could own property. A married woman could own property apart from her husband, and a woman's wages were not included in her husband's debts. A married woman could make bank deposits. A husband was not responsible for his wife's debts before marriage. Women could conduct their own suits for the recovery of property or money. This legislation was quite advanced for its time because in many countries women had no property rights whatsoever. That women owned property in frontier Calgary is revealed in receipts for taxes made out to women in the East, the United States, and England, indicating that there were absentee landladies who doubtless purchased the property for speculation.

Another factor to consider is the prevailing attitudes towards women in the nineteenth and early twentieth centuries. The most important function of women was to marry and bear children. They were set on a pedestal and assumed to be pure, ethereal, and spiritual, as opposed to the grosser, more beastly nature of men. They were fair, frail flowers, to be sheltered and protected. They should not trouble their pretty little heads with politics or business that were part of the man's world. This was the attitude the settlers brought from "back home", wherever that was.

One must not forget that women were in the minority. According to the federal census of 1911 there were 24,104 single males and 12,374 single females in Calgary, so the ratio of men to women was around two to one. Calgary, therefore, was a good place to find a husband. The frontierswoman was accustomed to being surrounded by chivalrous men who praised her appearance and her cooking. It might have been demoralizing for some of them to realize that the compliments they received from men were not simply because of their charms but also because of the scarcity of their sex. Women wielded little or no overt power in the community but they held considerable influence in subtle ways simply because they were women. They could not vote but they possessed two powerful weapons, tears and sharp tongues. We do not know how many of the decisions that were apparently man-made were influenced by a woman who encouraged, nagged, or turned on the waterworks.

There was a general pattern of immigration. Usually men arrived, established themselves, and then sent for their wives and children. Or a man would arrive and then send for his fiancee. She stayed in a hotel, or more than likely he made arrangements for her to stay with friends, a married couple, until plans were completed for the wedding. Brothers would emigrate and then send for a sister to keep house for them. Family groups arrived. These women were fortunate because they started their new life surrounded by people they had known most of their lives. Pioneer nuns came west, to serve as nurses and teachers. A few women, and they were considered very brave, ventured into the West alone, without family or friends to receive them, sought employment as teachers, nurses, or domestics, or looked for husbands. Prostitutes travelled west, for the discrepancy between the numbers of men and women was advantageous to their trade.

Women arrived in southern Alberta, a few at first and then in growing numbers. When they saw their first home in Alberta their immediate reaction, almost to a woman, was the same—they burst into tears. During their long journey across the country—and for some an equally long ocean voyage—their hopes had been buoyed by the promise of the future. Upon arrival, their dreams were pricked by reality's sting, so they wept. I read of a woman who wept for three months until she settled down and began to love southern Alberta.[3] Regarding her first home in Calgary, a woman railed against her husband, "Do you expect us to live in that? Why it's nothing but a cowshed," to which he replied, "Well, lassie, it's the best I can do."[4]

Women were the reluctant pioneers who followed their men—husbands, fathers, brothers, sweethearts. Before they left home they were given mementoes, religious books, a woolen shawl—lovingly given as protection against the cold—a lace tablecloth, a set of fine bone china, Mrs. Beeton's cook book, and recipes that were prized by mothers and grandmothers. They brought these precious belongings to the frontier so that they could look at them and dream of home, for homesickness and loneliness scourged the frontierswomen. If it were not for the patriarchal system of the time, their emotional attachment to their men, and the fact that few of them had any money, they would have turned around and gone straight back home. But they stayed, fortunately for us. Some spent a lifetime pretending the frontier did not exist. Truly, in their thoughts they were "back east", in Britain, in Germany or the Ukraine, and they behaved accordingly. And in the course of time they changed the frontier by introducing the cultures of their former homes.

They did this in many ways. For example, they changed men's speaking habits. Walking along the streets in Calgary's first years one saw very few women but a great many men, loud men, men whose vocabularies were larded with obscenity. A man who could swear for ten minutes without repeating himself was held in high esteem.[5] Even the missionaries were impressed. Now, in those days, men simply did not use profanity or obscenity in the presence of a woman. It had become so much a part of the speech of some of these tough frontiersmen they scarcely knew any other words. So when they were confronted by "a woman" they were struck dumb—they had no words to use. They just sat there looking at her, completely tongue-tied. If they decided they wished to associated with women they had to clean up their language—and many of them did. So, women were instrumental in changing the vocabulary of the frontier. It swung to the opposite extreme, for the Victorians were noted for genteel euphemisms. There really were women who referred to a stallion as a "big horse", and a bull as a "gentleman cow", but I don't think there were very many of them in the ranching district. The vocabulary changed, at least when women were present, from an explicit and forthright body language to speech patterns that completely denied human sexuality.

Men living alone, or in groups, were not very fastidious about their appearance. A Calgarian was proud to smell like his horse.

Calgary's first mayor recorded in his diary that he changed his underwear.[6] If this had been a daily, or even weekly, occurrence I doubt if he would have mentioned it. Then one day, he had a great clean-up and put all his clothes in a big tub and boiled them on the top of the stove. When men washed clothes—if they washed them—they hung them to dry on the fence or a bush or anything convenient. Women changed all that. They insisted that their husbands build a proper clothesline and they instituted the Monday-morning wash. People knew better than to call on a Calgary housewife on Monday morning for she would be busily engaged in washing clothes, with a washboard, or maybe with a washing machine which she turned with a handle. She wrung the clothes by hand or with a mangle. Then she hung the clothes on the line—the sheets, shirts, pillow cases (sometimes they were sugar or flour sacks with the labels bleached out), long-handled underwear, flannel petticoats, socks she probably knitted herself, dresses, blouses, pants. In winter the washing swayed stiffly in the breeze until she went out, and with fingers numb with cold, brought it in and strung it on lines around the kitchen to thaw and dry. Then she went to work with the sadiron that was heated on top of the stove. I don't think women enjoyed washday very much. Once they advanced up the socio-economic ladder they hired a woman to come in and do the wash or they sent it to a Chinese laundry. Some of these frail flowers earned a livelihood with the backbreaking job of laundresses. Women cleaned up the frontier in more ways than one.

Men on their own were not particular about privacy. They did not care who peered in the window at them. Women certainly did. One of the first things they did was put curtains on the windows. Curtains offered a colourful note in the otherwise drab interiors of the first dwellings. As well, the curtains afforded privacy and continued the illusion, as a woman looked around her little domain, that the frontier outside did not truly exist. Within the four walls of her home her family behaved according to the norms of the people "back home". If the family lived in a one-room house—and many of them did in the first years—she strung wires or ropes along the ceiling, under the sod roof, and suspended sheets or blankets from them, creating temporary partitions that afforded privacy for bathing, which some called a "sponge bath", dressing, or the connubial bed. Women insisted on the construction of outdoor toilets, preferably with a pleasant view from the open door, a design of some sort cut in the door, and a catalogue hanging from a hook, the latter for functional as well as educational purposes.

Men were not fussy about cooking or washing dishes. They served the entire meal from one dish. Women prided themselves on setting a good table. They washed the dishes and put them in the cupboard. Now, the cupboard might be a packing case covered with cretonne but it was still a cupboard. Denied the vote and positions of power in the community, they concentrated their energies on housewifely skills. Pioneers enjoyed their food, and some of the rich people enjoyed it to the point of gluttony. Women vied with each other, showing off their culinary skills. Yet not all of them were superior cooks, because in some cases the home-made bread had to be cut with an axe. They used recipes brought from "back home".

In the district around Calgary in the first years, many families lived off the land except for staples such as flour, sugar, oatmeal, spices, raisins, currants, syrup, and salt. It was not unusual for a woman to go out and shoot prairie chickens for supper. It was she who planted and tended the garden, and it was she who canned dozens of quarts of fruit and vegetables. When company came, she would raise part of the kitchen floor by means of a metal ring, go down the steep steps into the cellar, and point proudly to row upon row of Mason jars with the spring tops, or sealers with screw tops, filled with fruit, vegetables and meat, pickles, jams, and jellies. Cabbages hung from the rafters, and bins around the floor contained potatoes, turnips, and carrots. Crocks of meat and butter stood in a corner, or perhaps were kept cool in a nearby creek or an old, open well. Although her family ate good, wholesome food, the meals were a bit monotonous, for there was not the variety we have today.

When men, riding across the rangeland, saw the tell-tale signs of a woman's presence—curtains on the window and a clothesline at the back—they made a bee-line for the house. Of course they were invited to share a meal with the family. They washed up and slicked back their hair, cleaned up their language, and sat down at the table to enjoy a home-cooked meal prepared by a woman's hands. Simply to sit in a woman's presence was a treat, for the men were lonely too.

When you add the warm-hearted hospitality to men's carelessness about their persons, you get a simple answer—bedbugs. Bedbugs were everywhere in Calgary—in the hotels, in the humblest dwellings, and, yes, in the splendid mansions. Women waged a continuing war against the pestiferous little insects. One of the battle tactics was to leave the offending room in darkness and then to rush in, with a coal oil lamp in one hand and a rag soaked with coal oil in the other, and then dab, dab, dab. Here is a recipe that was used to eliminate bedbugs in Calgary around 1900: corrosive sublimate and alcohol, to be prepared by a druggist who would know the formula. Apply with a feather and in a few days make another application. This remedy would be effective, providing one could catch up with the bedbugs.[7]

The environment was unkind to women. Complexions suffered in the arid climate. In 1889 a visitor remarked, rather uncharitably I think, "Calgary girls are very pale faced, sallow or pasty faced. They lose colour because of the dry atmosphere."[8] Frontierswomen seldom wore cosmetics. They could dab their noses with talcum or rice powder with propriety, or pinch their cheeks before going to a party to give them a rosy glow, and girls might experiment with beet juice when their mothers were not looking. The obvious use of cosmetics, or "paint", signified that one was a prostitute. Girls dressed in much the same way as their mothers except their skirts were shorter. They wore their hair long, in ringlets or braids, perhaps with a bow at the back. When they were eighteen their parents held a coming-out party for them, at home, in the district school, or in some public place. At that time they lengthened their skirts and put their hair up, arranging it in the fashion of the time. This change in their appearance signified that they could participate in the adult functions of the community. It also indicated that a woman was of marriageable age. Thus one could tell at a glance a woman's status in the community.

The aridity was bad enough but the dust was worse. Black blizzards swirled over the frontier town. Herds of cattle being trailed around Calgary's perimeter raised more dust. "Dust storms were frequent and severe and made things worse," a woman wrote. "Before the streets were paved they were terrible. First a purple cloud would come up. Then the wind started. The air was so clouded with dust, all signs of houses, even those nearest, were blotted out. We could not keep the dust out. We wet strips of cloth and stuck them around the cracks of the windows, but they did not stop it. It seemed almost to come through the walls."[9]

The Chinook, the gentle wind of winter, is mentioned in almost every diary of that time. During a Chinook a woman could hang her clothes on the line and perhaps they would dry there. She could walk around Calgary in comfort or walk into the fields around the ranch house, and watch the cattle sunning themselves. The wind was a mixed blessing. Moccasins and woollen socks that kept feet warm in below zero temperatures, when soaked with water, became sodden and cold. Sleighs that glided over snow were stopped by patches of bare prairie. "Rotten ice" on rivers made transportation, which was always difficult, even more hazardous. Kells tells of a woman who was crossing the river on rotten ice with her three children in a buggy. The buggy broke through and she managed to get out with the baby. She carried it to what she thought was a safe place and laid it on the ice. Then she went back and rescued the other two children. When she went back for the baby, it was gone. There was a slope to the ice and the baby had squirmed around, slid down the ice and drowned in the river.[10] Each year the rivers took their toll of drownings as persons unsuccessfully attempted to ford them or cross on rotten ice.

Pioneer Calgary women were extremely conscious of the hazards of flooding which took place annually. In June of 1897 a cloudburst in the mountains precipitated a flood that rushed into town at ten o'clock one evening. The Fire Department and NWMP directed rescue activities, brought horses and wagons to save people and their furniture on the lower flats. Two of the city's bridges were wrecked and a third came close to going. All that could be seen of Prince's Island was the tops of the trees.[11] A letter from a visitor to Calgary in 1902 mentions settlers' homes as well as barns and outbuildings floating down the river.[12] Women and children were evacuated and stood watching in anguish as everything they possessed drifted out of sight.

Fire was another hazard that menaced rural and urban residents alike. Summer and fall skies were frequently clouded by smoke from prairie and forest fires. Menacing clouds of smoke stirred rural residents into emergency action. Fire guards were ploughed around buildings. Gunny sacks were kept on hand to be soaked in water, perhaps in a rain barrel or nearby creek and used to beat out the flames. Green cowhides were sometimes used for the same purpose. Children were put in the cellar for safety as women helped their husbands fight the flames. Horses and cows were taken from the barn and freed. Sometimes dwellings and outbuildings were razed and the unfortunate family sought shelter with neighbours.

Calgary, like most communities of that era, was far from being a model of sanitary procedures. It was a semi-rural community where civic officials continually coped with the problems of stray animals and filth. Dogs fought on sidewalks and in the main part of town. Horses could be purchased from the Indians for two or three dollars, or imported at great cost from eastern Canada and Europe. Many families kept horses in the town during summer and sent them to nearby ranches in winter. Women were not surprised to see curious horses looking in the kitchen window or standing on the verandah. One woman was somewhat taken aback, however, when she returned from a shopping expedition and found that a horse had wandered into the bedroom. Dead cows from ranches to the west floated down the river and lay on the banks, rotting and stinking. Dead horses were left to decompose until the town scavenger hauled them away. One can imagine the difficulties of women wearing long skirts picking their way around the town.

It was not surprising that the community swarmed with house flies. In 1889, J.H. Walker wrote to England, "The house fly is here all the time. There were really numerous flies on the table, so thick it looked like a black cloth with white spots." At first he tried to swat the flies or drive them away, but finding it futile he tried picking them out of the food. That proved to be too much trouble so he went on eating and did not look at them.[13] Although the story smacks of being a tall tale, it does indicate that flies were numerous and everywhere. They were considered a nuisance but were not particularly dangerous. On June 11, 1911 the *Albertan* editorialized:

The house fly is a criminal. . . .It was first suggested by Dr. Nicholas in 1873 that the house fly carried disease but only in the last few years has it been proved. Health officers are beginning to ask, "Why is typhoid fever?" Flies are the greatest criminal at large.[14]

Two weeks later, the Fly Committee of a local women's club issued a bulletin that they were beginning a war on flies.[15] Thanks to women's efforts, Calgary became a cleaner and more healthful place.

Girls in this dusty, arid place led sheltered lives, protected by their mothers, fathers, and brothers. This was part of the Victorian ethos but it was also necessary in a community where men outnumbered women. A girl was expected to be innocent of human sexuality. Mothers did not believe that their daughters should know the so-called "facts of life". One wonders if the mothers themselves knew any more than the basic facts of reproduction. Girls were advised to be cautious in their relationships with men, and were carefully chaperoned at parties. There was a polarization of women between good and bad. A respectable woman was expected to be superhumanly pure. Her opposite was considered to be the dregs of the gutter. Pioneer society simply did not recognize a woman who was somewhere in between. Married women established themselves as the guardians of public morals. If a couple was living together without marriage, or "living-in-sin", as it was called, the married women ostracized the woman concerned, or made life so uncomfortable for her the couple would move away, perhaps to another town. In 1911, out of a female population of 23,511, there were only four divorcees. Divorce did take place, but very infrequently.

A woman's sole function in life, according to public opinion, was to marry and raise a family. Clergy and press extolled the "joys of motherhood" yet there is no particular evidence the women themselves wanted large families. Birth control was practised to a limited extent but most women had no idea that conception could be prevented. When women met, they whispered so the children would not hear that Mrs. A was "expecting", "expecting a little stranger", in a "delicate or interesting condition", or "in-the-family-way". The word "pregnant," being an overt expression of sexuality, was taboo. Women viewed childbirth with philosophical resignation or dread. The use of anaesthetics in childbirth was debated at that time. Some people wondered about the safety of the mother and child. Others opposed anaesthetics on moral grounds. The pains of childbirth were part of the curse pronounced upon women in consequence of Eve's transgression in the Garden of Eden. The use of anaesthesia would interfere with the penalty. Fortunate, indeed, was the pioneer woman who had a physician in attendance to alleviate the pain with chloroform and deliver the baby. Most babies, even in Calgary, were born at home, where a room—a bedroom or the parlor, frequently called the "front room"—was set aside as a delivery room. In the district around Calgary, where there were no doctors and transportation to the town was painfully difficult, babies were delivered by practical nurses, midwives, or perhaps a neighbouring woman. One end of a sheet was tied to the bottom of the bed, the other end was thrust into the woman's hands, and she was told to "push hard". I have not been able to find statistics on the maternal mortality rate but there is every indication that it was high. After delivery the mother was expected to rest quietly in bed for ten days to two weeks. The rationale was that complete immobility would help her regain her strength.

There were women who, for one reason or another, did not wish to bear the child they were carrying. Self-abortion was practised, by means of a knitting needle, at fearful risk to the woman's life. Calgary's most notorious abortionist was a man who called himself "Dr. Lovingheart". He must have functioned quite openly because there is a reference to the Dr. Lovingheart Building in City Council Minutes.[10] In 1894 he was charged with the murder of a woman and child and was lodged in jail. For some reason, and this makes for all sorts of speculation, he got off trial and was charged with the lesser offence of practising medicine without a license. Dr. Lovingheart left Calgary with his wife, who was described as a pleasant woman, and a young German girl who seemed mesmerized by the man. The girl's parents were distraught, wondering what her fate would be.[11] It is impossible to present statistics on abortions but they did take place, either self-inflicted or performed by quacks.

Few mothers did not mourn the death of at least one child. Considering the flies and the filth around Calgary, it is not surprising that there were so many communicable diseases. In 1901 the Public School Board advised parents that their children should be vaccinated.[12] Apparently not all parents conformed to this suggestion, preferring to use home remedies that were completely ineffective. Some mothers put camphor around the children's necks to ward off disease. Others gave them Scott's Emulsion of Cod Liver Oil or sulphur and molasses. Innoculation was not practised in this era. Mothers watched their children choking away their lives with diptheria. Children died of whooping cough, scarlet fever, pneumonia, and infantile paralysis. Some simply died of a fever, for the diagnosis was unknown.

This is what a Calgary woman wrote in the 1890s: "Our dear little Ewen got septicemia and passed away on May 23. He was barely three years old. We laid him to rest in his little, white coffin ourselves and Dad and Charlie took him in the buggy to the cemetery where our clergyman and Mr. Rogers laid him to rest. It snowed that night and how my heart did ache to think of our precious little boy out there in the cold ground, though we knew his spirit had returned to God who gave him."[13]

These were the women of the frontier. They were the fair, frail flowers of western womanhood.

THE CHINESE EXPERIENCE IN FRONTIER CALGARY: 1885–1910

J. Brian Dawson

Over the first twenty-five years of Calgary's history a permanent Chinese residency was established in a Western Canadian city which was predominantly Anglo-Canadian in all important respects. The Chinese presence in this environment led to hostility and even violence towards the numerically insignificant Chinese population. This chapter attempts to provide an insight into the pattern of Chinese settlement in urban centres in western Canada and illustrates the types of responses by urban pioneers towards an essentially undesired ethnic group.

The years from 1885 to 1910 were distinctive ones in the historical evolution of Calgary and in the establishment of a local Chinese community. In 1885 Calgary was a small railway town with some likelihood of expanding into a major transportation centre. By 1910, however, Calgary had been an incorporated city for sixteen years and had experienced a dramatic population explosion which commenced roughly in 1904; some forty thousand people resided in the city as 1911 approached.[1] Within a generation a relatively insignificant prairie town had developed into a burgeoning financial and commercial metropolis.

The first Chinese pioneers arrived in Calgary at least as early as 1886, and thus the Chinese can claim a very long presence in the hundred-year-old city. There were only a handful of Chinese pioneers in Calgary during the 1880's and 1890's, but, as the city expanded increasing numbers arrived. Less than one hundred Chinese lived in Calgary in 1900, whereas by 1910 over four hundred resided in premises scattered throughout the city. The year 1910 was a very significant one, as in the fall months the third Calgary Chinatown, which still exists, began its construction. From this date a distinct, and therefore recognizable, Chinese community developed within the city. In Chinatown various businesses opened to serve the cultural needs of the local Chinese, and during the period after 1910 a considerable number of Chinese associations were formed for social, fraternal, and benevolent purposes.

*   *   *   *   *

During the nineteenth century there had been two large waves of Chinese immigration into Canada. The first wave occurred during the Cariboo Gold Rush of the 1850's in British Columbia, and in June, 1858, a number of Chinese from San Francisco landed at Victoria joining the throngs of eager miners. The following year more Chinese apparently arrived at Victoria directly from Hong Kong. When the mines were largely depleted in the mid-1860's some Chinese left Canada, but many decided to stay. They found jobs working as labourers, houseboys, coal miners, and gardeners, or opened up their own businesses, especially laundries. By the mid-1870's a moderately sized Chinatown had grown up in Victoria, and the Chinese presence in British Columbia was well established.[2]

The second wave of Chinese immigration was of course in the 1880's, when Chinese labourers arrived to build the British Columbia sections of the Canadian Pacific Railway. Andrew Onderdonk, the contractor responsible, arranged for over 18,000 Chinese men to come to Canada, and although some came from the United States, most arrived directly from China aboard chartered vessels. During 1883, the year of peak railway construction in the province, there were from 6,000 to 7,500 Chinese labourers working on the various sections at any one time. During the five years of construction an estimated 1,500 Chinese died in the course of work.[3]

Completion of the Canadian Pacific Railway in late 1885 resulted in mass unemployment for thousands of unskilled Chinese labourers. Neither Onderdonk their contractor, the Canadian federal government, nor the railway would admit any responsibility in assisting the men in securing employment or in returning them to their homeland. Within weeks after the driving of the last spike several thousand Chinese boarded ships bound for

China but several thousand others remained in British Columbia jobless and crowded into coastal Chinatowns. The province was in an economic recession at the time, which augmented the serious plight of the Chinese.[4] While many desperate Chinese crossed the border into the United States undetected, a small number crossed the mountains in search of employment on the prairies.

There is no written account of the arrival of the first Chinese in Calgary or in the territory of Alberta. It appears, however, that Chinese pioneers were in the Calgary area in early 1886 and perhaps in 1885. The Calgary *Herald* reported:

Mr. Amos Roscoe, as subcollector of customs for this outpost of Calgary, has been appointed comptroller of Chinese immigration in this district. Every Chinaman at present residing in the district has to pay a fee of $5. and everyone coming in hereafter $50. The latter have also to obtain a medical certificate that they are free from leprosy and other contagious diseases, and no Chinese prostitutes are to be admitted at all.[5]

It is probable that the Chinese residents referred to were local launderers, since the Chinese hand laundry, a hallmark of Canadian prairie settlement, made an early appearance in frontier Calgary.

By 1888 several Chinese laundries had been operating for some time in Calgary. In June of that year one Hop Sing arrived from Vancouver to open another laundry "where family and single persons' washing of all kinds will be done in first-class style at very low prices."[6] The established laundries were very shortly forced into a price war by the newcomer:

Calgary's Chinese colony is just now in the midst of a bitter trade war. A recently arrived immigrant from the flowery kingdom opened the ball by advertising. . .reduced rates. Joe George and Sam Lee, two old-timers, immediately raised him, coming out with a tariff which threatens ruination to the manipulators of the wash board and flat iron, if kept up for long.[7]

The price war did in fact continue into the fall season by which time Hop Sing was apparently forced out of business. In late September the four remaining laundries established fixed prices for laundering. Their new tariff was to come into effect October 1, 1888, and was advertised under the heading "Chinese Laundry Association Prices."[8] The stability of the laundry business in the town, however, was short-lived. The interloper again decided to upset the *status quo*:

Hop Sing informs us that the Chinese washing combination are not to have it all their own way, as he has made arrangements for a number of men to come in from Victoria, when he will resume work at his old stand near H. Collins' Ivy Goods store at old prices.[9]

The resulting events were not reported but it is probable that the enterprising Hop Sing transferred the base of his operations to an area of pure competition. This episode reveals that Chinese entrepreneurs had firmly established themselves in a particular service trade in Calgary in the 1880's. Also, the economic enterprise and competitiveness of the Chinese in the Canadian West is apparent.

During the next few years little notice was given to local Chinese by the press, but in 1892 it became dramatically evident that the Chinese were not welcome residents in Calgary. In April, 1892, the *Empress of Japan* docked at Royal Roads, British Columbia, and a case of smallpox was detected. Health measures were implemented but within a few months the dread disease had taken seven lives in Vancouver and Victoria. Although the disease had been carried aboard a ship from China to British Columbia, a bastion of anti-Orientalism, "there was surprisingly little anti-Oriental feeling generated by [the episode]."[10]

On June 28, 1892, it was discovered that a Chinese resident of Calgary was recovering from smallpox in a local Chinese laundry. The man had returned from Vancouver several weeks previously and when he fell ill was attended to by fellow countrymen. The building and all its contents were burned the same day by civic authorities and the occupants were quarantined outside the town in an empty shack. A detachment of Mounted Police guarded the shack to enforce strict quarantine measures and a town doctor was placed in attendance.[11]

The outbreak was taken very seriously, of course, as were all similarly contagious diseases which on occasion resulted in epidemics in the Canadian West.[12] Within a short time the Chinese laundries were inspected, disinfectants were employed, most of the citizens were vaccinated and "all of the lanes, yards and back premises in town. . ." had been inspected.[13] Throughout the prairies various precautionary health measures were implemented to check the spread of the disease. In Manitoba, medical examinations were instituted at the boundary with the North-West Territories "in the case of passengers going East."[14] At Banff, medical examinations were required before newcomers could enter the town and at Medicine Hat civic officials absolutely prohibited east-bound passengers from "entering the town and Mounted Police [were] on hand to enforce the order."[15] At Sheppard, Alberta, "the Canadian Pacific pay car was not allowed to stop."[16] During the scare only two cases of smallpox occurred outside Calgary and both patients recovered.[17]

In Calgary, nine persons eventually contacted the disease and by mid-August three had died. The town's citizens placed blame for the disease directly on the shoulders of the local Chinese population and it seemed that violence was imminent. The Calgary *Herald* issued a warning to civic officials:

The local feeling against the race is strong, and it is as well for the authorities to recognize the fact. If the Chinese now at the quarantine be sent back into the town there will be trouble.[18]

Interestingly, the Calgary *Herald* published a long editorial two days later which did not blame Chinese as the transgressors. Rather, the Canadian federal government and the Canadian Pacific Railway were singled out for severe criticism. A portion of the remarks follows:

There is a strong conviction throughout Canada and especially in these Territories, that the Government authorities are greatly to blame for the introduction of smallpox into British Columbia. . .it is almost impossible to prevent the Canadian Pacific railway carrying the disease along its entire system. . .the Government officials dealt too easily with the officers and property of this powerful company; and now all Canada is alarmed at the consequences of this fatal neglect of duty.[19]

During the following two weeks only one other indication of hostility towards Chinese appeared in print when a letter to the editor was published with the ominous title "The Chinamen Must Go." The writer contended that Chinese were "undesirable residents in any white community" and the only solution was to await release of the quarantined Chinese and then "let them and all the others be told that they must go."[20]

On the evening of August 2nd, the four Chinese in quarantine were released and went to a local Chinese laundry. On hearing the news, a mob of over three hundred men, led by seven or eight ringleaders, gathered in the streets to chase the Chinese population out of town. At about 10:30 PM, they proceeded to the laundry where the released men were residing, but the occupants escaped. Two other laundries were then visited and the doors and windows were smashed in. At the second laundry the men unsuccessfully "attempted to burn the place down" and subsequently:

[The mob] visited the Chinese store. . . .One or two Chinamen were badly treated in the melee, though no bones were broken and no serious injury was sustained. . . . The outrages might have been stopped at the outset by the prompt interference of the police, but they were not to be seen until too late. The Mounted Police were finally brought up, but by this time the excitement had spent its force.[21]

The total lack of any response by town authorities is revealed in NWMP. Inspector R.A. Cuthbert's report on the riot. As he had heard rumours that the Chinese "were to be driven from town. . . ." Cuthbert sent an officer on August 2nd to notify the mayor that the men were about to be released "in case he should deem it necessary to take some steps to anticipate a possible disturbance."[22] During the riot some of the Chinese being attacked fled to the Mounted Police barracks. Fearing further outrages, Cuthbert sent messengers to the mayor offering support; however, the mayor had "left town shortly after seeing my messenger from quarantine."[23] Although the NWMP rarely acted as town constables, "a squad of men" was dispatched into the town. The Inspector explained:

. . .the row seemed to continue and several persons asked me to take some steps to stop it. . .the matter seemed to be going too far; none of the municipal authorities were disposed to assume any responsibility in dispersing the mob which had gathered or in restoring order. . . .On arrival of the squad in town and the effecting of a couple of arrests the last of the crowd dispersed.[24]

It is beyond question that for a number of hours a large unruly anti-Chinese mob of men roamed the streets of the town at will. Fortunately, there were some coolheaded individuals present who checked the prospect of further violence from this mob.[25]

The Chinese were naturally very badly shaken up by the vio-

lence and during the next few nights a number of Chinese arrived to join their fellow countrymen in the Mounted Police
barracks.[26] Threats against Chinese continued and "the situation
was becoming absurd when the town authorities were urged to
take decisive action."[27] Finally, the mayor requested that the
Mounted Police patrol the town. After three weeks of day and
night patrols the NWMP contingent was withdrawn as there appeared to be little likelihood of renewed violence.[28]

The Calgary *Herald* deplored the incident as a "thoughtless
demonstration," adding that, "Everything approaching the mob
spirit is to be condemned."[29] But the newspaper made it clear
two days later that it sympathized with the motives of the rioting
element when it suggested the boycotting of Chineses businesses:

*[By boycotting the Chinese], in a short time, without violence, without any
interference with personal liberty, we can be rid of what the majority regard
as an obnoxious element. . . .If public opinion decides that he shall go the
country will not be a loser by his absence.[30]*

The Calgary *Herald* clearly sided with the views of the anti-
Chinese element in the town and such reporting, even encased in
editorial parlance, could only foster antipathy and hostility towards local Chinese. The abusive editorial policy of the Calgary
Herald lasted many years and was typical of virtually all Alberta
papers. Even before the arrival of the Chinese in 1885, an editorial condemned the presence of Indians in the town and blamed
residents who hired them for odd jobs. Such "bribery" it was
claimed explained "not only the Indian question in Calgary, but
the Chinese question in British Columbia. In both cases it is because the whites make use of them and pay them for staying that
they are not gone long ago."[31]

The Calgary *Tribune* expressed a more tolerant viewpoint than
its rival during the smallpox episode. Although the newspaper
felt that the alleged harbouring of smallpox was wrong, there
were no accusatory condemnations of the Chinese as a people.
The *Tribune* heartily denounced the rioters and from the outset
"called for the punishment of its ringleaders."[32] Also, a Winnipeg
Free Press editorial of August 5, 1892, was reprinted which condemned the un-British behaviour of the Calgary "cowardly
pack" and remarked on the "[Chinese] characteristics deserving
of admiration."[33] While positive aspects of the Chinese community were not praised by the newspaper, two letters to the editor

were published defending them. The first letter, submitted by
"JUSTICE", called upon all loyal Englishmen to honour Queen
Victoria's commitment to China whereby she expressly guaranteed the immigration of any number of Chinese into Canada and
promised that full legal protection for them would exist, unlike
the United States.[34] The second letter, submitted by "D.C.", advocated establishment of "a local Health Society" for all Calgarians' advantage and also related Lord [Garnet] Wolseley's opinions of the Chinese; Wolseley "believed the Chinese to be the
greatest race in the world; they possess all the elements of being a
great people; they have courage, physical power and absolute
contempt for death. . . ."[35]

It is probable, nonetheless, that a majority of Calgarians at
this time held the Chinese in derision and disrespect. In mid-August about six hundred citizens packed the Opera House to
listen to an anti-Oriental lecturer, one Locksley Lucas, whose
topic was "the Chinese question". Lucas spoke "at considerable
length into the reasons why Chinamen are not desirable residents
of any country,"[36] presumably excluding China. The audience
"frequently and forcibly expressed their approval of the views
promulgated by Mr. Lucas."[37] At the meeting's end a provisional
committee was formed to establish a branch of the Anti-Chinese
League and consisted of Mayor Lucas (no relation to Locksley)
and Councillors Orr and Freeze.[38]

Calgary's clergy gave the largest measure of support to the
Chinese. At a special meeting with the town council three representatives of the local clergy expressed concern that no prosecutions had been laid concerning the riot, although the leaders
were well known local citizens. Mayor Lucas calmly explained
that if prosecutions were laid, "it would be almost impossible to
keep the people quiet."[39] The clergy did not press the point and
no charges were laid. The ministers present, however, felt that
the town council should assure the Chinese that they could expect full and complete protection under the law. The clergymen's
petition condemning the riot was given some consideration by
council, but was not acted upon.[40]

Although the attitude of the town council was at least neutral
during the episode, Mayor Lucas's behaviour was, on the other
hand, openly hostile towards local Chinese. At a council meeting
he maintained that for concealing smallpox the Chinese "deserved to be punished."[41] Moreover, the mayor's calculated absence from town was hardly coincidental. Not only did a Mounted

Policeman warn him of the men's impending release, but Lucas blandly told council that "some of them [Chinese] had come to his house several hours before the riot and asked for him, intimating that there was going to be trouble."[42] Chief of Police English was out of town for the week and the mayor decided to absent himself as well and let events take their natural course. Councillor Wesley F. Orr offered a double lot free of cost to any white person who would thereupon construct and operate a laundry employing only white personnel. He hoped that this would "make the presence of Mongolians in our midst totally unnecessary."[43]

The 1892 Smallpox Riot was an isolated act of concerted violence against Calgary's Chinese population. It revealed that the majority Anglo-Canadian population regarded the Chinese as an undesirable group in "their" town. The incident and its aftermath seems to indicate the presence of a "garrison mentality"[44] in the town. In other words, the town's citizens held deep convictions as to what, and even who, was right, good and proper for the continuing community good. Also, prairie isolation in Calgary and other frontier towns reinforced the strength of existing principles and the sense of community. The Chinese were condemned by Anglo-Canadians in this instance as carriers of disease into "their" town, and it was not the sick man concerned who was blamed by all local Chinese.

The 1892 Smallpox Riot was the most dramatic example of widespread hostility to Chinese in early Alberta history. Dr. Howard D. Palmer has documented the pervasiveness of anti-Orientalism in Alberta up to 1920 and concludes that these prejudicial attitudes transcended political orientations and class allegiances, although anti-Oriental sentiment was stronger in southern Alberta.[45] He has illustrated that the press and politicians of the province were vehemently anti-Oriental on many occasions and that few citizens in the province expressed any public support for the Chinese.[46] These observations hold true in the main regarding the Chinese experience in Calgary to 1910 and later.

In the decade after 1892, Calgary's population showed virtually no increase and the number of Chinese in the city did not increase significantly; in 1901 there were only sixty-three Chinese enumerated as residents (see Table 1). Most local Chinese were engaged in business or service trades, and indeed the majority of Chinese who settled in the Canadian West were owners or employees of small businesses. This phenomenon resulted mainly from Chinese experiences in British Columbia where operating stores had proved "quite profitable [and thus] when the Chinese penetrated to the prairie and eastern provinces, most of them opened business for themselves."[47] Chinese businessmen took full advantage of any opportunities, and by patient work, long hours, and good service maintained their enterprises on a highly competitive basis in Calgary, as elsewhere.

TABLE ONE

Total Population, and Chinese Population in Calgary, 1881–1911

| Year | Chinese Population | | | Total Calgary |
	Female	Male	Total	
1881	0	0(unknown)	0	75
1891	0	-(unknown)	-	3,876
1901	0	63	63	4,091
1911	3	482	485	43,704

Sources: Census of Canada, 1881–1911; Calgary City Hall

Chinese businesses in Calgary consisted overwhelmingly of restaurants, laundries, and grocery stores. In order to make a profit, restaurants and grocery stores had to open early in the morning and close late at night. Laundry work was especially wearisome as during this period it meant the soaking, scrubbing, and ironing of clothing solely by hand; also, prompt service was necessary to keep the customers satisfied. Workers in laundries and groceries received the going wage of twenty-five dollars per month, and, despite long hours, the work-week was seven days.[48] For the majority of local Chinese, therefore, the daily routine was almost solely working, eating, and sleeping; very little time existed to pursue recreational interests.

There were a few other occupations available to local Chinese. Some were employed as hotel workers, labourers, and domestic servants. In the surrounding countryside, Chinese cooks were hired by ranchers on a seasonal basis and returned to the city during the off-season. It appears that after 1900 a greater number of Chinese were employed as domestic servants due to the needs of wealthy Calgarians whose spacious residences were increasing in number. Dr. Henry Klassen has noted:

Maids, Chinese houseboys, and coachmen were viewed as status symbols, and were also expected to lighten the domestic burdens of the family. [By the beginning of the twentieth century] more employers began to employ Chinese servants, who also were in short supply. Paid $25 a month, a Chinese house-boy was quick to give courteous service, and generally worked hard. Employers of houseboys as a rule had little difficulty in training them in the ways of servanthood.[49]

Their services were appreciated by their employers who frequently developed a sincere liking and respect for them.

Whenever a sufficiently large number of Chinese lived in a settlement in the Canadian West, they established a "Chinatown" which might, of course, consist solely of one combined restaurant-grocery store. Calgary's first Chinatown began in the early 1890's and was located on what is now the corner of Centre Street S. and Ninth Avenue E. across from the Canadian Pacific Railway station. By 1900 it consisted of two restaurants, a hand laundry, two groceries, and a twenty-bed rooming house.[50] The Kwong Man Yuen Restaurant at 815 Centre Street had a "community room" behind its premises where Chinese congregated after work to socialize, and drink tea or perhaps "Sam Suey", a Chinese whisky.

Why were Chinatowns established? Generally speaking, as an American writer has remarked, "Chinatowns grew out of vital and cogent needs of the immigrant Chinese."[51] In the first place there was a wide cultural gap between Chinese settlers and the majority Anglo-Americans in North America, or in the case of Calgary, the Anglo-Canadians. Most Chinese spoke their own language, ate their own national dishes, read Chinese newspapers, and associated with fellow countrymen in social activities. Secondly, "the Chinese sought refuge within the boundaries of Chinatown for their own protection from the persecution wreaked against them during the late nineteenth and early twentieth centuries."[52] Thirdly, a Chinatown met certain psychological needs of Chinese sojourners.

The majority of Chinese residents in the Canadian West were men whose goal was to save enough money so that they could retire in comfort or wealth in their native villages. While resident in Canada they sent home remittances to sustain their families, whether this meant parents and/or wives and children. Many Calgary men had wives in China but because of tradition and the very steep head tax, they stayed in China and almost without exception their husbands kept them well provided for. Most Chinese, however, did not accumulate enough funds to retire as respected men in their homeland and therefore spent their lives in what became their adopted country.[53] During their supposed sojourn Chinatown was also, then, a physical and functional area which preserved a few features of Chinese culture.

The language barrier certainly inhibited the establishment of better relations between Chinese and other residents, and it was also a barrier to Chinese commercial pursuits in the community. Around 1900 some young men began to attend Sunday School classes at Knox Presbyterian Church to learn English. However, at this time "any attempt made by interested persons to teach the Chinese people English and a smattering of the Scriptures was thoroughly thwarted by many Calgarians."[54] The minister of the church, Reverend J.C. Herdman, concluded that separate premises were required and the news reached Thomas Underwood, a devoted Baptist who was mayor of Calgary from 1902 to 1903. Mr. Underwood, who was a prominent contractor, provided a room at nominal rent for the classes and then in November 1901 built a two-room frame building at 215 Tenth Avenue S.W. The following year he added a second story in order to accommodate up to thirty-five pupils. "There were living quarters upstairs which included five bedrooms and a small kitchen."[55] Years later it was recalled that, "Mr. Underwood founded the mission with the object of bettering the relations between the white people and the Chinese, and at a time when feeling was very bitter against the Chinese here."[56]

After 1901 increasing numbers of Chinese arrived in Calgary and the need arose for a larger Chinatown to meet the increased demand for goods and services as well as rooming facilities. The first Chinatown could not expand, as, due to its restricted location, there was simply no adjacent unused land. Therefore, a second Chinatown came into existence in the immediate vicinity of the recently built Chinese Mission. Chinese businesses were established along Tenth Avenue and First Street. By 1910, Chinatown consisted of twelve businesses, several "community rooms", and rooming facilities.[57] Nonetheless, Chinese businesses in the first Chinatown continued to operate for some years after 1901, and most Chinese residents in the city lived in quarters behind their business premises which were scattered throughout the city.

The years 1901–1910 were dramatic ones for Calgary. Her population soared and many commercial and industrial enterprises were founded. People from all nations, cultures, and races poured into the expanding centre. During this rather chaotic boom-period, over four hundred Chinese settled in the city to take advantage of increased opportunities, and many new Chinese businesses opened their doors (see TABLE TWO). Because of cultural barriers and the continuing prejudice towards them, the

TABLE TWO
Chinese Businesses in Calgary, 1902-11

		YEAR		
Type of Businesses		1902	1906	1911
Grocery Stores	Chinese	unavailable	7	unavailable
	Other	16	38	unavailable
	Total	16 or more	45	104
Restaurants	Chinese	3	7	22
	Other	2	12	43
	Total	5	19	65
Laundries	Chinese	10	17	28
	Other	3	6	3
	Total	13	23	31
Tobacconists	Chinese	-	5	21
	Other	5	14	93
	Total	5	19	114

Sources: Gronlund's 1902 Directory, Henderson's Directory for 1906 and 1911. City of Calgary License Records for 1902, 1906 and 1911.

Note: In 1911 there were 114 grocery stores listed in the directory and of at least 3-4 Chinese groceries known to have existed none were listed; also, the license records were obscure for 1911 in this respect.

newly arrived Chinese worked in those occupations to which they had become reconciled. It was in this decade that the foundations, though not the substance, of a viable and thriving Chinese community were laid. The outlines of this are apparent in terms of population figures, the establishment of a moderately large Chinatown and in terms of Chinese business enterprises.

In 1910 Chinatown was forced to relocate, and this caused a minor local stir. In June 1910, the Canadian Northern Railway announced its proposed route into the city and plans called for the construction of a "mammoth" hotel-depot on the corner of Tenth Avenue and First Street W.[58] Property values in Chinatown soared and the non-Chinese owners of the real estate concerned sold their holdings. The Chinese decided the best course was to buy their own property and thereby have the say in the next Chinatown. Several wealthy Chinese purchased a site at the corner of Centre Street and Second Avenue, and, after submitting construction plans, they received a building permit.

However, on October 4, 1910, a deputation of angry citizens, represented by Alderman James Short, K.C., approached the city commissioners insisting on another site for Chinatown. The citizens, supposedly property owners near the site chosen, advocated a segregated Chinatown. Short's remarks included:

They have not the slightest idea of cleanliness or sanitation. Everywhere they go they are undesirable citizens. . . .It is for you to take up the question and set the Chinese in one section of the city as you would an isolation hospital.[59]

The city commissioners subsequently issued a temporary order to with-hold any further building permits to Chinese until the situation was clarified.[60] On their part the Chinese took into consideration alternate locations and expressed considerable interest in property between Seventh and Eighth Avenues across from Mewata Park, at the same time insisting that if a new site was chosen they must be fully reimbursed for their investment to that date.[61]

At an October 10th city council meeting in "respect to the Chinese puzzle" a petition presented by three citizens was approved which recommended "that the commissioners, twelve citizens appointed by the mayor and twelve representatives of the Chinese should confer within the next few days and report back to the council."[62] The so-called "Chinese question" at hand was: "What shall be done with the Chinese citizens of Calgary, will they be placed in a special quarter, or will they be permitted to go where they like?"[63] On October 13th the representative groups met together and discussed the Chinatown issue. Three white members of the Chinese Mission formed part of the Chinese delegation "while prominent among the Chinese were Luey Kheong, president of the (Chinese Empire) Reform Association of Calgary, and Ho Lem, representing the laundry interests."[64]

The conference passed "a resolution that no action be taken by the council in the matter of segregation but that they pass a by-law regulating sleeping and living space in houses."[65] Alderman Cameron stated after the meeting that, "Objection was taken to anything being said about segregation as we are all opposed to segregation."[66] A more careful reading of the episode reveals that whenever an alternate site was suggested there were objections from the aldermen or residents of the area where the proposed Chinatown might be located. Thus, to all intents, the Chinatown issue was settled and construction began shortly afterwards.

The relocation of Chinatown in 1910 revealed that, while anti-Chinese sentiment was still prevalent in the city, there had been a distinct improvement in the local standing of the Chinese population. A number of prominent citizens publicly supported the Chinese stand and maintained that they were desirable citizens. Alderman Stanley T. Jones remarked in part, "There is one reason the Chinese are unpopular and that is that they have got along well. . . .Those discriminating are against them on the grounds of religion and race."[67] The most revealing remarks during the controversy were those of Mr. H. Haskins, a member of the "white delegation", who felt compelled to remark during the August 13th conference:

Many of them (Chinese) are among our best citizens. The only solution I see is that we leave them completely alone. . . .They are a different class in Calgary to San Francisco and New York. We have some of the best of the boys. . . .They are better citizens than lots of people. . . .and I could point to some around me. If you want to do something good, let's turn to something else than getting after these hard-working honest citizens. [68]

At the same time, letters to the editor by prominent members of the Chinese Mission (J.B. Henderson and R.H. Standerwick) lauded the provident nature of the Chinese people. The former wrote that he had personally drawn up the specifications and plans for the proposed brick block which were "better than is actually required." He added, "[Let us abide] by the strictest letter of the law, and show the same faith in the law and its administration that these people (the Chinese) have done."[69]

This liberal conviction was borne out in a reply by Luey Kheong, a prominent Chinese merchant, during the relocation episode. In what was probably the first public rejoinder in a Calgary newspaper by a Chinese resident, the author demonstrated considerable political acumen and humour:

Calgary, Oct. 6 - To the Editor of the Herald *- I take your paper and see that some people in Calgary are saying some bad things about my countrymen here. This is not right. The Canadian government has given us the right to live here and pay our debts. We want to do honest business in Calgary, same as all men, and, Canada's law will protect us. You send missionaries to our homes in China, and we use them good; also English business men. If my people are no good to live here, what good trying to make them go to Heaven? Perhaps there will be only my people there. Thanking you for your trouble.*

I am, yours truly,
Luey Kheong

Chinese Merchant. Member Chinese Empire Reform Association.[70]

Such expressions of Chinese opinion rarely found their way into the local newspapers.

More common to the ambience of frontier-city journalism was the expression of segregationist opinion in favour of a relocated and distinctly homogeneous Chinatown. The Calgary *Albertan* for one feared that the city core would degenerate without segregation, "The Chinese are all right in their place, but their place is not in the heart of the business district of the city."[71] The Calgary *Herald*, on the other hand, regarded the recently acquired Birnie market site as the best Chinatown location and stated, "The Chinese, wherever they locate, should not be allowed to establish their centre on a main thoroughfare as Centre Street."[72] Yet, the unbending attitude of the local newspaper editors was not absolutely characteristic of broader civic opinion. A poll of Calgary's nine senior civic officials revealed that only one advocated segregation of the Chinese and then, "only if it were carried out properly."[73]

In conclusion, with the commencement of construction of the

third Chinatown, a distinct period of Chinese settlement in Calgary ended and another distinct period was just beginning. The Chinese, by 1910, had demonstrated that they were useful citizens engaged in essential services in the frontier community, and were moderately significant in the local world of small business. They had, in short, fully established themselves as a permanent component of the city's composition. In succeeding years, the institutional and associational structure of the Chinese community was established and, with the arrival of increasing numbers of Chinese, including women, the community's features changed.

By 1910, too, the pattern of responses towards the Chinese had changed significantly for the better. But, and this needs emphasizing, anti-Chinese sentiment was still pervasive and quite evident. The police raids of the 1910's instigated, co-ordinated, and led by Police Chief Alfred Cuddy, are a striking example of continuing hostility towards Chinese residents. Nonetheless, the "garrison mentality" of the early decades of Calgary's history had been transformed by 1910 into much more of an urban mentality with the beginning of a social consciousness appearing. It was urbanization which was assisting the creation of new attitudes, beliefs, and life styles in Calgary.

CALGARY: THE PRIVATE SCHOOLS, 1900–16

Douglas Coats

T hroughout its history, the city of Calgary has exerted a
strong metropolitan influence over southern Alberta, and
indeed over much of western Canada. In no respect has
this been more true than in the area of education, for from the
days of the Normal School, through the establishment of the Calgary Technical School, to the acquisition of autonomy by the
University of Calgary, the city has attracted youth from many
points in western Canada by its offer of the latest in educational
facilities. But perhaps at no time before or since has Calgary had
the pedagogical impact on the West that it enjoyed during the
period from 1900 to 1916, the halcyon days of private boarding
schools in the community.

No fewer than six such institutions flourished in the city during those years, a rather remarkable figure for a community
whose population in the period concerned began at only 4,400
and never exceeded 60,000,[1] particularly as that community was
also the possessor of a respectable public school system. Sacred
Heart Convent, Saint Hilda's Ladies' College, Western Canada
College, Bishop Pinkham College, Mount Royal College, and
Calgary College all were the products of, and in turn left their
mark upon, the society of Calgary and southern Alberta at that
time. This paper attempts a brief analysis of the society that
produced these schools, of the nature of the schools themselves,
and of the reasons for their decline.

In 1900, southern Alberta was still young enough that its native white population was very small. With few exceptions, the
adults of the district, and particularly the influential ones, had

come from Great Britain or eastern Canada. These people tended to fall into three categories. First, amongst the owners, the managers, and even the cowboys of the great ranches of Alberta, was a group used to travelling in the wealthy and well-to-do circles of old country and Canadian society.[2] In their rustic surroundings they did their best to carry on the grand life to which they were accustomed. An illustrative story is told of a number of young Britishers, quite possibly remittance men, who were wintering in the town of Okotoks in the 1890's, preparatory to establishing their own ranches:

Typically, they wanted some fun, some amusement, other than their poker games, so they decided to put on a. . ."Bachelors' Ball"; there were printed invitations, due regard was paid to all the niceties, and the entire function was planned with dash and verve. The young ladies of note in the town and area attended, suitably chaperoned, of course, and the affair was very well received. There was just one criticism—the young ladies felt that their evening gowns became slightly soiled as the gentlemen were not wearing gloves.[3]

Such people had been educated in the best private schools of England and Ontario, and naturally wished the same type of education for their children.[4] Their support of private education was undoubtedly also a reaction to the unimpressive state of rural public schools, particularly at the secondary level.

The second category in southern Alberta was also wealthy, but this wealth had come as the result of its possessors' own efforts in the new West. They were the "self-made men", the "nouveaux riches", including such notables as James Lougheed, Patrick Burns, William Roper Hull, and a host of lesser business and professional men. Most were Canadian, all had made their fortunes through opportunities seized on the frontier, and all settled in the towns and cities. Calgary as a particularly up-and-coming metropolis attracted more than its share of such people, and rapidly became a very wealthy city[5]: James Lougheed, for example, paid more money in municipal taxes than did the Hudson's Bay Company and the Alberta Hotel.[6] The Calgary *Herald* suggested a measurement of the number of such local aristocrats when it discussed financing the hoped-for university:

The city contains five men who could endow five chairs: it contains fifteen men who could subscribe $10,000 each: twenty-five who could subscribe $5,-000: and one hundred men who could easily subscribe $1,000. Let us hope this estimate errs, if it errs at all, on the side of conservatism.[7]

In an era when Calgary's labourers were content with thirty-seven and a half cents per hour,[8] this parvenue elite toasted itself and visiting dignitaries in the Ranchmen's Club[9] or in its baronial castles on Thirteenth Avenue and in Mount Royal. These patricians enjoyed and demanded the high life as much as did their more genuinely "noblesse" counterparts on the ranches. Modelling themselves upon well-to-do English and Toronto-Montreal society, they sought for their children the education they themselves, in many cases, had never had; the private school was the means of bringing up their offspring in the ways of ladies and gentlemen in the midst of the uncultured frontier. That the private academies were supported by these men is clear from a glance at the composition of their boards of directors: most of the big names were there.[10] Beneath this urban elite was an upper middle class, the up-and-coming storekeepers and real-estate men, many of whom could not afford private schools but some of whom tried.

The third type of person in Calgary and southern Alberta society is of little concern to this study. He was the "average citizen", of the middle or lower class, whose children attended the public schools. Always in the large majority, he nonetheless was greatly overshadowed in terms of political and economic influence by the small group above him. When we read, then, of private schools created by "popular demand", it was in fact the popular demand of a relatively small part of the population.

Another aspect of life in southern Alberta that greatly aided the development of private education was the religious orientation of the upper classes. It is interesting to note that the urban aristocrats in Calgary were, to a man, not merely active but were virtual dynamos in their respective congregations. Denomination did not seem to affect their status (Burns was Roman Catholic, Lougheed Methodist, and Cross Anglican, for example) as long as they were involved *somewhere*. Undoubtedly they were sincere believers, a fact which explains their support of denominational private schools as much as does the probability that their church activities gave them connections and an air of respectability that served them well in the business world.

It is likely, too, that these men took an interest in private education simply because they were not satisfied with the public school system of the day. Well into the period of study there was no separation of elementary and secondary students in Calgary, and leading citizens were of the opinion ". . .that Calgary was not doing the educational work it should. . .that Calgary was behind as an educational centre."[11] No real matriculation program to prepare students for university existed, and this, to the upper class, who regarded a university education as desirable, was a most unhappy situation.

These, then, were the people, and this was the social, religious, and educational background behind the development of private schools in Calgary.

The first such school was established in 1885 at Sacred Heart Convent on present-day Eighteenth Avenue S.W. beside St. Mary's Cathedral. Founded by Reverend Mother Greene of the Faithful Companions of Jesus, the institution was both a boarding school and a day school for Roman Catholic girls. Until after 1900 the area south of Seventeenth Avenue was not a part of Calgary, but was named Rouleauville after the Supreme Court justice who lived there; it was a Roman Catholic community built around the site of Father Lacombe's mission, and contained a number of French-speaking citizens. For this reason the school offered a full education in both English and French, and by 1913 was teaching "plain and ornamental needlework, pianoforte playing, singing, painting, stenography, and elocution."[12] At its peak in 1913 Sacred Heart Convent was instructing seventy-five boarding students and a number of day students with a staff of fourteen teaching sisters.[13] The girls were from Catholic families from all over southern Alberta.

Not to be outdone, local Anglicans raised in English and Ontario denominational schools started a private girls' school in 1889. Classes met in the Parish Hall beside the Cathedral of the Redeemer, at Seventh Avenue and First Street S.E., under a Miss M. Crawford. The girls' parents were not prepared to finance the school adequately, however, and after two years the first private Protestant girls' academy in the North-West Territories was forced to close.[14] But the idea of an Anglican girls' school appealed to the Bishop of Calgary, Cyprian Pinkham, and when in 1904 a Mrs. Corrie Smith from Ontario failed in a venture to establish a girls' school in Calgary, Bishop Pinkham was quick to suggest that she try again, this time under the patronage of the Church of England.[15] Mrs. Smith accepted the offer, a classroom building and dormitory were constructed on Twelfth Avenue at Eighth Street S.W., and St. Hilda's Ladies' College was born. While the school was under the control of the Anglican Church, there was to be "no interference with the religious preferences of the pupils as indicated by their parents."[16]

That the girls' parents wished the school to be an oasis of culture in the primitive West was made clear in the institution's stated aim: "The College combines thoroughness in Education with all wholesome and refining influences, and aims to develop such strong, intelligent, cultured and useful Christian womanhood as all parts of Canada, and especially the West, urgently require.[17]" The Board of Governors was composed of fourteen men, eight of whom were Anglican clergymen.[18]

St. Hilda's taught vocal culture, art, physical culture, French and German conversation, and music, as well as all subjects needed for university entrance. Its pupils learned tennis, croquet, and field hockey from England, and baseball and basketball from the United States.[19] A graduate of the class of 1905, however, when asked "What did the girls study"?, responded, "The boys from Western Canada College." She remembered that the most thrilling aspect of life at the school was to be invited by the Western boys to skate on the rink at that male institution.[20]

During the first year of operation, St. Hilda's taught twenty day students and twenty resident students, the latter mostly from southern Alberta ranches. The girls were between the ages of five and eighteen. By 1908 the enrollment had risen to eighty,[21] and this number remained constant until the First World War. In 1916 there were only forty students, and only a quarter of them were boarders. By 1924 the school was in financial trouble and was forced to become non-denominational. It was reorganized as St. Hilda's School for Girls, but was little more than a shadow of its former self. It closed in 1949 when tax exemptions were lifted from private schools by the city.[22]

Western Canada College, already mentioned as an attraction for the young ladies from St. Hilda's, was a boys' school established on Seventeenth Avenue in 1903. Like St. Hilda's, it was "founded in response to the demand for such an institution in the far West."[23] But unlike St. Hilda's, it was not a denominational school. While the promoters of the institution, Reverend J.C. Herdman and Dr. A.O. MacRae, its first principal, were both Presbyterian ministers, no clergymen were put on its Board of Trustees, and its constitution stipulated that "The College shall be distinctly Christian, but no religious test or qualification, save the profession of Christianity, shall be required of any Trustee, Teacher, or other official of said College.[24]"

The money for the classrooms and dormitory, proudly acclaimed as being "lighted with electricity and heated by the hot-water system,"[25] was raised on a joint-stock basis by local businessmen.[26] The Board of Trustees was like a Who's Who in Calgary: Pat Burns, P. Turner Bone, William Pearce, T.J.S. Skinner, and Thomas Underwood were there to maintain ties with the business community and to make sure their money was being wisely spent. Instruction was given in classics, English, history, modern languages, mathematics, science, commerce, writing, music, and physical training.[27] The boys were also permitted to take dancing lessons at St. Hilda's.[28]

Western Canada College was equally innovative in its teaching methods. The Principal visited schools in Montreal, Ottawa, Boston, and New York to study new techniques,[29] and originated a rudimentary individual progress system. Any boy deficient in a particular subject was not put back with those younger than himself, but was tutored individually by the staff. One did not have to pass all his courses at one level all at once: the College's calendar reported that "No backward boys will be required to keep abreast of all the work of any one form."[30]

College graduates achieved a reputation for hard work:

Every year the college has sent forth a large number of lads to take places in business offices, wholesale establishments and banks. Excellent reports are being received of their progress. The college has achieved success because, as the boys themselves testify, they are made to work. Great care is taken with the discipline, the training, and the preparation of the boys.[31]

The discipline, training, and preparation stood the boys in good stead with the advent of the war: over four hundred "Old Boys" enlisted, a record unequalled by any other school of its kind in Canada.[32] The list of volunteers included sons of some of the city's best-known citizens.[33] The war took its toll on the College, however, as a peak enrollment of one hundred and fifty (one hundred of whom were boarders)[34] dwindled severely. After a financial reorganization, Dr. MacRae left, the secretary-treasurer absconded with much-needed funds, and the institution was finished. Closed in 1924, the school was bought in 1926 by the Public School Board for thirty-five thousand dollars, barely enough to cover its debts.[35]

Western Canada College was not the only private school for young men. Pleased with the success of St. Hilda's, the local Anglican community decided a denominational boys' school was desirable, not only for teaching university entrance courses but for producing a native clergy. In 1909 land for such a venture was donated by Ezra Riley, a prominent local Anglican, who stipulated that the school built upon it was to be named Bishop Pinkham College.[36] The Bishop "strongly opposed the idea of the institution bearing his name, but to no avail,"[37] and Bishop Pinkham College it became. A building fund was taken up, with fifteen thousand dollars being donated in England and the remaining nine thousand collected in Calgary.[38] Pending construction of the new quarters, classes were held in Sub-Warden Canon d'Easum's house and by correspondence for those out-of-town scholars who later would be boarding at the college.

Bishop Pinkham's sixteen-man Board of Governors was entirely Anglican, and fully half of it was composed of clergymen. Other Governors included William Roper Hull and Ezra Riley.[39] The school's aims were well set out:

[It was to be] a Diocesan Institution, in which men could be specially, and, if necessary, generally trained for the work of the Sacred Ministry in this important part of Canada. . .Side by side with this great work and in connection with the College, it was thought advisable to establish a boys' school, which would provide not only a thorough high-class education on definite Church of England lines after the types of the great English and Eastern Canadian schools, to fit boys for professional and commercial careers, but also, by special attention being given to the inculcation of refining, moral and religious principles, equip them to take part in life as Christian gentlemen, by combining refining and religious influence with thoroughness of education.[40]

Although the school was under the direction of the Anglican Church, there was to be "no interference with the religious preferences of pupils as expressed by their parents."[41]

The new building was located in Hillhurst at Eighth Avenue and Thirteenth Street N.W., and opened in 1911. There were forty-one pupils that year,[42] and applications from interested parties were more plentiful than space. The curriculum included Greek, Latin, French, German, English, history, science, and sports. Principal Reverend A.P. Hayes requested of Cambridge University that Bishop Pinkham be designated the local centre for writing the entrance examinations to that institution, and when this request was granted, the College gained a great deal of prestige. Graduates of the school gained entrance into Cambridge, McGill, and, more often, the new University of Alberta.[43]

Perhaps owing to its staunch Church of England affiliation, Bishop Pinkham was the most "English" of the private colleges. The boys wore a uniform consisting of Eton jacket, collar, and tie, and mortarboards and tassels adorned their heads. This apparel promoted almost daily fights with the boys of Hillhurst Public School across the street, who were not prepared to tolerate sissies in any form. One "Old Boy" reflected years later that "Perhaps the intention of the authorities was to establish something of the snobbishness and exclusiveness of an elite corps, and in this I am afraid they succeeded."[44] Cricket, football, and boxing were emphazised to "build character." The Headmaster wrote that "It is our endeavor not only to impart bare facts but to train the boys to think for themselves." To this end they were encouraged to read, and every Saturday two boys were dispatched to the Public Library to bring back books for the whole school. To make sure that the students were behaving themselves, the masters slept in the student dormitories.[45]

The coming of the war in 1914 affected Bishop Pinkham as it had affected Western Canada College. Every able-bodied student of age enlisted in the Bishop Pinkharm Cadet Corps and then went off to war.[46] The school was forced to close in 1916.

Chronologically the next private school to be established was Mount Royal College, founded by the Methodist Church in 1911. The brainchild of Dr. George W. Kerby, minister of Central Methodist Church, the College had its future virtually guaranteed when the Alberta Conference and the General Council of the Methodist Church agreed to give it an annual grant. This in turn led many citizens to support the institution. The Board of Directors consisted of thirty-two men, none of whom were clergymen, and many of Calgary's leading citizens were represented—W.H. Cushing, Melville Scott, O.G. Devenish, O.S. Chapin, and E.H. Crandell, all pillars of Methodism.[47]

Mount Royal differed from the other private academies in that it was co-educational. "Designed by its promoters to give a first-class college education to young people of both sexes, under the best influences and at a moderate cost,"[48] it offered courses in English, history, mathematics, science, French, German, Latin, Greek, commerce, household science, and primary and junior subjects.[49] Sports included hockey, rugby, and basketball. Residential students numbered over one hundred and came from all parts of the province;[50] there was classroom space for another two to three hundred day students.[51]

Of all the private schools in Calgary, Mount Royal College was the lone survivor into the 1970's. It endured the First World War, perhaps because of the Methodist grants and its co-educational nature; it lasted through the 1920's, and then in 1930 became affiliated with the University of Alberta as a junior college. This enabled Mount Royal to offer the first two years of a university program, but the move forced the abandonment of the primary and domestic science courses[52] as well as eventually its private denominational status.

The last of the pre-First World War private schools to be established was Calgary College, somewhat unique in that it was an attempt at a full-fledged university. Calgary had been rejected by the provincial legislature as the seat for the University of Alberta, and had received no compensation save the Provincial Normal School in 1906. By 1912 a number of prominent Calgarians, led by Dr. T.H. Blow, had become concerned enough to decide that Calgary should have its own university regardless of provincial support. Their motivation was not purely altruistic, however, as the College was organized as a joint-stock company with an eye toward issuing dividends from the money collected in student fees.[53] Stockholders and members of the Advisory Board included R.B. Bennett, James Lougheed, A.B. Cushing, E.H. Riley, and F.G. Beveridge.[54]

The institution they established was refused the right to confer degrees by the provincial legislature, which feared that the fledgling University of Alberta would not be able to withstand such competition. Thus, despite the pleas of Bishop Pinkham College, which petitioned the government on its behalf, Calgary College was not in effect a university. This, however, did not deter the school's promoters from opening it in 1912.[55]

Classes were held in the Carnegie Library in the late afternoon to facilitate the attendance of teachers and office workers. A Faculty of Arts under Dr. E.E. Braithwaite was serving two hundred and seventeen students by 1913, and a Faculty of Law under Mr. Kent Power served another fifty-one.[56] In 1915 the College was forced to close, again due to the war and the resulting drop in finances from tuition fees.[57]

Since the prime reason for its existence had been the civic pride and spite of its founders, Calgary College never re-opened after the province granted the city a Technical School in 1915. Despite attempts by the academics on its Advisory Board to make the best of a bad situation and affiliate the College with the Technical School, its original promoters and shareholders wrote it off as a bad investment and allowed it to close altogether.[58]

By 1916, then, only Mount Royal College and St. Hilda's Ladies' College continued to exist in their original form, and by 1930 these too had been changed beyond recognition. There were other private schools that grew up after 1916, but they were never on as large a scale as the institutions that began before the war. The year 1916 was very definitely a watershed in the story of private education in Calgary.

One may wonder why the era of the large, denominational, segregated, English-style private school ended so suddenly. The war clearly was the immediate cause, but surely if the schools had been serving a useful purpose they would have resumed operation in 1918. Perhaps it can be argued that the whole nature of southern Alberta society changed between 1900 and 1916, and that that change rendered unnecessary the private college as it existed before the war.

In 1900, the West lacked an indigenous white population. By 1916, the children of the pioneers were growing up, and, having been raised on the frontier, consciously or unconsciously were undoubtedly less interested than their forebears had been in perpetuating the ways of England and Ontario. When they returned home from the war and had children of their own, they did not send them to private schools; even amongst those who had attended the private colleges there was no demand that they reopen after 1916. The second-generation Albertans were very different in outlook from their parents.[59]

If one reason for the decline of the private schools was the Westernization of the children who had attended them, another was that the type of elite that had required them was not regenerated after the war. Homesteaders had replaced the British ranchers; and, in the city, the Burns, Hulls, and Lougheeds were not as young as they had been in 1900. They had made their fortunes by providing much-needed services in a frontier community, and had succeeded largely because they were the first ones to offer those services; but by 1916 Calgary was no longer a frontier town, and the amassing of private fortunes was no longer possible on the same scale. Not until the oil boom of the 1950's did a new group of self-made financial empires develop in Calgary. In the intervening years no class of Calgarians comparable to the old aristocracy was there to demand private education for its progeny.

Perhaps even more basic to the collapse of the private schools was the fact that by 1916 very few Calgarians were acquainted with them. New techniques in agriculture, the closing of the American frontier, industrialization in Europe with its corresponding increase in overseas demand for farm products, improved transportation technology, and the energetic immigration policies of the Canadian government combined after 1900 to make the prairies an attractive home for newcomers from Europe, the United States, and eastern Canada.[60] Between 1901 and 1920, Alberta's population increased from 73,000 to 588,000,[61] and that of Calgary rose from 4,400 to nearly 60,000.[62] The overwhelming majority of these people were of the middle and lower classes, and on the whole had no sentimental feeling for the English or Ontario private school. Those who were educated tended to have been educated in public schools, and found the same quite adequate for their children. The same great influx of immigrants ended the hold of the rancher in southern Alberta, and the old British landowner and remittance man were replaced by homesteaders who did not need or wish private schools. And by this time rural schools had become increasingly numerous, rendering the urban residential schools less necessary than had previously been the case.[63]

Then, too, government attitudes toward private education were not positive after the war. The U.F.A. government was of the opinion, as expressed by Minister of Education Perrin Baker, that: "it was not wise nor in the interests of the development of the best Canadian citizenship that children should be educated in segregation–away from the Public School system."[64] Yet another factor, and perhaps the most important, in the demise of private education, was the increasing improvement of Alberta's public school system. Particularly in the large urban centres like Calgary an effective education system, for its day, was beginning to be offered to all children. Teacher qualifications were improving, facilities were becoming more modern and better equipped, curricula were broadening, high schools were being built, and, in short, the public school was drawing ever closer toward offering virtually everything that the old private schools had. The one possible exception was in religious activities, as the public schools were non-denominational; but they were undisputably Christian enough for most parents.

The years from 1900 to 1916 had provided Calgary with educational facilities of a type it would not see again. The society of 1916 was not the society of 1900, and that difference was what spelled the end of the large, denominational, private schools. They simply had outlived their usefulness.

THE RESPONSE TO URBAN GROWTH: THE BUREAUCRATIZATION OF PUBLIC EDUCATION IN CALGARY, 1884-1914

Robert M. Stamp

S peaking before a Calgary audience in the spring of 1971, Canadian historian Maurice Careless[1] concluded his analysis of urban growth in western Canada with these words:

Lifestyle in the western cities had very soon become largely a counterpart of eastern. This simply indicated the common conditions of modern living for the urban West had virtually become contemporaneous with the urban East by 1914. . . .[Western cities] had in a few short decades compressed a century or so of eastern growth. . . .[2]

The purpose of this chapter is to test the Careless hypothesis on one facet of development in one western Canadian city—the public school system of Calgary. From rudimentary beginnings in the winter of 1884, public schooling in Calgary grew rapidly in both size and complexity in the thirty-year period leading up to the First World War. "A century or so of eastern growth" was indeed compressed "in a few short decades."

It is not difficult to document the physical growth of the Calgary Public School system during these years. Detailed records are readily available on the number of pupils, number of teachers, and number of school buildings which provide annual or even monthly comparisons.[3] It is however an anlaysis of the growing *complexity* and bureaucratization of public schooling in Calgary, developments that resulted from the school board's response to the pressures of urban growth, that would best serve to test the Careless hypothesis.

Between 1884 and 1914 public schooling in Calgary passed through five different stages of development. Each successive stage produced its unique "pattern of social organization" in response to the growing complexity of providing schooling in a rapidly developing urban centre. The first stage comprises the thirteen-month period from February 1884 to March 1885, and is characterized by a voluntary approach to education through the vehicle of a small private school. Stage two lasts from 1885 to 1892 and witnesses the establishment of a public school board and a large central school. The third stage occupies the period from 1892 to 1903 and is highlighted by successive administrative regulations that increasingly remove the management of schools from the direct concern of ordinary citizens. Stage four spans the years from 1903 to 1911 and sees public schooling move from the casual and informal pattern of a nineteenth-century frontier community to the more bureaucratic pattern of a twentieth-century commercial centre. The final stage, evident in the three years preceding the First World War, ushers in the full flowering of a complex, urban school system. It was the "special kind of environment" produced by urban growth that led to the increasingly complex and increasingly bureaucratic five patterns of school system management.

I

It would be flattering to report that formal schooling arrived early in the little community huddled around Fort Calgary. But this is not the case. The town boasted several general merchants, grocers and dry-goods firms, livery stables and blacksmiths, doctors, jewellers, and preachers, even a photographer and a sign and showcard writing firm, before the first school began in 1884. Schools were dependent on two ingredients—a sufficient number of white children and, even more important in the initial stages of support, a sizeable group of white women—wives, mothers, and homesteaders—who saw certain advantages in the socializing and civilizing role that schools could play on the frontier.

Not till the spring of 1882 did the first white woman homesteader arrive from the East. But it was the women who soon added a tone to pioneer society that created the necessary climate for schooling. As W.B. Fraser writes in his history of the city:

Many of Calgary's pioneer women. . .had come from good homes in the East. Although they were prepared to rough it for a while, they had no intention of allowing their new home to remain a frontier town forever. Women were active in every educational and cultural movement of the day . . . . Often it was the pioneer women who first realized that a wholesome community needs more than just a healthy economy. They wanted, and they built, a better society in which their children could grow.[4]

The usual view of a frontier town is that women remained very much in the minority for years to come. Yet Max Foran's research on early Calgary shows that by 1891 "the town had a far more balanced proportion of women to men in the twenty to forty age bracket" than did most of the North-West Territories.[5]

By the beginning of 1884 Calgary was moving from the stage of frontier settlement to organized community. The arrival of the railway, the growth of the population to five hundred, and the continued influx of wives and families led community leaders to take the first step in organizing education. At a public meeting on February 6 a citizens' committee was formed and 125 dollars subscribed towards the cost of a private school.[6] Less than two weeks later, on February 18, twelve children showed up for instruction at Calgary's first school.[7] The classroom was ungraded, the supplies scanty and the furniture home-made; but the trustees were able to boast that their teacher, J.W. Costello, possessed a "first class certificate from Ontario."[8]

Two months after opening day, the school celebrated with a public examination of the pupils. "A few friends of the children were present to witness the proceedings," reported the Calgary *Herald*, "and at the close expressed great satisfaction at the general proficiency of the pupils. The progress made by the pupils while under the tuition of Mr. Costello reflects great credit upon him."[9] It was good that the pupils had made progress during the two months. School was promptly dismissed after the examination, since there was no more money forthcoming from the "few friends of the children". But the *Herald* was not discouraged:

Looking into the dim future when Calgary shall possess colleges, when degrees shall adorn the names of its citizens; when this town of the far west shall furnish statesmen, educated here, to administer the laws of our Province, it will be a pleasant reminiscence to these children to remember their little rough school-house and this first examination within its walls.[10]

Thus ended, temporarily at least, the first stage in the institutionalization of schooling in Calgary. The establishment of a private school had been considered necessary to meet the learning needs of an increasing number of families arriving from the East. To progressive civic leaders of the day, a school was essential for attracting still more settlers to bolster Calgary's chances of replacing Fort Macleod as the major distributing centre for southern Alberta. Yet from the beginning, the management of education passed quickly into the hands of the "better classes" of the community. The three "trustees" of the private school were a lawyer, a government agricultural inspector, and a stage-coach owner. Ever present in the background was a fourth leading citizen—Colonel James Walker, onetime NWMP superintendent, former manager of the Cochrane Ranch, up-and-coming local timber baron. Walker's domination of schooling in Calgary began with his call for the formation of a citizens' committee in 1884; it continued with his push for the establishment of a public school district the following year. Over the next thirty years Walker emerged as the most influential educational policy maker. He was a member of the board for fourteen years, and chairman for six. He was the one individual whose public involvement in education spanned the full sweep of urban growth, from the frontier learning of 1884 to the large school system of 1914.

II

The establishment of a public school district was the second stage in the institutionalizing of learning in the small town of Calgary. This grew naturally out of the work of the private school, which had re-opened in September 1884 in a new location, with a new teacher, and a total of fifty pupils. In January of the following year James Walker circulated a petition among the ratepayers which led to an affirmative vote for a school district. Accordingly, on March 2 the executive council of the North-West Territories officially constituted Calgary Protestant Public School District No. 19.[11] Local boosters saw a rosy future for the board and the community. An 1885 town directory made this forecast:

The school accommodation of Calgary are yet very limited. The expense so far has been borne by private subscription confined to a few friends of education. . . .[But] last month voting took place on the erection of a school district and the district has been formally organized so that in a short time a fine school house will be built and a first-class school running.[12]

The new board simply took over the work of the private citizens' committee. The pupils must have noticed little change as they continued with their same teacher, their same meagre supplies and equipment, in their same building. This building—the second school house and the first public school—was located on the north-west corner of Ninth Avenue and Fifth Street S.E. Although some distance from other buildings at the time, the location midway between the old tent town east of the Elbow River and the new town centre around the CPR station proved acceptable to both sections of the community.[13]

The major challenge faced by the board in its early years was the rapid increase in the demand for schooling caused by urban growth in the late 1880's. Between 1884 and 1890 Calgary's population increased sevenfold, from around 500 to slightly over 3,500. Incorporation as a town, the completion of the transcontinental railway, and the planning of branch railway lines to Fort Macleod and Edmonton enabled the community to consolidate its role as the marketing and distributing centre for southern Alberta. More people meant more children to be educated; by 1892 a total of 397 pupils appeared on the attendance roll of the Calgary Public School Board. The board's response to this growth was twofold: the construction of a large central school and the beginning of high school instruction.

The one-room school at Ninth Avenue and Fifth Street S.E. provided sufficient accommodation for just one year. In the fall of 1886 a second classroom was opened in rented quarters on the second floor of the I.S. Freeze building on Eighth Avenue S.E. But with 104 pupils on the register during the winter of 1887, and 171 that summer, it was obvious that the school system needed more than temporary accommodation. Civic pride was also at stake—Calgary's enrollment was second to Regina's among territorial towns, and Regina already boasted a large modern school. Debentures of eight thousand dollars were promptly issued for the building of a four-room school. By November of 1887 the southern half of the "Old" Central School was in operation on Fifth Avenue just west of Centre Street.[14] Central included many of the features associated with urban school development: the division of the curriculum into grades, the division of the children into rigidly graded classrooms, and the clear division of function—female teachers for the primary grades supervised by a male principal who also taught the senior class.

Rising elementary enrollment led naturally to pressure for more advanced work at Central School. The first high school class began in 1891, with a second added three years later. For a ten-year period the two high school teachers taught the entire curriculum to their Standards VI through VIII pupils. It was a curriculum that included reading, dictation, composition, writing, arithmetic, ethics, drill, grammar, geography, history, literature, book-keeping, drawing, algebra, geometry, agriculture, physiology, hygiene, Latin, botany, and chemistry. But the provision of high school work, no matter how rudimentary or superficial, was a demand that had to be met by any urban school board of the day. Civic pride would not long tolerate children being sent away to Winnipeg or the East for an expensive secondary school education.

A sense of distance and remoteness soon developed between the board and the ratepayers of Calgary. Citizen interest in the formation of a school committee, then in the establishment of a public school board, quickly gave way to seeming indifference. Only three persons showed up at the first annual ratepayers meeting in November 1886—the three trustees.[15] This situation is consistent with Careless's analysis of citizen participation in early western urban centres:

The sense of common achievement in city-building often displayed at civic celebrations and community social occasions, did not go far enough to sustain a lively common interest or participation in municipal political affairs. In general, government in the cities was soon left in the hands of an elite in-group. . .who made a fairly regular profession out of directing government for a citizenry that normally preferred to be left alone.[16]

Part of the blame for the ever-widening gulf must rest with the trustees themselves. At least this was the view expressed by "A Citizen" in a letter to the Calgary *Herald* in 1891:

The School Trustees of this town have to do with important matters, the dis-

cussion of which should be opened to the public. Thus far they appear to operate in secret; their proceedings at their meetings are a sealed book; and the people, who are most interested in these proceedings, seldom hear of the trustees' decisions until too late to modify their action. . . .Certainly the citizens have a right to know from one meeting to another everything that is done by them in their official capacity. . . .They are a public body dealing with weighty matters and with large funds and they should be most anxious to take the citizens into their counsels, as they go, instead of withholding this information. . . .[17]

During the early 1890's Calgary moved from a relatively open and fluid society of the frontier period to a more stratified society of town and city. The school trustees continued to be drawn from the ranks of the middle and upper-middle classes of business and professional men. As with most urban school systems of the day, it was not unusual that a more formal and distant relationship developed between the board and the more socially mixed general population of the community.

III

The third stage in the evolutionary development of an urban school system in Calgary begins with the construction of the first "ward" school in 1892 and continues for the next eleven years. This period roughly coincides with a slowdown in the community's rate of growth. Calgary languished during the 1890's, despite the completion of rail lines to Edmonton amd Fort Macleod, the coming of city status, and the beginnings of an industrial base built on the products of the surrounding agricultural region. Not till after the turn of the century would Calgary share in the prosperity of the "Laurier" boom. In the meantime the population crept from 3,876 to 4,091 between the census years of 1891 to 1901, quite a contrast with the preceding and following decades.

The slower rate of growth had its effects on the public school system. Unlike the 1885–90 and 1904–14 years, the period from the early 1890's to 1903 was one in which the trustees were not constantly preoccupied with the problem of providing accommodation. The opening of the one-room East Ward (later Alexandra) School in 1892, and the two-room South Ward (later Haultain) School two years later, provided enough classroom space to

house the additional children from newer homes east of the Elbow River and south of the CPR railway tracks.[18] In fact the slow-
ness of the population growth barely justified these two new
schools. During most of the 1890's the now eight-room Central
School was almost sufficient in itself; usually only one room at
South Ward School was used, and occasionally the East Ward
School was closed for brief periods.

But the construction and operation of the ward schools reveal
two important aspects of institutional growth. First, the Calgary
Public School Board now possessed three tracts of land, enough
to make it a very visible property owner in the small town of the
1890's. In 1894 these three pieces of real estate were valued at a
total of 10,850 dollars. With buildings valued at 13,000 dollars
and equipment at another 1,500 dollars, the board had tangible
assets of 25,350 dollars, which placed additional responsibilities
on the part-time, non-paid trustees.[19] Secondly, the operation of
three schools led to the establishment of rigid attendance boundaries between the different institutions. School boundaries are
but one example of increasing institutionalization of schooling
during this period. The trustees passed a host of restrictive administrative regulations during the decade—regulations govern-
ing attendance and truancy, entry of beginning pupils, duties of
teachers, and teachers' contracts.

Staffing and financing were the major concerns of the Calgary Public School Board during the 1890's. There was certainly
no shortage of applicants for teaching positions—forty-six applied for one advertised vacancy in 1892 alone. The problem
arose over the board's preference for experienced Ontario teachers versus the insistence of the territorial administration on con-
didates possessing valid North-West Territories certificates.
Many eastern-trained teachers were at first given only temporary
letters of authority; to renew their certificates, these teachers had
to attend a session at the Regina Normal School. But costs deterred many from doing so, and the few graduates of the regular
program in Regina could not begin to fill the territorial demand.
In 1893, D.J. Goggin, superintendent of schools for the territories,
warned the Calgary board that five of its nine teachers "were
practically teaching without a certificate." This placed Calgary
in a dangerous situation "for if any member of the Executive at
Regina desired to do so, he would stop the payment of the grants
on account of these teachers."[20]

Finances were, at best, shaky during these years. Territorial grants were small, and up to seventy percent of operating costs had to be raised through the local property tax. Records from the period constantly attest to the backlog of unpaid taxes and the need for a "diligent collector of overdue moneys". The minutes for the March 1893 board meeting are particularly discouraging; at that time the trustees authorized the payment of certain accounts "as soon as there were sufficient funds in the Treasury." Again in January 1896 the mere breakdown of the furnace at Central School threatened to throw the trustees into a financial panic.[21] Not till the new century brought increased territorial and provincial grants and a broader local tax base would the board be out of financial danger.

In 1893 the board adopted an organizational pattern that continued without major change during this third period of urban growth. On the first Thursday of each month, the five trustees gathered in the "library" of Central School for their regular monthly meeting. They were joined by a part-time supervising principal, whose duties also included teaching the senior class at Central School, and a part-time secretary-treasurer. To handle routine business between meeting, four standing committees were structured—finance, school management, school buildings, and property and supplies. Compared with the private citizens' committee of 1884, the management of education in Calgary had become more complex and efficient; but in terms of what would follow, it was still rather casual and simplistic.

IV

The fourth stage in the development of the Calgary public school system lasts from approximately 1903 till 1911. This period coincides with years of spectacular population growth; between 1901 and 1911, Calgary's population increased by elevenfold—from 4,000 to 44,000. During this time Calgary changed from a frontier town to a commercial centre of major importance in the West. Not only was the city the marketing centre of a prosperous agriculture and ranching area, it also became the focal point to which new immigrants flocked. And the exploitation of such resources as coal, oil and natural gas in the surrounding countryside increased the possibilities of further urban growth.

Such a dramatic period of growth quickly rendered obsolete the casual and informal attitude towards education taken by the school board in the 1890's. A spirit of optimism and a vision of big-city status permeated Calgary's citizens; in 1903 this spirit and vision caught up with the trustees. As the *Morning Albertan* remarked:

The schools of Calgary are in a transitory stage. They are not as popular as they should be, and whether there may or may not be a reason for it, people in Calgary have a habit of depreciating anything local, which is unwestern and unwise. This is particularly the case with the schools and one hears on all sides, 'The schools here are no good.' Such a statement as that is unkind and untrue. Yet at the same time the schools of Calgary are not as pre-eminently in advance of those in other parts of the Territories as they should be in a city like Calgary.[22]

Were Calgary's schools lagging behind those of other Western centres? That same year a transplanted easterner, Mrs. G.W. Kerby, could remark that "the schools of Calgary are equally as good as our eastern counterparts, though somewhat hampered by their crowded conditions, owing to the rapid growth of the city."[23] Yet concerned citizens were also aware of the board's repeated failure to separate elementary and high school instruction, and the frequent departure of able principals for careers as rural school inspectors or lawyers. And citizens with friends on the board also heard rumours of critical inspectors' comments on the quality of teaching and school administration. To gauge public feeling and elicit support for future moves, board chairman A.L. Cameron called an open meeting for April 24, 1903.

That night marked a turning point in the history of the Calgary Public School Board. Comments from citizens present indicated unanimous support for a two-pronged response to the challenge of urban growth: a quantitative increase in accommodation and a qualitative improvement in instruction and administration. Some excerpts from the Calgary *Herald's* account of the meeting:

Dr. Herdman: Calgary was not doing the educational work it could. They should get the best system, employ the best teachers and engage the best principal to work it out. A few hundred dollars should not stand in the way. Calgary should take a high stand in educational matters and make itself known as such and get on a right footing now.

R.J. Hutchings: The difference in cost between a good and poor school was so small that it was false economy to stop at a few dollars of proper expenditures. The best was none too good for growing Calgary, and we must have the best schools and the best system.[24]

What did it mean? "The board is evidently preparing for a progressive movement as regards the schools of Calgary," declared the *Herald*, "and from the tenor of the speeches made by the citizens present, it will receive hearty and earnest support." And the editorial writer went on to warn: "If the expression of opinion of those present can form any gauge of public opinion, *the board will have to move.*"[25]

The first obvious manifestation of the board's shift to the next stage in its development was its decision to separate elementary and high school instruction. In September 1903 the high school classes were transferred to two adjoining frame buildings on Seventh Avenue S.E. behind the old city hall. The school was officially known as City Hall School, although pupils always called it "Sleepy Hollow" High School. Perhaps the nickname was a means of masking the school's less-than-prestigious location, surrounded as it was by the police station, livery barn, and dog pound. "It was like stepping backwards in time," recalled a student in later years. "Our schools in Woodstock, Ontario had all been big modern buildings. I wasn't prepared for the change when we moved to Calgary, but I soon got used to it. Sleepy Hollow had no inside toilets, no running water, no science labs. Students from outlying areas rode in on horseback, and they just tied their horses to the fence in the back yard."[26]

The primitive state of Sleepy Hollow High School in the early years of the century—four frame buildings joined by covered passageways—is indicative of the still light demand for secondary education in Calgary. The *Morning Albertan* attributed "low attendance in the higher grades" to the fact that "Calgary furnishes excellent business opportunities for boys of the High School age, and most youths are lured away from the paths of education for positions in offices and stores."[27] Yet the fact that Sleepy Hollow served the city's needs for only four years attests to the rapid increase in demand for secondary schooling during the first decade of the century. In 1907 Calgary's high school pupils moved into larger, more impressive accommodations at Calgary Collegiate Institute. This impressive sandstone building at Thirteenth Avenue and Eighth Street S.W. gave a new status to secondary education.

The construction of a new Central School—a three-storey, palatial sandstone structure costing seventy thousand dollars—was the second major step taken by the board during this period. At the laying of the cornerstone in 1904, chairman R.J. Hutchings reaffirmed that "it was the intention of the school board to be in front as far as educational matters were concerned. They would never be satisfied until they had everything of the best."[28] At least the problem of overcrowded classrooms had been temporarily solved; by 1905 the Calgary Public School Board could boast three large schools—the "Old" and "New" Central Schools plus Alexandra (an enlarged East Ward School)—and two smaller structures—Sleepy Hollow and South Ward.

The appointment of a full-time superintendent of schools was the third and most significant step taken during this fourth stage of development. The move was advocated in April 1906 by Winnipeg School Superintendent Daniel McIntyre, who had been commissioned to prepare an "independent" evaluation of Calgary schools. The *Morning Albertan* printed *verbatim* McIntyre's arguments for a superintendent:

However well the plan of combining the duties of superintending and teaching may have worked when the city was smaller. . .your school system has passed the stage when such provision for direction can be held to be sufficient. . . .

The duty of such an official would be to direct the whole work of organization, classification, teaching and discipline of all the schools, to determine the standard of attainment in the several grades, guide the pedagogical reading of the teaching staff. . .and be a leader in everything that would make for the efficiency of the schools.[29]

Just two days after McIntyre's report was released, the *Morning Albertan* ran a page one photograph of Melville Scott, announcing his appointment as superintendent of Calgary public schools. It was obvious that McIntyre had been used to lend outside credibility to the board's decision to employ a full-time administrator. Scott was a surprise choice to many Calgarians; a professor of chemistry at the University of New Brunswick, he had had but three years teaching experience in rural Ontario schools, and no previous contact with western Canada. Yet Scott possessed those characteristics the trustees felt were lacking in the primitive Calgary school system of 1906. Scholarship: an honours degree from the University of Toronto and a doctorate from Goettingen. Authority: pupils and teachers were terrified of him and hesitated to question his word. And above all, respectability: as a staunch Victorian Methodist, Scott gave his full support to the civilizing and moralizing mission of the public school on the prairie frontier.

In his study of the municipal reform movement in early twentieth century Canada, Paul Rutherford describes the impact of the full-time professional administrator:

This was the beginning of the age of the specialist and the professional. . . .To a degree, this appeared to be a devolution of authority; in fact it was a centralization of authority in the hands of professionals, well-nigh independent of the electorate. . . .The latent authoritarianism was tempered by the assumption that the bureaucrat would move in accordance with a right-thinking public.[30]

The appointment of Melville Scott was the most dramatic indication to date of urban complexity and the increasing bureaucratization of public schooling in Calgary. Scott's presence represented a further level of executive and administrative decision-making between the ratepayers who elected trustees to formulate educational policy, and the teachers who were charged with executing those policies at the classroom level. The fact that Scott was an outsider who had not come up "through the ranks" added a further degree of isolation and remoteness to the situation.

V

The fifth and final stage in the institutionalization of public schooling in pre-First World War Calgary was evident by 1911. Calgary was in the midst of the greatest economic boom in its history, sustained initially by wild speculation in real estate and then by early oil discoveries in the Turner Valley area. Between 1910 and 1912 Calgary had the largest percentage increase in population and construction of any Canadian city. The value of building permits in the latter year was more than fifty million dollars, a figure not exceeded until 1950. In the years immediately preceding the war, Calgary had become a commercial centre of major importance in western Canada.

During these hectic years the trustees of the Calgary Public

School Board faced a constant battle in providing accommodation; new classrooms and new buildings for the expanding school enrollment did not materialize out of nowhere. Scott's monthly report for September 1911 is typical of the period:

Considerable numbers of pupils have been unable to gain admittance in some parts of the city. In Hillhurst there are three rented rooms, and yet no adequate relief can be given until the new school is ready. In Riverside and Crescent Heights it is imperative that some steps be taken to meet requirements which will be pressing long before new schools are built.[31]

It would have been easier if all the new pupils had been Grade One beginners enrolling on the first school day in September. But they were entering at all grade levels, in every month of the year. "One-third of our present pupils are new to Calgary schools this year," Scott lamented in April 1913.[32] "Only one-quarter of our Grade Eight pupils began school in the primary grade in Calgary," he reported two years later.[33]

Second only to the problem of accommodation was the task of staffing every classroom with a qualified teacher. Applicants appeared regularly, especially from eastern Canada, but they left the board's employ with almost equal speed. As the *Herald* remarked in 1913: "There are many conditions about Calgary which serve to attract young women teachers from Eastern centres, but. . .the opportunities of matrimony are so many and so attractive that it is a somewhat difficult matter to maintain permanent staffs."[34] Consequently, anyone with a year or two of experience in the Calgary system was regarded as a veteran. Of the one hundred and twenty two teachers in January 1912, for example, fifty-nine had been employed by the Calgary board for less than a year, while only twelve had been on staff more than five years. "The work of the teacher here is much more trying than in a settled community," reported Scott. He listed the problems as: "the never-ceasing interruptions owing to the opening of new classes, the removal of pupils from one school to another to avoid overcrowding, the coming into the city of new families, and the incessant moving from one part of the city to another."[35]

Problems of providing classrooms and teachers are certainly indices of urban growth, but more fundamental indices of urban complexity were two additional challenges facing trustees in the 1911–14 period: bureaucratic remoteness and the extension of the traditional role of the school. Board minutes for August 8,

1911 contain in one short paragraph a revealing commentary on how the growth of the school system had changed the management of education:

The Chairman expressed a wish that the members of the Board endeavour to visit the schools and become acquainted with the teachers, and Colonel Walker very kindly placed his car at the disposal of the Board when they desired to visit the schools together as a Board.[36]

Only eight years before, board chairman Herb Sinnott had been principal of tiny Sleepy Hollow High School. At that time he and his elementary school counterpart, Hugh Parker, had felt no isolation from the trustees. On the contrary, their major complaint concerned the constant meddling of the trustees in the daily business of running the schools. But the situation had changed dramatically by the time Sinnott returned as a trustee.

Even more dramatic were the changes observed by veteran decision-maker James Walker in his thirty-year involvement in Calgary education. Three decades of urban growth had forced the public school system to radically change its pattern of operation. Between 1884 and 1914, pupil population grew from 12 to 7,451, teaching staff from 1 to 198, and school buildings from 1 to 34.[37] The policy setting and executive functions of this sprawling enterprise grew into a complex organization of paid trustees, endless board and committee meetings, and full-time administrators, supervisors and secretaries. A symbolic move occurred in 1911 when the board transferred its offices from crowded quarters in Central School to a modern suite on the third floor of the new city hall. Increasingly, one found a board of trustees and a supervisory staff removed from the lives of the average citizen and also removed from the day-to-day concerns of the schools.

Further evidence of growing complexity is found in the response of the Calgary Public School Board to three early twentieth century urban challenges. The challenge presented by the city's growth as a commercial and industrial centre was met by the introduction of courses in business and technical education; that of urban crime and juvenile delinquency by the appointment of a full-time truant officer; and that of urban poverty and slum living conditions by the establishment of a medical inspection department.[38] Each of these moves significantly expanded the role of the school system beyond that of catering solely to the academic needs of its clients. But in each case the board's decision met with a favourable community response; the majority of citizens gave at least tacit support to the idea that an urban school system should address itself to the needs and problems of an urban community.

By 1914 Calgary had risen to become an "economically affluent, technologically advanced, and socially fast-maturing urban centre." Rapid growth and the increasing complexity of city life forced its school system, along with other public services, to move quickly beyond the frontier stage of the 1880's and 1890's and into the urban stage of the twentieth century. In this sense, the former social differences between Calgary and eastern cities diminished quickly. The Calgary public school system between 1884 and 1914 illustrates perfectly the Careless hypothesis:

Lifestyle in the western cities had very soon become largely a counterpart of eastern. This simply indicated the common conditions of modern urban living, for the urban West had virtually become contemporaneous with the urban East by 1914. . . .[Western cities] had in a few short decades compressed a century or so of eastern growth. . . .[39]

With the exception of a provincially dictated curriculum, the Calgary Public School system manifests this similarity with its eastern counterparts. Complete with its large school buildings, well-trained teaching staff, a hierarchy of full-time administrators, and constantly confronted by the problems of urban life, it had "compressed a century or so of eastern growth" in three short decades. It had become increasingly bureaucratic by acquiring those characteristics which sociologists would generally agree mark bureaucracy: for instance, hierarchy, division of function, specialization, precision, continuity, rule-following and discretion.[40] And increasingly, the pupil populations of the neighbourhood elementary schools reflected the socio-economic divisions and the class structure representative of large urban centres. By 1914 the Calgary Public School system had more in common with school boards in Toronto, Hamilton, and Ottawa, than with boards in Trochu, High River, and Okotoks.

THE EARLY HISTORY OF THE CATHOLIC CHURCH IN CALGARY

M.B. Byrne

The first permanent Catholic Mission was established in southern Alberta in the spring of 1873, two and a half years before the Mounted Police established their fort at what was later Calgary. Father Lacombe had been going on summer missions to the Blackfoot from St. Albert since 1865, and indeed had previously even visited them during the epidemic of 1857, but he left western Canada in 1872 and was gone for ten years.

This left the Blackfoot without a missionary, and the only person available was Brother Scollen, a young Irishman who had been making his studies for the priesthood when he could spare time from teaching at the first school in Edmonton, teaching Cree to the new missionaries, going on missions to the prairies, working with Father Lacombe on a Cree grammar and diction-ary, and acting as secretary to the Bishop and bursar to the Mis-sion. He was ordained priest on Easter, 1873, and the following Tuesday he set out for his new Mission in the South.

The previous year in November Alexis Cardinal, a Métis whose mother tongue was Cree, had built for the Mission a small hut on the Elbow River about twenty-five miles up from the pres-ent site of Calgary. The spot seems to have been chosen because it was the country of the winter camps of the Blackfoot. During the winter some of the buffalo left the open prairies for the shelter of the wooded country of the foothills. It seems also to have been on the trail from Rocky Mountain House to the Peigan country and Fort Benton.

The hut which Alexis Cardinal built was modelled on the

Métis winter shelters, and usually not used for more than one season.[1] According to a later description by Father Doucet, the walls were of trunks of trees, the roof branches covered with pine bark. The floor was bare ground, the windows covered by canvas sacks or skins, and the door was a skin stretched on poles. It was heated by a chimney of flat stones and earth. The whole was no more then fifteen feet square and was surmounted by a cross. Later a small alcove was added which served as dormitory and chapel.

This spot has been marked by a cairn, the base of which is built with the chimney stones of the original building. It is situated on the north bank of the Elbow River in Section ten. This was the first chapel, Our Lady of Peace, in what was later the Calgary Diocese.

Father Scollen spent his summers on missions to the Indians on the prairies, no doubt in the same manner as had Father Lacombe, whose assistant he had been. His work would have been impossible without the help of the Métis, the sons of French-Canadian "Voyageurs" or Company "servants", who acted as interpreters, guides, and provided liason with the Indians. They had their eccentricities; Alexis Cardinal, for example, regarded himself as a missionary and wore a semi-clerical gown of black stroud made for him by a Métis woman on his instructions. According to Father Doucet he would preach in Cree to the Blackfoot (and of course was little understood). He boasted to them that he was more powerful than the Bishop and could teach the Fathers a lot. He liked to be admired and flattered by the Indians and at times would lose his head completely.[2] Nevertheless he was a faithful helper. Louis Dazé hunted for the missionaries and kept them supplied with game. He was lost in a blizzard in the winter of 1873–74 and was frozen to death. Jean L'Heureux was apparently not a Métis, but was born in Quebec and educated there. He had been a helper to Father Lacombe and took his assumed vocation very seriously. He also wore a soutane, and when he was alone with the Indians baptized, preached, blessed marriages, heard confessions, and made the appearance of saying Mass. In the circumstances episcopal discipline was obviously impossible, and the missionaries did not hesitate to make use of him in spite of his oddities. He was an interpreter with Father Scollen at Treaty Number Seven in 1877, and in 1884 was at Blackfoot Crossing to persuade the Indians to send their children to Dunbow School.[3]

Two years after Father Scollen came to what is now southern Alberta he met the Mounted Police in Macleod and heard of plans to establish a fort. It was probably from Jerry Potts that he heard of its likely location. When he returned from Fort Macleod on July 10 he immediately instructed Alexis Cardinal to build a dwelling at the confluence of the Bow and Elbow. Father Scollen left on July 12 with Father Touze, newly arrived from St. Albert, for his mission on the prairies with the Indians. Alexis Cardinal left for the Bow River where he built the Mission hut. Father Doucet, who had also come that spring from St. Albert, was left alone at Our Lady of Peace Mission.

The missionaries were almost alone in this vast country. In 1871 Fred Kanouse, an American trader, had built a fort or post a few miles up the Elbow from the Bow. He had with him three other men and an Indian woman, considerable ammunition, and trading goods, including whisky. Before long they were in a fight with a party of Bloods which lasted for three days, in which one of the whites and several Indians were killed. The fort was abandoned. In 1872 another trader named Berry attempted to build a post where Kanouse had been but was chased off by the Bloods. He then built a post twelve miles up the Elbow, but a Blood ambushed him, shot him dead, and scalped him after stabbing him repeatedly.[4]

This was the country in which Father Doucet remained alone that summer of 1875; his only neighbour, Sam Livingston, was some miles down the Elbow. Father Doucet was a small man, extremely shy and retiring, and suffered terribly from the solitude and extremely primitive conditions of the Indian country after having arrived so recently from the civilization of France. His notes give some picture of the hardships:

Grizzly bears. . .mosquitoes. . .solitude. . .grasshoppers. . .flies. . .vermin crawling everywhere. . .a storm and nearly wounded. . .wolves howling. . .Oskijik stole a horse of Livingstone's. . .courage!. . .the garden nearly destroyed by grasshoppers and then by gophers and then by rabbits, etc. . . .nearly six months of solitude. . .ennui. . .nothing to read. . .isolated. . .hostile Indians. . .bandits of all colours of skin. . .anxiety. . .nights of insomnia. . .[5]

These last notes suggest severe psychological distress from loneliness. Nevertheless Father Doucet remained on the Indian Missions in southern Alberta for nearly seventy years, and was the first Catholic Missionary to the Blackfoot Reserve in 1881.

The building on the Bow River was of the same rough construction as their former mission, about nine feet square, set near the bank of the Elbow River. The Mounted Police when they came in September began building their barracks somewhat to the west of it.

Finding unsuitable the site of the little house built by Alexis Cardina, Doucet's journal notes "we lent our shack to the Mounted Police who were at first living in dug-outs. . .we chose another spot about a mile up the Elbow. . ."[6] It was of the same rough construction and was set on a little plateau (which has since been razed) approximately where the Nurses' Residence of the Holy Cross Hospital now stands.

In 1876 Father Scollen was at Fort Carlton where he was a witness to Treaty Number Six with the Wood Crees, Plains Crees, and the Willow Crees. At that time he was requested by the Minister of the Interior, the Honourable David Mills, to make a report on the character, habits, and conditions of the Blackfoot. At the end of the report he submitted, Father Scollen added a postscript: "I am also aware that the Sioux, now at war with the Americans, have sent a message to the Blackfoot tribe asking them to make an alliance, offensive and defensive, against all white people in the country."[7] It will be remembered that this was the summer of the massacre of General Custer and his troop directly to the southeast of the Blackfoot territory. Father Scollen was also a witness to Treaty Number Seven in 1877 at Blackfoot Crossing.

It should be noted here quite clearly that in these early missionary days Father Lacombe was *not* here. Overcome by the legend of his personality, painters, sketchers, and writers-after-the-fact often attribute Scollen's accomplishments to Father Lacombe. This is an error through negligence or ignorance, but should in justice be cleared up. Father Lacombe returned to Calgary in 1882 after it was evident that the Canadian Pacific Railway would be built through Calgary, and he then began to build from what had been virtually an Indian Mission.

From 1877 to 1881 the Mission to the Indians had been severely hampered by the disappearance of the buffalo. By the Treaty Number Seven of 1877 the Indians were to be settled on reserves, educated, and given a small living allowance. But it took years to implement this and in the meantime the Indians were short of food. In October, 1879, Chief Crowfoot, learning that buffalo had been seen grazing in Montana, let the Blackfoot stay there, where they remained until the spring of 1881 when the American government forced them to return north of the border. It was at this time that the Indians first began to settle on the reserves: the Blackfoot, the Peigan, the Blood, and Sarcee; and Morley for the Assiniboines. During this time the missionaries had to serve them as best they could and try to act as ambassadors for them with the Indian agents.

The other congregation of the missionaries were the Métis. In 1879 Father Scollen reported to his superiors:

Our Lady of Peace, the only Mission on the Bow River, includes nearly ten thousand souls in its boundaries. . .About six thousand Blackfoot. . .The remainder is composed of about fifty Catholic Métis families, five or six hundred Assiniboines, nearly all Protestant. Add to that a rabble of nearly every nationality, and about sixty soldiers of whom some are Catholics.[8]

The chief care of the missionaries, then, aside from the Indians, were the Métis who settled around the Mounted Police posts. Their chief occupation was supplying and freighting by wagon trains from Fort Benton and Edmonton. They caused considerable worry to the missionaries with their free way of life.

The mixture of opposed customs and values, the Indian as against the French-Canadian, undermined the foundation of tradition among the Métis that left them floating without a real base for their culture. They suffered with the Indians when the buffalo culture was destroyed, but they were too far removed from the French-Canadian culture to fall back on it as a support for their lives. Thus, while in the early days they were essential to the missionaries as interpreters and guides and hunters, later in the urban centres their rootlessness caused grave problems.

II

In the spring of 1881 Bishop Grandin of St. Albert visited what was called the Southern Mission and brought with him two lay brothers, carpenters, to build residences on the three principal reserves. From this visit dates a great change in the missions. The settling of the Indians, and the rumour of the building of the railway and the consequent increase in the white population, necessitated a changed plan. Father Legal came as Superior in November, 1881, Father Scollen returned to Edmonton in the summer of 1882, and Father Lacombe came in August as Superior of the Southern Missions and began a considerable building program. The second era of the development of the future Calgary Diocese began.

Within a month he had begun a new residence and chapel in Calgary on the site of the present Sacred Heart Convent on Nineteenth Avenue and First Street S.W. He spent the winter in Macleod with Father Legal working on a Blackfoot Dictionary, caring for the Indians on the Blood and Peigan reserves, building a new mission building at Macleod, and arranging with Sir Alexander Galt to have sawn ten thousand board feet of lumber for his new missionary buildings.

During the building of the Canadian Pacific Railway through what is now Alberta, the Oblate missionaries cared for the workers on the various contractors' gangs strung along the right-of-way from Maple Creek to Golden. The labourers were of many nationalities, including a large proportion of French-Canadians. Father Claude, the parish priest in Calgary, was appointed chaplain to the "Cheminots", as the French called them. Where the line was finished the missionary travelled by train or hand car, then went ahead on foot, or by horseback when lucky, with a pack on his back through the brush or the clearings in all kinds of weather to hear confessions and say Mass. Then he packed up and went on to the next camp. This mission lasted from early in 1883 until October, 1884 when the railway line reached Golden, beyond what is now the Alberta border and outside the St. Albert Diocese.

With the coming of the railway the community that had settled in what is now east Calgary moved across the Elbow River, and those that did not buy lots in the CPR's Section Fifteen began squatting on Crown lands. Father Lacombe with his characteristic vision and energy at once made claim to two "homesteads" under the Act of 1871. Without waiting for permission from his Superior he left for Ottawa at the end of 1883 and called upon Sir David McPherson, then Minister of the Interior, requesting two quarter sections immediately south of Section Fifteen in the name of Father Leduc, Superior of the Missions, and himself. This was the land on which the Mission buildings were standing, and it has been called the Mission District ever since. The Minister indicated that the request would be received fav-

ourably and would be confirmed in due course. To this Father
Lacombe replied:

*Non, Monsieur, I cannot go until I receive that settlement of our land. I came
hundreds of miles just for this. I will wait here with your permission. . .I am
used to camping on the prairie, on the floor, anywhere. . .I will just camp
here until I get my papers. . .[9]*

These two homesteads comprised the west half of Section Ten except for that part east of the Elbow River and north of Twenty-
sixth Avenue which had already been ceded to Paul Fagnant.
They extended from Seventeenth Avenue to Thirty-fourth Avenue S.W., and from Fourth Street W. to Second Street E.

On the same visit to Ottawa he arranged that three Industrial Schools for Indians be built by the government: one Protestant, at Battleford; and Catholic, at Qu'Appelle and at Dunbow
near the confluence of the Highwood and the Bow Rivers. The
idea was to bring the very young Indian children to the school to
teach them English and trades, along with the regular schooling,
so that they might fit into the community of Europeans that now
controlled the country. But the Indians resolutely refused to give
up their young children, and in the end fifteen boys from 15 to 17
years of age were assembled. These youths of course were already
formed in the Indian way of life and there was no way of changing them. As Father Lacombe said, they were like wild cats in a
beaver den.

The Grey Nuns of Montreal came to Dunbow in September
of 1884 and gradually some younger children came to the school.
Little by little the nuns gained their affection and established a
regular school routine in which manual training, household
economy and agricultural techniques were taught. The school
lasted for forty years until government schools were well established on the reservations, and then was closed in 1922.

When it became apparent in the spring of 1885 that because
of the Riel Rebellion the Sisters, the Faithful Companions of Jesus, would be forced to leave St. Laurent in what is now Saskatchewan, they were invited to Calgary. Father Lacombe arranged
to give them the Mission residence and chapel for their home
and school and immediately set about building another mission
residence for the Oblates. In November of 1883 the residents east
of the Elbow had built a chapel, St. Patrick's. In the spring of
1884 this had been moved across the river to the northeast corner

of the Mission homestead where the fire station on Second Street E. is presently located. In June of 1885 it was again moved with the help of the local garrison to a spot somewhat west of the present Cathedral. A contract was given on June 12 for a two-storey house to be attached to the chapel, and the community was able to move in on July 12, a month after signing the contract. It was apparently in this manner that early Calgary was built. This was the fifth location of the Mission of Our Lady of Peace.

The Faithful Companion nuns arrived in Calgary on July 26, 1885 and opened their school on September 1 to 15 pupils. Separate School District Number One was established a month or so later. The nuns immediately began building a convent for resident pupils, and by 1888 there were ninety pupils attending. The teaching staff was exceptional for the North-West Territories at that time. All had taught in England, Ireland, and France where the standard of achievement was high.

According to Mrs. A.G. Plunkett, one of the earliest natives of Calgary, the nuns were born teachers—the Inspectors who came to the Convent said they came to learn how to teach and not to inspect. The nuns taught music and drama as well, and, according to the same Mrs. Plunkett,

Mother Bernard was a wonderful musician—a real musician. She played the harp and the organ and everything. She was terribly bad tempered. . .I liked Mother Bernard. She was a fat little tub and homely as all get out, but her hands were beautiful. Reverend Mother Green was a real lady with a beautiful speaking voice.[10]

On March 31, 1886, in the Townsite Ledger it is recorded that the CPR had set aside lots Sixteen to Twenty in Block Fifty of Section Fifteen as a free gift to the Roman Catholic Church. These were on the southwest corner of Seventh Avenue and Centre Street S.[11] The Oblates apparently preferred to build a larger and more suitable church on their own homestead, and the old sandstone church was built in 1889 with great pride and enthusiasm. This was the sixth and last location of Our Lady of Peace, and when the parish was canonically erected in 1910 it was under the name of the Immaculate Conception.

In 1888 Bishop Grandin asked the Grey Nuns of Montreal to staff a hospital in Calgary. It was not until late in 1890, however, that they could supply personnel. Father Leduc had a house built for them twenty-four feet square with two stories, the upper floor for the nuns' quarters and the lower floor for the hospital.

This was built on Eighteenth Avenue near the present St. Mary's Hall.

On the 30th of January, 1891, three sisters and an Assistant Superior arrived in Calgary at two o'clock in the morning in bitterly cold weather and deep snow. Train schedules in the early days were not reliable or accommodating. The nuns had been accompanied from St. Boniface by Father Leduc, but there was no-one to meet them in Calgary and they had to carry their luggage from the station to the Mission. They received their first patient in April, but it was at once apparent that a small hospital of six beds was not sufficient, and the townspeople began asking them to expand. But the next year a large hospital was built on the present Holy Cross property. In those days fees were one dollar a day for those who could pay and nothing for those who could not. Indigent patients from outside the city were paid for by the Government at forty cents a day. That same year the nuns staffed a smallpox hospital three miles from the city where they remained in tents for about five weeks until the epidemic passed. The following year the top floor of the hospital was arranged as an isolation ward during a diphtheria epidemic. At the same time the nuns provided home nursing wherever a nurse was required. In 1969 the Grey Nuns sold the hospital complex to the provincial government when medical care became the concern of the state.

To return to 1884, in August the Oblates had the northwest part of their homestead surveyed and the sale of the lots began immediately. Seventeenth Avenue was called Notre Dame Street, and the avenues south from there were St. Joseph, St. Mary, Oblate, Lacombe, Doucet, Rouleau, Grandin, Scollen, and Legal. Fourth Street was called Broadway. This district came to be called Rouleauville, undoubtedly because Chief Justice Charles Rouleau, who came to Calgary in 1886 and built his house at the northeast corner of Broadway and St. Mary Street, which he called "Castel aux Près". There was still a fair proportion of French-Canadians among the congregation, and a strong community spirit around the church. According to Mrs. Plunkett the Oblates were all liked. As she said, they never had better priests.[12]

III

After the completion of the Canadian Pacific Railway in 1885 the settlement of the West was slow until Sir Clifford Sifton became Minister of the Interior in 1896. His dynamic campaign in Europe and the United States brought more than two million settlers to the prairie provinces in the next fifteen years. This, together with the development of the Canadian Northern Railway in the western Provinces, brought tremendous growth to the cities and towns, of which Calgary was a prime example. City growth in turn sparked the third era in the growth of the Catholic Church in Calgary.

The Oblate missionaries made a brave attempt to cope with growth in the cities as well as in the rural communities that were springing up everywhere with the opening of land for homesteads. As well as forty-seven churches in rural areas when the Diocese was formed in 1912, three new parishes had been established in Calgary and schools built to service the children of the new families.

For the north hill parish of St. Benedict (now St. Joseph's), Benedictine monks were brought from England. They came on an invitation of the Oblate Bishop to establish a college as well as to do parish work, and had at first planned to establish their school in Edmonton to care for the English-speaking boys of the Catholic community. This was not carried out and they settled in Calgary in 1912. Due to various difficulties and misunderstandings the college in Calgary was not completed either and the Benedictines withdrew in 1914—a great loss to the Catholic community and to the whole of the West. For the Benedictines are historically known as the civilizers of western Europe, and even today their schools are pre-eminent in England.

The comments of Father McLaughlin O.S.B. regarding his parish bear some interest:

The eastern flat—Riverside—is the foreign quarter pre-eminently. There are endless German Protestant churches in it, and a large Russian population. But to us it is the Italian quarter. There must be over a thousand Catholics in this part alone. I said to a politician, "There must be hundreds of Italians there." He answered, "There are more than six hundred men alone. I've naturalized more than four hundred of them in this election."

The mixture of nations is not all a difficulty; in some ways it is a great encouragement. It gives a new and actual sense of the catholicity of the church. . .In Holy Week there was a Japanese kneeling beside me and praying most devoutly. At a Ruthenian funeral, in the snow, where no one could understand me an old Indian woman came to the graveside, and when she saw the child's coffin, knelt down and made a great sign of the Cross, pointed upwards, and began evidently some hymn of praise; and then the Ruthenians followed her example in their own tongue, while I said the Latin prayer.

But what moved me most was meeting the fully-educated of the different nations, and finding in all of them the Church had taken these utterly diverse characters, and developed them into the perfect type of Catholic. I met such people from the continent of Europe, from the United States, from the Maritime Provinces, from middle Canada and the West.[13]

In 1905 a sandstone parish hall was built east of St. Mary's Church, and part of it was rented to the school board. The lots on Seventh Avenue given by the CPR in 1886 were sold in 1908 for what must have seemed a phenomenal sum of 25,000 dollars. In the same year twelve lots were bought in what is now called the Eau Claire district, and a small church was built, but was used only once. In the height of the development euphoria of 1911 and 1912 the Canadian Northern Railway bought St. Mary's parish hall as a temporary station and considered building a large terminal in Calgary. The Canadian Northern had been responsible for much of the prosperity of the West by opening branch lines, providing transportation for goods and services, populating large tracts of land, and pouring millions of dollars into their railway construction. But by 1911 the servicing of their debt was becoming expensive and European money markets with their own political problems were becoming wary. There was also anxiety about international political tensions. Very little appreciation of this reached Calgary, but it affected the plans of the Canadian Northern Railway. Their large plans for a terminal in Calgary which would have required most of the St. Mary's and the Oblate property had to be shelved. But in the meantime, on the expectation that the St. Mary's property would be sold for several hundreds of thousands of dollars, the parish purchased new property for a Cathedral and rectory. This was the property of Patrick Burns, a city block at Twelfth Avenue and Fourth Street S.W. which is now the property of the Colonel Belcher Hospital. The first Catholic Bishop of Calgary, John T. McNally, arrived on the heels of the collapse of the real estate boom, and one of his first tasks was to arrange for the return of this property to Patrick Burns, one of his parishioners. And the Cathedral and Oblate property remained where it was.

The great increase in population in the province between 1900 and the establishment of the Diocese in 1912 put a severe strain on the personnel of the Oblates, and Bishop Legal found it necessary to provide the minimum of spiritual care for the new communities by inviting other religious orders into the missionary district. To the Grey Nuns, the Faithful Companions and the Sisters of Providence who staffed Lacombe Home, the orphanage, and the old people's home, were added the Benedictines and six French orders for teaching, nursing, and parish work. Although large numbers of Germans and some Russians were among the homesteaders, and Belgians and various Central Europeans were among the mining communities, religious orders from these countries were not so available, and there is some evidence that Bishop Legal took what orders were available even though French-Canadians were not disposed to pioneer in what they considered the forbidding West.

Besides the work in Calgary there was much to be done in the rural areas. The missionaries made trips out from their Indian missions or other mission centres on horseback or by buckboard and team, sometimes on foot, to visit the isolated farmsteads or sod huts of the newly arrived settlers, said Mass in their houses, sometimes stayed for several days instructing the children and the adults in their catechism, and then made their way to another homestead. In time the Catholics of a neighbourhood began to meet together to decide how they could build a church. Many of these early rough churches were built by the cooperative labour of the parishioners, who cut and hauled the logs, planned the site, and built the church itself. The community was greatly benefitted and welded together by the common efforts to raise money by picnics, concerts, dinners, plays, and dances over many years. Notes were given at the local bank by the various parishioners and later redeemed as they were able to raise the money, often from very meagre returns.

This was the state of the Southern Mission after forty years of work by the Oblate missionaries when the Diocese of Calgary was established in November 1912 and handed over to its first Bishop, John McNally D.D., in July 1913. It had developed from a wild and lonely territory inhabited by a few thousand Indians and herds of buffalo and hardly a hundred white traders and prospectors, to a well organized and growing community based upon land settlement, railway development and immigration.

CENTRAL METHODIST CHURCH BEFORE WORLD WAR ONE

J. Fraser Perry

This chapter is not concerned with theology, nor particularly with congregational records such as membership totals, or Sunday-by-Sunday collection figures. The real question which has been asked is, "What did Calgary Methodist Church (as it was until 1905) mean to the non-Methodists of Calgary?"

Unfortunately the question is more easily asked than answered, because few congregations, of whatever complexion, kept records indicating the views of their members, never mind the non-members. What must be done, then, is a good deal of imagining, reading between lines, and synthesizing.[1]

Church histories tend to run by the tenures of ministers, just as British history is sometimes still taught by reigns. Historians of older schools sometimes forget that many of the men who flourished and found fame under the Tudors were born and educated under the Plantagenets.

To consider the history of Central Methodist Church before the First World War, minister by minister, would be to ignore the fact that while ministers came and went, the congregation remained and continued. It would also be pretty disjointed because by 1914 there had been no fewer than twelve ministers—and there was another change that year. On the average, each lasted only three years.

This does not mean either a fickle congregation or a succession of incompetent ministers. The simple fact is that the Methodist Discipline, as the church manual of the period was called, limited the tenure of a minister to four years. And it is not surprising that in the changing climate of the frontier, few of them stayed that long.

That period in the history of Central Church makes a lot more sense in terms of the fact that it is more than spanned by the career of one man—Rev. Dr. John McDougall. McDougall was on the Bow River at Morley with his father in 1872. He was in Fort Calgary within weeks of its founding, and conducted the first Methodist services—possibly the first services of any kind—within the Fort. He served the Methodist congregation of Calgary as minister until 1883. His hands helped cut the logs for the first church building, and to raise them as well. And even though he went on to other appointments in the church, he was associated with Central Methodist until his death during the First World War.

During the more than thirty years from the time McDougall was succeeded by Rev. James Turner to McDougall's death, the congregation had occupied four increasingly large buildings. Its membership had grown from 14 to about 1,250, and had declined only slightly when new churches were formed and some members transferred to them. As a matter of fact, Calgary Methodist Church "swarmed" five times to create new churches in outlying parts of the city so that it became the central church among several. Hence the change of name.

That, in brief, is the story of the organizational church, and it is dramatic enough. But during the same interval equally important events had taken place which are not so easy to quantify, and not nearly so dramatic.

Central unquestionably played a role, for example, in the development of what is called the social gospel. Unfortunately, the record of that role is incomplete, and a good deal, as suggested earlier, must be synthesized. But that story is a little beyond our scope here today. And whatever its role in the larger church, the role of Central in the growing Calgary community changed surprisingly little during the first forty years.

It is true that the first Methodists in Calgary formed, in organizational terms, a mere outpost of the mission at Morley. It is true that Calgary Methodist Church called its own minister after only eight years, became self-sustaining in another four, and soon after that was contributing both mission funds and missionaries to the larger church—a complete change of status.

But whether Calgary Methodist was performing its parochial, pastoral and community functions with the help of subsidies, or contributing to subsidies for other churches after providing for the discharge of its own local responsibilities, these responsibilities were recognized and met. And while they grew, they did not materially change.

This was, from the beginning, what is now called a gathered congregation. In fact, there are members today who live outside the present city limits, and there were members then living in approximately the same places. But those places were then a lot farther from town, and the members travelled to church by live horsepower over prairie trails. So did the minister when he went visiting his flock. Those Methodist preachers were not called circuit riders for nothing. They had to be familiar with local geography, because the early membership lists give many addresses in terms of section, township and range, or of miles upriver from the Fort.

So Central had never been a "parish" church, serving an area circumscribed by metes and bounds, and relating only to that area. At the same time, Central has been involved, from its earliest days, in the kinds of problems associated today with the inner city church. This is another aspect of the urban-rural duality which Grant MacEwan refers to in his chapter.

There are many mentions, in the earliest records still surviving, of funds being used to assist those in want. Not that the poor in today's ordinary sense have always been with Central in great numbers. But the frontier had its share of transients. And there were those who arrived in Calgary seeking new opportunity, who were also, for the moment at least, at the end of their financial resources. There were those, as well, who had to go broke before it came home to them that they were not going to be successful as ranchers or farmers or general merchants.

All these needed help, and Calgary Methodist Church was, for many, the source of help from cash to counselling. Dr. George Kerby, who served Central toward the end of the period we are discussing, and at the beginning of the boom which caused Calgary's population to soar during the decade before World War One, wrote a book called *The Broken Trail*. In it he describes his encounters with several of the desperate people cast up at his door. And in a commentary at the end of the book, he talks about the problems which they represented:

Within every city, large and small, there is another city—a city within a city—a city without a church, without a child, without a home, as old as the

first civilization and as new as our own.
    What has the church done for the city within the city?
    It seems to me there is but one way out. It may not be through the church as an organization.
    . . . .as long as one stone of this inner city stands upon another your mission and mine to the world remains unaccomplished, and our Christianity incomplete.

That could have been written yesterday. It is quoted here not to show that the Christianity of Central and the Methodists is still incomplete, but rather to suggest that Kerby was expressing what has been a major theme in the life of Central Church.

By the mid-1880's, alcohol had become a social problem on the Prairies, and one has only to read James Gray's book *Booze* to get a pretty clear idea how great a problem it was, how badly it was mishandled by various authorities, and what a vocal role the churches played in the struggle for (and against) change. Rev. Joshua Dyke, who served Calgary Methodist Church from 1884 to 1886, is mentioned in Gray's book in this connection. At the time he received even more prominent mention: two full columns, on one occasion, in the Calgary *Herald*. For details of the consequences of Rev. Dyke's sermons, I refer you to James Gray's book. There is no doubt that the church, through Dyke, had an impact in the community, and that his sermons about the liquor laws and their administration are representative of the fact that Calgary Methodist Church and its clergy very often voiced strong views on temporal affairs.

These views did not always carry. As one instance of failure, imagine if you can, Seventh Avenue S.W., with Central Church where it is now, but First Baptist Church across the avenue to the north where the new Alberta Government Telephones building is nearing completion. The two churches joined forces in an attempt to persuade city council that it should reject a proposal to run street cars along First Street W.

The street cars ran, and the buses still do. Central is still there, having survived sixty-some years of transit traffic. (Let me say by way of clarification that First Baptist moved not because of the street cars but because of a fire.)

Not in every instance is it recorded whether the minister agreed with a statement passed by the official board, or whether some members were faint-hearted in their support of a public statement made by the minister. But certain it is that they were not always in agreement. At the same time it must be said that the members were not always agreed among themselves on matters of current concern, whether liquor laws or street cars.

The lay leadership in early years included a number of men like R.B. Bennett, W.H. Cushing, and James Lougheed, who were often heard in the community both as businessmen and as politicians. Most of these men took the same stand on any given issue, speaking in public and as elected officeholders, as they did behind closed doors in the councils of the church. But the membership also included numbers of people who were infected with the social Darwinism of the period, and exhibited a degree of ambivalence toward "lesser breeds".

This was really a WASP congregation, and while the McDougalls, for example, were on terms of real friendship with the local Indian population, the very presence of the McDougalls in Alberta reflected the attitude of a WASP church toward such people as the Indians: they were first and foremost a subject of concern because they were not Christians, and especially not Methodists. Tolerance, in particular tolerance of paganism, was not listed among its virtues, and the Indians were seen not only as pagans, but as savages, no matter how noble. They were feared and mistrusted even before the rebellion of 1885.

A little later on, these attitudes were modified somewhat with respect to the Chinese immigrants who gathered in Calgary. They were invited to become Christians, certainly, and numbers of the young men attended Bible classes at Central, where they received at least as much instruction in English as in theology. This was perhaps not as generous as it sounds, because most of the pupils could get little out of the Bible until they had learned some English.

In any event, these classes continued into the late 1920's, with the result that the room where they were held is still known as the Chinese room. The other results do not, however, include a continuing Chinese-Canadian element in the congregation. The chief reason seems to have been the existence of a Chinese Presbyterian church where Chinese Methodists found a home after the union of 1925.

Whatever the whole explanation, the Chinese United Church of today remains something of a monument to the idea of more or less equality, as long as it was separate. It must be mentioned also, however, that by no means all of the congregation tended to keep the Chinese people at arm's length. There was one incident, a sorry chapter in the history of the community, the smallpox riots of 1892, when a number of Chinese people were threatened with violence. And a member of Central Methodist sheltered them in his home until the danger was past.

Still another incident under this general heading helps give some idea of the attitudes of the period under discussion which do not prevail today to nearly the same extent, or are nowadays directed toward different groups. When Calgary Methodist Church was busy helping new churches get started, one of the first was in the general area of Bridgeland. After it had been in existence for a year, one of the members of the official board at Central was asked to report on its progress. Things were moving but slowly, he reported—which was quite understandable because those people over there were Germans. Martin Luther might have been surprised to hear that. Such comments suggest that while it might have been important to be a Christian, preferably a Methodist, it was still more important in the minds of some Methodists to be Anglo-Saxon as well. From either the chicken or the egg point of view, Rudyard Kipling came out ahead of St. Paul.

In this set of circumstances it might seem slightly surprising that the Central congregation had a part in developing the social gospel. Of course it may be true that the frontier produced the social gospel in the churches, rather than vice versa. Calgary was subject to the same pressures which produced, in many smaller centres on the Prairies, the local union churches. There is evidence in plenty that a strong spirit of co-operation was abroad among the churches in frontier Calgary. And this went beyond the fact that if a Baptist church or a Methodist church were destroyed by fire, there were immediate offers of the use of other sanctuaries. At one time, the Methodists and the Presbyterians literally shared the same tent.

The frontier influences may well have extended to those suggesting new roles for the church. It must be remembered here that the various Methodist churches in Canada had been going through a series of unions which finally brought them all together early in the life of Central Church, and that the Methodist Church in Canada had but recently taken over such concerns as missions from the parent church in England. There was bound to be new emphasis here and there.

This is clearly evident in the field of education. The Methodist Church world-wide has always had a strong interest in education, and in the field of secular education has supplied the state with a number of Caesars over the years. But only in Canada did the Methodist Church have Egerton Ryerson. Two things are important here about Ryerson. One is that he developed in Ontario the system of universal, compulsory, tax-supported education which became the model for most other parts of Canada. The other is that he turned from that accomplishment, as Superintendent of Education for Ontario, to the development of Victoria College.

The roll call of Victoria College graduates who served Calgary Methodist Church, as ministers, is significant. They brought with them not only Methodist theology, but Ryersonian thinking on education. It is more than coincidence that the same George Kerby who was voicing concern seventy years ago about the role of the church in the inner city was the builder of Mount Royal College.

Of course, there was a general concern among settlers of all faiths for the education of their children. Best evidence of this is probably the fact that at many points on the prairies the first unit of local government to be established was the school district. And there was also the concern of the federal and later the provincial governments that provision should be made for the instant Canadianization, through schooling, of the children who came with their parents as immigrants from Europe, and came in increasing numbers as the nineteenth century gave way to the twentieth.

All these factors reinforced one another, but that takes nothing from the importance of the Methodist zeal for education. On the other hand, what is probably sometimes exaggerated is the role of George Kerby in the founding of Mount Royal College. Once the decision was taken to establish the school, he took over the primary leadership role, and his was a great accomplishment. But he did not do it alone, and there were certainly more laymen than clergy involved during the stages which led up to his appointment. It may reasonably be assumed that these laymen had derived some of their thinking on education from long exposure to the sermons and conversation of a succession of Ryersonian ministers.

Such community involvement was in the tradition of Central. When John McDougall was felling logs and raising them for the first Calgary Methodist Church, he worked side by side with a carpenter named Andrew Sibbald. It is generally accepted that

Sibbald was the first teacher in the Calgary area.

There is no better example of the church in action as a community institution than that of Sibbald and Kerby in the field of education because they really represent group action by the members of the congregation or other units of church organization—group action by way of putting beliefs into practice, of proving on Monday and Friday that what is professed on Sunday can be realized.

A long list could be made of Central Church members who served the larger community as school trustees and aldermen and members of the Legislature. Another list could be drawn, showing how many had taken part in non-political activities in the community. It would be much more difficult, but an attempt could be made to show how much aid had been given the needy prior to 1914, how much counselling had been done by the clergy, how many youngsters and young adults had been influenced by the teaching of the Sunday school and adult bible classes. An estimate might even be made of the influence of Central Church members in deciding the outcome of the liquor law dispute or women's suffrage or any number of things. And from all these it might be deduced that the Methodist church meant this, or that, or the other thing to the Calgary community at large.

I strongly suspect, however, that its presence and its works were taken for granted, and much of its influence unrealized. That's nothing new in the social role of the churches. Strangely enough, it was probably with respect to its contribution to the cultural life of the community that Central Methodist Church was best recognized.

In a frontier community such as Calgary, the largest auditorium which is available for general use tends to become the community concert hall. And in many prairie communities it was a Protestant church sanctuary which assumed this function, because Catholic and Anglican churches are not, by tradition, so often made available for secular purposes. Thus, the church calendars, newspapers and reports contain a representative list of all the various concerts and other performances held in Central Church prior to 1914. And they would also represent a substantial percentage of all the performances held in the city during the same period.

But this was not just a matter of making the sanctuary available. Many of the concerts involved the church organist, or choir, or both, or were sponsored by the church. At one time Central even had an orchestra. All performances had, of course, to be approved by the executive committee of the official board. And they could strictly enforce the moral standard of any public performance, the nature of its profane content, and even such mundane matters as dress. On more than one occasion, female operatic soloists being checked out for possible booking into Central were vetted for *décolletage*. But music was important, and there are recorded instances in which a prospective new minister received an extra vote or two because he had a fine singing voice.

Calgary's pioneer Methodists had either a lot of nerve or a lot of faith back in 1883 when they called their own minister to serve a congregation of only fourteen members. And some think they still had a lot of nerve a few years later when they granted only provisional membership to a newly arrived couple because they were Baptists. I have a hunch they were accepted on any basis only because they could sing. So the hymn "Shall We Gather at the River" becomes a part of the history of Central Church.

CALGARY'S EARLY ANGLICANS

The Very Rev. David J.Carter

The Church of England came to Calgary through the initiative of the Mounted Police, who used the Prayer Book for church parade services. The first official Anglican service was conducted by the Rev. J.W. Tims in the Mounted Police barracks in 1883. The first church was built in 1884 and was succeeded by the present Cathedral Church of the Redeemer in 1904–05. From the beginning the Anglican church has been part of the growing community of Calgary. Many of the laity and clergy gave leadership with others in the development of Calgary. Many well known members of the community were also Anglicans—Macleod, Pinkham, Cross, Jephson, Paget—and they participated with others in the founding of services and organizations that added the necessary balance to community life. Education, social concern, hospitals, literary endeavours, music, writing, art forms were all activities that became part of the growing Calgary experience. The daily ministry to the lonely, the shut-ins, the homeless, the transient, the natives, the old, the young, the infirm, the living and the dead—all were part of the everyday experience of the Anglican church and its people as they worked together with other citizens of Calgary within Calgary's first one hundred years.

* * * * *

The first Anglican services in what is now Canada took place in a tent at Frobisher Bay in the summer of 1578. The minister was a chaplain on board ship; his name was the Rev. Robert Wolfall.

From about 1701 onwards other clergy came with the fishermen to the outports of Newfoundland. On October 10, 1710, the Rev. John Harrison, chaplain to Commodore Martin, conducted a service of thanksgiving in Annapolis Royal, Nova Scotia. The sermon was preached by the Rev. Samuel Hesker, chaplain to Colonel Reading's marines.

In the years that followed, the Anglican church moved into what is now known as "Eastern Canada", with a strong base in the Maritimes and Ontario. Later the Church, with the aid of the Church Missionary Society and the Society for the Propagation of the Gospel in Foreign Parts, would follow the trade route around the Horn and be established on the west coastal region of British Columbia.[1]

The area known as British North West America was left alone by the Anglicans for some considerable time. To aid in the missionary thrust into British North West America, the Church of England had a number of groups supporting its work. These groups were the SPCK (The Society for the Promoting of Christian Knowledge); the SPG (The Society for the Propagation of the Gospel in foreign parts); the CCCS (The Colonial and Continental Church Society); and the CMS (The Church Missionary Society).

The SPCK was founded by Thomas Bray and four laymen in England in 1698 to promote charity schools in England and Wales and to disperse, at home and abroad, bibles and tracts of religion. In later years, its educational and printing work was absorbed by the SPG. The SPG was formed in 1701 to assist in missionary work initiated by the SPCK. It existed to provide ministrations of the Church of England for British people overseas and, secondarily, to evangelize the non-Christian races of the world. The CCCS was founded in 1838 to enable Evangelicals of the Anglican Church to take an active part in the work of church extension in the British colonies. But the group which supplied the strongest force of Anglican missionaries on the prairies in the early days was the CMS. The Church Missionary Society was the outgrowth of a group of dedicated Evangelical laity and clergy who banded together in 1799 to form the Society for Missions in Africa and the East. It counted as one of its founding members, William Wilberforce; and the CMS became the most effective organ of the Church of England in foreign missions.

In 1820 the first Anglican missionary to western Canada arrived. He was the Rev. John West and had been sent out by the predominately "low church" evangelical missionary group, the CMS. He travelled via Hudson Bay and into the Red River system. Settling in the Red River colony, he worked there for a period of three years before returning to England. Later he worked in the Maritimes. While at Red River he established not only the Church of England but a system of education and an approach that showed concern for the whites, the Indians, and the métis. In addition to preaching the work of God, he performed the services of baptism and marriage, and the funeral rites. He worked with both boys and girls in religious and general instruction and the latter tended to include the necessary subjects that one would find at Cambridge, England. Greek and Latin were taught as well as mathematics and history! He initiated the pattern of taking children into supervised dormitory living, first in private homes at the colony. This of course meant that often white, Indian, and Métis lived and were educated together. Rudimentary medical attention was part of the expected skill of the missionary. Often the missionaries not only encouraged the natives to settle onto plots of land but acted as resource persons to the new farmers in terms of growing crops. One Anglican clergyman near Red River developed one of the first strains of earlier-maturing wheat, cross bred to withstand the vagaries of our western Canadian climate.

Due in part to a lack of funds, manpower, and a falling out with Governor Simpson, the Anglican mission work did not move out much beyond Red River. Governor Simpson denied the Anglican missionaries the right to travel with the Hudson Bay Company's boats into the Saskatchewan country. The Governor was not too pleased that the missionaries were seeking to have all the country-marriages legalized—at least that is the reason that has been handed down.

But by 1856 the Anglicans started to move westward into the Saskatchewan country with the building of a mission post at Fort Stanley (approximately 150 miles north of Prince Albert). Today that church is the oldest wooden structure in the province of Saskatchewan, and has had continuous Anglican services since 1856.

The first Anglican work in Alberta was carried out by William Carpenter Bompas (later Bishop of Athabasca), who arrived in 1865 and worked in northern Alberta and the Yukon and Mackenzie areas. He celebrated the first Anglican church service in the present province of Alberta at Athabasca Landing in 1867.

In 1875, the Rev. Dr. William Newton (an ex-Unitarian minister) arrived at Fort Edmonton to work with the whites and the Indians. He was sponsored by the SPG.

In the southern Alberta area it can safely be assumed that

wherever the Mounted Police went, Sunday church services were held. These services were conducted by the senior officer of each denomination and the men fell out according to denomination. In this manner the Church of England Prayer Book came to save the situation for many a "C of E" officer as he was called upon to take the Church Parade for his men. The following excerpt is from an NWMP Memoir:

Tuesday, 28th., 1874: (Roche Percée)
The third day after our arrival being a Sunday, and, as everybody is aware, the Sabbath Day being consecrated in the British Dominions to rest and prayer, we were that morning ordered to get ready for Church parade. This was the first divine service held since our departure from Dufferin. As the Mounted Police was composed of men belonging to different denominations, and there being no chaplain attached to the corps, I was wondering who would act in their stead. But I soon heard that, under such circumstances, it was the duty of officers to act in the place of ministers of the gospel. At ten o'clock a.m. as the six divisions stood ready for orders, Colonel French, who was an Episcopalian (Anglican Church of England), called for the men that belonged to his denomination, and Roman Catholics, Methodists and Presbyterians were called for, in like manner by officers of their respective creeds. Some denominations held their meeting on the hills, others in the valley. And it was a grand sight to see 300 men standing in the wilderness, several hundred miles from civilization, giving thanks, in different manners, and offering prayers to their Creator.[2]

In 1878 the Rev. George Mackay arrived at Fort Macleod from Stanley Mission in northern Saskatchewan and educated at Cambridge, England, before going to Stanley. He arrived in the Fort Macleod area to open a mission with the Peigan Indians and the people of Fort Macleod.

In 1880 the Rev. Samuel Trivett was sent from Stanley Mission to the Fort Macleod area by the CMS. He was sent originally to Blackfoot Crossing but the Indians had more or less dispersed. He heard of the Blood Indians having settled in the area of the Belly Buttes southeast of Fort Macleod so he settled there and homesteaded a big island in the Belly River. He took up work with the Blood Indians and carried on the usual Anglican missionary tasks of homesteading, feeding himself, building his home and later schools, acting as preacher, baptising, marrying, burying, offering medical aid, teaching school to boys, then girls, visiting all over the countryside, and occasionally helping with services in Fort Macleod. He also looked after the people in Pincher Creek for a time and was to guide them in the construction of their church—which still stands, as the oldest Anglican church building in southern Alberta. It dates from 1884.[3]

What has all this to do with the Anglican church in the Calgary area? It is the past which is prologue to the church's early development in Calgary. For example, when the Mounted Police came to Fort Calgary one may assume, although as yet there is no evidence to offer as proof, that the Mounted Police on occasion had services of worship. A fairly normal pattern of Protestant worship with men in the forces has been and still is to use the Anglican Prayer Book. Thus Anglican services were probably held on the Calgary site from 1874 and conducted by laymen.

The first Anglican work in southern Alberta bypassed Calgary, even though Samuel Trivett was supposed to have started Anglican work with the Blackfoot Indians near Gleichen in 1880. However, in 1883 the Rev. J.W. Tims was sent out by the CMS and he established the Church of England mission at the South Camp near Gleichen.

In August, 1883, the Anglican Bishop of Saskatchewan made a tour through southern Alberta which was a part of his jurisdiction. He camped in a small tent on land covered with scrub and brush just west of the old NWMP barracks—a site that is within the legal parish limits of today's Cathedral Church of the Redeemer. A few people met with Bishop John McLean and they appointed a committee to raise subscriptions towards building a church structure and to pay the stipend of a clergyman. But an early minute book records that "This committee failed to accomplish anything."[4]

In October 1883, seven men met around a stove in G.C. King's general store in east Calgary and sent a letter off to Deacon Tims at the Blackfoot Reserve. They requested him to come to Calgary on occasion to take Church of England service. Tims agreed to come, although it meant a trip of eight days and time away from his own mission responsibilities. Tims came, and the first regular Anglican church service in Calgary was held in the orderly room of the NWMP barracks, the first Sunday in November, November 3, 1883:

A number of civilians attended this service and members of the Mounted Police came in force under the command of the late General Steele. Seats were improvised by using nail kegs upon which planks were placed. The organ used was borrowed and on the evening before was wheeled down Ninth Avenue on a wheelbarrow from the vicinity of the C.P.R. depot, the parson walking beside to steady it. The instrument was played by S.W. Shaw of Midnapore, and the singing was led by Sergeant-Major Lake.[5]

Tims soon established the pattern of travelling to Calgary every two weeks for services. On Easter Day 1884 there were eighty people at service and a meeting was held to see about a church building. A new committee was struck—J.G. Fitzgerald (Secretary); G.C. King (Treasurer); Messrs. Geddes, Pettit, and Thomas; Dr. Lindsay; and Sergeant-Major Lake. This committee functioned well, and within a space of four months the first Church of the Redeemer was built on the site of 218 Seventh Avenue S.E., the site of Paget Hall just to the east of the present Cathedral. The architect was a Mr. McCroskie. His design was to be copied in the miniature of St. Paul's Anglican Church, Fish Creek-Midnapore, in 1885 and at St. Andrew's, Gleichen, in 1886.

The year 1884 was good for Anglican church construction; in fact there was a race on! While the Calgarians were building, so were the people at Pincher Creek under the direction of Samuel Trivett. Pincher Creek church was finished and opened on August 17, 1884. But the church in Calgary was officially opened August 3, 1884 and the congregation was able to get hold of Bishop McLean before the Pincher Creek people.

On May 24, 1884 the Rev. Edward Paske Smith, M.A., arrived in Calgary as the first Incumbent of the City of Calgary. On August 3, the first Church of the Redeemer opened its doors for worship. Smith had been born in India and educated at Oxford before coming to Calgary under the sponsorship of the SPG. While in Calgary he also supervised the construction of St. Paul's Church, Midnapore. He resigned in 1887 to return to England where he later served as a chaplain in the British army.

The impermanence of the early church was not relieved when Bishop John McLean died in November, 1886 as a result of being thrown from a buggy in Edmonton. But, in 1887, he was replaced as Biship of Saskatchewan by the most durable force in the far western field for the next generation—the Rev. William Cyprian Pinkham.

Pinkham was born in Newfoundland and was a graduate of St. Augustine's, Canterbury. He served at Red River from 1869 as Incumbent of St. James', Winnipeg. From 1871 to 1883 he was

Superintendent of Education for the Protestant schools of Manitoba. He served the Anglican church as Archdeacon of Manitoba from 1882 to 1887. After his appointment as bishop, he immediately moved his headquarters to Calgary and his family joined him in 1889.[6]

In 1888 Bishop Pinkham promptly reorganized his jurisdiction and had the area of southern Alberta, Diocese of Calgary, divided from the Diocese of Saskatchewan. He continued to serve as bishop of both dioceses until 1903 when sufficient funds were accumulated to allow both districts to have their own bishop. Bishop Pinkham then chose Calgary as his diocese, and did so again when in 1914 the Diocese of Edmonton was carved out of Calgary's jurisdiction. It was here that he served until his retirement in 1926 and his death in 1928.

The church achieved some stability in its formative years by the appointment of the Rev. Alfred William Francis Cooper, M.A., T.C.D., as the first Rector of the Church of the Redeemer, Calgary. Born in Ireland and educated at Trinity College, Dublin, he served in Ireland for ten years before coming to Yorkton in western Canada. He then came to Calgary where he was to stay for eleven years and to earn a number of "firsts"—first Rector of the Church of the Redeemer; first Rural Dean of Calgary; and first Archdeacon of Calgary. During his incumbency the Church had to be enlarged to keep up with the growth of church population. In 1898 he resigned to return to Ireland to care for his elderly father.

The early years of the Boer War were unstable ones for the Anglican congregation. Cooper was succeeded by the Rev. Henry Percy Lowe, M.A. Lowe had been born in England and in 1890, under the sponsorship of the SPG, had served in central Ontario, particularly as assistant curate at St. George's church, Toronto, from 1892 to 1898, before moving to the Church of the Redeemer, Calgary. His ministry in Calgary was to be brief; he died of pneumonia in June, 1899.

In January of 1900 the Rev. Herbert F.E. Whalley moved from the Cathedral in Fredericton, New Brunswick, to become Rector of the Calgary church. But he resigned the following August and returned to England, his birthplace.

Into this rapidly changing merry-go-round then came the famous Dean Paget. The Rev. Clarence Edward Paget was to serve the Church of the Redeemer and Calgary from 1900 until his retirement in 1926. Paget was born in England, trained at Oxford, and served for a time in the Diocese of Gloucester. He then spent a year with the Choir School of St. Paul's Cathedral, London, before moving on to be principal of a missionary college at Dorchester, near Oxford. He served in that capacity for six years and then moved to Montreal for reasons of health. In 1886 he moved to the staff of the Cathedral at Davenport, Iowa. In 1899 he took on the parish at Revelstoke, B.C., and came to the Church of the Redeemer in September 1900. On January 1, 1901, he was appointed as the first Dean of the Diocese of Calgary. In 1899 Bishop Pinkham had named the Church of the Redeemer as a Pro-Cathedral—a temporary cathedral. That designation held for the small wooden church and it was carried over to the sandstone church building in 1904. The Church of the Redeemer became a full-fledged Cathedral on June 8, 1949, and as a result lost its loving title "the Pro". In August, 1974, the building was designated a Registered Heritage Site of the Province of Alberta.

Dean Paget became a well loved, familiar figure on the streets and in the homes of Calgary. He was author, traveller, mountaineer (Paget Peak near Wapta Pass is named after him), scholar, and builder. He was a benefactor of the community and the cathedral in particular. Under his leadership the present aesthetically pleasing cathedral was built in 1904–05. Paget not only donated the funds for one-third of the building, but he also directed the construction together with a firm of architects from Victoria, B.C. Under his guidance and supervision the cathedral grew as a house of worship, as an art form, as a centre of instrumental and vocal music, as a place of ministry, and as a place of community interest groups. Under his leadership the Pro-Cathedral parish also grew, and new parishes such as St. John the Evangelist in east Calgary, St. Stephen's, and St. Barnabas sprang up. Often he contributed much of his own income to the church-building projects. In 1904 the cornerstone for the new church was laid and the church opened in July, 1905. This present Cathedral Church of the Redeemer is one of the oldest and best preserved of that Calgary era when the city was known as the Sandstone City.

But the growth of the Christian church should never be measured by clergy and bishops alone. The laity have a most important part to play in the foundation work and growth patterns of the church. So too with the Anglicans in Calgary!

After the men of the Mounted Police, came others. In 1883 William Roper Hull came to Calgary for the first time. He was in the stock business and had just driven one thousand two hundred head of cattle from B.C. via the Crow's Nest Pass. He had been born in Devonshire, England in 1856 and arrived in Kamloops in 1873 via Panama. He was attracted to Calgary and in 1886 established a meat business which in the course of time was sold to Pat Burns. W. Roper Hull became involved in construction and was responsible for the construction of such buildings as the Grain Exchange Building, the Alberta Block, the Victoria Block, and the Albion Block. Calgarians are familiar with the name of the Hull Opera House. Through his ranching, financing, insurance, and construction interests a considerable estate was built up. His estate made generous awards to the Anglican Diocese of Calgary and to the founding of a home for orphans. The family home was a well known city landmark, although it has since been demolished for an apartment block.

John Pascoe "Jermy" Jephson was educated at Cambridge, England. He arrived at Red River and married Christina Drever. In 1886 the Jephsons moved to Calgary where he was admitted to the Bar. In his role as solicitor and barrister, he was one of Calgary's early legal fraternity. He was a charter member of the Ranchmen's Club and served as Solicitor for the Anglican Diocese of Calgary.

Another interesting Calgary Anglican layman was William Pearce. He was born in Dunwich Township, Ontario, in 1850. Following education at the University of Toronto he took up his profession as a civil engineer and land surveyor. By 1874 he was in Winnipeg and was one of the first ten surveyors in the West. He even helped establish the location of the 49th parallel. In 1882 he was appointed Inspector of Land Agencies and a member of the Dominion Lands Board. In these appointments he was responsible for the supervision of lands, forests, minerals, and waterways. In 1884 he was named Superintendent of Mines. Three years later he moved his office to Calgary where he had jurisdiction over the land from Red River to the Rockies and from the 49th parallel to the 56th parallel. In this area of approximately four hundred thousand square miles he was also involved in homestead and railway grants.

By 1892 William Pearce was also touting the prospects of coal and oil in the Turner Valley and Athabasca Tar Sands. He was a strong advocate of irrigation. He also had an aesthetic avocation—planting trees in Calgary. It is an endorsement of William Pearce to see the welcome plantings of trees in the inner city of Calgary in this Centennial year. In 1904 William Pearce joined the CPR as an advisor on land management and natural resources. The Pearce family lived on what is known as the Pearce Estate along the Bow River near St. George's Island—the family name for their home was "Bow Bend Shack". During his lifetime William Pearce showed himself to be very much a public-spirited citizen. He chose the site of Calgary's General Hospital, and he was instrumental in setting up Banff National Park and St. George's Island, Calgary. He was a charter member of the Calgary Kiwanis and a member of the Ranchmen's Club.

Jephson, Bishop Pinkham, and Colonel James Farquharson Macleod were all related by marriage. Macleod was really only in Calgary a short while prior to his death but his name commands great respect in western Canada. He was born in 1836 on the Isle of Skye. He was educated as a lawyer and was a graduate of Queen's University, Kingston, and Osgoode Hall, Toronto, 1860. In 1870 he joined the Wolseley Expedition to Red River. Four years later he was appointed Assistant Commissioner of the newly formed North-West Mounted Police. He joined in the great trek across the southern prairies, and supervised construction of Fort Macleod. In 1876 he married Mary Isabella Drever and resigned from the Force to become a Stipendiary Magistrate. That only lasted six months, and in July of 1876 he was appointed Commissioner of the Mounted Police. In this capacity he negotiated Treaty Number Seven, in 1877. He retired in 1880 and became Stipendiary Magistrate at Pincher Creek. At the formation of the Supreme Court of the North-West Territories in 1887 he was appointed Justice at Fort Macleod. The Macleods lived in the south country until 1894, when they moved to Calgary. He died on September 5, 1894, a poor man without pension, and is buried in Union Cemetery near his wife and Bishop and Mrs. Pinkham. Today the grave marked by a lonely flagpole without flag stands overlooking Macleod Trail.

Bishop Pinkham's wife was Jean Drever, daughter of William Drever, a Red River merchant. Mrs. Pinkham's sister Mary married Colonel James Macleod in 1876; her younger sister Christina married Mr. John P.J. Jephson who also came to Calgary as a barrister. Thus within a few families were contained the church, the Mounted Police, and the legal profession, all working together for the growth of their adopted community.

In 1890 Mrs. Pinkham helped to start what was to be the

forerunner of the first Calgary General Hospital: In her memoirs
she comments on the beginnings of the hospital:

*There were no hospitals when we came here and one heard of some appall-
ing cases of accidents on ranches, and of sad maternity cases. I believe the
first person on record to do anything for a hospital was a Chinaman who
died in one of the Hotels, leaving a suit of clothes to the clergyman who visited him, and one hundred dollars to start a hospital. I got to work as soon as
I could and was able to collect some money towards starting a Cottage Hospital. However, some people thought that might mean an Anglican institution, so I persuaded the Mayor to call a meeting in order that people might be
interested in starting a General Hospital, and I undertook to turn over the
funds I had in hand. We had quite a good meeting and we soon started in a
small way by securing a frame building on Seventh Avenue, with Mrs.
Hoad as the first matron. We formed a Women's Hospital Aid Society. I
was elected President and Mr. A. Allen, Secretary. . . .*[7]

Mrs. Pinkham founded the Women's Auxiliary of the Anglican
Diocese in 1891 and became its first president. It was reorganized in 1904 and she became Honorary President and continued with her interest in that vital church women's organization until her death in 1939. In addition to her interest in starting a Calgary General Hospital she helped organize the founding
meeting of the Alberta Division of the Canadian Red Cross. After the First World War she was awarded the Order of the British
Empire for her work with the Red Cross and the war effort. She
was decorated with the Order of St. Sava for her efforts with the
Serbian government for the relief of Serbian refugees. In addition
she presided over the founding meetings of the Local Council of
Women and the Victorian Order of Nurses, and was a moving
force in the Imperial Order Daughters of the Empire.

Church construction did provide facilities for worship, facilities for the hearing of the word of God, but it was also an aesthetic place in which to hold baptisms, weddings, confirmations, funerals. It was a mark of a community's growing sophistication, if
not civilization. In time it was also a place for meditation, for
small groups to be held with the whole spectrum of Bible study,
youth groups, men's groups and women's groups, groups concerned about spiritual growth, groups concerned about social is-
sues such as the welcoming and welfare of immigrants, the care of
single and wayward girls, and the problems of gambling, prostitution, and transiency. Within the building itself came the early

traditions of music. Old pump organs could still yield melodies to warm the inner soul with the breath of nostalgia and appreciation of the finer things of life as experienced in other far-off-places. The growth of choirs together with organ music laid the foundations for church choirs and also for choral groups such as the Calgary Philharmonic Orchestra and choir. In addition there were the beginnings of youth work that would result in the Cathedral being the birthplace of the scouting movement in Calgary. There was work with Little Helpers (pre-school children) that later would evolve into the Girls' Auxiliary, Scouts, Cubs, Guides, Brownies, Rangers. These groups encouraged self-development, and of course it was a part of many of these mini-committees to develop the skills of cooking and mending. Some people trod upon the stage for the first time in the parish halls of various Calgary churches; Paget Hall was one such popular place for young and old Thespians. There would be the socials, which would probably include a great feast followed by guest speakers or debating societies or dances. The church was often one of the very popular (albeit sober) places of community social life. Then too the development of athletic endeavours could be found within the orbit of such groups. It could be anything from lawn tennis to cricket to rugger to badminton. It was a broad spectrum that the early church covered, and of course it was as good a place as any to meet that "special someone" in terms of wanting to settle down and raise a family!

Paget Hall became one of the forerunners of the public school system in Calgary. Classes were held in the first church hall on what is now the front of the present Paget Hall at 218 Seventh Avenue S.E. Later in 1904 St. Hilda's Ladies College was formed by Bishop and Mrs. Pinkham and in 1909 Bishop Pinkham's College for boys. There was a strong emphasis upon education, and the Anglican Church provided leadership both in terms of buildings and educators following the missionary tradition of the church in all parts of the world.

The Anglican community had thus continued to grow in response to the changing social composition of south-central Alberta. The first Anglican missionaries had been sponsored by English missionary societies, not by Canadians of the area nor Canadians from eastern Canada. The first Anglican missionaries in southern Alberta had been sent to work primarily with the native people. They were expected to convert, to preach, to baptize, to minister and to teach. Through education they were also to train the native people in farming, and to show by example that a settled educated way of life was a good alternative to the nomadic way of life. But with the tide of white immigration the role of the Anglican missionaries slowly changed. They had begun to work with the whites in terms of taking church services and helping in the supervision of church and church hall construction. Inevitably they received more response from expatriate whites who, wished to have religious services as part of the way of life in new settlements. But, as the clergy began to work more and more with the white communities, more men were enabled to come into the settled areas and in time they were financially supported locally. Slowly more and more clergy were available. At first most were born and educated in England but later a few men were born and trained in western Canada.

The great tide of immigration that struck western Canada in the last years of the century and the early years of this century included a considerable number of men and women who had worshipped with the Church of England in other places. They looked to the Anglican Church here and helped in its growth. Then the First World War broke out and brought about a tremendous drain of manpower from the prairies as men joined up to go fight for King and Country. A tremendous number of clergy and laity from the Church of England enlisted and very few of them returned. The Anglican Church in western Canada would take a long time to recover from that manpower and dollar drain of the First World War.

LAND SPECULATION AND URBAN DEVELOPMENT: CALGARY 1884–1912

Max Foran

C algary's frantic rush from frontier town to boom city in the first decade of the twentieth century was probably the greatest phenomenon of its kind in western Canada. The burgeoning economic growth which paralleled the population influx culminated in 1912 when the city reached an economic pinnacle not surpassed until the second land boom of the 1950's.[1] The more than forty thousand souls, still clinging to the apron strings of the business section, were being beckoned up and over the bluffs which guarded the Bow valley by the exotically named subdivisions that stretched onto the prairie in true suburban fashion. In the commercial section of the city the one hundred odd wholesale houses vied with the rising business blocks to give downtown Calgary an image that differed greatly both in size and nature from that of the 1890's. Yet the economic impetus which resulted in the zenith of 1912 was of relatively short duration, and in this respect contrasted sharply with previous years.

Indeed Calgary's growth before 1911 was steady rather than spectacular, and was probably exaggerated by speculative activity in the real estate market. The city expanded in a response to a multiplicity of factors. The CPR, for example, determined the pattern of wholesale development in the city. Geographical considerations dictated the basic pattern of settlement, although speculative zeal and transportation exigencies had begun to modify this somewhat by 1912. Overseeing the whole process was an often beleaguered city council, whose pragmatic attitudes typified only too well the inveterate optimism of the period.

In its first twenty years Calgary did not grow appreciably. The population totalled 504 at incorporation in 1884. It grew by only 1,000 in the years 1890–1900 and by 1901 according to the Dominion Census numbered a modest 4,091. It is difficult to assess exactly when the population began its rapid increase. Local census were taken by various groups, foremost among which was the police department, but such head counts were hardly accurate, as witness the discrepancy of 5,000 between the unofficial and the Dominion Census of 1906.[2] What is of note, however, is that these unofficial census or estimates first appeared with regularity in 1904,[3] and it is probably valid to assume that this year marked the real acceleration in population influx. Furthermore, Calgary at incorporation included only sections fourteen, fifteen and sixteen within its corporate limits, and by 1904 these boundaries had been extended only slightly.[4] The significant annexations which indicated the city's rapid expansion did not begin until 1906. The period 1884–1904 may thus be described as the first or static period of physical growth.

Calgary's business section during this period consisted essentially of retail stores with some commercial institutions and was located on Section Fifteen. This section, owned by the CPR under terms of contract, was administered by the Townsite Trustees whose policies were designed to protect company interests as much as they were geared towards the needs of the infant town. The Trustees withheld from sale certain blocks along Tenth Avenue south of the railway, and by utilizing arbitrary powers with regard to closing certain thoroughfares were able to encourage retail activity north of the tracks. The retail business section thus radiated from the railway station east along Eighth Avenue and Ninth Avenue to about Third Street E. The area immediately to the north along Sixth, Fifth, and Fourth Avenues was utilized as a prime residential area. Indeed some of the finest residences in the city continued to be located in an area where today stand towering office structures.[5]

The very compact nature of the small business section was disturbed in 1889 when real estate speculators began buying and building west of Centre Street and more particularly on Eighth Avenue.[6] This "western expansion" aroused much controversial reaction as property owners east of Centre Street viewed the tendency with mounting alarm. More than one hundred letters were sent to Ottawa when the Dominion Government was considering a western relocation of the post office,[7] and William

Pearce, Dominion Superintendent of Lands and Mines, and a large property owner in east Calgary, advised the Federal Government that such a move was contrary to the majority of vested interests.[8] Further testimony to the depth of local sentiment is provided by Wesley Orr, another interested party:

...*While I do not want to force development at a loss I know it is most important to keep on fighting or we will be left entirely out of the race. Neither. . . .has the slightest idea of the fierceness of the fight. . .on the part of the west to move the present business centre two or three blocks west. We hold meetings in some important office two or three times a week and sometimes twice a day.*[9]

In spite of Orr's fears, however, the extension of the building centre was not to affect east Calgary businessmen, at least not in his lifetime. The depression of the nineties froze future expansion, and beyond consolidating Eighth Avenue as the main business street of Calgary, the flurry of speculation and building in the years 1889–92 stood as an isolated reminder of what the future might bring.

Residential expansion during this period extended south to Seventeenth Avenue, east to the Elbow River, and west to about Eighth Street. To the north of the tracks the area between the business section and the Bow River was fairly well settled. Luxurious residences were erected along Twelfth, Thirteenth, and Fourteenth Avenues south, and indeed when the Public Library was being erected in Central Park in 1908 the comment was elicited that the class of people who lived near the library were well able to buy books of their own.[10] The CPR's reservation of the south-east quarter of Section Fifteen was in hopeful anticipation of an eastward expansion of the town. Such was not to be however, and in 1892 these lots were placed on the market specifically for the working man at the very low price of fifty dollars each.[11] The little residential occupation of land on the north side of the Bow River was on the flats adjacent to the two bridges which spanned the river during this period. The Hillhurst-Sunnyside community grew up in the vicinity of the Bow Marsh bridge while the residential area on the flats near the brewery was appropriately if unimaginatively named Breweryville.[12]

Some people, mainly Roman Catholics, took advantage of the very low terms of purchase to buy building sites south of the corporate limits in the area popularly known as the Mission property. By 1899 the value of buildings in this settlement was estimated to be in excess of fifty thousand dollars, and to protect their investment the five hundred residents incorporated themselves into the village of Rouleauville in October of the same year.[13]

Near the Langevin Bridge, Calgary's second bridge across the Bow, a considerable concentration of German-speaking residents occupied the area known as Riverside. In 1902 the district was referred to in the plain language of the day as Germantown.[14] Here, Galicians allowed their cows to run at large, the city by-laws were held in scant respect, and the Lutheran and Moravian Church signified that at least on the north side of the river the Anglo-Saxon pantheon did not hold complete sway.

Calgary's other ethnic group, the Chinese, concentrated themselves on Tenth Avenue in a small area directly opposite the business centre. These "nests of celestials and their rabbit warrens of opium smokers"[15] continued to be a recurring source of concern to civic officials well into the twentieth century. This small Chinatown was an obvious deterrent to retail expansion across the line to Tenth Avenue. Indeed it was in this specific area that land prices in Calgary showed their sharpest reduction in the years 1884–95.[16]

With poorly graded streets that were impassable much of the time, and with only two railway crossings west of First Street W., people were most reluctant to live far from their places of work. The need for a street railway was apparent and a company had been formed in 1889 to provide the town with this very necessary service. But it was not until 1909 that street cars were to operate in the city, and throughout the period under discussion Calgary residents were fairly restricted in their mobility. The sinuous meanderings of the inadequately bridged rivers, and the formidable inclines which hampered services and defied loaded drays decreed the static population cluster around the business section. In fact one could argue that it was mild speculative activity rather than demand for residential land which saw the many quarter sections beyond the corporate limits begin changing hands by 1905.

Land within the corporate limits of Calgary was owned in large part by local residents, whether private individuals or real estate agents, by 1894. Only in Section Fourteen were there large private holdings, and these owners had had title to their properties before incorporation. On the other two sections, Fifteen and

Sixteen, only R.F. Moody and T.S.C. Lee acquired land in large parcels, although it is true that other locally based real estate agents controlled individual blocks, particularly in Section Sixteen, and indeed this latter section was completely bought up by 1887.[17] What speculation occurred during this period was on a small scale and mainly by local residents. The superintendent of the NWMP post in Calgary reported in 1893 that deposits in the division bank were low owing to the penchant of his men to invest in town lots.[18] The Voters' List of 1894 showed 609 owners of land on Section Fifteen and 319 in Section Sixteen. In the same year there were only forty-three owners of land in Section Fourteen.[19] A resident reported in 1891 that the average man bought his lots in threes and fours[20] and same were usually bought on terms repayable at six percent interest. These lots were not paid off easily. Land sale records reveal that time periods of up to ten years were not uncommon, while in 1889 some 260 would-be speculators lost their lots at a sale for unpaid taxes.[21] Absentee land holders were definitely in the minority, increasingly so after 1889, rendering more than a little prophetic the *Tribune*'s comment in 1886, "Calgary is too far removed for people in the east ever to go crazy over town lots in the Bow River valley."[22]

In spite of comments to the contrary in the booster magazines of the 1890's,[23] speculators large or small did not make much profit during this period. The general pattern of land transactions revealed falling sales and prices. For example, Block Eighty-four directly north of Central Park was not sold until 1903, and then at an average price of one hundred dollars[24] per lot. In 1890 Senator James A. Lougheed paid an average price of 750 dollars each for four lots on Block Sixty-five between Eighth and Ninth Avenues and Second and Third Streets W. In 1902 he bought seven more lots on the same block for 220 dollars each.[25] In 1892 property was advertised in the heart of the business area on Eighth Avenue near the Post Office at the low price of fifty dollars per frontage foot,[26] while two years later one could still buy ten lots on Eighth Avenue between Fifth and Sixth Streets W. for a total of 220 dollars.[27] The *Tribune* carried an advertisement in 1891 offering for sale on the corner of Seventeenth Avenue and Fourth Street S.W. eight lots and a five-roomed house with fence and well for the total price of 1,600 dollars.[28] In spite of such bargain prices, sales were few, as witness the two real-estate agents who advertised every week in the *Herald* for six months between March and August, 1892. In that time they disposed of two lots between them. Even local advertising trailed off markedly from the year 1895 into the 1900's. In fact real-estate activity at the turn of the century was directed mainly at placing people on farms in the Calgary district. Interest in local real estate was moribund.

The emergence of a small manufacuring base in east Calgary during this period was in part due to aggressive policies by east Calgary landowners. Faced with the potential threat of a westerly commercial and residential expansion, the largest holders of property on Section Fourteen consciously followed policies designed to locate industries east of the Elbow River. William Pearce, one of the chief spokesmen for east Calgary interests, was probably not completely tongue in cheek when he advised his superiors in 1892 that "Calgary's future as a manufacturing centre dictated that further expansion be eastward. . .and that if vested interests be considered there are more [of them] in the east than in the west."[29]

The most significant move initiated by east Calgary property owners came in 1887, when Major James Walker was instrumental in persuading the town council to purchase part of the northeast quarter of Section Eleven for stockyard purposes.[30] Being school land this strategically located square mile directly south of Section Fourteen was neither the property of the CPR nor open to normal homestead entry, and it is interesting to note that soon after the above purchase the rest of the section fell into the hands of east Calgary owners for prices that averaged less than fifteen dollars per acre.[31] The subsequent location of the stockyards on Section Eleven ensured that the resultant meat packing and processing plants would arise in east Calgary and not to the west of the city limits as had been the CPR's and the Council's original choice.

Wesley Orr, another east Calgary property owner, entered civic politics in 1888 with the sole idea of protecting his vested interests. It was Orr who introduced the industry bonusing resolution into Council, and four years later revealed both the depth of his commitment and the singlemindedness of his intentions when he wrote that "unless we can foster factories, mills, and shops in the east. . .I will throw in the sponge."[32] The presence by 1893 of a brewery, tannery, and soapworks on Section Eleven just outside city limits for tax exemption purposes was solid evidence of Orr's dominating influence on Council. A donation of thirty-five acres of land to the Calgary and Edmonton Railway Company for freight yards in 1890 also helped consolidate east Calgary's role as manufacturing centre.[33] That the city's future industrial expansion was to be south and east seemed further assured in late 1894 when the Council made application to purchase the northeast quarter of Section Thirty-five a mile south of Section Eleven for 800 dollars.[34] It was certainly no coincidence that when the first major extension of the city's boundaries occurred in 1903 it was to take in, not the new residential subdivisions, but the northeast quarter of Section Eleven.

The expansion of Calgary's residential suburbs in the period 1905–12 followed a pattern that was not dictated by real-estate speculation. The rising population and the expanding business area decreed that new residential areas be opened up; geographical and transportation factors decreed where. In fact one could argue that the many houseless subdivisions that crouched on the city environs epitomized the misplaced visions of grandeur that preceded the bursting of the real-estate bubble in 1913.

Although cheap lots and boundless opportunities were being paraded by real-estate agents in the five years 1905–09, there continued to be a housing shortage in the city. In 1905 an American visitor reported—somewhat erroneously, according to an irate *Herald*—that there was not a vacant house in the city and that upwards of one thousand people lived in tents, barns, and sheds.[35] Less than six months later the *Herald* was forced to admit that demand for rented houses outstripped supply by a ratio of ten to one in spite of spiralling rental rates.[36] In 1907, despite the 396 building permits issued in the first seven months of the year, the housing famine continued, with scores of citizens forced to keep their families in the east because of insufficient residences.[37] When the privately owned Centre Street bridge opened in 1907, scores of tents appeared on the bluffs north of the river inhabited by irate individuals who could or would not meet the exorbitant rent demands created by the acute housing shortage.[38] Indeed the acceleration in housing construction after 1908 probably resulted from the easier financial terms offered by builders to their customers.[39] It was certainly not resultant from more generous terms available in the real-estate market.

Speculative activity on the city environs in the period 1905–11 resulted in the transfer of most holdings from private to corporate interests. Bowness Estates passed through several hands before being sold to a British syndicate for over one million dollars in 1912.[40] Fred C. Lowes, Calgary's most sucessful real-estate speculator, acquired land in south west Calgary from various private sources, and in 1911 his holdings which stretched from Mission to Windsor Park were estimated conservatively at two million dollars.[41] Land was usually acquired by the acre ranging from approximately twenty-four to two hundred dollars, depending on the distance from the city limits,[42] and by 1911 virtually all land within three to five miles of the post office was in the hands of local real-estate agents who attempted to dispose of building lots at prices between fifty to three hundred dollars per lot. These local agents represented eastern Canadian, British, American, and local syndicates who pursued policies designed to raise the appeal and value of their somewhat peripheral holdings.

Typical of the initiative displayed by local landowners was that which involved the construction of the first Centre Street bridge in 1907. In that year the Bow River Bridge Company was formed and capitalized at $18,000 dollars by local businessmen including J.A. McArthur, owner of the property known as Crescent Heights; A.A. Dick, lumber merchant and owner of the quarter section between the Langevin Bridge and Twelfth Avenue; the German American Colonization Company, which owned the Belfast subdivision; and B.A. Stringer, another extensive property holder. The Bow River Bridge Company, convinced that the bridge would pay for itself in toll money and lead to the opening of north Calgary, made little effort to inform the city of its exact plans and virtually ignored the Council's request for information concerning the venture.[43] Although the need for the bridge was recognized by the city in 1911 when it took it over for the modest rental fee of five hundred dollars per year,[44] the speculative venture had largely failed in its objective of encouraging settlement north of the river.

Other real-estate interests financed smaller bridges across the Elbow; American planners were brought in to design new subdivisions; trees were planted and hills were washed away by investors in an effort to maximize the attractiveness of their holdings. The proposed Chestermere Lake Aquatic and Boating Club, held to be the last word in luxury, apparently justified the sale price of three hundred dollars per lakeside lot.[45] W.J. Tregillus, an extensive property owner in the west of the city, offered one hundred acres near Shouldice Park for the removal of the Exhibition grounds.[46] Doubtless there was more than philanthropy be-

hind Tregillus's offer of land in west Calgary for university purposes. The proposed but unbuilt suburb of Varsity Heights in the
area west of present-day Wildwood is probable evidence of that
fact.

Yet actual residential expansion was fairly restricted during
this period. North of the Bow River, the Hon. E. Riley, provincial member for Gleichen, used his influence to secure legislation
which saw Hillhurst-Sunnyside, his former property, become
part of the city in 1907, in return for a tax exemption of two
years. The village of Crescent Heights, incorporated in 1908
amid much local sentiments respecting pride of individuality,
made application to be annexed by the city in 1910.[47] The promises of the much desired public utilities overrode the voices of
official opposition. By 1912 there were houses in Mount Pleasant; Rosedale, where lots were sold on a plan of co-operative
ownership; the CPR subdivision of Bridgeland; and Balmoral.
Sparsely settled Mount View was paraded as the coming suburb,
while farther north was the nationally promoted suburb of Tuxedo Park Estates. Indeed, in spite of the little real building activity north of the river, there were upwards of a dozen subdivisions
more than ten miles from the city centre.

The main concentration of residential activity, however, was
in a south westerly direction. Quarter-sections in this area had
been changing hands since 1905. The CPR used restraint in opening up its subdivisions, chief of which during this period was
Mount Royal. Initially, in 1906, lots on Seventeenth Avenue
were advertised at 475 dollars each,[48] but the strong lobby on
Council saw Mount Royal become the city's only true luxury
suburb when building restrictions were placed on all residences
erected thereon.[49] By 1910 the average price for a building lot
with fifty foot frontage was fifteen hundred dollars.[50] The building of houses had extended to the Knob Hill and Sunalta districts by 1912, and along the Elbow River the suburbs of Elbow
Park, Elboya, Roxborough, Glencoe, and as far south as Windsor
Park were being built upon. The ubiquitous subdivisions were
present, though, more than ten of them south of Kingsland, and
indeed the suburb touted as Hiawatha in 1912 had to wait till
the late 1960's to be built up and renamed Bayview.

The most significant aspect of development east of the Elbow
was the rise of industrial activity, and in 1910 it was estimated
that almost eight hundred men worked in nine industrial
plants.[51] Subdivisions sprang up in response to the new demand.

Foremost among these were the former properties of Colonel James Walker and William Pearce. The Mills estate on Section Eleven and Albert Park across the Bow River were two more suburbs which specialized in cheap lots "at prices within reach of the working man."[52] Determined to shake off the area's image as an adjunct of the brewery, an east Calgary association was formed in 1909 to promote the needs and aspirations of the district.[53] For a while in 1909 east Calgary was the fastest growing area in the city, a phenomenon which the *Herald* duly noted and congratulated.[54]

The built-up areas in the years 1905–12 were serviced with water and power, and these years saw an intensified effort to supply the needs of the citizens in this regard. Road paving and sidewalk laying were also carried on in the areas adjacent to the downtown section, and it was the former, together with the CPR's agreement to construct subways under its tracks, which led to the feasibility of a street railway system. Calgary's first transportation system of this type began in 1907 when three motor buses plied the mud between Bankview and Breweryville.[55] Two years later, amid much opposition, and prompted in part by a real estate lobby on Council, a municipally owned street railway system opened in Calgary. The street cars initially traversed seven and a half miles of main thoroughfare along Eighth and Ninth and Seventeenth Avenues between Eleventh Street W. and Fifteenth Street E. This service was immensely popular by 1910, carrying a quarter of a million passengers a month, and according to the *Herald* "created a marked movement suburbanward. . .and close in property no longer has a monopoly of the market such as it possessed when the working man was forced to walk to work."[56] A working man wrote in 1908 that the street railway would enable him "to build a modest home for himself in the suburbs where lots are reasonably cheap."[57] Real-estate investors and speculators used the advantageous presence of the street railway to increase the value of their holdings. The transaction which saw real-estate at Bowness change hands in 1912 was linked to the potential street railway service which would link the district with the city.[58] The owners of property in the Ogden area and Tuxedo Park were willing to pay for the cost of extending the city's system to their subdivision, while the proposed suburb of Railston near Chestermere Lake was sold on the assumption that it would be serivced by the soon-to-be-constructed line to Chestermere Lake.[59] It is also noteworthy that the opening of various apartment buildings coincided with the arrival of a viable public transportation system.

In spite of the many subdivisions and the very active real-estate market after 1910, the main residential area of the city continued to be in the districts described above. The advertising columns were full of "good houses" in the area which by today's standards were contiguous to the business area. When the CPR placed some lots in Sunalta on the market in 1912, men stood in the rain all night to buy a maximum of two lots at an average price of eleven hundred dollars each.[60] The opening of schools in Bankview, Riverside, Mount Royal, and east Calgary during these years showed more clearly than any other factor wherein lay the concentration of population.

Before 1910, then, it could be argued that land speculation anticipated areas of future expansion, and that those with capital to invest were in a sense gambling on the future. As long as the speculative market was healthy, real-estate firms flourished, particularly after 1909 when Council reduced licences by fifty percent.[61] The fifty-four firms which advised clients to "deal in Calgary real estate and grow wealthy"[62] had swelled to 443 at the beginning of 1912.[63] The two thousand odd men who owed their livelihood to the real estate industry reflected the buoyancy of 1911–12, Calgary's only true boom years.

The rapid spurt in real-estate activity in 1911–12 was precipitated by two factors, both of which involved railway activity. The CPR's decision to build its car shops at Ogden provided an immeasurable impetus to the local economy, while the projected arrival of the Grand Trunk Pacific and Canadian Northern railways sparked off an unprecedented movement in land transactions.

The magnitude of the CPR's Ogden project was certainly impressive. The shops were to employ upwards of five thousand men and the locomotive sheds alone were to cover six acres.[64] Small wonder then that the new subdivision directly to the south of the shops was gratefully named Ceepeear. In a transaction described as "the most important real-estate deal ever put through in Calgary" this subdivision was sold to F.C. Lowes for 775,000 dollars.[65] Within the year at least a half a dozen subdivisions surrounded the shops and the route of the projected street railway which would connect the district with the city. In April, 1912, a syndicate consisting of eastern Canadian and local interests acquired a section of land five and a half miles east of the city for a reputed one million dollars.[66] The proposed Grand Trunk Pacific ran right through this section, while at least two streetcar extensions were planned for the area. The pioneer Tractor Company of Minnesota, it appears, was prepared to develop the whole section named Victoria Square, as an industrial and residential area.[67] In Calgary itself the interest generated by the arrival of the Grand Trunk Pacific evoked the shades of a bygone era. Real-estate interests used their influence with a too co-operative Council, according to the *Herald*, to secure advance information as to the railway's exact route into Calgary.[68] The terminal was to be situated at the east end of the Mounted Police barracks, and was to be an elaborate affair costing upwards of 300,000 dollars.[69] By the time the Order-in-Council was passed by the defeated Liberal Government authorizing the purchase of the barracks property, land prices in the vicinity had risen to one thousand dollars per frontage foot.[70] This entry of the Grand Trunk Pacific brought fruition to the three-year-old real-estate campaign to raise the value and appeal of east Calgary to prospective investors.

Of equal import was the entry into the city of the Canadian Northern. The site of the proposed terminal was south of Seventeenth Avenue in the vicinity of St. Mary's Church, and to secure a right-of-way the company bought up over three hundred thousand dollars worth of real-estate.[71] Following the disclosure of the railway's choice of site, property along Seventeenth Avenue spiralled. A building lot opposite Sherman's rink sold for the astronomical price of 37,000 dollars,[72] while 150 acres in the surrounding Mission district changed hands for 150,000 dollars.[73] Other lesser deals involved sums which totalled several hundred thousand dollars, as Calgary's newest hot-property district came into its own.

The euphoria which accompanied this boom called out schemes of grandeur whose prospects shone bright in the undiscerning light of optimism. The Inter Urban Railway Company, formed in Calgary, was to deliver produce via electric trains daily from Carbon, Banff, Pincher Creek, Lethbridge, Taber, Strathmore, and Medicine Hat.[74] The terminal was to be in the Calgary Market, and the main controversy in 1912 centered not around the viability of the venture but the direction the first line from Carbon was to take in entering the city. The somewhat Baroque Mawson Plan for the development of the city and the opulent designs for a huge civic complex provide further examples of ambitions that knew no bounds. The idea of diverting the course of the Elbow River to accommodate the Canadian Northern,[75] or of extending subdivisions into areas not bounded by the city of 1975 were to prove unreasonable only in the aftermath of worsening global economic conditions. Before the boom of 1911–12, Calgary's speculative promise had outstripped its achievements. Who could blame those who thought in 1912 that their hour was finally at hand?

The years at 1905 saw a marked transformation in the face of down town Calgary. The frontier image was being happily exchanged for one which spoke of urban affluence. The business section began its irrevocable encroachment on the surrounding residential area and as early as 1906 the *Herald* reported that

the 1st Street E. and W. residential portion of the city is rapidly giving way to the spread of stone buildings. On 1st. Street W. the retail stores have passed south of 12th. Avenue and threaten to invade the block adjacent to St. Mary's church. This tendency of the business section to encroach upon that portion of the city hitherto regarded as essentially residential suggests the growth of the municipality as no other development can.[76]

Two years later a visitor to the city lamented the absence of a civic policy which would concentrate on encouraging people to build farther away from the business section.[77] The main extension of the business section was along Eighth Avenue, and most of the real-estate activity in the downtown area involved properties on this street. One could still purchase lots on Eighth Avenue in 1905 for between 2,500 and 3,500 dollars.[78] By 1909 the figures ranged from 500 to 1,800 dollars per frontage foot,[79] and in 1912 a lot on the corner of Eighth Avenue and Fifth Street S.W. sold for 100,000 dollars.[80] In the same year the *News Telegram* reported that three thousand dollars per frontage foot had been refused for property on Eighth Avenue.[81] The commercial blocks which sprang up cost on the average well over one hundred thousand dollars and rose as high as five storeys. Along Eighth and to a lesser extent Ninth Avenues, retail, wholesale, and commercial establishments competed for prime space. The result was the westward expansion of the business centre, the nemesis of the east Calgary property owners of 1889–90.

The reasons for this pattern of western development was probably associated with the emergence of a wholesale district south and west of the railway tracks, together with the increasing importance of First Street W. This latter street, described as the Portage Avenue of Calgary in 1908,[82] was the first north-south thoroughfare to achieve commercial prominence. That Second Street E. was expected to fill this role was evidenced when the CPR chose it as the site of the first subway under the tracks. The poorly constructed grades led teamsters to ignore the subway in favour of the level crossings on First Street E. and First Street W.[83] The fact that the latter street connected with the Macleod Trail, combined with the substantial building impetus supplied by Thomas Underwood, gave it the edge over First Street E. In 1907 a survey indicated that in one day over one thousand vehicles crossed the tracks via First Street W. compared to approximately seven hundred on First Street E.[84] In the same year the CPR disputed the city's right to demand subways under both First Street E. and First Street W. The railway company freely admitted to the priority of the latter, but argued that a subway under the former would be uneconomical given the city's continuing westward focus.[85]

Indeed, the influence of the CPR was fundamental in more than one way to determining the westward pattern of commercial development. In 1903 the CPR constructed its freight sheds between First Street E. and W. In 1905 these sheds were extended east of Second Street E. All trains coming from either direction were uncoupled in these yards and switched to the spur lines which served the wholesale district. Thus east of First Street W. there was a tremendous amount of shunting, and it was precisely this heavy traffic which necessitated the construction of subways.[86] The spur lines and therefore the wholesale district had to be west. By 1912 there was a substantial concentration of warehouses north and south of the tracks west to Eighth Street which was the limit of the area served by the spur lines. Enough of this concentration was south of the railway to warrant Tenth Avenue being termed in 1909 "the coming wholesale street".[87]

The commercial establishments in areas outside the downtown core followed the street railway routes after 1909. Building activity was brisk across the Tenth Street bridge, in east Calgary, and along Eleventh Street and Seventeenth Avenue W. By 1910 Seventeenth Avenue had laid its claim to the much-bandied soubriquet "the coming business street",[88] as its boosters indicated proudly the four hundred dollars per frontage-foot that was being paid for business sites. The mounting pressure to have the building restrictions removed on Seventeenth Avenue proved to be a reliable gauge to the future.

Local government had a difficult role to play during these years of expansion. Committed to a policy involving large-scale annexation, the designers of civic policy were more concerned with keeping up with rather than controlling or even regulating growth.

Council was forced to bow to the wishes of large property owners on more than one occasion. In 1907 Council passed a motion allowing the widening of Seventh Avenue for easier access, and refused to issue building permits unless structures were placed six feet back from the street line.[89] Large property owners protested strongly maintaining that land values were being depressed, and that the motion was an act of bad faith against those who had already erected buildings. Faced with such opposition, Council quietly withdrew the enabling by-law.

In 1910 City Council requested legislation to bring the rest of township twenty-four within the corporate limits. Large property owners thus affected protested strongly, and demanded that their holdings not be subject to the normal assessment. Pat Burns was most vociferous and stated that since it was he who had made the city he had the right to expect something in return.[90] The Assessor apparently did not agree and in the subsequent assessment Burns's holdings were assessed in the vicinity of three million dollars, while property belonging to Colonel and Mrs. James Walker was assessed at one million dollars. The Court of Revision, in an effort apparently to pacify the irate owners, reduced Burns's assessment by about 99.7 per cent to eight thousand dollars.[91] That the Council was depriving itself of about five and a half million dollars of assessment mattered enough for a private citizen to appeal the Court of Revisions' action. The appeal was upheld by the Supreme Court and the original assessments were allowed to stand.[92] The *News Telegram* triumphantly noted that through the determined efforts of a few citizens the tax burden to the average ratepayer was reduced by about ten percent.[93] The main issue that the civic leaders were so easily swayed by the wishes of the powerful ratepayers was not noted in the sweet light of victory.

One of the most enduring themes during the whole period before 1914 was the ongoing dispute with the CPR over the latter's arbitrary right to close crossings. Whenever news of a projected opening or closing was disclosed there were the usual ramifications in the real-estate market. The example of 1906 provides an excellent case in point. In that year the CPR wished to effect closure on Seventh and Tenth Streets W. The railway company gave as its reason, and probably legitimately so, the fact that spur lines were needed on those crossings. The Council contested the CPR's right to do so and pointed to a promise extracted from the Railway in 1889 to the effect that the crossings would be kept open. In the meantime the locals became increasingly disgruntled and real-estate prices fell. Since the spurs needed were on Seventh Street, the CPR was able to compromise, and as a result opened crossings on Eighth and Eleventh Streets.[94]

Another recurring issue of contention between the City and Railway concerned taxation. Ever since the days when the Canadian North-West Land Company claimed tax exemption under contract in the 1880's, the Council had had to deal with the evasive tactics of the CPR. When the latter rented land along its right-of-way in Calgary to various business firms, it apparently assured its tenants that they would be exempt from taxation, as was CPR land under terms of contract. The City, however, acted boldly and assessed both—the CPR as owners and the different businesses as occupiers. Both parties contested the action in the courts but to no avail. Judge Sifton agreed with the City's reasoning that if such lands were used for anything other than for railway purposes they were liable to taxation.[95]

The City did make some attempt to regulate the action of the developers. In a test case in 1908, the owners of the Westmount subdivision contested their assessment, maintaining that the value placed on the land was too high. By a neat political ploy the civic authorities asked the owners to swear to a statement that the lands were not worth that much. This the owners refused to do for obvious reasons. The appeal against the assessment was subsequently dismissed.[96] In 1910 the legislative committee of the City Council recommended that owners of new subdivisions be requested to donate one-tenth of their subdivisions for park purposes.[97] Civic officials treated with the utmost caution those offers by subdivision owners to build street railway extensions to their properties, and refused to be pressured with regard to erecting bridges to encourage building development.[98] Similarly, in its disposal of public buildings the local authorities acted judiciously. Realizing that the choice of these sites had a marked effect on surrounding real-estate values, the Council followed generally impartial policies. The site of the Central Library, for example, developed purely out of economic considerations. The

Central Park site was free, whereas all twenty-four of the other suggested sites would have had to be purchased.[99] Although there was the allegation that interested parties had received advance knowledge of the site of the Normal School,[100] its western site was held to be a fair choice. The retention of the current City Hall site for the new structure was an obvious tribute to the maintenance of the east-west balance.[101] The alternative site was on Centre Street at Sixth Avenue. Even the location of schools on high pieces of ground was probably part of a policy of impartiality.

Although the city had long since abandoned its former policy of granting new industries generous bonuses and tax exemptions, it remained committed to a policy of aiding and therefore directing the location of commercial establishments. The city held many mortgages on businesses operating in the city.[102] These mortgages were carefully examined with respect to location and financial viability. The Al Azhar Temple, the Riverside Lumber Company, and the R.C. Thomas Block represented some of the more substantial mortgages,[103] but there were many others, which although on a much more modest scale, did indicate that the city had found a way in which it could exercise some control over the city's commercial expansion. If the terms of mortgage could not be met, the land reverted to the city.

Real-estate speculation was probably the most tangible expression of the boosterism characteristic of the whole period under discussion. The town was born in an atmosphere of promotional zeal that manifested itself in a healthy real-estate market. The land speculation of the 1889–90 period coincided with the projected construction of the Calgary Edmonton railroad and its promise of opening the area to the north. Depressed economic conditions limited further economic growth beyond 1892, and without an external "rallying point" both the boosters and the real-estate market were silent. The period 1905–09 was not one of continued prosperity. It was punctuated by mildly depressive economic conditions in 1906–07 despite the relative prosperity brought on by the population influx. In the latter years the real-estate market was very quiet. The strident voices of the boosters began again in 1909 and rose immeasurably with the news of the Ogden shops and the entry of the two transcontinental lines. If these short bursts of economic activity are discounted one finds the real-estate market in Calgary to be far less active and only modestly speculative.

This speculative activity certainly was a dominant theme in the period 1905–12. In these years the land around the city was bought up at reasonable prices by local and outside syndicates who waited for the "rallying point" which would sky-rocket the value of their holdings. It was the same with individual lots where private citizens were encouraged to make their fortunes by investing in town property. Thus it could be argued that many of the sales which were boosted as indicating the growing prosperity of the town were merely stages along the escalating path of speculation.

Calgary's commercial and residential expansion before 1912 began in 1884. As indices of general prosperity, the real-estate market, like the magnified statistics given by an exultant press, should be treated with caution, for these crested and dipped according to moods suggested by the promise of immediate things to come. Instead one should look to the gradual extension of the business section to take in a substantial wholesale district, or the location of an increasing number of industries across the Elbow River, or even to the heroic efforts of an harassed City Council to cope with strident demands and new problems. The pattern of real-estate activity did show one significant development, however. Local ownership of land was fast disappearing in the wake of outside capital investment. A phase of the frontier had passed.

IN SEARCH OF WEALTH AND STATUS: AN ECONOMIC AND SOCIAL STUDY OF ENTREPRENEURS IN EARLY CALGARY

Paul Voisey

Much evidence of wealth could certainly be seen in Calgary in the decade preceding the Great War. A visitor then might marvel at activity in the business district where buggies, streetcars, and automobiles thronged the narrow streets. Office buildings, banks, and shops all teemed with busy customers. Striking advertisements glared from the windows of countless real-estate firms. A frantic construction boom swallowed up wagon-loads of building materials, and the clatter of workmen's tools filled the air. To the south, wholesale houses nestled against narrow railway sidings. To the east, there were flour mills, meat packing plants, breweries, sprawling stockyards, and railyards. A stroll along Twelfth and Thirteenth Avenues S. revealed the fruits of this newly acquired wealth. Few eyes could miss the castle-like mansions of this neighbourhood or the ornate homes which studded the Mount Royal hillside farther to the south.

In the 1880's, the scene had been substantially different. Calgary had been a rough outpost and her men of wealth had little money. In fact, early business activity was monopolized by outsiders; Calgary's very creation in 1875 was the outcome of Ottawa's decision to build police forts in the West. The Hudson's Bay Company and I.G. Baker, a wily trader based in Fort Benton, Montana, foresaw that the Mounties and any who followed them would need supplies. Rival trading posts were quickly established. For years Baker's plodding oxen provided most of the freight transportation in the region. After 1875 a few shacks were added to the settlement—nothing more.

The arrival of the transcontinental railway in 1883 injected new vitality into the stodgy community. Between then and 1914, three types of businessmen invaded the city: the salaried managers of Eastern-based firms, the small retail merchants, and the more ambitious wholesalers, real estate developers, and manufacturers. It was the latter group, the entrepreneurs, that dominated local business and garnered most of its profits. Their spectacular rise to fortune owed much to the settlement of the agricultural frontier around them, and the newness of both their wealth and their community pervaded their way of life.

The most successful entrepreneurs of nineteenth-century Calgary were the manufacturers. Some processed prairie agricultural products. Donald McLean built a flour mill in 1893. A.E. Cross made beer. The son of a prominent Montreal jurist, Cross came to Alberta in 1884 to work as veterinarian and bookkeeper for Senator Cochrane's horse ranch. But Cross wanted a spread of his own and soon quit the job. In time, four huge ranches would sprawl over tens of thousands of acres.[1] Visiting his native city, he was intrigued by operations at the Montreal Brewing Company. He rushed back West in 1892 and launched the Calgary Brewing and Malting Company. That year a dozen employees churned out ten thousand barrels of beer.[2] He quickly organized Calgary Beverage Ltd., a subsidiary that manufactured soft drinks. By 1901 the capitalization of the brewery had swelled to 200,000 dollars and the annual value of its products to 35,750 dollars. Employees numbered thirty-four.[3] To guarantee a market for his beer, Cross started buying hotels throughout the West.[4]

William Roper Hull was a meat packer. He was only seventeen when he and his brother left England in 1873. They sailed round Cape Horn to the west coast of British Columbia, trudged inland to Kamloops, and started ranching. A slaughtering business began in 1883 when they agreed to supply beef to all the CPR construction gangs in British Columbia. An occasional supplier of horses to Alberta, Hull started a ranching and meat-packing business near Calgary in 1886.

Pat Burns, a tough-minded Ontario Irishman, was penniless when he arrived in Manitoba in 1878. To raise cash for his homestead, he worked as a railway labourer, but soon turned to buying and selling cattle. He was the first to ship livestock to Eastern markets.[5] Finding the business lucrative, he pursued it further in Winnipeg, and, like Hull, was soon supplying meat for railway gangs. This enterprise brought him to Calgary in 1890 where construction had started on the Calgary and Edmonton Railway. When fire destroyed his slaughter house in 1892, he built a larger one. He won contracts to supply meat to the Blood Reserve, and to the lumber, railway, and mining camps in the Kootenay region of British Columbia, where he built sixteen retail meat stores.[6]

Burns was dressing six hundred head a month when the Yukon gold rush started.[7] He guessed that rich claim-owners would pay a fortune for beef, but the problem of delivery was staggering. He sent live cattle to the coast by rail, shipped them north to Skagway, and drove them over the coastal mountains. They were slaughtered and floated into Dawson City by raft.[8] The profits were subsequently ploughed back into the business. In 1902 Burns bought a ranch, slaughter house, business block and several retail meat stores owned by Hull.

McLean, Cross, and Burns started processing food at a time when new railways were flexing north and south of the city. Others attempted to manufacture durable goods that could be marketed along those lines at a cost low enough to compete with Easterners. Most failed. Discriminatory freight rates and an abundant supply of capital, labour, power, and markets favoured the growth of secondary manufacturing in the St. Lawrence-Great lakes region. Western manufacturers could only compete, even in their own regional market, by concentrating on products requiring little capital or technical expertise, or on goods that were too bulky in relation to their value to justify the cost of importing them.

Sporadic efforts to manufacture leather goods and simple hardware bore some fruit, but most of the durable goods produced in Calgary before 1900 were made of wood. Lumber was a precious commodity on the treeless plains and W.H. Cushing knew it. A builder by trade, he opened a mill in 1885. Its fifteen employees made not only lumber but sashes and doors.[9]

Sharp competition came from I.K. Kerr and Peter Prince, two eastern Canadians who emerged from the Wisconsin forests armed with capital and experience. They started the Eau Claire and Bow River Lumber Company in 1883, and three years later, they opened a mill manned by seventy-five employees. Logs from the foothills were floated down the river in summer and processed in winter. The partners figured that excess power generated by their electrical plant could be used to generate extra money as well. In 1889 they secured a franchise from the city to supply street lighting, and the Calgary Water Power Company was born. Ingeniously, they burned sawdust to produce electricity; it ran the mill by day and lit the city by night.[10] Responding to increased demands for power in 1893, Prince and Kerr later built the Hillhurst dam and installed two water wheels.

Through lack of capital, markets, or expertise, many early manufacturing projects in Calgary fizzled. In 1891 factories numbered twenty-eight; by 1901, only ten. These failures served to strengthen the companies that survived. Whereas the average factory in 1891 employed only six men, it employed thirty-one a decade later. A wildly expanding market between 1900 and 1915 boosted the number of factories to sixty-nine and the average number of employees to forty-four. In the same period, capital invested in factories swelled from four hundred thousand dollars to 14.5 million, and the annual value of output from six hundred thousand dollars to 11.1 million, highest on the prairies after Winnipeg.[11] These figures also reveal that increasingly it took more capital to produce a dollar's worth of goods. The upshot was that manufacturers well established prior to 1900 were better able to glean profits from the new market. If one uses labour strength as a yardstick of growth, Cushing Brothers Ltd. employed 225 men by 1914; the Eau Claire company, 206; P. Burns Company, 350; and Cross's brewery, 142—all well above the city average for factories.[12]

But these figures only hint at the rampant pace of expansion. In the case of W.H. Cushing, the capital invested between 1905 and 1910 in his plant soared from twenty thousand to five hundred thousand.[13] He acquired timber rights in British Columbia and elsewhere. He built a new mill in Calgary in 1908; branch factories cropped up in Edmonton, Saskatoon, and Regina. Retail outlets dotted the province. A wider range of building materials was offered for sale, and by 1910 four hundred doors alone tumbled from the home factory each day.[14]

No-one expanded faster than Pat Burns. His plan was to build a fully integrated meat industry. In the first phase, he rapidly acquired twelve huge spreads, which at their peak in 1917 were estimated at 450,000 acres.[15] He bred cattle, fattened them, and slaughtered them. The Calgary plant was enlarged and modernized in 1906. When it burned down in 1913, it was said that Burns gave the command to build a larger one before the flames had died.[16] He processed every kind of domestic animal including poultry, and sold hides, fertilizer, and lard as by-products. He bought out rivals across the West and built packing plants in six other cities.[17] Dressed meats went to Burns's cold-storage warehouses and from there to his retail meat stores. In addition, he bought cheese factories and dairies and added wholesale fruit and vegetable outlets to his empire.[18] One of the few prairie manufacturers to crack world markets, Burns opened offices in London, Liverpool, Paris and Yokahama to market his exports.

While Calgary's earliest manufacturers prospered in the new century, so did a few newcomers. Many factories built after 1900 were, of course, simply eastern branch plants, but some sprang fresh from entrepreneurial initiative, particularly lumber mills. W.A. MacKinnon arrived in 1905 and started the Western Planing Mills, "manufacturers of sashes, doors, and other home furnishings."Within a decade its labour force spiralled from twenty to one hundred and fifty.[19] The Austrian-born Sereth brothers dwarfed this achievement. A 15,000 dollar investment launched the Riverside Lumber Company in 1905, and seven years later they were turning out annually 360,000 dollars worth of assorted wood products.[20] Two mills had been thrown up in British Columbia and retail lumber yards were scattered in numerous towns. Six hundred men in all were needed to run the Calgary-based enterprise.[21]

After 1900 a growing urban market also made it profitable to manufacture a wider variety of goods. The demand for iron and steel products swelled. It was possible for local companies to compete with eastern farm machinery manufacturers, but success blessed those who concentrated on the technologically simple and the inexpensive products. Edward Knape, for example, started the Union Iron Works about 1909. His custom foundry works, employing thirty men, made horseshoes, doors, ore cars, fire escapes, well drills, tanks, and structural iron.[22] Leather-workers were among those who accumulated fairly large-scale operations. Riley and McCormick began making saddles and harness for the pioneer farm and soon opened a branch plant in Lethbridge. Robert J. Hutchings, an early wholesaler of leather goods, started the Great West Saddlery Company in 1899. It employed one hundred men and had three branch factories by 1914.[23]

The growth of wholesaling after 1900 was equally spectacular. The number of jobbers rose to eighty in 1907, and nearly doubled in four short years.[24] Many specialized in agricultural supplies, and seventeen sold only farm machinery.[25] While the wholesaler seldom duplicated the glittering success of the big manufacturer or real-estate developer, a few giants emerged. James Wheeler Davidson arrived in 1905 and organized Crown Lumber. His firm opened forty-six lumber yards in Alberta before 1910.[26] By 1914 William Georgeson, owner of the Tuxedo Coffee and Spice Mills, exployed one hundred labourers and fourteen salesmen in his mammoth grocery house.[27] R.C. Thomas sold a wide range of goods. He had farmed near Calgary for a decade before taking his chances in the city. After 1894 he started selling coal, ice, lumber and farm machinery. He bought real estate and owned and managed all sorts of commercial buildings.

Burgeoning wholesale expansion went hand in hand with the thrust of new railways into frontier markets. Wholesalers were delighted in 1902 when the CPR made Calgary the cheapest point to ship all goods bound for southern Alberta. After 1905 railway construction in the region accelerated, and their steel cords firmly tied Calgary wholesalers to new customers. Links with two new transcontinental railways were secured when the Canadian Northern and Grand Trunk Pacific entered the city in 1913. But the CPR retained a mighty grip on the economy of both the city and its hinterland. Calgary became headquarters for its irrigation projects in 1895, and, in 1912, Western head office for the Department of Natural Resources, a division of the company that developed Western coal, petroleum, timber, irrigation, farm land and real estate. The year 1913 witnessed the construction of the huge Ogden rail shops. The CPR was easily the largest employer in the city; thousands of workers were on its payroll by 1914.

The rapid settlement of southern Alberta after 1900 stimulated Calgary's transportation, wholesaling, and manufacturing functions so vigorously that the city itself grew explosively; it jumped from almost nothing to a regional metropolis of 56,000 in a span of 15 years. The "instant city" phenomenon was only possible (but not unusual) on or very near rapidly-settled frontiers. In Calgary it opened two new avenues to wealth: real estate and construction.

Mushrooming growth transformed Calgary into a contractors' paradise. Between 1904 and 1912 the value of building permits soared from just under a million dollars to twenty million.[28] Builders like McDougall and Forster, and T.F. Hook employed two hundred to four hundred men at the peak of the construction season.[29] While Calgary lumbermen welcomed the boom, manufacturers of more substantial building materials arose solely to exploit the new urban market. Sandstone quarries had been operating since the 1880's but large-scale organization came in 1905 when E.H. Crandell started the Calgary (Crandell) Pressed Brick and Sandstone Company. It employed one hundred men and its furnaces spewed out 45,000 bricks a day.[30] W.J. Budd started cement factories throughout the province, and another cement manufacturer, Geoffry Silvester, formed the Calgary Silicate Pressed Brick Company in 1910.

The opportunities that arose in construction, real estate, wholesaling, and manufacturing were so tempting that some entrepreneurs invested ubiquitously in several enterprises. T.J.S. Skinner worked on survey crews and carried the mail across the Rockies before settling in Calgary in 1887. He started a real-estate business, then plunged headlong into wholesaling, soap manufacturing, flour milling and petroleum exploration. The business interests of Colonel James Walker of the NWMP were even more far-flung. A Canadian-born Scotsman with some business training, he left the Force in 1880 to manage the Cochrane Ranch. Two years later he bought its sawmill and began supplying timbers for railway ties and bridges. He became a building contractor. He prospected, acquired coal mines, started ranching, dabbled in city real estate. Two lots bought for three hundred dollars in 1883 were valued at fifty thousand dollars during the boom[31] He owned and operated the city's first telephone system in 1884. He started a fire insurance company, and by 1914 was deeply involved in the new petroleum industry.

R.B. Bennett also prospered mightily. He brought his talent as a corporation lawyer to Calgary in 1897 when he entered into partnership with James Lougheed. His best customers were the Hudson's Bay Company and the CPR; the latter was soon paying ten thousand dollars a year for his services.[32] Bennett organized the schemes of others, and in return, he retained directorships and blocks of stock in the most promising companies. This list was exceedingly long; by 1914 his interests spanned real estate, lumber mills, cattle, mining, finance, irrigation, cement, paper, electrical power, petroleum, grain elevators, and newspapers.

By 1914, then, a small group of men wielded enormous control over the business life of Calgary. Two factors in their rise to power should be summarized. They did not have to claw their way into established markets; a new one emerged on the frontier around them.[33] Secondly, the earlier a man established his business, the better his chances were.[34] But these favourable circumstances existed for thousands of prairie businessmen. Why did some rise faster, more successfully than others?

In part, it was their ability to forge business connections that effectively linked opportunities to capital. Sometimes they pushed each other up the ladder of success—Cross started his brewery with the financial backing of Hull and three other ranchers. More often someone dropped them a rope from above. William Mackenzie, architect of Canadian Northern Railways, was a boyhood pal of Pat Burns back in Kirkfield, Ontario. He gave Burns his first contract to supply meat to railway workers.[35] A contract to build new NWMP barracks helped launch the business career of former officer, Colonel James Walker.[36]

The career of R.B. Bennett neatly illustrates how a growing circle of powerful friends made some Calgarians rich. Determined to regain the family fortune swept away by the death of the Maritime ship-building industry, Bennett worked at odd jobs and taught school in order to attend Dalhousie University. While articling in a New Brunswick law office, he met a young man named Max Aitken, who, as Lord Beaverbrook, would become the kingpin of London's Fleet Street and one of the richest men in the British Empire. James Lougheed, meanwhile, was looking for a young law partner. When he asked Dean Weldon of Dalhousie for suggestions, Weldon gave him Bennett's name. Following his friend to Calgary, Aitken made a quick profit in a real-estate deal and headed for Edmonton where he met James Dunn, another New Brunswick lawyer—this one destined to become the steel titan of Canada. Together they hurried back East and met other industrialists. This connection was vital, for Aitken helped Bennett and his Calgary friends organize Calgary Power in 1909, and was able to bring Montreal millionaire Herbert Holt, Canada's richest and most powerful man by the twenties, into the project. Considering the enormous expansion of the company, it is unlikely that Calgary money could have done the job alone.[37]

Yet Bennett was not a gambler, preferring instead to invest in dreary bank stocks. And it almost seemed as though Aitken had to drag him by the heels into profitable risk ventures.[38] One was the formation of the Canada Cement monopoly; another involved the amalgamation of ninety-four grain elevators in the Alberta Pacific Grain Company, a venture, according to Aitken, that yielded Bennett a capital gain of 1.35 million dollars.[39] Meanwhile, a girl friend of Bennett from back home had married Ottawa lumber baron E.B. Eddy. Through her influence, Bennett was appointed a director of the Eddy company in 1906. Eddy died, leaving his wife controlling interest. When she and her brother died in the 1920's, Bennett inherited stock valued in the millions.[40]

Illustrious connections such as these not only gave Calgary entrepreneurs direct access to capital, but convinced bankers that local enterprises were a good risk. The growth of financial institutions in Calgary was stupendous. In the three years between 1909 and 1912, bank clearings tripled from 98.8 million to 275.5 million dollars.[41]

A close examination of the social backgrounds of forty prominent Calgary businessmen (See Table One) provides more general clues to their success. Contrary to local myth, they did not

TABLE ONE

Forty Prominent Entrepreneurs and Their Primary Businesses, 1883–1914, Selected for a Study of Social Origins.

These men were selected for the survey because of their importance, because they are representative, and because information about them is available. Lack of information prevented the inclusion of Van Wart, Judge Travis, and a few other prominent businessmen.

Armstrong, W.C. (real estate)
Bennett, R.B. (corporate law and organization)
Beveridge, Thomas (real estate)
Budd, W.J. (cement, finance)
Burns, Patrick (meat packing, ranching)
Cameron, Arthur L. (wholesaling, real estate)
Carson, William (flour milling)
Crandell, E.H. (canvas and brick manufacturing)
Cross, A.E. (brewing, ranching)
Cushing, W.H. (lumber milling, wood products)
Davidson, James W. (lumber wholesaling)

Denby, W.A. (canvas and mattress manufacturing)
Dowler, Leo (construction)
Georgeson, William (grocery wholesaling)
Hatfield, Thomas A. (real estate, general merchandising)
Hook, T.F. (construction)
Hull, William Roper (real estate, ranching)
Hutchings, Robert J. (leather manufacturing, general merchandising)
Irvine, John A. (real estate)
Jacques, Leopold (real estate)
Kerr, I.K. (lumber and wood products, electric power)
Knape, Edward (iron and steel foundry)
Lott, C.S. (real estate)
Lougheed, James A. (real estate, law)
Lowes, F.C. (real estate, general broker)
McCormick, Eneas (leather manufacturing)
McDougall, David (real estate)
MacKinnon, W.A. (lumber and wood products)
Newburn, Lloyd T. (grocery wholesaling)
Prince, Peter (lumber and wood products, electric power)
Reilly, W. Barrington (cement, general wholesaling)
Sayre, A. Judson (farm real estate)
Sereth, Alexander (lumber and wood products)
Sereth, H.N. (lumber and wood products)
Silvester, Geoffry (cement and brick manufacturing)
Skinner, T.J.S. (real estate, finance, general wholesaling and manufacturing)
Thomas, R.C. (real estate, general merchandising)
Toole, William (real estate)
Underwood, Thomas (real estate, construction)
Walker, Col. James (real estate, ranching, lumber, mining, petroleum)

---

all come from England and the United States. Only one-quarter of them were born in the British Isles, and only six in England. Only five were born in the United States.[42] More than half of them were Canadian-born, a reflection not only of the numerical strength of Canadians in the city, but of their early arrival in

Calgary. American businessmen arrived too late to reap full benefits from the great boom.

The same problem faced the continental European who soon stumbled over other obstacles: the language barrier, a lack of capital, discrimination—perhaps a peasant background that left him ill-equipped for rapid advancement in an industrial urban society. Leopold Jacques, however, became successful precisely because he was European. The son of a French postman raised in Italy, he quickly added German and English to his native tongues of Italian and French. He worked as an interpreter at luxury hotels in New York, London, and Paris before becoming a furniture maker in England. In 1903 he came to Calgary and started a similar business, but quickly realized that his command of foreign languages could be turned to profit. He became a real-estate broker who bought property for speculators in Europe, and in the process acquired much land for himself.[43]

Of the forty entrepreneurs examined, nearly all were Protestants, with Anglicans, Methodists, and Presbyterians heading the list. With the possible exception of teetotaling Methodists like Bennett and Cushing, it seems unlikely that religion played an important role in the lives of the elite, but the broad connection between Protestantism, Anglo-Saxon culture, and capitalist achievement was well exemplified in early Calgary. Only a few of the forty were Roman Catholic, but one of the most prominent entrepreneurs, Peter Prince, was among them. And Pat Burns, both an Irish Catholic and Calgary's wealthiest resident, might be regarded as a cultural oddball. But as one Chicago cattleman observed, ". . .he resembles the proverbial Scotchman who keeps the Sabbath Day and everything else he can lay his hands on."[44]

T.W. Acheson's study of Canada's industrial elite of 1885 concludes that formal education was not a prerequisite to business success.[45] The genteel tutoring of A.E. Cross at private schools in Montreal and England, followed by studies at Canadian universities, was not the experience of his peers. No more than one in seven prominent Calgary businessmen had even attended college or business school. The majority never survived high school, but none were as poorly educated as Pat Burns. Reporters loved to record the popular rumour that he made a million dollars before he learned to read or write. At least one successful entrepreneur in seven had served an apprenticeship, an education that often promoted manufacturing success by teaching industrial skills at a tender age. Prince, like his father before him, had been trained as a millwright, a useful background for a lumber manufacturer.

If entrepreneurs in Calgary did not come from wealthy families, neither did they come from destitute ones. Pat Burns, always the exception, was so poor that after picking out a Manitoba homestead in 1878, he walked 160 miles back to Winnipeg because he had no money for train fare.[46] But only three prominent businessmen in the list of forty came from homes where the breadwinner was a common labourer. The social background of well over half of them might be described as lower-middle class. Their fathers were farmers, skilled craftsmen, or small businessmen. Before coming to Calgary, most entrepreneurs pursued occupations similar in status to their fathers. Indeed, this information describes the type of individual that migrated to frontiers generally. The rich and successful had no reason to go there; the very poor could not afford it.[47] There was a significant degree of social equality on the frontier and when an elite did emerge, it was nouveau riche.

Another myth, widely believed at the time and not yet entirely dead, was that businessmen owed their success to a childhood of hard work and virtuous upbringing on a farm. Only a quarter of these men were raised on farms at a time when three-quarters of the national population was rural. At the other extreme, only five of the forty grew up in large metropolitan centres. The majority were raised in towns or small cities. Another valid generalization may thus be drawn. Urban folk migrated to the urban frontier; rural folk to the rural frontier.

From this survey it is possible to draw a portrait of the successful Calgary entrepreneur of the 1883–1914 period, one that, at a glance, seems apt for contemporary entrepreneurs in other prairie cities. He was an Anglo-Saxon Protestant from a town or small city in Ontario or the Maritimes. His formal education ended shortly after grammar school. His father's occupation was lower-middle class, and so was his, prior to arriving in Calgary as a young man.

This background was likely to instill a powerful hunger for material success and the entrepreneurial instincts to achieve it. Individual traits might vary widely. Pat Burns was described as a warm, jovial man.[48] Bennett was cold, self-righteous, given to temper tantrums. Everyone respected him; no one liked him. (Reporter: "It is almost impossible to get any human interest stories about you." Bennett: "There are none.")[49]

But Bennett, Burns and other successful entrepreneurs could deal intelligently—ruthlessly, if necessary—with associates, competitors and employees to achieve their goals. Bob Edwards, editor of the Calgary *Eye Opener*, reportedly said that Burns' idea of a good time was ". . .attending the funerals of rival butchers."[50] Evidence suggests that his rampant expansion after 1906 was triggered by fears that the Chicago "Beef Trust" was out to crush him.[51] He raced to take over small companies or establish plants in key areas in advance of giant competitors like Swift, and was so successful that the Alberta government ordered an investigation in 1907 to determine if Burns operated a monopoly powerful enough to control the price of Alberta cattle.[52] Similarly, Prince and Kerr waged a short, bitter war in the 1890's to crush a rival power company.[53] Cross, on the other hand, did not seem anxious to buy out the competing breweries that opened in Calgary, probably because he feared the growing prohibition movement. He invested his money elsewhere.

Few particulars are known about the treatment afforded the working man in Calgary, but clearly his life was not easy. Unskilled workers were packed into dilapidated boarding houses that lacked running water, proper heating, and privacy. True, the frontier scarcity of labour forced higher wages; in 1911 the average worker in the West received 15 to 18 dollars a week compared to $14 a week in Ontario,[54] but employers tried to keep wages as low as possible. When Prince and Kerr secured a power monopoly in the 1890's, electricity rates shot up but wages remained the same.[55] The cost of living was higher in the West, and the emphasis on extracting and processing natural resources often meant seasonal employment and little need for skilled workers. Laws governing working conditions were inadequately enforced. Prevailing business attitudes towards labour movements probably found their sharpest expression among nouveau riche employers. ("I built this company with years of sweat and no union is going to wreck it for me now.") Using lockouts and blacklists, Hutching's Great West Saddlery Company zealously fought efforts by employees to unionize. Pat Burns, on the other hand, was cagey; he was usually benevolent enough to avoid ugly confrontations.[56] But if the horror of labour exploitation described in Upton Sinclair's *Jungle* was less apparent at the Burns packing plant, the organization of industrial processes and labour was the same.[57]

Another tactic of entrepreneurs was the manipulation of local government for private purposes. To gain access to municipal coffers, members of the elite sometimes ran for city council. But, more often, small businessmen eagerly did their bidding at City Hall.[58] Enterpreneurs of every stature exerted potent influence through the Board of Trade and other business associations. Yet, the rule of City Hall by business interests was not as despotic as it seems. Few criticized its activities. Intoxicated by the boom, nearly everyone hoped to benefit from the prospect of economic growth.

Everyone agreed that railways and farmers were crucial to economic growth. The Board of Trade clamoured constantly for lower freight rates and the construction of more branch lines in the hinterland. In 1898, the City handed the CPR a 25,000 dollar gift to help build its repair shops.[59] In 1884 an annual Agricultural Fair was organized to squash the belief that southern Alberta was unproductive, and from its formation the Board of Trade enthusiastically advertised the region. After 1904 it issued about 25,000 promotional pamphlets annually and scattered them across the continent.[60] The pamphlets portrayed southern Alberta to the intending farmer as the Garden of Eden:

Climatically, Alberta is the most wonderful province or state on the continent. . .ours is doubtless the most healthful climate in Canada. . .and from an agricultural standpoint, the country surrounding our city cannot be surpassed. . .the quality of grain grown in Alberta is undoubtedly the highest, and. . .southern Alberta is one of the finest stock producing districts now available.[61]

The pamphlets questioned the fertility of soil in the Edmonton, Regina, and Saskatoon hinterlands, but promised a bonanza of wealth to the pioneer of southern Alberta. Other advantages included a strong moral and religious atmosphere, therapeutic drinking water, and probably long life. Such boosterism was heavily subsidized by the public. In 1906 the Board of Trade received 15,000 dollars for advertising purposes.[62]

City Hall gave manufacturers advantages that were perhaps vital to the establishment of many local industries. Direct subsidies? In 1892 Donald McLean received five thousand dollars to help build his flour mill, and another man got eight hundred dollars to start a tannery.[63] Tax concessions? Cross's brewery was typical; it paid only $2.50 in 1901.[64] Land grants? In 1911 a manufacturer could buy a spacious lot from the city for only two

hundred dollars.[65] Two years later, City Council borrowed 250,-
000 dollars to construct a massive building to house industries at
public expense.[66]

Merchants, realtors, and builders anticipated the flow of
wealth from new industries. They encouraged its advent through
the City's Committee on Railways and New Industries which
was formed to ". . .advise City Council how to secure or assist the
above,"[67] and through the 100,000 Club, which vowed to
". . .induce Manufacturers and capitalists to locate and thus increase the population to 100,000."[68] To advertise Calgary, manufacturing displays were added to the annual Agricultural Fair,
and the city authorized special "Made in Calgary" shows. In
1906 the New Industries Committee received a city grant of five
thousand for a publicity campaign,[69] and the pamphlets issued
by this and other promotional organizations generally exaggerated the importance of Calgary's rail connections and enticed
manufacturers with cash, land, and tax incentives.

A booming frontier economy, convenient business connections, and aggressive ambition; the ability to trounce competitors, bully labourers, and seduce governments; hard work, and
luck—these were the prerequisites of success for Calgary's early
entrepreneurs. The elite itself did not think so. It was fashionable
for businessmen and professionals to pay the costs of publishing a
book if the writer agreed to include biographical sketches approved by the backers. A typical example read as follows:

*Charles S. Lott is a typical representative of the spirit of the age, the spirit
which leads out into new and untried fields of labor, utilizing natural resources and the advantages which the times and conditions offer in the development of large enterprises and business interests. His name is an honored
one in financial circles, and the extent and importance of his operations directed by him indicate marked mental force and discernment, combined with
an executive ability which recognizes in obstacles and difficulties only an impetus for renewed effort. There is in the anxious and laborious struggle for an
honorable competence and a solid career of the business or professional man
fighting the every day battle of life, but little to attract the idle reader in
search of a sensational chapter, but for a mind thoroughly awake to the reality and meaning of human existence there are noble and immortal lessons in
the life of the man who with a clear head, a strong arm and stalwart purposes makes steady advancement in the business world, winning not only success, but also the deserved respect and esteem of those with whom the years of
his active life have brought him in contact.*[70]

In these biographies, great riches were acquired through thrift, industry, intellectual wisdom, and the moral virtues of honesty and fair play. They implied that poverty resulted from slovenly morals and laziness. But most of all, they conveyed a frantic plea for public recognition and respect.

This obsession, argued Thorstein Veblen in the *Theory of the Leisure Class* (1899), drove men to acquire more wealth than they needed to satisfy their material desires. Immense riches brought social status. A brief comparison of commissioned biographies in eastern and western Canada suggests that the desire for status may have been more powerful on the frontier. Dreams of its attainment help explain why many people headed west, and why their entrepreneurial drive was so strong. The urban frontier presented lower-middle class pioneers with a unique opportunity to become members of an elite. They would not have to fight their way into an established upper class—they could build one from scratch.

But the quest for status presented a quandary. Since social backgrounds were similar, the only real difference between pioneer classes was money. Other distinctions had to be invented. Veblen noted that the wealthy often distinguished themselves from the common herd by acquiring skills that obviously took years to develop, but which were totally useless for any economic purpose: learning dead languages, cultural history, or better yet, thousands of rules on social etiquette. These preoccupations proved that you didn't have to work—that all your time was leisure time. The impression could be enhanced by wearing clothing that would render manual work impossible.

But how was the frontier elite to learn the proper behaviour of rich folks? Veblen observed that most people mimicked the class just above them. To do so, the elite in Calgary had to look eastward, and as creatures who clung conservatively to hometown traditions, they did so willingly. Eastern elites had exclusive social clubs; Calgary would have one too: the Ranchmen's Club. Problem: how should it be structured? Solution: copy the St. James Club of Montreal.[71] To keep it exclusive, membership was restricted to 250, fees were two hundred dollars the first year (three months' wages for many Calgarians) and fifty dollars a year thereafter. One blackball in seven was sufficient to deny entry to any man.[72] The club featured a library, private dining chambers, and a bar that ordered ten-year-old Scotch directly from Edinburgh.[73] Because the club was founded so early (1891), some prominent entrepreneurs never got the chance to join, but some prominent ranchers and professionals did. Those left out quickly gravitated to the Alberta Club and the Calgary Golf and Country Club.

Most businessmen belonged to an astonishing number of voluntary organizations. Between 1883 and 1914, A.E. Cross joined at least seventeen and served as an officer for at least eleven. W.H. Cushing and Colonel James Walker served on almost every civic board in the city. Yet one questions how much leading businessmen enjoyed the work and fellowship of these organizations. Look at the favorite recreations of some of them: Bennett, reading; Cross, shooting and horseback riding; Hull, travelling and horticulture; Skinner, gardening; Burns, racing in cars at high speed.[74] They preferred private activities to public ones, since forays into the community spotlight were bids for status.

The elite enjoyed socializing in less formal settings, at the clubhouse, at private parties, or at the Alberta Hotel. The largest ranchers stayed there when they came to town. R.B. Bennett took all his meals there, and held luncheons to solicit political support from businessmen. In the bar, the most stimulating entertainment in town was provided by the lively conversation of editor Bob Edwards and Calgary's famed criminal lawyer, Paddy Nolan.

The elite tried desperately to imitate the cultural life of the East. Numerous literary societies were formed, and their children were shunted off to colleges and private schools in eastern Canada and England.[75] The affront of losing the provincial university to Edmonton prompted Bennett, Cushing, Skinner, and other leading entrepreneurs to take a leading role in the establishment and support of Mount Royal College. A Symphony was founded in 1913. Plays at the Hull Opera House, built in 1893, were staged mainly by local amateurs, but the elite strutted to its performances dressed in the formal fashions of the East. It was said that R.B. Bennett was the first Calgarian to wear a top hat and all his clothes were tailor-made in the East.[76] The elite was so purse-proud in its social pretensions and cultural creations that industrial pamphlets and directories always devoted several pages to highbrow affairs.

The elite embellished their domestic activities with conspicuous consumption. While they spent lavishly on automobiles and clothing, their primary indulgence was their homes. Sandstone gave Calgary the appearance of solid respectability that was lacking in most western cities. It became a prestigious symbol for the very rich. The Burns mansion, built in 1901, cost 32,000 dollars, excluding furnishings, land, and landscaping.[77] Although his family consisted solely of his wife and one son, the mansion had ten bedrooms and four bathrooms. Heavy paintings and stuffed animal heads adorned its oak panels. At the height of the real-estate boom, Burns valued the property at 150,000 dollars.[78] Lougheed's home nestled amidst landscaped terraces and ornate fountains. Inside, there was Italian marble, Spanish mahogany, and antique furniture from England.[79] To furnish his new mansion, William Roper Hull spent three thousand dollars. He greeted his guests in a red velvet jacket and rushed them to the third floor for a game of billiards.[80] William Pearce, a prominent government official who built one of the most elaborate mansions ever erected in this city, called his home "Bow Bend Shack",[81] but few businessmen shared his frontier sense of humour. Lougheed lived at "Beaulieu," Hull at "Langmore," E.H. Rouleau at "Castel-Aux-Pres".

Wealth, luxury, and extravagance. They were paraded before admiring crowds at the mansion garden party. On one occasion Hull entertained seven hundred guests.[82] An orchestra played music while the guests played tennis, croquet, and lawn bowling. Lunch was served to all. Lougheed held such parties frequently; he entertained prominent visitors like the Duke and Duchess of Connaught, Princess Patricia, and the Prince of Wales.

Inspired by the automobile and enforced by zoning regulations, residential segregation by social class was coming more into vogue throughout North America. When the CPR developed Mount Royal as an enclave for the rich, the attempt to copy its Montreal namesake was exacting in every detail. But residential segregation was still relatively new, as many millionaires continued to live along Twelfth and Thirteenth Avenues S. and elsewhere in the city.

The urban elite did not look exclusively to the East for patterns of behaviour, but to a unique group in their own community as well. Many ranchers in the region came from prominent families in England. And, the pretensions of the English ranchers were not without effect on the business elite.[83] They awarded high status to the sporting horseman. Businessmen sometimes joined polo teams, the Calgary Turf Club, or the Calgary Hunt Club, whose members mimicked the traditional English fox hunt, substituting the prairie coyote for the fox. Realtor

F.C. Lowes and wholesaler Lloyd Newburn figure prominently at all equestrian events. Burns, Cross, and Hull were ranchers from the start; entrepreneurs like Prince and Kerr probably bought ranches for status rather than economic gain.

It is tempting to overestimate the aristocratic origins of Calgary's English ranchers. Few could legitimately claim such origins and many exaggerated their former status. As one early Westerner said to the English tourist who bemoaned the lack of historic castles on the prairie landscape, "Wait til we git to Calgary. We got lots of English ruins there, only we call 'em remittance men." In spite of the appearance of the gentleman-rancher in early Calgary, the statement that the social origins of most frontiersmen were very ordinary remains valid.

Two influences conspired to foil the attempts of Calgary's business elite to ape the behaviour of the Eastern elite successfully—the frontier and their *nouveau riche* status. As has been shown, these factors are almost impossible to separate. Much leisure time was essential to develop social and cultural grace; old wealth in the East had it, new wealth on the frontier did not. These men were directly engaged in building business empires—no time for much else. Cross frequently excused himself from social functions on account of business.[84] From early childhood Calgary's prominent businessmen were conditioned to hard work, and once rich, many were unable to break the habit. Pat Burns had no hobbies, took no vacations.[85] Only the largest real-estate developers like Lougheed and Hull found much time for gentlemanly pursuits.

Leisure time was more often the luxury of wealthy businessmen's wives. To show that they had a maid or Chinese houseboy to do all their work, they wore the most impractical clothing of all. Parodying the society columns of other newspapers, Bob Edwards carried the practice of describing their clothing to an absurd conclusion: "Among those present were: a beautiful gown of blue satin with net trimmings and touches of gold. . .and a gorgeous creation from Paris, Saskatchewan, of sequin trimmings and sage and onion stuffing."[86]

Wealthy women were free to focus all their attention on social niceties, parties, charitable organizations, music clubs, and the Calgary Women's Literary Club, formed in 1906. But even for the women and few businessmen who were able to spend all their time developing social and cultural grace, their social and educational backgrounds doomed them from the beginning. And in a frontier city, lacking a cultural heritage or leadership of its own, there was no-one to provide the necessary daily instruction. Edwards justly lampooned their cultural pretensions: "At the Browning Club an interesting paper was read by Miss Lizzie Hargadine on the subject of grease-spots and their eradication."[87]

Yet, only one prominent businessman in Calgary could legitimately claim a literary background. James Wheeler Davidson of Crown Lumber was an American educated at an Illinois military school. In 1893 he joined Peary's scientific expedition to the Arctic. Between 1895 and 1905 he served with the United States consul in various parts of China. He authored four books on the history of Formosa and wrote a number of scientific and geographical papers. Among Calgary businessmen, he was a rare bird indeed.[88]

Calgary's elite was forever revealing tattletale signs of their humble origins. What guardian of old family wealth in Montreal's Westmount would keep a milk cow in the city? Pat Burns kept one in Calgary.[89] Calgary's Edwardian mansions were an ostentatious mishmash of freely borrowed and poorly interpreted styles from many historic periods. They possessed little continuity of style and exhibited little aesthetic taste. The interiors were cluttered with incongruous objects. Even the quest for status could assume different shapes on the frontier. Charity, for example, was a common way to win community esteem. But generosity towards the disadvantaged is often generated by millionaires in old age. Before 1914 Calgary's rich were mostly young men still actively engaged in expanding their estates.

The frontier city, growing wildly, booming magnificently, feeding on a large and rapidly settled hinterland, offered its pioneers exceptional opportunities to get ahead. Through well honed entrepreneurial skills and special advantages some surged well ahead of the rest. Unable to launch such large capital enterprises, they grew rich from a modest start in wholesaling, light manufacturing, real estate, and construction.

They came West seeking not only wealth but status. In many respects, the first goal was obtained more easily. The relative egalitarianism of the frontier combined with their own middle-class origins to thwart the re-creation of an Eastern elite. Because the social distinctions they raised were alien fabrications, they were paraded ostentatiously in the hope of imparting a convincing impression of authenticity. But if the dignified and cultured model they aimed at more often resulted in the unrefined, city-boosting, consumerism of a George Babbitt, they nonetheless convinced themselves and their fellows that their social position was as superior as their bank accounts.

FROM NEW BRUNSWICK TO CALGARY—R.B. BENNETT IN RETROSPECT

George F.G. Stanley

When a person endeavours to recall events far in his past, he must inevitably face the question whether his recollections are really the product of his memory, or whether they are recalled because his parents or other people have frequently talked about them. It is therefore difficult for me to be certain when I am drawing upon my own memory and when I am drawing upon my parents' recollections of my own experiences. I am sure that I do not personally recall the time when R.B. Bennett presented Connaught Public School with autographed photographs of the Duke and Duchess of Connaught, when they visited Calgary in 1914. After all, it was not until the next term that I entered Grade One at Connaught School. And yet I do recall the photographs—the Duke in his military uniform, the Duchess with a coronet in her hand, and the autographs, "Arthur" and "Louise Margaret". They hung on the wall for all to see; and I attended Connaught School between 1914 and 1920. I wonder if the photographs are still there? Incidentally, when the Duke visited Calgary he was taken to Turner Valley to see the Dingman well and presented with a miniature solid gold oil derrick and an illuminated address. I wonder what has happened to the oil derrick!

The earliest recollection of Richard Bedford Bennett that I can positively draw from my own memory is that of meeting him in the autumn of 1923 on the stage of the Assembly Hall in the old, grey, sandstone Central Collegiate institute, still standing, facing Thirteenth Avenue between Eighth and Ninth streets. It had been my good fortune to win a scholarship offered by Mr.

Bennett for the highest standing attained by a male student in the provincial examinations in Calgary for Grade XI. Mr. Bennett had been invited by the school principal to make a formal presentation of the award before the assembled student body. I went forward to receive my cheque for one hundred dollars—a mighty sum for a school boy in those days. At that point, without any prior warning, Dr. J.M. Hutchison, the principal, asked me to say a few words of thanks on behalf of the student body for Mr. Bennett's generosity in offering these scholarships for annual competition. Somehow I managed to say something, appropriate to the occasion or not, and returned to my seat clutching my hundred dollars, while Mr. Bennett strode ahead with his talk extolling the virtues of diligence, hard work and application to studies. Perhaps Mr. Bennett's words made some impression on me. I do not know. But I do know that the manner in which he expounded his familiar platitudes did.

I had, of course, been aware of R.B. Bennett long before this particular meeting. My father was an active worker for the Conservative party, and from an early age I reflected my family's faith in the Conservative party, and their respect for R.B. Bennett in particular.

In the autumn of 1925 I registered as a student at the University of Alberta. My original intention was to study law, particularly after my father told me that he had spoken to Mr. Bennett about my future, and that R.B. had expressed his willingness to take me into his office after graduation.

Because I went to Edmonton early in September I remember very little of the election of October 29, which saw Mr. Bennett returned to Parliament as member for West Calgary, and a substantial improvement in the Conservative representation in the House of Commons in Ottawa. I do, however, recall hearing stories of how R.B. would come out on the platform with a large red book under his arm which, according to one observer, "showed up like a lighthouse in a fog." J.D. Matheson of Macleod, later Judge Matheson, once said to Mr. Bennett, "You want to be careful R.B. that you don't lose that big red book, for if you did it would sure put your speeches on the hummer." The story is also told of how, during the campaign, an angry Liberal got up to leave while R.B. was speaking, making as much noise and confusion as he could. R.B. stopped speaking and said, "Hurry up, my friend, they will be closing very shortly, so don't let us detain you here listening to us." By implying that the deserter was rushing off to get a drink before closing time, R.B. provoked a good laugh at the poor man's expense.

At the end of the year I was approached by the head of the two-man History Department, Professor A.L. Burt, who persuaded me that my aptitudes really lay in the field of history. This meant, of course, that I would have to make my career at the blackboard rather than at the bar.

The next year, 1926, I did have a chance to see politics at close quarters. I recall vividly the excitement aroused by the Customs scandal, by Governor General Lord Byng's refusal to grant a dissolution to Mackenzie King, and the Prime Minister's subsequent resignation. Arthur Meighen's acceptance of office was regarded by my father and myself almost as a family triumph. I listened critically to Mackenzie King and sympathetically to Arthur Meighen when the two party leaders stumped the country in the late summer of 1926. But I was disappointed. Mackenzie King seemed to have the better of the exchange. I was not impressed with his oratory; but I was impressed by the casual way in which he waxed eloquently indignant about the threat to responsible government implied in Lord Byng's action. Meighen, who could out-talk Mackenzie King, and usually did, was suffering from a bad cold when he arrived in Calgary, and croaked his way through a speech which dismissed the constitutional issue as a piece of verbal chicanery. Meighen was not, however, effective on that occasion. Not, at least, in my opinion. The audience dutifully applauded. They applauded, however, much more enthusiastically when the Conservative lawyer Fred Shouldice stood up and angrily grasped the hat of a man sitting in front of him who had made a nuisance of himself by heckling Arthur Meighen, pulling it down over his ears and nose. There might have been trouble, but Fred Shouldice looked pretty formidable to the heckler, who left the hall, much to the amused delight of most of the members of the audience who witnessed the episode.

My role in the election of 1926 was that of a canvasser in the region of Calgary bounded by the Elbow River, Second Street E., and Twenty-Sixth Avenue. It was a region of small houses, many of them occupied by railway men. Despite the fact that they lived close to the CNR tracks, a number of these railway workers were CPR men, and I therefore found myself generally with a sympathetic audience. In any event, I was young and enthusiastic, and though I was not old enough to vote, I was not too young to accept an occasional drink from some of the more bibulous party supporters. I enjoyed my electioneering, that early autumn of 1926, almost enough to induce me to continue my law studies—but the Conservatives, as you all know, were defeated. And that was a damper. Meighen gave up the seals of office, and on September 25, Mackenzie King was back in power once again. Perhaps that is why I turned to study history, resolved to continue in an honours history course at the University. The only satisfaction I derived from the election was the fact that Calgary proved itself once again to be a good Conservative town. And the vote in the region I canvassed? I wonder if I am right in recalling that it gave Bennett a majority.

In 1929 I entered Keble College at Oxford as an undergraduate in History. Just one year later R.B. Bennett, now Prime Minister, arrived in England to represent Canada at the Imperial Conference of 1930. I had, by this time, become a strong Canadian nationalist, and I was therefore happy that it should be my friend Mr. Bennett, who had always been pictured as a strong Imperialist, who should have come to England to put Canada's seal of approval on the recommendations embodied a year later in the Statute of Westminster, a document I have always looked upon as the charter of Canadian nationhood. I was even happier to hear that Mr. Bennett was coming to Oxford and would like me to join him at lunch.

The group which gathered at the Mitre Hotel, on that occasion, included my mother, who was in Oxford at that time, Miss Millar, R.B.'s secretary, Burton Kierstead, a Rhodes Scholar from New Brunswick, Hugh Morrison, another Rhodes Scholar from Alberta, and myself. While standing in the anteroom, waiting to be conducted to his table in the dining room, Mr. Bennett gave the three Rhodes Scholars a short lecture on the virtues of temperance and the evils of strong drink. It was an old theme, one on which he had rung all the changes ever since he was a young man teaching school and studying law at Chatham, New Brunswick. Then, just after we seated ourselves in the dining room, Mr. Bennett turned to us with the question, "Now, would any of you boys care for a drink?" Cowards we were. All three of us. Lacking courage and leadership we stuttered something about ginger ale. And that was what we got.

The lunch was followed by a sightseeing tour of the three Oxford colleges we represented, Merton, Keble, and Exeter. While Mr. Bennett was examining the portraits hanging in the dining hall at Keble, my mother drew his attention to a large painting of Charles I, bearing the caption, "Charles the Martyr". My mother was a good Cavalier; she knew what Mr. Bennett's reaction would be. It was the reference to "Charles the Martyr" that did it. Bennett muttered some kind of a protest in his throat and then launched into a lecture, this time on the virtues of Oliver Cromwell. Cromwell was, of course, one of Bennett's hero-figures; Cromwell, the man of action, the man of strength, the sword of Jehovah. Bennett's admiration for Cromwell was self-revealing.

In passing, I might mention another episode which occurred during the Imperial Conference of 1930. Maurice Dupré, a forty-two year old lawyer from Trois-Rivières, who was Solicitor-General in the Bennett administration, had accompanied the Canadian Prime Minister to London. He too paid a visit to Oxford and met a group of Canadian students. With the brashness usually associated with a younger man, Dupré told us that he would be the next leader of the Conservative party after Mr. Bennett. It was part of a discussion in which Dupré stressed the importance of the Conservative party having a French-Canadian leader. He believed that if the Conservatives were to survive, particularly in Quebec, they would have to prove that they were truly a national party. The Conservative party needed a new image in Quebec, where, Dupré suggested, many voters were still voting for the ghost of Sir Wilfrid Laurier. Dupré was right in pointing out that it was the Macdonald-Cartier and Macdonald-Langevin alliances that had ensured the long tenure of the Conservative government in Canada in the nineteenth century; where he was wrong was in believing that he would be the man who would replace Laurier in the minds of the people of Quebec. Fate never gave him the chance. He was killed in an accident in 1941.

In 1936, I graduated from Oxford with a D. Phil. degree. When and where was I going to obtain a teaching appointment? That was the question I constantly asked myself. From Dr. R.C. Wallace of the University of Alberta, the university from which I had graduated, I received a particularly chilly brush-off. Queen's University seemed to offer some hope; but this hope vanished when the History Department discovered that I had never taken any courses in American history. Nobody seemed to need me; certainly nobody wanted me. What was I to do? Finally, almost as a last resort, I wrote to R.B. Bennett, explaining my predicament and soliciting his aid. Despite the fact that this was 1935, when he was absorbed with the time-consuming task of fighting an election, Mr. Bennett paused long enough to write a letter to Mount Allison University, in Sackville, New Brunswick. It happened that the Professor of History at Mount Allison was due to retire in 1936, and when the President of Mount Allison received Bennett's letter, he sent me a telegram offering me a one year appointment at a salary of 1,500 dollars. I lost no time in accepting the offer. Then I set out to see if I could find a Rhodes Scholar from Mount Allison who could tell me where his *Alma Mater* was located and what it was like.

I was, you must realize, extremely grateful to Mr. Bennett for his assistance at this very critical point in my life. I had no desire to remain in Great Britain. I had a strong affection for my own country and I felt a sense of obligation to return to it. It was Bennett's intervention that made my return home possible. This I know because the fact was revealed to me several years later by the President of Mount Allison, Dr. George Trueman. He had just learned that R.B. Bennett was interested in endowing a chair in History at Mount Allison in memory of his father and his mother. Dr. Trueman apparently believed that my presence at Mount Allison had something to do with this, and was congratulating himself on not having rejected the great man's request in giving me an academic appointment.

The ironic thing is that I never occupied the Stiles-Bennett Chair of History at Mount Allison. By the time it was established, Canada was at war with Germany and I had left the University to serve in the Canadian Army.

II

Richard Bedford Bennett was born on July 3, 1870, in his mother's family home at Hopewell Hill, Alberta county, New Brunswick. The Bennetts were of English stock, coming to Nova Scotia by way of Rhode Island during the American Revolution, and subsequently moving to New Brunswick. R.B. was thus of U.E.L. stock and was proud of it! His father, Henry Bennett, was a sea captain, an easy-going, cheerful man who was not averse to alcohol, a Baptist because his parents had been Baptists, but not one to take his religious obligations too seriously. Henry Bennett had inherited the family shipyard at Hopewell Cape and was believed by his neighbours to be comfortably off. In actual fact, he was feeling the consequences of the changes from sail to steam, and from wood to steel, and his means were steadily dwindling. For that reason it was fortunate that he married a frugal wife.

R.B.'s mother, Henrietta Stiles, was a woman cast in a mould different from that of her husband. She was a woman who worked hard and believed that everyone else should do the same. As the years passed, she was disposed to look upon her husband as a failure. He might sire her sons and daughters, but he would never serve as an inspiration to them. Henrietta therefore set out to instil *her* ideas and ideals in her offspring. Richard, probably more than any of the other children, was the one on whom she centered her hopes and her aspirations. He, she believed, might be shaped into the kind of man she would have liked her husband to have been. And Richard was a ready and apt pupil. He had both the natural gifts and the acquired qualities which would enable him to realize his mother's ambitions.

After completing Grade Eight at the local school, young Bennett—he was always called "Dick" in his boyhood—went to the Provincial Normal School at Fredericton at the age of twelve. Four years later, equipped with a first-class certificate, he accepted a teaching appointment at Irishtown, near Moncton, at an annual salary of 160 dollars. Two years later, at the age of eighteen, he was appointed Principal at Douglastown, near Chatham on the North Shore, at a stipend of five hundred dollars. This marked a considerable increase over the earlier salary, but R.B. had his mother's frugality, and he managed to save at least half his income. To increase it further he enlisted in the local militia. It was his only experience of military service. Apparently he made an indifferent soldier and was soon transferred to the pay office, where he was happier and where his talents could be put to better use. As a schoolteacher Bennett took his responsibilities seriously, if we may judge from the rather unusual report he addressed to his trustees at Douglastown:

During a stay of nearly two years in this place, I have come to the conclusion that the material is not lacking here to produce pupils of more than ordinary ability, but while I feel that such is the case I cannot but remark that unless the parents are aroused and awakened from the apathy with which they now view all matters connected with the school work, the fine abilities of their children will never be shown.

While in Chatham, young Bennett became acquainted with Lemuel Tweedie, Q.C., a Conservative lawyer who was later to become Premier of New Brunswick and Lieutenant-Governor of his native province. Bennett had already come to the conclusion that school teaching offered little prospect in the way of achieving wealth or public recognition, and when Tweedie suggested to him that he should study law in his office, Bennett adopted the suggestion. Teaching during the day, he worked in Tweedie's law office under his employer's direction in the evenings and during the vacation. Tweedie was much impressed with Bennett's industry, and promised his young student-at-law a junior partnership as soon as he should be admitted to the provincial bar. Bennett, with some justification, believed that the best and quickest way to achieve that desired goal would be to go to the Dalhousie Law School, then in the period of its greatness under Dean R.C. Weldon. He had saved enough money from his small salary as a teacher to pay his fees and his board and room, and Weldon, interested in the ambitious young New Brunswicker, helped him along by arranging for an appointment for him in the Dalhousie Law Library. Finally in 1893 Richard Bedford Bennett graduated from the Law School in Halifax and returned to take up his promised partnership in Chatham.

According to his contemporaries, Bennett had his eyes upon a political as well as a legal career. Mr. Justice W.H. Trueman of the Manitoba Appeal Court, who was a student at Dalhousie in Bennett's day, tells the story of how he and Bennett went to hear Sir John A. Macdonald give a political address in Halifax. Returning from the meeting, Trueman noticed that Bennett was very quiet, apparently mulling over in his mind what Sir John had talked about. Then, suddenly, he turned to Trueman and said, "I'm going to be Premier of Canada." Prophetic inspiration or mere boastfulness? Perhaps something of each.

During the next few years nothing occurred that would seem to suggest the likelihood of Bennett achieving his casually expressed ambition. And yet, during these early 1890's, R.B. was unconsciously moving in that direction. The things he did, the people he met, the friends he made, all came together to form a pattern recognizable only at a much later date. He entered politics by securing election—albeit by a one-vote majority—as an alderman in Chatham; he strengthened his friendship with Jennie and Harry Shirreff, both of whom were later to leave him substantial legacies in the form of shares in the E.B. Eddy Match Company of Hull, Quebec; he became the close friend of young Max Aitken, who entered the law firm of Tweedie and Bennett; and finally he met Sir James Lougheed of Calgary, who was looking for a promising young lawyer to assist him in his expanding law practice in Calgary. Lougheed had initially approached Dean Weldon, who wrote to him, "I think I have just the young man you want." The two men, Lougheed and Bennett, met in Ottawa, and again later in Saint John. Finally a satisfactory agreement was arrived at—it lasted until 1922—and, in February 1897, Bennett boarded a train bound for a part of the world with which he was wholly unfamiliar, but which was to become his second home. To Tweedie, Bennett was throwing away the certainty of a good legal practice and an assured political career in New Brunswick for the gamble of an uncertain future in the North-West Territories. What Tweedie did not understand was that the very fact that Bennett was prepared to take the gamble was the best promise of his success in the Canadian West. Bennett did not come to Calgary with a bundle slung over his shoulder. He may not have had much in the form of this world's goods, but he was well endowed with a determination to succeed, and the judgement to enable him to grasp opportunities when they arose. Speaking some years later, in 1914 to be exact, Bennett told a Calgary audience of his first impressions of his new home:

I remember it as though it were today. There were over 3,000 persons here and the city was spread over a rather wide area, in which there were a large number of vacant houses and shacks. The principal buildings were the Bank of Montreal, the Alberta Hotel, the Roman Catholic Church and the Post Office. The principal occupations in those days—well, the people were like Micawber, waiting for something to turn up. And things did turn up once the start was made.

It was, of course, Lougheed who gave Bennett his start. It was also Lougheed, so the story goes, from whom R.B. picked up that grandiose style of oratory which was the characteristic feature of his public speeches. Lougheed never used a single syllable word when a three-syllable word would do as well. It is said that Lougheed, when a schoolboy, when asked to define marriage, replied, "Marriage—ah—is a corporation of two persons, with—ah—power to increase its numbers." Lougheed was an Ontarian who had come to Calgary in 1883, made a fortune in real estate, been admitted to the Territorial Bar, and, in 1889, been called to the Senate of Canada. He was, by 1897, less interested in the practice of law than in the practice of politics, and he needed a junior partner to handle his business obligations. And in Bennett he found the right man. Conscientious, thoroughgoing, and ambitious, Bennett immersed himself in the work of his new firm, Lougheed and Bennett. The qualities which had made him a successful schoolteacher in Chatham stood him in good stead as a lawyer in Calgary. An infinite capacity for taking pains, a rare ability to sort out detail, an exceptional memory, these were all part of the intellectual equipment which Bennett employed with skill and spirit. It did not matter that he never quite caught the feel of the West—the sea was in his blood and he always loved it—he was prepared to lose himself in his work, identify himself with his client, and make himself at home in his office in the Clarence Block on Eighth Avenue. I believe he always remained at heart a Maritimer. Not long ago another expatriate Westerner, Lt. Colonel Donald MacLauchlan, remarked to me that eastern Canada was always more formal than the West, but that R.B., with his clean, pink, cherubic countenance surmounting his starched collar, always appeared a little too formal even for eastern tastes. A portrait of him as a member of the Alberta legislature shows him with a broad-pointed wing collar and a bow tie. Later he dropped the bow tie in favour of a long cravat, but he continued to wear a wing collar for the rest of his life. Because he would not conform to the outward patterns of Calgary life, Bennett must have cut a strange figure in the bar room of the Alberta Hotel where, despite his strict views on temperance, he frequently went to meet his clients.

But even conceding that Bennett never really became a Westerner, I believe that Calgary and the West did leave its mark upon him. It did dilute some of his formality and it unquestionably added a vaster horizon to his vision of Canada. On one occasion he told my mother, when we were dining with him at his brother's house in Sackville, New Brunswick, that it always gave him a special kind of experience, a lift, to arrive in Calgary, to breathe the fresh, invigorating mountain air, to see the bright sunshine and the vividly clean outlines of the foothills and the Rocky Mountains in the distance. Calgary gave him new life after months spent in the humid atmosphere of Ottawa.

At the turn of the century, R.B. was living at 222 Fourth Avenue W., in a house belonging to Joseph Stanley. He still obtained his clothes from eastern Canada—not long ago I came across a letter written by R.B. to F.O. Patterson, a tailor in Chatham, New Brunswick, ordering a new suit of clothes. In addition to buying clothes, Bennett was also buying books and building up a personal library which is to eventually become the property of Mount Allison University. In 1899 he ordered Rapelje and Meach's *Digest*, and *An Encyclopedia of Pleadings and Practice* from an American publishing house for 138 dollars. From Morang in Toronto he obtained a set of the works of Rudyard Kipling, and in 1900 a set entitled *Masterpieces of the World's Literature* from a Montreal publisher. Over the years he accumulated collections of the works of Shakespeare, Shelley, Macaulay, Irving and Whittier, together with numerous books on history and travel. Biographies of famous men were always his favourite reading, men like Richelieu, Cromwell, Chatham, Peel, Palmerston, Disraeli, Nelson, Napoleon, and, of course, John A. Macdonald. During a visit to Sackville he gave me a copy of Professor Waugh's *James Wolfe*, a book I still have in my possession. If one may generalize about a man's interests from his library, then one would note, in R.B.'s case, the heavy emphasis upon English political history. R.B. was always a firm believer in the virtues of the British Empire—his early purchase of Kipling is evidence of that. Speaking to the Canadian Club in Calgary in 1912, he publicly stated what I would call the principal article of his political faith:

I will confess that I have had an overwhelming passion to advance the interest of the British Empire ever since I was a boy, and I cherished the hope that, some day and somewhere, I might be useful in the furtherance of the cause of the organic union of the British Empire. If I can serve that great passion better by doing it somewhere else than here, I shall do it with the profound conviction that Providence has given us no greater implement to further the interests of mankind than the British Empire.

On another occasion he said:

I will not yield the right to be called a Britisher to those only who were born in the British Isles. I hold myself as much a Britisher as if I had been born within the sound of Bow Bells.

Admitting that he thought of himself as a Britisher when he made these last remarks at a banquet in Toronto on May 26,

1914, I cannot believe that he thought of himself as a Cockney! I still wonder at his reference to Bow Bells.

With his background and his ambitions, it was in the natural order of events that R.B. Bennett should become involved in western Canadian politics. Had not Tweedie and Lougheed found law the road to a political career? Why should not he, Bennett, tread the same path? And had not part of his agreement with Lougheed been that he should be allowed a "free hand in public matters"? It was equally natural that he should choose the Conservative party as the political organization with which he would identify himself. Not because of any strong philosophical convictions—Bennett never had a philosophical turn of mind—but because his views had already been shaped by men like Tweedie and Weldon. And the Conservative Party in Calgary welcomed him when, shortly after his arrival in the city, he put down Frank Oliver, the Liberal stalwart from Edmonton, in a sharp verbal exchange. Frank Oliver was a pretty hard man to put down, and for a relative stranger to succeed in doing so, was a source of delight to the Conservatives and of satisfaction to Bennett himself. This probably explains why Bennett had no difficulty in getting a nomination for Calgary in the Territorial election of 1891, less than two years after he had stepped from the CPR train at the Calgary station.

Bennett opened his campaign at a large political meeting held in the Hull Opera House at Sixth Avenue and Centre Street. All the local worthies were on the platform: Senator Lougheed, A.E. Cross, Colonel Wyndham, James Reilly. The chairman was the Mayor of Calgary, A.L. Cameron. Bennett spoke first, setting out his platform as provincial status for the North-West Territories and Calgary as its capital. "In the East," he said, "Calgary is always spoken of in terms of praise as an enterprising city with fine buildings and energetic citizens." This kind of thing pleased the audience and they were disposed to ask what Bennett's opponents, Stuart and Muir, had ever said or done for Calgary? Bennett knew that he was regarded as pretty young for a political career, but he argued that capacity counted more than age in a member of the legislature, and as for his opponents' charges that he was inspired by ambition, he admitted frankly that he was. "I left no blighted ambitions in the East," he said. "My ambition is to grow up with this country which I have made my home and advance its prosperity. I have no ambitions for judgeships. . . .As long as I live, this is my home and I will work for and serve this country on all occasions to the best of my power." The Opera House meeting was only one of several held in various parts of the constituency, and in each he repeated much the same speech, stressing above all the need for provincial status, irrigation, and the extension of the Calgary and Edmonton Railway to the United States frontier to link up with James J. Hill's Great Northern.

When the votes were counted, Bennett was the victor. Recalling this election in a letter to Lord Beaverbrook in 1941, Bennett attributed part, at least, of his success to the help afforded him by Beaverbrook, then Max Aitken, his young friend of Chatham days, who had followed him from Tweedie's office to Calgary. Some of his success, too, was due to George Cloakey, who worked hard for Bennett in Olds. In Calgary, Bennett and Muir ran neck and neck, and it was only the strong Bennett vote in Olds which carried the day.

In Territorial politics, government was conducted along non-party lines, and the Territorial Premier, F.W. Haultain, was determined to keep it that way. Personally, I believe the Territorial Legislature was a more truly democratic body, certainly a more independent body than it would have been had it been dominated by a party government; but R.B. did not see it that way. He was a strong exponent of party politics and was determined to introduce political parties into the North-West Territories. In 1903 a convention of Territorial Conservatives met at Moose Jaw. They demanded provincial autonomy, an end to the policy of land grants to the railways, a railway to Hudson's Bay (Louis Riel had made the same demand in 1884), and a protective tariff. These are all good Conservative ideas and Bennett was in the forefront in advocating them. But above all he fought for the formation of a Territorial Conservative party and its active participation in the next Territorial election. He laid into Haultain (who supported the Conservatives federally) with such vigour that Robert L. Borden was moved to write to Bennett, telling him that Haultain was "extremely sore over the attacks made on him by the Conservatives" and asking him to restrain himself and those of his friends who might be "inclined to be too impulsive in dealing with Haultain." Borden was afraid that if the Territorial Conservatives did not let up on their attacks, they might well drive Haultain out of politics. He wanted them, he said, to co-operate with the Territorial Premier and seek his assistance, and not to make an enemy of him. This was not a policy to Bennett's taste. To Bennett, politics involved more than the needs, real or imagined, or any particular constituency, and the only way to raise politics above the purely local level was to form political parties. Politics were to R.B. a matter of principle, and, in his own case, this meant the principles of nineteenth-century British Conservatism. To Bennett, democracy was simply the right of the people to be governed by the law and not by public officials.

As far as provincial status for the North-West Territories was concerned, Bennett and Haultain saw eye to eye. But the two men parted company over the question of whether the Territories should be constituted into one province or two. Haultain favoured the erection of a single province. He argued that the desire for more than one province was prompted only by the ambitions of certain towns to become provincial capitals. It was a not unfair assessment of the situation, if we are to judge from the stand taken by Calgarians. They wanted two provinces, divided by a boundary line running either east and west or north and south. In either case, Calgary would have to be a capital, and Calgarians prepared to do battle either with Regina or Edmonton for that honour. But when autonomy came in 1905, Calgary lost out. It was Edmonton, not Calgary, that was given the dignity of becoming provincial capital of the new province of Alberta.

With the formation of the provinces of Alberta and Saskatchewan, Haultain's non-party system disappeared from western Canadian history. In Alberta, the Liberals elected A.C. Rutherford as their leader and the Conservatives, R.B. Bennett. But Bennett, however, failed to secure election and his party made no showing at all. It was not until four years later that he succeeded at the polls, when he entered the Alberta legislature as the junior member for the two-member constituency of Calgary. But leadership of the provincial Conservative party held no bright future for Bennett. He was only one of two Conservatives elected in 1909. The other was George Hoadley of Okotoks. A third, Edward Michener, was elected for Red Deer, but since he called himself an Independent, he could be regarded only as a half-hearted Conservative. With so few men to back him there was little Bennett could do in Edmonton. He did succeed in bringing about A.C. Rutherford's resignation by attacking the Liberal premier's dealings with the Alberta and Great Waterways Railway; even so he failed to bring about the defeat of the Liberal Government. Perhaps the Calgary *Herald* reporter put his finger on Bennett's lack of success as a party leader:

Bennett has a handicap, which is granted to few men in debate. His ability is recognized to such an extent that even when he lays a problem bare, talking in language that any man can understand, the rank and file of the remaining Government supporters, though they can see the picture of what he painted as clearly as if it stood before them, refused to be influenced by him because they feared his cleverness was simply twisting things to appear his way.

Ernest Watkins, Bennett's biographer, put it more succinctly when he wrote "It was not that he was too good to be true. It was that he sometimes seemed too clever to be right."

It is possible that had Bennett decided to remain in provincial politics, he might have led his Conservatives into office in 1911 or 1913. But he was not prepared to make the effort. Instead he chose to retire from the provincial field. The Alberta Conservatives were disappointed. Francis Fatt wrote to him from Medicine Hat:

We appreciate in a very deep measure, the help and assistance which you have given in the most trying and thankless period of our young provincial life. It requires somewhat the heroism of a Crusader in going against such odds as you have had to contend with, and the faith of a Christian martyr to be content with the plaudits of future generations.

Bennett replied, explaining his decision to retire as the result of "the pressure of my business." Then he wrote, somewhat wistfully if a little sourly, "I have not been used to receiving more than abuse since I have been mixed up in politics, and it is refreshing to know that one's efforts are appreciated." Perhaps, he added, he would return to politics "in a few years hence." When he quit the provincial Conservative party in 1910, Bennett left it in a shambles. There was no one to take responsibility for its future. Bennett remained apparently unmoved when A.C. Calderon of Edmonton wrote to the provincial secretary of the Conservative Association, complaining that the party, lacking leadership, programme and organization, was being "ridiculed" by the Liberals, who were predicting that unless some saviour could come along and breathe life into the Conservative party, another party would "come into existence" and supersede them. And this, of course, is what happened with the organization of the U.F.A.

When Bennett hinted that he might return to politics, he was telling the truth. But not to provincial politics. He had his eyes on the federal scene. He was now forty-one years of age, with a good practice and a good income. His investments, including Calgary Power, Alberta Pacific Grain, Rocky Mountain Cement, and others, had prospered, more so than some of his early flyers in New Brunswick mining stocks. He had comfortable quarters in the Palliser Hotel, a reputation as a good speaker, an industrious worker, and a cheerful host, even if he was, as he called himself, "a cold water man". And yet he felt that he had not been a success. Perhaps his future lay in the federal field.

In 1911 Bennett was elected for the federal seat of Calgary West with a majority of 2,855 votes, the sole Conservative to win a seat in Alberta. "Bonfire" Bennett, the man who could speak 220 words a minute without mispronouncing a syllable, was now ready to make his mark in the nation's capital. He wondered if he might be appointed a minister in the new Conservative government of Robert Borden; but Borden, instead, chose Senator Lougheed. Admittedly Lougheed had served the party longer than Bennett, but R.B. felt that his law partner had not put his whole weight behind the Conservative party in the election in Alberta and did not deserve preferment. Moreover, there was that young upstart, Arthur Meighen, who had been elected for Portage la Prairie, and who, as ambitious as Bennett and equally eloquent, seemed to have caught the Prime Minister's eye. Perhaps that is why only shortly after the election Bennett wrote to Max Aitken:

I am sick of it here [Ottawa]. There is little or nothing to do and what there is to do is that of a party hack or departmental clerk or messenger. I will probably leave here. There must be something more doing that counts than is at present apparent. I really cannot tell you what I think of the Government. I will do that later on when I have more adequately sized up the situation.

When in 1913, Arthur Meighen was appointed Solicitor-General, Bennett was ready if not to tell Aitken, at least to tell Borden what he thought of the Government. For some years he had regarded those two titled scalawags, Sir William Mackenzie and Sir Donald Mann, with great suspicion. It did not lessen his jealousy of Meighen that Meighen should have chosen to defend their actions, to become "the gramophone of Mackenzie and Mann" in the House of Commons. It is hardly surprising, therefore, that when Borden and Meighen asked the Canadian Parliament to approve a resolution endorsing the federal Government's willingness to make a deal with Mackenzie and Mann's Canadian Northern Railway, Bennett should take the floor of the House and hold it for four and a half hours. During those hours he revealed the long history of "political corruption, of lobbying, of degradation of parliamentary institutions and of the lowering of the morale of public life" by Mackenzie and Mann; he belaboured the Government, the Conservative Government of which he was normally the supporter, for suggesting that these two dubious creatures should be relieved of their obligations to pay their debts. When Meighen interrupted him, Bennett snapped back, "I will not be diverted from my argument by the impertinent interruptions of this young man." And he wasn't.

Bennett's speech was a magnificent effort. It displayed a mastery of facts and figures; it was free of the exaggerations of earlier efforts; it was unmarred by partisanship; and it was marked by plain speaking about the past of both the Liberal and Conservative parties. Through it ran a note of sincerity and honesty. It was a terrible arraignment of those "M and M mendicants" who had done nothing for Canada but "get down on their knees and beg." From east to west, Bennett's speech received the plaudits of the press. The Saint John *Globe* called it "one of the masterpieces of Canadian Parliamentary debating" and heaped praise on the "former Albert County man". The Calgary *Albertan* looked upon it as "the most telling assault upon railway piracy" heard in Canada "since the Dominion began." But it did not bring down the Government. Nor did Bennett want it to. He was always, as he said himself, "a firm believer in party government" and proud to be a member of the Conservative party.

But, party man or not, R.B. Bennett at this time more nearly attained the unanimous support of the people of Calgary than at any other time in his career. That, at least, is what my father believed, and I know that his view was shared by others. Certainly it was shared by those who attended the great reception which was held in the Sherman Rink on Seventeenth Avenue, in honour of Bennett, when he returned from Ottawa in the summer of 1914. The Rink was filled. On the platform were the chairman, acting Mayor M.C. Costello, T.M. Tweedie, M.L.A., Dr. Blow, George Hoadley, M.L.A., and Aldermen E.H. Crandall and W.G. Hunt. As the crowd gathered, the band of the 103rd Calgary Rifles played such classics as "The Maple Leaf Forever", "The British Grenadiers", "The Camptown Races" and "She's My Great Big Blue-Eyed Baby". On this occasion R.B. did not deliver a political speech. He sensed the non-partisan nature of his audience, and talked about his vision of Canada as a nation of fifty million people, about Canada's imperial heritage, and about Alberta's future in oil, "the great wealth which underlies the country" and which, he maintained, "must be regarded as ours in trust, for the benefit of generations yet to come, as well as ourselves." His remarks were well received, and the *Herald* observed, "There is great need for such men in Parliament and the people recognize the need, which is the reason why Mr. Bennett is unique and invincible." "Richard the Lionhearted" was how he was caricatured in the press.

It was a busy summer for R.B., that summer of 1914. He spoke at the closing of Bishop Pinkham's College, at Connaught School and at the unveiling of the South African War memorial in Central Park, designed and executed by the French Canadian sculptor Phillippe Hébert, and unveiled by the Garrison Commander, Colonel Ernest Cruikshank.

During his period in Chatham, Bennett had served in the local militia. On the outbreak of war in 1914, he volunteered for service with the P.P.C.L.I. His services were, however, refused. The Patricias were looking for men who had served in South Africa or in some other part of the Empire, and R.B. wrote to a friend:

I and men of my type can best assist the Empire by doing that work at home for which we are equipped. . .At any rate they do not want me or men like me for foreign service.

At that point Bennett threw himself into the activities of the Canadian Red Cross. In 1916 he was appointed Director General of the National Service Board. This was a political appointment. A year later, however, he parted company with the Government. When in 1917 Borden set out to form a coalition including both Liberals and Conservatives, Bennett refused to go along with him. Bennett had been opposed to party coalitions on principle during the days of Haultain, and he was not prepared to abandon the principle for the benefit of Borden. And his determination not to participate in the Union Government was reinforced by the current rumours that the Siftons were. Bennett was a good hater, and the Siftons, of all people, he disliked the most. Whatever his reasons, R.B. did not choose to run in the wartime election of 1917. Neither did he seek a seat in the Senate; certainly not in the "dear old Senate" which he once described as "that body of manufacturers and millionaires sent there by Laurier to be his mouthpiece." Not until the coalition was at an end in 1921, when his old adversary Arthur Meighen, who had succeeded Borden as Prime Minister, offered him the Ministry of Justice in his caretaker cabinet, did Bennett agree to return to politics.

R.B.'s acceptance of public office in 1921 meant that he had once again, to offer himself to the electorate of Calgary West. The election of December 1921 has sometimes been called the fountain-pen election, because a number of ballots were marked with coloured pencils, while still others were marked with a I instead of an x, simply because Alberta had adopted the system of proportional representation and voters forgot that in federal elections the traditional system of marking ballots had still to be used. All ballots thus marked were rejected. Had they been counted, Bennett would have emerged with a narrow majority. As it was, he lost his seat to Joseph Shaw, a man of whom little was ever heard afterwards in political circles. Bennett knew that the vote would be a close one, a battle virtually between the Conservative and Labour candidates, but he had never believed that the voters of his adopted city would fail to elect him. My father, who worked on Mr. Bennett's behalf in this election, told me afterwards that Mr. Bennett's defeat was due largely to his disposition to take Calgary West for granted. He spent too much time speaking on behalf of other Conservative candidates in the West, all the while neglecting his own campaign in Calgary. After all, my father maintained, the local machine could only do so much. The candidate's presence was needed in the constituency. And this was particularly true in those days before television, when door to door campaigning was the most effective way of winning votes. I still recall my shock at Bennett's defeat.

I believe I would have been even more apprehensive about the future of Canada had I known that in his humiliation, Mr. Bennett was thinking in terms of leaving Calgary and taking up residence in Great Britain. However, he changed his mind when he learned, while in England, that Senator Lougheed had dissolved the legal partnership between himself and Bennett. Full of fire and determination, Bennett hurried back to Canada. He looked upon Lougheed's action as a stab in the back; and he was never a man to forget an injury or forgive an attack upon his honour. He organized his own firm, Bennett, Hannah, and San-ford, and refused to be reconciled with Lougheed. The dispute between the two men dragged its intermittent way through the courts until the old Senator died, three years later, in 1925.

Meanwhile, since he had chosen to remain in Calgary, Bennett made up for any sins of omission in the electoral campaign of 1921. During the next four years he mended every political fence. He would never ignore his constituency again. Not a single Conservative had been elected in the prairie provinces in 1921, and Bennett was determined to see to it that when the next election was called, he at least would be sent back to Ottawa. He therefore never lost an opportunity to appear in public; never turned down a request to speak, even if only to schoolboys and to parent-teacher groups. He presented scholarships and took an active part in the life of the city. In short, he did everything he could to recover the confidence and affection Calgarians had afforded him in pre-war days. Hence, when he offered himself again for election in 1925, he emerged victorious with a majority exceeding four thousand votes. It is said that old Senator Lougheed on his death bed, when he heard the news of Bennett's success, said, "Isn't that fine." He at least could overlook their differences in a party victory. Bennett was the leading Conservative in Alberta, and Lougheed was a Conservative to the end.

In 1926 Bennett won again—this was the election in which I played my small and insignificant role. In the same election Arthur Meighen lost his seat in Portage la Prairie and never again sat in the House of Commons. Bennett was clearly the strong man in the party, and when the Conservative Convention met in Winnipeg in October, 1927, Richard Bedford Bennett of New Brunswick and Alberta was chosen to head the federal Conservative party. Three years later he was again elected for Calgary West; this time with a majority of 8,072 votes. His Conservative running mate, Dr. George D. Stanley, was also elected in Calgary East. The success of the Conservatives in Calgary in 1930 was repeated elsewhere in Canada, and on August 7, just a month after his sixtieth birthday, Bennett became Prime Minister of Canada.

On the 22nd, R.B. was back in Calgary. The warmth and the volume of acclaim accorded him was only equalled by that which he had received sixteen years before, in 1914. Once again he was honoured at a dinner, this time in the Palliser Hotel. Covers were laid for 650 in the main dining room and within five minutes of the opening of the doors, the room was packed to capacity. After dinner had been served and consumed, a number of tables were taken out and room was made for an additional 150 people. Decorating the head table was a miniature oil derrick bearing the words "Canada First".

Of course R.B. made a political speech; I think he could be pardoned for that. After all, it was a political celebration. But he was visibly moved by his reception and spoke too in a reminiscent vein of his thirty-three years as a resident of Calgary.

III

With the exception of the dinner in Oxford in 1930, to which I have alluded, I did not see Mr. Bennett until after I returned to Canada in 1936. But I heard a great deal about him. Normally the English press contained little news of Canada; but after the Ottawa Conference of 1932 the English papers were filled with attacks on the Canadian Prime Minister. Lord Beaverbrook attributed this unhealthy "hate-Bennett" campaign to the malevolence of the British Prime Minister, Stanley Baldwin, who, he claimed, deliberately misrepresented what had happened at the Ottawa Conference in 1932 to cover his own reluctance to negotiate honestly with the Canadians. That Baldwin was not above distorting the truth is now well known. Unfortunately for Bennett, Canadians accepted Baldwin at his word and promptly blamed their own Prime Minister for the failure of the Conference. The fact is, if Beaverbrook is telling the truth, Bennett approached the Conference honestly believing in the possibility of making the British Empire a viable economic unit. Under Bennett, wrote Beaverbrook, "Canada appeared to be emerging as the heart and spirit of a United Commonwealth. The march of the Empire was westward and Ottawa the new capital of the new movement." But the British, however, could not bring themselves to accept Bennett's leadership or to become members of a new British Empire. Whoever was responsible, Bennett or Baldwin, one thing is clear, and that is that after the failure of the Ottawa Conference of 1932, American influence in Canadian economic affairs began to grow at an ever-accelerating rate up to the present day.

In the summer of 1934 I spent several months in Canada. Part of that time was spent on my aunt's farm in southern Saskatchewan. There I heard Bennett denounced as heartless, arrogant, and dictatorial; I heard all the ills of the country, the unemployment, the drought, the dried-up sloughs, the stunted stalks of grain, the grasshoppers, all blamed upon the Prime Minister; I rode in a Bennett Buggy and in the local Saskatchewan version known as the Anderson cart. While in Calgary I heard Aberhart and about Aberhart. Some of my friends expressed the hope that I might come back to Alberta and resume my study of law and go into local politics. But my purpose in 1934 was to look for historical material for my doctoral thesis on Louis Riel. I had no intention of going into Canadian politics. I wanted to become a professor of Canadian history.

I did, however, see Mr. Bennett several times in Sackville after I received my appointment to Mount Allison in 1936. I remember when, at Camp Sussex in 1938, he presented new colours to the New Brunswick Rangers, the local militia unit in which I had accepted a commission. I remember, too, when I first heard that Mr. Bennett was going to leave Canada and go to live in England. The news came as a great shock to me. Because I was a nationalist, I had always chosen to see Bennett in a nationalist light, the man of "Canada First." I was not blind to his imperialist inclinations, but I never thought that they were strong enough to pull him away from his native land. I never thought they were strong enough to pull him away from Calgary. I agreed with the columnist who, when Bennett was in Calgary for a brief visit in April, 1937, wrote in the *Albertan*, a newspaper never sympathetic to R.B.,

Your coming makes us feel better for we recall that you made a success of it in this western country where you came as a stranger and the circumstances and outlook were far less hopeful than they are now. We don't expect you to talk politics to us now when there is no election going on. At the moment none of us are fussed up at all over such things. Take a stroll out among us and let yourself be greeted by those of all walks of life and shades of thought, because we all like you, even if you make us cross now and again. You are not only of Calgary, but in the eyes of those in all parts of the world you are Calgary itself, the very essence of it. There wouldn't be any Calgary, as we oldtimers remember it, if there wasn't any you.

For years I had heard people accusing Bennett of being no more than a transient, pausing in the West while treading the road to his true home in England; but he had not left Calgary. I did not think he would go this time. I realized, after the Stevens rebellion within the Conservative ranks and the Conservative defeat in 1935 (Calgary West, be it said to its honour, did not abandon Bennett), that in all probability there would be a change of leadership in the party. The Conservatives have always been noted for dumping their chiefs. However, I saw Bennett following in the footsteps of Sir Robert Borden, retiring from politics, playing the role of an elder statesman. Partisan though he had been during his political career, Borden had succeeded in rising above political partisanship after 1920; he had become the sage, the oracle, the voice of experience and wisdom in public affairs. Could not Bennett do the same? When you understand my feelings towards R.B. Bennett you will, I am sure, appreciate why I deeply regretted his decision to leave Canada; why I was disappointed at the bitterness and petulance which accompanied his going. It was hard to believe that he would brush aside the tributes which he received from various gatherings across Canada from friends and former political foes alike, with the sour remark, "I am quite certain that the politicians opposed to me would not have taken part in these gatherings, had they not assumed that I was permanently taking up my residence in England." Because Canada did not appreciate him he would go elsewhere. I felt it was unworthy of him. I felt let down by the man whose courage, ability and high idealism I had always admired.

In 1939 Bennett sailed for England. He had bought a property called Juniper Hill. It was close by Cherkley, Lord Beaverbrook's estate, not far from the village of Mickleham in the county of Surrey. When war broke out in 1939, Bennett became chairman of the London Advisory Committee of the Canadian Red Cross; he looked into the matter of employing interned enemy aliens in Beaverbrook's Ministry of Aircraft Production, and made a speaking tour across Canada. In 1941 he received a peerage, a viscountcy, and took his seat in the House of Lords. He had, for some years, been the honorary colonel of the Calgary Highlanders, but when the regiment arrived overseas, the Commanding Officer, a former political opponent of Bennett, made no effort to get in touch with him. Not until there was a change of command was Bennett given a personal invitation to visit his Regiment. This he did in 1944, inspecting the Highlanders at Bognor Regis shortly before they crossed the Channel to fight in Normandy. But by this time the old man had lost interest in the Highlanders and was disposed to regard his belated invitation with mild cynicism. He clearly enjoyed himself much more when he was asked to dine with the North Shore Regiment from New Brunswick, when they were on their way home after hostilities had ceased. He made a good speech, displaying some of the old fire that had been his political trademark in earlier days. The story is told that after the regimental chaplain, Mgr. Hickey, had sung "Molly Malone," Bennett, catching the spirit of the evening, turned to the troops and asked, "What will you have next?" With a shout, they replied, "More beer!" Bennett, the teetotaller, the "cold water man", amidst even louder shouts of approval, cried out to the waiters, "More beer!"

I never did see in him that mood, for such occasions were rare for him in those war years. But I did see him once at Canadian Military Headquarters in London in 1944. He was looking tired and disillusioned. He reminded me of a man whose dreams had lost their magic and whose success had turned to failure. And failure is life's bitterest experience. We talked briefly about Sackville and Calgary, and about the Stiles-Bennett Chair of History at Mount Allison. He offered me a few words of encouragement and an invitation to visit him at Juniper Hill. And then it was all over. I had a hundred questions I should have liked to ask him but I did not do so. I was not aware of the fact that he was suffering from diabetes; but I thought he looked like a sick man. I suspected, too, that he was grieving over the death in Normandy of his brother Ronald's two sons from Sackville.

Today when I think of Mr. Bennett, or rather of Viscount Bennett of Hopewell, Calgary and Mickleham, I prefer to recall a great service which he rendered me in 1937. When *The Birth of Western Canada* appeared in 1936, I sent Mr. Bennett a copy. It was my first-born effort and I was very proud of it. I wanted everybody to read it. Then, to my great distress, I received a letter from my publishers, Longmans Green of London, telling me that a firm of lawyers had taken out an injunction against the book on the grounds that it had contravened copyright of title. The lawyers claimed that they held the copyright, and therefore the publishers and author should assign them a certain percentage of the royalties. I knew of no other book with the same title, neither did anybody else. But I had no idea what to do. Finally I decided to go to Ottawa and consult Mr. Bennett. He was a lawyer of distinction; he knew the book; he would advise me. He received me in his office—he was then Leader of the Opposition—and I told him the story and turned over to him the letter I had received from Longmans Green. He replied that he would look into the matter and that he would call me when he had collected the necessary opinions. A week or ten days later, I was asked to come to his office. When I was ushered into the inner sanctum he threw a bundle of papers down on his desk and said, "You can read these over at your leisure. They are the opinions of the law officers of the Crown. Briefly their advice to you is to defy the injunction. If the firm in Edmonton chooses to take you to court, institute a countersuit for damages for loss of sales during the period of the injunction. They haven't a leg to stand on. It is all sheer bluff. You are fortunate that you did not sign anything away to them." I read the opinions and sent copies of the documents to London, instructing the publishers to follow Mr. Bennett's advice. The book then reappeared in the bookstores. And it is still there. It has been reprinted several times in paper back editions. When any one of you buys a copy of *The Birth of Western Canada*, just remember that it was Richard Bedford Bennett who made it possible for you to obtain it.

THE *BOND OF BROTHERHOOD* AND CALGARY WORKINGMEN

Henry C. Klassen

F ew aspects of frontier Calgary have been as much over-looked in historical writings as the condition of the working class. Unlike businessmen and politicians, the workers seldom excited the imagination of historians. Virtually untouched, Calgary's working class belongs to the category of forgotten history. Yet the working people were an essential part of the city's life, and they deserve to be rediscovered.

The working class in frontier Calgary is defined here as those men and women who shared the fundamental experience of selling their labour to employers. In their search for work and their preoccupation with job security and a living wage, the workers found themselves drawn together in a community of interests. It is misleading, however, to see these workers as a homogeneous social class. They were often conscious of distinctions among themselves in terms of traditions, outlook, skills, aspirations, and status. The story of the working class in frontier Calgary is thus a study of complex relationships shaped by a sense of identity as well as by different attitudes.

Though both men and women in the work force require attention, the comment in these pages is restricted to workingmen. Concentrating on the workingmen in the years 1903–04, as this discussion does, seems appropriate because of the conspicuous place they were then beginning to occupy in Calgary society. With the rapid commercial and industrial growth of the city, which by 1904 had a population of well over nine thousand, they were entering the labour force in ever larger numbers. They also made their presence felt by organizing unions. By the beginning of 1903, the membership in the various trade union organizations affiliated with the Calgary Trades and Labor Council had risen to about 1500.[1] The prominence of workers in these years can, above all, be attributed to strike activity and the appearance of a weekly labour newspaper, the *Bond of Brotherhood*. An examination of the *Bond*, besides providing hints of the complexity of the labour scene, reveals the radical element in the working class. But it has little to say about the conservative labour element. A look at the *Bond* alone would obviously be inadequate in attempting to understand the world of labour. Yet, when read together with other available materials, it sheds considerable light on the thinking of workingmen.

Lasting from May, 1903 to June, 1904, the *Bond* prided itself in being the first and only labour newspaper in the Northwest Territories. Its founders and editors were James Edward Worsley, a metal worker, and Alfred Palmer, a CPR clerk. Worsley, the senior editor, was the guiding spirit behind the paper. Born in Manchester, England, in 1867, he was the son of a platelayer. Leaving Manchester in 1897, he migrated to Winnipeg and in 1899 moved to Calgary. Worsley, like many other immigrant workingmen from Britain, brought with him to Calgary his trade union experience. Shortly after his arrival, he became an active member of the Allied Metal Workers' Union in the city. In 1901, as president of the Metal Workers' Union, he took a leading part in organizing the Calgary Trades and Labor Council. At Calgary's first Labor Day celebration on September 2 of that same year, Worsley, a good speaker, made an effective speech on the burdens of the workingman.[2] His zeal for improving the conditions of workingmen, coupled with his organizational and speaking ability, made him a natural candidate for the top position in the city's labour movement, and in January, 1903, he was elected president of the Trades and Labor Council. Several months later, in association with Alfred Palmer, Worsley brought out the first issue of the *Bond*. Endorsed by the Trades and Labor Council, the paper set itself the goal of educating and organizing workers. The main factors contributing to its demise in mid-1904 were lack of funds, insufficient subscribers, opposition from employers, and the departure of James Worsley for England. Although he would return to Calgary in 1920 and again become prominent in the local labour movement, his departure in 1904 left a large gap in the ranks of organized labour.

In spite of the short career of the *Bond*, it made an important impression upon labour circles in Calgary. Its influence among workingmen was at once unifying and devisive. As an agent of labour unity, it fostered the growth of existing trade union organizations including carpenters, railway carmen, machinists, retail clerks, leatherworkers, and general labourers. In addition, Worsley, as editor of the *Bond* and president of the Trades and Labor

Council, was instrumental in 1903 in organizing several new unions like the stationary engineers and the stone-cutters. Similarly,
the conciliatory policy of the *Bond* during the prolonged teamsters' and carpenters' strikes in the summer of 1903 tended to
have a unifying influence on labour.[3] Coming out firmly against
strikes and revolutions as a means of settling industrial disputes,
it advocated the establisment of a permanent conciliation board
in the city, representing both union workers and employers and
acting under the authority of the Department of Labour in
Ottawa.[4]

The *Bond's* emphasis on socialism, however, proved to be a
source of disunity within the labour community. Worsley and
Palmer made no secret of their socialism and of the fact that their
paper was a socialist labour journal. Believing socialism to be
"the only hope of the worker," they expressed their admiration
for the teachings of Karl Marx and the principles of the International Socialist Party of America and the Socialist Party of
Germany.[5]

While such a statement struck a sympathetic chord in a number of Calgary's workers, it alienated others and made the *Bond*
suspect. Indeed, the *Bond's* attempt to radicalize the trade union
movement through the promotion of socialism met with a good
deal of resistance. Many conservative workingmen could identify
more easily with William M. Davidson, Liberal editor of the
Albertan and a friend of labour, and they looked to Liberals like
him to advance their interests.[6] Moreover, almost all the unions
in the city were affiliated with the conservative American Feder-
ation of Labour. The socialists nonetheless continued to maintain
a significant following in the Calgary labour community.

Workingmen were more inclined to be of one mind when it
came to municipal politics. Labour had come forward with an
aldermanic candidate for the first time in the civic election of December, 1902.[7] Richard A. Brocklebank, a native of Bruce
County, Ontario, and a carpenter representing labour in Ward
Three in south-east Calgary, had been elected to city council by
acclamation. He was the sole labour alderman in the nine-
member council of 1903. His aims were municipal ownership of
utilities, the abolition of the property qualification of 1,000 dollars for civic elective office, and manhood suffrage. Under the existing system, the property qualifications of voters excluded numerous workingmen from the vote. While the electoral laws thus
severely handicapped the working class, they strengthened the

hands of the larger property holders by permitting them to vote for aldermen in all the wards in which they held property.

The disproportionate electoral power of property was evident in the civic election of December, 1903. Although labour with the support of the *Bond* again united behind Brocklebank, he was defeated by the combined forces of property owners and employers who had not yet forgotten the part he had played in the recent carpenters' strike through his role as president of the United Brotherhood of Carpenters and Joiners.[8] Fortunately for labour, the relations between employers and workers gradually improved. In the following municipal election Brocklebank, strongly backed by labour, headed the aldermanic poll in Ward Three and once more took his place in city council.[9]

Under the stress of civic elections and strikes, the *Bond* was quick to remind Calgary workingmen that they were engaged in a bitter class struggle against capitalists. "The one great lesson which organized labor learned here in 1903," wrote the *Bond*, "was the fact of the class war existing here as naked and unashamed as in the older cities most of us have recently left."[10] In the eyes of the *Bond*, the solution to labour's problems was political action—the organization of a labour party in Calgary in order to place a candidate in the field during the federal election of 1904. Nothing came of the proposal, though a feeble effort was made to collect funds to run Richard Brocklebank as a labour candidate on a platform adopted by the Calgary Trades and Labor Council.[11] Workingmen at this time appeared to lack the political vigour necessary to bring forward a labour candidate. Equally, class warfare, as the *Bond* saw it, seemed to be a minority idea in Calgary. Many workers were probably familiar with the concept of class conflict, but there is little evidence to suggest that the whole working-class community was bound together by the notion of class struggle.

Working-class awareness, however, was another matter. Calgary workingmen in these years displayed a certain degree of class consciousness in their popular labour day parades and celebrations, their trade union activities, their preference for union-produced goods with a union label, and their support of a labor newspaper.[12] The existence of all these working-class institutions gave rise to a feeling of class among workingmen. The strike activities of 1903 had a similar unifying effect. Yet these institutions and activities did not embrace the entire community of workers. Other conditions, moreover, actually tended to discourage the development of working-class awareness. Not all the employers exploited their employees. Frequently, employees thought of their employers more as individual human beings than as representatives of the middle-class. In the smaller establishmens like bakeries, foundries, and blacksmith shops, employers and employees usually worked side by side at the same tasks. Employers in Calgary's small industrial comunity, unlike those in the larger eastern Canadian industrial centres, often took a personal interest in the problems of their employees. Many workingmen, having left the United Kingdom in order to escape the rigid class system, shook off much of their class feeling in the freer atmospher of Calgary society. Thus, despite the appearance of class distinctions in frontier Calgary, the youthfulness of the city and the numerous opportunities to get ahead led to a less rigidly defined class structure.

The workingmen of frontier Calgary, with their various problems, convictions and aspirations, are worth remembering. They contributed not only to the preservation and collapse of old values and traditions but also to the building of a new social milieu. They disagreed as much among themselves as they did with their employers. In their ranks there were agitators, thinkers, and men who simply minded their own business. And in their own day they were much more visible than contemporary publications would lead us to believe.

NOTES

Birth To Boom To Bust:
Building In Calgary, 1875–1914
J.P. Dickin McGinnis

1 Harold Kalman, "Recent Literature on the History of Canadian Architecture," *Society of Architectural Historians Journal*, XXXI (December 1972), 315.

2 For a discussion of various phases of Canadian architecture, see Alan Gowans, *Looking at Architecture in Canada* (Toronto: Oxford University Press, 1958).

3 K.E. Liddell, *This is Alberta* (Toronto: Ryerson, 1952), p. 83.

4 Kenneth Coppock, "Calgary and the Company," *The Beaver* (March 1941), 43.

5 Grant MacEwan, *Calgary Cavalcade, from Fort to Fortune* (Edmonton: Institute of Applied Art, 1958), pp. 11–3.

6 T.T. Johns, "History of Calgary" in the Morning *Albertan, The 100,-000 Manufacturing, Building and Wholesale Book Edition* (Calgary: *Albertan*, 1914), p. 6.

7 See map of the Old North Trail in Richard P. Baine, *Calgary, an Urban Study* (Toronto: Clarke Irwin, 1973), pp. 16–7.

8 From 1909 Anniversary *Albertan*, p. 4. Quoted in Lawrence H. Bussard, "Early History of Calgary" (unpublished M.A. Thesis, University of Alberta, 1935), p. 22.

9 Bussard, p. 23.

10 From *Herald*, 1923 Anniversary Edition, p. 5. Quoted in Bussard, p. 24.

11 MacEwan, p. 17.

12 Hugh A. Dempsey, "Calgary's First Christmas," Calgary *Herald*, 22 December 1956.

13 Bussard, pp. 25–6.

14 James G. MacGregor, *A History of Alberta* (Edmonton: Hurtig Pub., 1972), pp. 115–6.

15 Robert J.C. Stead, "Calgary—City of the Foothills," *Canadian Geographical Journal*, XXXVI (1948), 157.

16 MacEwan, pp. 29–33.

17 Leishman McNeill, *Tales of the Old Town, Calgary, 1875–1950* (Calgary: *Herald*, 1951), p. 10.

18 Bussard, pp. 40–1.

19 Quoted in Calgary *Herald*, 28 September 1913. Unfortunately his name is not given.

20 Bussard, pp. 52–63.

21 *Ibid.*, p. 68.

22 Maxwell L. Foran, "The Calgary Town Council, 1884–1895: A Study of Local Government in a Frontier Environment" (unpublished M.A. Thesis, The University of Calgary, 1970), pp. 10–11.

23 Douglas Coats, "The Economy of Calgary, 1884–1895" (seminar paper, The University of Calgary, 4 April 1974), p. 5.

24 For all pre-1904 street names see Henderson's City Directory (Calgary), 1908 or Calgary *Albertan, Sketches of Early Calgary* (1963), no. 1.

25 Bussard, pp. 63–7. On Stephen (Eighth) Avenue and Osler (First) Street E.

26 J. Brown, "Calgary—the City of the Foothills," *The Beaver* (April 1922), 2.

27 Quoted in Alfred H. MacKay, *History of Calgary* (Weekly *Herald*, 8 July 1909), p. 8.

28 Bussard, pp. 67–8, 85–7.

29 *Ibid.*, pp. 72–5.

30 *Ibid.*, p. 84.

31 Calgary Fire Department, Fire Prevention Bureau, "History of the Calgary Fire Department, 1885–1966," p. 1. Pamphlet printed by fire department.

32 McNeill, p. 25.

33 MacEwan, pp. 91–3; Johns, p. 8; Bussard, pp. 117–9.

34 Calgary *Herald*, 23 January 1973. S. Arnold Wark, *The City of Calgary Yearbook* (1919), p. 97.

35 J.G. Fitzgerald, *Calgary Business Directory*, 1885 (Calgary *Herald* Printing and Publishing Co., 1885).

36 Thomas S. Barwis, *Calgary, Alberta, and the Canadian North-West. Valuable information for intending settlers* (n.p.: n.p., 1884?).

37 George B. Elliott, *Calgary, Alberta, her industries and resources*, compiled and ed. by Burns and Elliott (Calgary: n.p. 1885).

38 Glenbow Archives. J.H. Walker, "Calgary District Observations, 1889–91."

39 Canadian Pacific Railway, *Harvest News, 1890, The Calgary District, Alberta* (Winnipeg: The Company, 1890).

40 *Calgary route to the Klondyke gold fields; description of routes; miners' and prospectors' outfitting guide* (Calgary: n.p., 1898).

41 A.O. MacRae, *History of the Province of Alberta*, Vol. 1 (n.p.: Western Canadian History Co., 1912), p. 428.

42 MacEwan, pp. 65–9.

43 Bussard, pp. 41, 52, 58. Additional information is available on the mill in J. Walker, Bow River Saw and Planing Mills. Letterbook of Lumber and Contracted Business, Calgary, 1885–1903. Glenbow Archives.

44 Foran, p. 33; Bussard, p. 70.

45 Parker Kent, "The Calgary Story," Calgary *Herald*, n.d. See also T. Strom, Reminiscences Re: Eau Claire Lumber Company. Glenbow Archives. Also, Theodore Strom, "With the Eau Claire in Calgary," *Alberta Historical Review*, XII (1946), 1–11.

46 Richard Cunniffe, *Calgary—in Sandstone* (Calgary: Historical Society of Alberta, 1969), p. 3. M.B. Venini Byrne, *From the Buffalo to the Cross. A History of the Roman Catholic Diocese of Calgary* (Calgary: Calgary Archives and Historical Pub., 1973), p. 68.

47 Cunniffe, p. 6.

48 *Ibid.*, pp. 6–7. *Albertan, The 100,-000 Manufacturing. . .Edition*, p. 51.

49 *Calgary, the Denver of Canada* (Calgary: Calgary *Herald* Printing, 1895), p. 5.

50 Cunniffe, pp. 3–6.

51 Including the old Victoria Block (not to be confused with the also defunct Victoria Apartments housed in the David Block) and an old building last used as a Provincial Treasury Branch on the southeast corner of Eighth Avenue and Centre Street, both of which were considered to be architecturally important by the Canadian Inventory of Historic Building.

52 P. Jules le Chevalier, *Esquisse sur l'origine et les premiers développements de Calgary (1873–1913)*

(Calgary: la Paroisse Saint-Famille, 1936), pp. 79–80.
53 *Herald*, n.d., 1950.
54 For example, *Herald*, 17 January 1900.
55 *Herald*, 12 February 1895.
56 *Municipal Manual* (1914), pp. 108–9.
57 Cunniffe, p. 5.
58 Calgary Board of Trade, *The Famous Calgary District: The Land of Golden Wheat, Fat Steers, Industrial Opportunities and Unequalled Climate* (1906), p. 49.
59 A valuable source for the lifestyle of laborers is John Gillespie, Diary of a Calgary Stonemason, 1893–1915. Glenbow Archives. It is interesting to note that the list of workers set in the cornerstone of City Hall lists, out of fifty-three men, only six with obviously non-British names. By far the majority were Scots. City Clerk's records.
60 As advertised in Henderson's City Directories, 1907–15; *Albertan, The 100,000 Manufacturing...Edition*, p. 55, 56, 116, 139; "Why go to Canada," supplement to Calgary Daily *Herald* (June 1910).
61 For example, the Customs Building on Eleventh Avenue and First Street E.
62 Calgary Board of Trade, *The Famous Calgary District*, p. 4; Henderson's City Directories; Calgary City Council, *Calgary, the land of plenty* (Calgary: City Council and Calgary Board of Trade, 1907), p. 2; Royal Architectural Institute of Canada, *Souvenir, sixth annual assembly, Calgary, Alberta, Sept. 15 and 16, 1913* (Calgary: Maurice J. Connolly, 1913), pp. 19 and 31.
63 Much of the architectural information used in this paper was obtained by personal interview

and correspondence. These are examples.
64 *Sessional Papers of Canada, 1914*, Chief Architect's Reports, Report of Minister of Public Works for fiscal period ended 31 March 1913. Paper 19, Vol. XLIX, No. 13, p. 51.
65 J.A. Clark in "Why go to Canada," n.p.
66 *Albertan*, 7 December 1919.
67 *Architects and Builders Edition*, p. 67. Cited by Lorne E. Render, Script talk on Calgary architecture, 1884–1915, Glenbow lecture series (Winter 1968), p. 15. Glenbow Archives.
68 Ernest L. Richardson, *Calgary, Alberta, commercial metropolis of Western Canada* (Calgary: Hammond Litho., 1907).
69 *Calgary and sunny Alberta illustrated: the official souvenir of the Dominion Exhibition, Calgary, Alberta, June 29th to July 9th, 1908* (Calgary: *Herald* Job Printing Co., 1908).
70 *One Thousand Facts about Calgary*, compiled and published by the Hundred Thousand Club, Calgary (Calgary: *Herald*-Western Printing Co., 1909).
71 *Census of Canada, 1911*, Vol. 1, p. 554
72 *Ibid.*, Vol. 1, p. 531.
73 *Ibid.*, Vol. 6, pp. 342–3. It must be remembered that there was little automation in building at this point. Mortar and concrete were mixed by hand and all hauling and hoisting done by horses.
74 *Albertan*, 28 February 1911.
75 S.L. Bensusan, *Twentieth Century Cities: Calgary* (London: Hodder and Stoughton, n.d.), pp. 42–7.
76 P.J. Smith, "Change in a Youthful City: the case of Calgary, Alberta," *Geography*, LVI (January 1971), 7–10.
77 P.J. Smith, "Calgary: A Study in Urban Pattern," *Economic*

Geography, XXXVIII (October 1962), 319.

78 For the latter see International Realty Ltd., *Bowness, Calgary's Finest Residential Sub-Division* (Calgary: n.p. 1912).

79 "Why go to Canada," n.p.

80 *Albertan* Anniversary Number, 28 February 1911.

81 *Calgary, the City Phenomenal* (Calgary: n.p., 1912), p. 16.

82 Rupert Brooke, *Letters from America* (London: Sidgewick and Jackson, 1916), p. 126. Although not as nice as those of new Zealand.

83 Only one survived to see the more sober days of the Depression by which time the era of its purchase was referred to bemusedly as the "Spendthrift Boom Days." *Albertan*, 21 September, 1935.

84 The Mawson plan represents in printed form the quintessence of the term "picturesque eclecticism" in architecture. Almost any architectural style or gimmick that could be borrowed, was borrowed. T.H. Mawson and Sons, *The City of Calgary, Past, Present and Future* (City Planning Experts. London, Lancaster, Vancouver and New York: City Planning Commission of Calgary, 1914).

85 "Building Code of Calgary Most Advanced of Western Cities," *Albertan* Anniversary Edition, 28 February 1913.

86 *The City of Calgary, the commercial capital of sunny Alberta* (Calgary: Linton Bros., 1911).

87 *Calgary, sunny Alberta, the industrial prodigy of the great West; her phenomenal progress, thriving industries and wonderful resources* (Calgary: Jennings Pub. Co., 1911).

88 Adam Shortt and A.G. Doughty, eds., *Canada and Its Provinces: The Prairie Provinces*, Vol. XX (Toronto: Glasgow, Brock and Co., 1914), p. 403.

89 *The Story of Calgary—Alberta—Canada; progress—opportunities* (Calgary: Western Standard Pub. Co., 1914).

90 For, of all things, a federal prison farm. Fred Kennedy, "Events Moved Fast Locally in 1913 Boom," *Herald*, 15 February 1936.

91 *Albertan* Anniversay Edition, 28 February 1913.

92 Cunniffe, p. 6.

93 Calgary Board of Trade, *Calgary, Alberta, Canada's most progressive city; presenting interesting information regarding Calgary, the industrial metropolis of Alberta* (Calgary: n.p., 1918).

94 MacEwan, p. 220.

95 Figure arrived at by comparing Henderson's City Directories for 1915 and 1973. Also *Municipal Manual, 1914*, pp. 64–8.

96 At 1216 Thirteenth Avenue S.W. according to L.P.V. Johnson and Ola MacNutt, *Aberhart of Alberta* (Edmonton: Institute of Applied Arts, 1970), p. 34.

"Kootsisaw": Calgary Before The Canadians
B.O.K. Reeves

1 James G. MacGregor, *A History of Alberta* (Edmonton: Hurtig, 1972); Irene M. Spry, *Papers of the Palliser Expedition* (Toronto: Champlain Society, 1968).

2 H.M. Wormington and R.G. Forbis, *An Introduction to the Archaeology of Alberta, Canada* (Denver Museum of Natural History, Denver, 1965).

3 J.L. Rogers and M. McIntyre, Archaeological Investigations in the Proposed Bow-Highwood Reservoir Area: Preliminary Report, 1972. Manuscript on file, National Museum of Man, Ottawa.

4 J.L. Rogers, Archaeological Investigations in the Calgary Area: Preliminary Report, 1971. Manuscript on file with the author.

5 M. Wilson, "Fossil Bison and Artifacts, *Plain Anthropologist*, 19 (63) 1974, 34–45.

6 H.M. Wormington and R.G. Forbis, *An Introduction to the Archaeology of Alberta, Canada* (Denver Museum of National History, Denver, 1965).

7 A.M. Stalker, "Geology and Age of an Early Man Site at Taber, Alberta," *American Antiquity*, 34 (4) 1969, 425–428.

Briscbois: Calgary's Forgotten Founder
Hugh A. Dempsey

1 Minnedosa *Tribune*, Feb. 13, 1890.

2 Letter, J.H. Mousseau to John A. Macdonald, Dec. 11, 1879. Macdonald Papers, Vol. 360, No. 168187. Public Archives of Canada.

3 RCMP Papers, RG–18, A–1, Vol. 3, file 48A. Public Archives of Canada.

4 R.B. Nevitt, *A Winter at Fort Macleod* (McClelland & Stewart West, 1974), 80–81.

5 Cecil Denny, *The Riders of the Plains* (Herald Press, 1905), 59.

6 "Return to order. Expenditure for North-West Mounted Police, 1876–7–8; and of all Amounts Paid to I.G. Baker & Co."

Sessional Papers of Canada, No. 188, 1879, p. 70.

7 Letter, Leslie Wood to Richard Hardisty, Dec. 15, 1875. Hardisty Papers, Glenbow Archives.

8 RCMP Papers, RG–18, A–1, Vol. R–4. No copy of the actual charges appear to have survived.

9 *Ibid.*

10 Denny, *op. cit.*, 55.

11 Letter, Wood to Hardisty, *op. cit.*

12 Letter from E.A. Brisebois, Dec. 20, 1875. Macdonald papers, Vol. 324, p. 301. Public Archives of Canada.

13 Letter, in French, from Bishop Grandin to Father Albert Lacombe, Jan. 8, 1877. Testement de Mgr. V. Grandin, Vol. 1, Ob-

late Papers, Provincial Archives of Alberta.

14 John D. Higinbotham Papers, F–20, Vol. A, 62. Glenbow Archives.

15 Letter, John Bunn to Richard Hardisty, Jan. 13, 1876. Hardisty Papers, No. 765. Glenbow Archives.

16 Letter, A.G. Irvine to Minister of Justice, Feb. 19, 1876. Copy to Glenbow Archives.

17 "The Naming of Calgary" by G.F.G. Stanley. *Alberta History*, Summer 1975.

18 Letter, A.G. Irvine to Deputy Minister of Justice, April 25, 1876. Fort Macleod correspondence book, RCMP Museum, Regina.

19 Letter, E.A. Brisebois to A.G. Irvine, Jan. 9, 1876. Fort Macleod correspondence book, *op. cit.*

20 Letter, Irvine to Deputy Minister

of Justice, *op. cit.*

21 L.F.R. Masson to Macdonald, Oct. 30, 1880. Macdonald Papers, Vol. 228, No. 98727. Public Archives of Canada.

22 Brisebois to L.F.R. Masson, in French, Oct. 25, 1880. Macdonald Papers, Vol. 228, No. 98720. Public Archives of Canada.

23 D.O. Boudreau to Macdonald, June 20, 1879. Macdonald Papers, Vol. 359, No. 166051. Public Archives of Canada.

24 Brisebois to Masson, *op. cit.*

25 Minnedosa *Tribune*, Dec. 23, 1887.

26 *Idem*, April 4, 1889.

27 *Idem*, Sept. 19, 1889

28 *Idem*, May 8, 1885.

29 *Idem*, July 3, 1885.

30 *Idem*, Nov. 14, 1889.

31 Montreal *Gazette*, March 10, 1890.

Spatial Aspects Of The Cattle Kingdom: The First Decade, 1882–1892
Simon Evans

1 Paul F. Sharp, *Whoop-Up Country: The Canadian American West, 1865–1885* (Minneapolis: University of Minnesota Press, 1955), p. 228.

2 H.S. Arkell, "The Cattle Industry," in Henry J. Boam (ed.) *Twentieth Century Impressions of Canada* (Montreal: Sells Limited, 1914), pp. 247–54.

3 Gerald L. Berry, *The Whoop-Up Trail* (Edmonton: Allied Arts Products Ltd., 1953), p. 95; Reverend James MacGregor, "Lord Lorne in Alberta," *Alberta Historical Review*, 12 (Spring, 1964), p. 9; and Canada, *Sessional Papers*, 3

Part 2, Vol. 14, 1881, p. 24.

4 Sharp, *Whoop-Up Country*, p. 223.

5 Order in Council, May 20, 1881, *Department of Interior*, Vol. 3, pp. 611–13.

6 Canada, *Sessional Papers*, 23 Vol. 10, 1883, p. 136; and computation from Orders in Council, *Department of Interior*, Vol. 4, 1882.

7 Canada, *Sessional Papers*, 7 Vol. 20, 1887, pp. 36–38.

8 John Stewart Marsh, "The Chinook and its Geographic Significance in Southern Alberta," (Unpublished M.Sc. Thesis, University of Calgary, 1965).

9 W.G. Hardy (ed.), *Alberta: A Natural History* (Edmonton: M.G. Hurtig Publishers, 1967), pp. 256–265.

10 Alexander Begg, "Stock Raising in the Bow River District compared with Montana," Chapter 16 of J.S. Macoun, *Manitoba and the Great North-West* (Guelph, Ontario: World Publishing Co., 1882).

11 D. McEachran, "A Journey over the Plains from Fort Benton to the Bow River and Back," Montreal *Gazette*, November 4, 1881.

12 Order in Council, December 12, 1882, *Department of Interior*, Vol. 4, p. 631; and Order in Council, May 26, 1885, *Department of Interior*, Vol. 7, p. 163.

13 Canada, *Sessional Papers*, 7 Vol. 20, 1887, p. xxix.

14 Canada, *Sessional Papers*, 7 Part 1, Vol. 20, 1887, p. 19.

15 Public Archives of Canada, RG 15 B2a Vol. 170 f 145330 part 1, letter from C. Drinkwater to Minister of Interior, February 28, 1886.

16 Order in Council, May 24, 1886, *Department of Interior*, Vol. 8, p. 425.

17 Canada, *Sessional Papers*, 4 Vol. 21, 1888, p. viii; and summary of Quarantine Regulations, 7 Vol. 26, 1893, pp. 100–103.

18 Canada, *Sessional Papers*, 7a Vol. 20, 1887, p. 7; and D.H. Breen, "The Mounted Police and the Ranching Frontier," in Hugh Dempsey (ed.), *Men in Scarlet* (Calgary: McClelland and Stewart West, 1974).

19 W. Turrentine Jackson, "British Interests in the Range Cattle Industry," in Maurice Frink, W. Turrentine Jackson, and Agnes Wright Spring, *When Grass Was King* (Boulder: University of Colorado Press, 1956).

20 Robert H. Fletcher, *Free Grass to Fences: The Montana Cattle Range Story* (New York: University Publishers Inc.,1960), p. 48.

21 PAC, RG B2a Vol. 3, f. 11007, letter from Assistant Commissioner of Customs to Burgess, March 12, 1885.

22 Ernest Staples Osgood, *The Day of the Cattleman* (Chicago: University of Chicago Press, 1929), p. 217.

23 Moreton Frewen, *Melton Mowbray and Other Memories* (London: Herbert Jenkins Ltd., 1924), p. 222.

24 *River Press*, September 1, 1886.

25 Orders in Council, *Department of Interior*, 1886, Vol. 8.

26 *Stockgrowers Journal*, September 18, 1886.

27 Canada, *Sessional Papers*, 7 Vol. 20, 1887, p. 19.

28 Canada, *Sessional Papers*, 7 Vol. 20, p. xxix; and 4 Vol. 21, p. ix.

29 Robert S. Fletcher, "That Hard Winter in Montana, 1886–87," *Agricultural History*, 4 (October, 1930), 123–130.

30 *River Press*, February 23, 1887.

31 *Macleod Gazette*, August 9, 1887.

32 *Fergus County Argus*, October 27, 1887.

33 Osgood, *The Day of the Cattleman*, p. 223.

34 PAC, MG 26 A1(d) Vol. 418, Macdonald Papers, Evans to Macdonald, August 20 and 28, 1885.

35 M. Frink, *When Grass Was King*, p. 154.

36 Order in Council, October 12, 1892, *Department of Interior*, Vol. 14, p. 537; and D.H. Breen, "The Canadian Prairie West and the 'Harmonious' Settlement Interpretation," *Agricultural History*, 47 (January 6, 1973), 63–75.

37 Order in Council, January 11, 1886, *Department of Interior*, Vol. 8, p. 41.

38 Order in Council, April 7, 1887, *Department of Interior*, Vol. 9, p. 245.

39 Order in Council, March 1, 1886, *Department of Interior*, Vol. 8, p. 127.

40 Canada, *Sessional Papers*, 14 Vol. 12, 1888, p. xx.

41 C.M. MacInnes, *In the Shadow of the Rockies* (London; Rivington's, 1930), p. 206.

42 F.W. Godsal, "Oldtimes," *Alberta Historical Review*, 19 (Autumn, 1964), 19–24.

43 Edward A. Ackerman, "Geography as a Fundamental Research Discipline," Department of Geography Research Paper No. 53, University of Chicago (June, 1964), p. 28.

44 William Trimble, "Historical Aspects of the Surplus Food Production of the United States, 1862–1902," *Annual Report of the American Historical Association*, 1918, Vol. 1, p. 229.

45 Canada, *Sessional Papers*, 10 Vol. 20, 1886, p. ix; and Allan Bogue, "The Progress of the Cattle Industry in Ontario during the Eighteen Eighties," *Agricultural History*, 3 (July, 1947), 163–169.

46 John Warkentin, "Steppe, Desert, and Empire," in A.W. Rasporich and H.C. Klassen (eds.), *Prairie Perspectives 2* (Toronto: Holt, Rhinehart, and Winston of Canada Ltd., 1973), pp. 80–101.

47 Walter Prescott Webb, *The Great Frontier* (Boston: Houghton Mifflin, 1952).

48 Simon G. Hanson, *Argentine Meat and the British Market* (Stanford University Press, 1938).

49 Mary W. Hargreaves, *Dry Farming in the Northern Plains, 1900–1925* (Cambridge, Mass.: Harvard University Press, 1957).

The Social Elite Of The Ranch Community And Calgary

Sheilagh S. Jameson

1 F.W. Godsal, "Old Times," *Alberta Historical Review*, XII, Autumn, 1964, p. 19. Often quoted is Lord Lorne's statement, "If I were not Governor General of Canada, I would be a cattle rancher in Alberta."

2 Sir Francis W. de Winton, military secretary to the Governor General on the expedition, and Lord Lorne himself, became owners of the Alberta Ranche.

3 *Canada Sessional Papers*, No. 13, 1885, pp. 31–32. Leases up to 100,000 acres were made available at the rate of one cent per acre per year.

4 David H. Breen, "The Cattle Compact: The Ranch Community of Southern Alberta, 1881–1896," unpublished M.A. Thesis, The University of Calgary 1969, and "The Canadian West and the Ranching Frontier, 1875–1922," Unpublished Ph.D. Thesis, University of Alberta, 1972. In these studies the writer has established the political, economic and social importance of the ranching community in Canadian history.

5 Glenbow-Alberta Institute—Archives, Mrs. Charles Inderwick papers, "Hope" to "Dearest," p. 25.

6 Sheilagh S. Jameson, Notebook, "Reminiscences of Oldtimers," c. 1940's. A stranger approaching a home in the Millarville area commenced conversation by saying, "The Man who chose this site for a house certainly had an eye for beauty." (In writer's possession.) Also Lewis G. Thomas, "The Rancher and the City: Calgary and the Cattlemen, 1883–1914," *Transactions of the Royal Society of Canada*, Vol. VI, June 1968, p. 205.

7 Glenbow Archives, Sheilagh S. Jameson, "George Scott," Interviews, 1957–9, p. 5.

8 This was a nutritious mixture of blue grama, June grass, spear and other grasses.

9 Glenbow Archives, Rev. James MacGregor, "The Marquis of Lorne's Tour in Manitoba," *Edinburgh Courant*, 28 Oct., 1881. In scrapbook, Lord Lorne's Expedition to the West.

10 Moira O'Neill, "A Lady's Life on a Ranche," *Blackwood's Edinburgh Magazine*, Jan. 1898, pp. 1, 2. Moira O'Neill, noted Irish poetess, and her husband, Walter C. Skrine, spent the years 1895–1902 on their ranch west of High River.

11 See for example Glenbow Archives, Pioneer Interviews by Edna Kells, c. 1935. See also Thomas, pp. 204–9.

12 Glenbow Archives, Scott, p. 2.

13 O'Neill, p. 3.

14 Public Archives of Canada, RG 18, Vol. 80, f262, 1893. A list of names, addresses and occupations of ex-members of N.W.M.P. in N.W.T.

15 *Calgary Herald*, November 12,

1884. Others expressed the same opinion, see Kells, pp. 64, 72–73.

16 Mrs. Algernon St. Maur, *Impressions of a Tenderfoot* (London, 1890), p. 47.

17 L.V. Kelly, *The Range Men* (Toronto, 1913), pp. 140–148.

18 See for example C.M. MacInnes, *In the Shadow of the Rockies* (London, 1930), pp. 328–9. Also Kells, p. 96. Specific references are not easy to find, partly perhaps because of the stigma that became attached to the practice. The writer bases this statement partly on memories of stories told by parents and other old timers and on some personal knowledge of families of the Foothills area.

19 After some controversy an upright log church was constructed. See Glenbow Archives, Charles Schack letter, 1938.

20 Donald E. Brown, "A History of the Cochrane Area," Unpublished M.A. Thesis, University of Alberta, 1951, p. 2.

21 N.B. James, *The Autobiography of a Nobody* (Toronto, 1947), pp. 81–2.

22 Glenbow Archives. Mrs. Charles Inderwick papers. Mrs. W.F.N. Scobie to Mrs. C. Inderwick, Oct. 12, 1891. Also S.S. Jameson. Interview with Miss Arabella Welsh, 1960.

23 A strongly built two-wheeled cart well upholstered and equipped with leather mud guards over wheels.

24 See for example, Mrs. C. Lynch-Staunton, *A History of the Early Days of Pincher Creek* (Women's Institute of Alberta), p. 9. W.E. Smith, "Smitty," "one of the Cochrane outfit. . .never attended a dance in anything but a regulation dress suit." Also Jameson, Notebook. Story of three cowboys with dress suits on saddles riding

to Okotoks to attend a ball. One, recklessly, in his own words, "plunged into the sunkissed stream," completely soaking himself and his suit, so was unable to continue. The other two took a longer, safer route.

25 Glenbow Archives, Mrs. H.O. Boyd papers. From the Misses Wainwright, Royal Hotel, Calgary, formal letter of regret re attendance at The Country Bachelors' Ball, Pine Creek Hall, Dec. 11, 1889, because of "a disappointment about a chaperone."

26 Kells, p. 9.

27 Glenbow Archives, G.H. Gooderham's Papers. From information obtained from Douglas Hardwick, rancher, Calgary.

28 Inderwick, "Hope" to "Dearest," p. 12. See also Kells, p. 14.

29 Kells, interview with Mrs. Alex Thompson, High River, p. 12. Also p. 116.

30 *Ibid.*, interview with A.L. Freebairn, Pincher Creek, p. 82. "Cowboys never played baseball."

31 Boyd, from Mrs. Emily F. Austin to Mrs. Boyd, June 7, 1900.

32 *Calgary Weekly Herald*, June 28, 1900.

33 Thoroughbred horses imported by some of the big ranches, notably the Quorn, helped raise the standard of horses in the Foothills region. See Sheilagh S. Jameson, "The Quorn Ranch," *Canadian Cattlemen*, VIII, Sept. 1945, p. 69.

34 Brown, pp. 153–4.

35 High River Pioneers' and Old Timers' Association, *Leaves from the Medicine Tree* (Lethbridge, 1960), p. 364.

36 Glenbow Archives, Denny Layzell, "Millarville Races." Script of article, Jan. 22, 1952.

37 O'Neill, p. 6.

38 Jameson, "The Quorn Ranch," pp. 68 & 96.

39 Kells, p. 4.

40 Jameson, Notebook.

41 Glenbow Archives, Eleanor Luxton, "Polo in Calgary," 1960. Ms. From interviews with Frank McHugh, High River, 1958. The Irish team consisted of Dublin Rodgers, Millarville; Hon. F.A. McNaughton, Calgary; Addy Hone, Fish Creek; Justin Deane-Freeman, Millarville. The latter usually credited with being Alberta's greatest polo player, was killed while playing in Coronado, California, in 1910.

42 Boyd, from Mrs. Emily F. Austin to Mrs. Boyd, June 7, 1900.

43 Thomas Jameson diary, 1904 - Mar. 1905. Also Jameson, Notebook (in writer's possession).

44 Kells, p. 64.

45 Inderwick, Mrs. J.F. Macleod to Mrs. C. Inderwick, n. d.

46 Inderwick, Mrs. W.F.N. Scobie to Mrs. C. Inderwick, Oct. 12, 1891.

47 This tradition continued. The writer knows a Welshman, now living on Vancouver Island, who went home "for good" three times. Good-bye parties almost became an embarrassment.

48 Glenbow Archives, J.L. Douglass, Ms., 1886. "Journal of four months' trip across Canada and U.S., 1886."

49 Inderwick, April 9, 1889. See also St. Maur, p. 43. "It gives some idea of hardship when one sees ladies obliged to do everything for themselves. . ."

50 Kells, p. 47. Also John D. Higinbotham, *When the West was Young* (Toronto, 1933), p. 203. One rancher decorated his cotton panelling with charcoal drawings of horses and other animals.

51 Inderwick, "Hope" to "Dearest," p. 2.
52 Higinbotham, pp. 203–4.
53 *Ibid.*, p. 203.

54 At times John Ware also gave his services as a caller for quadrilles at dances. See *Calgary Herald*, Feb. 19, 1885.

Alberta Ranching In Literature
Ermeline Ference

1 Marc Bloch, *Apologie pour l'histoire ou Métier d'historien.*
2 C.M. MacInnes, *In the Shadow of the Rockies* (London: Rivingtons, 1930), p. 195.
3 *Loc. cit.*
4 Moira O'Neill, "The North-West—Canada," *Songs of the Glens of Antrim* (London: William Blackwood and Sons, 1910), pp. 58–59.
5 Mrs. C. Inderwick, Diary and Personal Letters from the North Fork Ranch, p. 26.
6 E. Lynch-Staunton, "Ranching in Southern Alberta" (unpublished manuscript, Glenbow Archives).
7 Edna Kells, Pioneer Interviews, p. 42.
8 Mrs. C. Inderwick, *op. cit.*
9 Moira O'Neill, "A Lady's Life on a Ranche," *Blackwood's Edinburgh Magazine*, pp. 7–8.
10 F. Ings, Tales from the Midway Ranch (Unpublished manuscript, Glenbow Archives 1933), p. 87.
11 *Ibid.*, p. 146.
12 *Loc. cit.*
13 Rhonda Sivell, "The Hard Winter," *Voices from the Range* (Toronto: William Briggs, 1912), pp. 88–92.
14 D.H. Breen, "The Cattle Compact: The Ranch Community in Southern Alberta, 1881–1896"

(Unpublished M.A. Thesis: The University of Calgary, 1969), p. 136.
15 J.W. Hugill, "The Rose Ball," Poem re: Military Ball (Calgary: Unpublished manuscript, ca. 1911).
16 "Hermit," "Polo," *Macleod Gazette*, Jan. 5, 1894.
17 R.B. Spackman, "The Creamery Handicap, Black Diamond Races, 1912" (manuscript).
18 F.G. Roe, "Remittance Men," *Alberta Historical Review* (Edmonton: Vol II, No. 1, January, 1954), p. 23.
19 L.G. Thomas, "The Ranching Period in Southern Alberta" (Unpublished M.A. Thesis, University of Alberta, 1935), p. 206.
20 J.R. Gordon, "The Old Cowpoke," *Rhymes of the Range* (n.p., n.d.).
21 M. Mau, *Meet Southern Alberta* (Calgary: John D. McAra, 1954), chapter entitled "Ranching."
22 G. MacEwan, *John Ware's Cow Country* (Edmonton: Institute of Applied Art, 1960).
23 R.E. Gard, *Midnight, Rodeo Champion* (New York: Duell, Sloan and Pearce, 1951).
24 R.H. Imes, "A Range Ridin' Cowboy," *Brooks Bulletin*, December 5, 1957.
25 W.J. Wilde, "The Round-Up,"

Wilde Collection, Glenbow Archives.

26 C.M. MacInnes, *op. cit.*, p. 241.

27 Anonymous, *Sixteenth Annual Old-Time Range Men's Dinner Programme,* July 8, 1947.

28 A.L. Freebairn, *Kootenai Brown and Other Western Poems* (n.p., n.d.), p. 30.

29 G. Weadick "Alberta Cow Country" (unpublished manuscript 1953) preface.

30 E.A. McCourt, *The Canadian West in Fiction* (Toronto: Ryerson, 1949), p. 13.

31 J. Mackie, *The Heart of the Prairie* (London: G. Newnes, 1901).

32 Luke Allan, *The Lone Trail* (London: H. Jenkins, n.d.), p. 48.

33 *Loc. cit.*

34 *Ibid.*, p. 42.

35 Ibid., p. 68.

36 *Loc. cit.*

37 *Ibid.*, p. 51.

38 Ralph Connor, *The Sky Pilot, A Tale of the Foothills* (Toronto: Westminster, 1899), p. 25.

39 *Loc. cit.*

40 *Ibid.*, pp. 26–27.

41 Ralph Connor, *op. cit.*, p. 27.

42 D.E. Brown, "A History of the Cochrane Area" (Unpublished M.A. Thesis, University of Alberta, 1951), p. 37.

43 C.B. Dick, *Trails I've Ridden* (Calgary: J.W. Dick, 1946), p. 15.

44 W.J. Wilde, *op. cit.*

Policemen And Poachers
John Jennings

1 Macleod *Gazette*, May 14, 1883.

2 *Ibid.*, July 14, 1883. See also *Gazette*, June 26, 1890.

3 See Calgary *Herald*, May 20, 1887 and Sept. 9, 1887.

4 Calgary *Herald*, Feb. 12, 1885. Stimson described the Stonies as the best Indians in the territory and warned that if the government did not feed them better they would either starve or kill more cattle. Stimson was considered a great friend of the Indians and often treated them better than he did his cowboys. Glenbow Archives, Reminiscences of W.E.M. Holmes in Eleanor Luxton, History of Ranching in Alberta.

5 Glenbow, Fred Ings Papers, Tales from the Midway Ranch.

6 Glenbow, J.D. Higinbotham Papers.

7 *Ibid.* Maunsell was one of the early members of the N.W.M.P., serving from 1874 to 1877. He started ranching in 1878, one of the first on the Canadian frontier.

8 Glenbow, Diaries of H.M. Hatfield, 1893–1900. On May 17, 1895, Hatfield stated in his diary a typical ranching sentiment: "Some Stonies came last night and wanted Grub. I did not give them any as they are little better than tramps and I wish the Government would keep them on their reserve."

9 See Glenbow, Henry Sharples Papers; Frank White diary; A. Stavely Hill, From Home to Home; John McHugh, Reminiscences of H2 Jack; A.E. Cross Papers; Letterbook of Stair Ranch, 1890–1893.

10 Glenbow, Kenneth Coppock Papers, p. 109.

11 Glenbow, Sheilagh Jameson, Biographies of Pioneers.

12 *Ibid.*

13 Thomas Bland Strange, *Gunner Jingo's Jubilee* (London: Remington, 1893), pp. 386–7.

14 *Ibid.*, p. 401.

15 Glenbow, Cochrane Ranch Letter Book, 1884–1885. On Jan. 28, 1885, Cochrane wrote to J.M. Browning that he had paid seven chiefs ten dollars each for the right to graze the cattle on the reserve.

16 Canadian Sessional Papers, Annual Report of the North West Mounted Police, 1879, p. 3. Colonel Macleod, the commissioner, stated: "It is undoubtedly the case that they [Indians] killed some, but nothing like the numbers claimed. It is the opinion of many respectable stockmen that whites had more to do with it than the Indians."

17 D.H. Breen, "The Cattle Compact: The Ranch Community in Southern Alberta, 1881–1896" (Unpublished M.A. thesis, The University of Calgary, 1969), p. 8.

18 C.S.P., 1881, Report of N.W.M.P., Report of Major Walsh for 1880.

19 John Jennings, "The Plains Indians and the Law" in *Men in Scarlet* (McClelland and Stewart, 1974), pp. 61–63.

20 Detailed crime reports are listed in the back of each annual report of the N.W.M.P.

21 D.H. Breen, "The Canadian West and the Ranching Frontier, 1875–1922" (Unpublished Ph.D. thesis, University of Alberta, 1972), p. 174.

22 Public Archives of Canada, Record Group 18 (Mounted Police Papers), Vol. 1085, 1887, file 544.

23 Breen, "Canadian West," p. 174.

24 P.A.C., R.G. 18 (Mounted Police), Vol. 80, 1893, file 262.

25 See early annual reports of the N.W.M.P

26 Indian scouts were responsible for making many arrests and in the notable case of the arrest of the murderer Charcoal, it is unlikely that he would have been captured without massive Indian support.

27 On numerous occasions Chief Crowfoot, particularly, aided the Police in making arrests. References to the help of chiefs in making arrests are scattered through the Mounted Police annual reports. In 1889 Crowfoot was given a reward by the Government for helping in the arrest of the notorious Indian runner Deerfoot, who was continually in trouble with the Police. P.A.C., RG 18, Vol. 33 (1889), file 350.

28 See Frank Gilbert Roe, *The Indian and the Horse* (Norman: University of Oklahoma Press, 1955), and John C. Ewers, *The Horse in Blackfoot Indian Culture* (Washington: U.S. Government Printing Office, 1955).

29 P.A.C. RG 18, Vol. 39 (1890), file 137. One Indian, Trembling Man, who was caught red handed with eight Cree horses, testified in court, "I took them all right enough, but nobody saw me do it."

30 See crime reports in the annual reports of the Mounted Police.

31 First mention of passes, or the permit system as it was first called, is found in the annual report of the Department of Indian Affairs for 1882. A report to the Privy Council from the Governor General in Council dated 24

April, 1882, advocated this policy so that Indians would settle on reserves and discontinue their border raids.

32 Annual report of Indian Affairs Dept., 1889, report of Hayter Reed, Indian commissioner for North West Territories, p. 167. This method was also used to "persuade" Indians to become monogamous and send their children to school. See also P.A.C., RG 18, Vol. 1100 (1888), file 134, and Vol. 56 (1891), file 696.

33 P.A.C., RG 18, Vol. 84 (1893), file 505, Steele to Commissioner, June 9, 1893.

34 Annual reports of the Department of Indian Affairs, 1884, p. xlviii; 1887, p. lix; 1889, pp.

82–4; 1890, p. 62; 1892, p. 47; 1894, pp. 85–91; 1895, pp. 73–5.

35 P.A.C., RG 18, Vol. 101 (1895), file 38. Superintendent Steele to Commissioner of Mounted Police, June 9, 1894.

36 *Ibid.*, Vol. 1295 (1894), file 82, part II. Commissioner of Mounted Police to assistant commissioner of Indian Affairs, July 8, 1894.

37 *Ibid.*, July 8, 1894.

38 *Ibid.*, Vol. 101 (1894), file 38. Report of T.P. Wadsworth to Indian Department, July 27, 1894.

39 *Ibid.*, Aug. 27, 1894.

40 Annual reports of the Department of Indian Affairs, 1883, p. x; 1891, p. x and p. 190; 1892, p. xii and p. 47.

The Not So Peaceable Kingdom: Crime And Criminal Justice In Frontier Calgary
T. Thorner

1 G.F.G. Stanley, "Western Canada and the Frontier Thesis," *C.H.A. Report*, 1940, p. 111.

2 D. Breen, "The Cattle Compact: A History of Ranching in Southern Alberta," Unpublished M.A. Thesis, The University of Calgary, 1968, pp. 14, 109, 116.

3 *Calgary Weekly Herald*, November 12, 1884. Hereafter cited as *C.W.H.*

4 *C.W.H.* Feb. 6, May 28, 1884; Feb. 12, 1885; Dec. 28, 1887; Jan. 15, 22, 1890.

5 Another problem with these records is that many justices often failed to file returns. See *C.W.H.* May 1-7, 1895.

6 *C.W.H.* Feb. 17, 1889; similar

complaints March 18, 1891 and continuing until after the turn of the century, see *C.W.H.* May 26, 1904.

7 *Canada Sessional Papers* (C.S.P.), 1889, XXII, Vol. 13, No. 17, "Annual Report of Superintendent McIllree," Appendix C, , Dec. 14, 1888, p. 37; *C.S.P.*, 1890, XXIII, Vol. 10, No. 13, "Annual Report McIllree," App. C, Calgary, Dec. 13, 1889, p. 25; *C.S.P.* 1888, XXI, Vol. 17, No. 28, "Annual Report Inspector T. Wattam," Calgary, Dec. 1, 1887; *C.W.H.* Aug. 31, 1883; Jan. 23, 1886; March 20, 1890; July 8, Jan. 28, 1891.

8 *C.W.H.* Aug. 13, 1893.

9 *C.S.P.*, 1893, XXVI, Vol. 10, No. 15, "Annual Report Inspector R. Cuthbert," Appendix J, Calgary, Dec. 1, 1892, p. 128.

10 T.B. Strange, *Gunner Jingo's Jubilee* (London, 1894), p. 389, 391; and in D. Breen, "The Canadian Prairie West and the 'Harmonious' Settlement interpretation," *Agricultural History*, LXXIV, January 1973, p. 6.

11 It is not clear whether this is the only explanation for this phenomenon. H.C. Klassen in "Social Troubles in Calgary in the mid-1890's," *Urban History Rev.* (Feb. 1975, p. 8) claims that the influence of a depressed economy encouraged more prostitution. Such an explanation though does not take into account the increase of other moral offences and the proliferation of municipal by-laws on the subject. The relationship between fines and by-laws is a possibility discussed below.

12 Sources include the annual reports of the N.W.M.P., returns of the Calgary Police Court and the returns of Calgary's Justices of the Peace found in the Provincial Archives of Alberta and Saskatchewan.

13 *C.S.P.*, "Royal Commission on Liquor Traffic," 1894, XXVII, No. 14, Vol. 3, p. 404. Hearings took place in Calgary on November 7, 1892.

14 Royal Commission, *op. cit.*, p. 386; and similar examples in L.V. Kelly, *The Range Men* (Toronto, 1913), p. 222.

15 *C.S.P.*, 1891, XXIV, Vol. 15, No. 19, "Annual Report Superintendent McIllree," Appendix C, Calgary, Dec. 1890, p. 36.

16 *C.W.H.* Feb. 20, 1884.

17 *C.W.H.* Aug. 13, 1886.

18 *C.W.H.* Feb. 13, 1884; also in

S.B. Steele, *Forty Years in Canada* (Toronto, 1973), p. 179.

19 T.B. Strange, *op. cit.*, p. 389, 391.

20 *C.W.H.* Jan. 30, 1890.

21 L.V. Kelly, *op. cit.*, p. 175; confirmed *C.W.H.* May 7, 1884; Feb. 12, 1885.

22 L.V. Kelly, *op. cit.*, p. 135.

23 *Ibid.*, p. 15, 150, 301–2; *C.W.H.* Dec. 29, 1895.

24 *C.W.H.* Nov. 23, 1883.

25 *C.W.H.* Jan. 22, 1885; Nov. 27, 1887 and in G. Barrass, "Calgary Jails and Police Force," paper prepared for the *Historical Society of Alberta*, 1956, p. 1.

26 *C.W.H.* Jan. 27, 1885.

27 M. Foran, "The Calgary Town Council, 1884–1895," (Unpublished M.A. Thesis, The University of Calgary, 1969), p. 20, 77. Foran cites the City Council Minutes, March 16, Aug. 15, 1887; Jan. 18, 1888; July 28, 1891; Aug. 9, Oct. 8, 1892.

28 *C.W.H.* Nov. 11, 1885.

29 *C.W.H.* Dec. 10, 1890.

30 Royal Commission, *op. cit.*, p. 375.

31 *Ibid.*, p. 236.

32 *C.W.H.* April 22, 1884.

33 *C.S.P.*, 1893, XXVI, Vol. 10, No. 15, "Annual Report Inspector Cuthbert," Appendix J, Calgary, Dec. 1, 1892, p. 126.

34 Rev. A. Sutherland, *A Summer in Prairie Land* (Toronto, 1882), p. 52.

35 *C.W.H.* May 28, 1884.

36 *C.S.P.*, 1889, XXII, Vol. 13, No. 17, "Annual Report of Superintendent McIllree," Appendix C, Calgary, Dec. 14, 1888, p. 37.

37 *C.W.H.* Feb. 27, 1889; Dec. 3, 1890.

38 D. Breen, *Cattle Compact*, p. 55; L.V. Kelly, *op. cit.*, p. 226.

39 *C.S.P.*, 1890, XXIII, Vol. 10, No. 13, "Annual Report of Superintendent McIllree," Appendix C,

Calgary, Dec. 13, 1889, p. 25.

40 *Ibid.* p. 31.

41 *C.S.P.*, 1891, XXIV, Vol. 15, No. 19, "Annual Report of Superintendent McIllree," Appendix C, Calgary, December 1890, p. 37. And in *C.W.H.* Nov. 30, 1883.

42 *C.W.H.* Aug. 13, 1886.

43 Royal Commission, *op. cit.*, p. 391.

44 *C.W.H.* Feb. 13, 1886 and *Calgary Tribune* Dec. 16, 1885 cited in M. Foran, "The Travis Affair," *Alberta Historical Review*, 1971, Vol. 19, No. 4, p. 3.

45 *C.W.H.* April 20, 1895.

46 *C.W.H.* Feb. 19, 26, 1885.

47 *C.W.H.* March 10, 1890.

48 Glenbow-Alberta Institute Archives, G. Murdoch papers and diary observations as mayor 1884–85, p. 26.

49 *C.W.H.* Oct. 26, 1883; Oct. 29, June 25, 1884; March 5, 1885; Complaints regarding the delay of the courts continued throughout the early years of Calgary's development, see *C.W.H.* Dec. 28, 1894; March 31, 1900; Dec. 9, 1901.

50 Glenbow-Alberta Institute Archives. E. Dewdney Papers, Vol. III, J.A. Macdonald to Dewdney, Sept. 17, 1883.

51 *C.W.H.* Aug. 5, 1885.

52 *C.W.H.* April 4, 1888.

53 *C.W.H.* Feb. 19, 1885.

54 *C.W.H.* Jan. 11, 1885

55 J. Gray, *Red Lights on the Prairies* (Toronto, 1973), p. 162.

56 *C.W.H.* April 27, 1891.

57 Glenbow-Alberta Institute Archives, G. Murdoch papers and diaries, p. 26. The loss of floating capital due to fines was also noted in *C.W.H.* April 23, 1884.

58 *Calgary Herald*, Nov. 5, 1935, "Police Life Grand Riot During 80's."

59 D.M. McLeod, "Liquor Control of the North-West Territories," *Saskatchewan History*, Autumn 1963, p. 82; *C.W.H.* March 12, 1884.

60 *C.W.H.* Aug. 6, 1904; also *C.W.H.* July 19, 1902.

61 *C.S.P.*, XII, Vol. 8, No. 27, "Report of Inspector of Penitentiaries," Feb. 28, 1879; and subsequent reports of Inspector Moylan through 1885.

62 R.B. Deane, *Mounted Police Life in Canada* (London, 1916), p. 285; and in *Western Law Times*, Vol. I, p. 86.

63 T.B. Strange, *op. cit.*, p. 391.

64 *C.W.H.* April 20, 1895 and Aug. 16, 1893.

65 *C.W.H.* Dec. 9, 11, 30, 1885; Nov. 18, 25, 1885; Feb. 6, 1885; Jan. 6, 1886; Nov. 11, 1885; and *Calgary Tribune*, Feb. 13, 1886 cited in M. Foran, "The Travis Affair," *Alberta Historical Review*, 1971, Vol. 19, No. 4, p. 5.

66 H. Dempsey, *Crowfoot* (Edmonton, 1972), p. 142 and in *C.W.H.* May 7, 1884.

67 *C.S.P.*, 1885, XVIII, Vol. 8, No. 15, "Annual Report of the Minister of Justice for Penitentiaries," Ottawa, June 30, 1884, p. 81; *C.S.P.*, 1888, XXI, Vol. 11, No. 11, "Annual Report of the Minister of Justice for Penitentiaries," Ottawa, Nov. 5, 1887, p. xᵃ xiii.

The Fair, Frail Flowers of Western Womanhood
Catherine Philip

1 In 1917 two Albertans became the first women elected to any British or Canadian assembly. They were Nursing Sister Roberta McAdams and Mrs. L.C. McKinney. James G. MacGregor, *A History of Alberta* (Edmonton: Hurtig Publishers, 1972), p. 237.

2 The five women were Emily Murphy, Irene Parlby, Louise McKinney, Nellie McClung and Henrietta Edwards.

3 Edna Kells, "Interviews with Southern Alberta Pioneers," Unpublished Manuscript, Glenbow Collection, p. 53.

4 Phyllis A. Haight and Muriel Holden, "Sit Down While You're Standing," Unpublished Manuscript, Glenbow Collection, p. 28.

5 John D. Higinbotham, *When the West was Young* (Toronto: Ryerson Press, 1933), p. 115.

6 George Murdoch, Diary, September 9, 1883, Glenbow Collection.

7 H.L. Toews, circa 1900, Glenbow Collection.

8 J.H. Walker, *Wallasey and Wirral Chronicle*, June 15, 1889, Glenbow Collection.

9 Edna Kells, "Interviews with Southern Alberta Pioneers," Unpublished Manuscript, Glenbow Collection, p. 182.

10 *Ibid.*, p. 31.

11 Wesley Fletcher Orr, Correspondence, Vol. 5, p. 559.

12 H.L. Gray, letter, July 9, 1902, Glenbow Collection.

13 J.H. Walker, *Wallasey and Wirral Chronicle*, Oct. 9. 1889, Glenbow Collection.

14 *The Albertan*, June 11, 1911.

15 *The Albertan*, June 26, 1911.

16 City of Calgary Papers, Vol. 5, p. 118, Glenbow Collection.

17 W.F. Orr, Correspondence, Vol. 4, p. 232, Glenbow Collection.

18 Calgary School District #19, Notes, 1885–1952, Minutes 1885–1900. Originals in the possession of the Calgary Public School Board. Microfilmed by Glenbow Archives.

19 Mrs. Henry A. George, Reminiscences, Unpublished Manuscript, Glenbow Collection, p. 33.

The Chinese Experience in Frontier Calgary: 1885–1910   *J. Brian Dawson*

1 Calgary's population was 43,704 in 1911. See *Census of Canada*, 1911.

2 See James Morton, *In the Sea of Sterile Mountains: The Chinese in British Columbia* (Vancouver: J.J. Douglas Ltd., 1974), pp. 6–45.

3 See Pierre Berton, *The Last Spike* (Toronto: McClelland and Stewart Ltd., 1971), pp. 194–206 and James Morton, *ibid.*, pp. 79–139.

4 See James Morton, *ibid.*, pp. 131–142.

5 Calgary *Herald*, January 23,

1886. The $50 referred to in this article was a "head tax" payable by every Chinese immigrant, exempting a few in certain privileged categories. The fee levied increased to $100 in 1901 and to $500 in 1904.

6 Calgary *Herald*, June 6, 1888.
7 Calgary *Herald*, June 13, 1888.
8 Calgary *Herald*, October 3, 1888.
9 Calgary *Herald*, October 10, 1888.
10 James Morton, *op. cit.*, p. 172.
11 Calgary *Herald*, July 5, 1892.
12 It should be noted that sanitary conditions in prairie towns were practically unbearable. Typhoid fever "was endemic to all the cities. . ." James H. Gray, *Booze* (Scarborough: The New American Library of Canada Limited, 1974), p. 35.
13 Calgary *Herald*, July 15, 1892.
14 Calgary *Herald*, July 19, 1892.
15 Calgary *Herald*, July 20, 1892.
16 Calgary *Herald*, August 3, 1892.
17 Calgary *Herald*, August 13, 1892.
18 Calgary *Herald*, July 19, 1892.
19 Calgary *Herald*, July 21, 1892. The *Empress of Japan* was, of course, a Canadian Pacific ocean liner.
20 Calgary *Herald*, July 23, 1892.
21 Calgary *Herald*, August 3, 1892.
22 N.W.M.P., *Reports*, 1892, p. 128.
23 N.W.M.P., *Reports*, 1892, p. 128.
24 N.W.M.P., *Reports*, 1892, p. 128.
25 See Calgary *Tribune*, August 3, 1892.
26 N.W.M.P., *Reports*, 1892, p. 128.
27 N.W.M.P., *Reports*, 1892, p. 128.
28 N.W.M.P., *Reports*, 1892, p. 128.
29 Calgary *Herald*, August 3, 1892.
30 Calgary *Herald*, August 5, 1892.
31 Calgary *Herald*, March 5, 1885.
32 Calgary *Tribune*, August 10, 1892.
33 *Ibid.*
34 *Ibid.*
35 Calgary *Tribune*, August 17, 1892.
36 Calgary *Herald*, August 17, 1892.

37 *Ibid.*
38 *Ibid.*
39 Calgary *Herald*, August 24, 1892.
40 *Ibid.*
41 Calgary *Herald*, August 10, 1892.
42 Calgary *Tribune*, August 10, 1892.
43 Calgary *Herald*, August 19, 1892.
44 The term "garrison mentality" has been employed by Northrop Frye as a concept of considerable importance in analyzing Canadian cultural history. See Northrop Frye, "Conclusion" in Carl F. Klinck, *Literary History of Canada: Canadian Literature in English* (Toronto: University of Toronto Press, 1965), esp. pp. 830–834.
45 Dr. Howard D. Palmer, "Anti-Oriental Sentiment in Alberta, 1880–1920," *Canadian Ethnic Studies*, Vol. II, No. 2, December 1970, pp. 47–48.
46 *Ibid., passim.*
47 Cheng Tien-fang, *Oriental Immigration in Canada* (Shanghai: Commercial Press, 1931), p. 181.
48 Calgary *Albertan*, Centennial Edition, May 1975, 7B.
49 Dr. Henry C. Klassen, "Cultural Life in Frontier Calgary," *Western Canada, Past and Present*, ed. A.W. Rasporich (Calgary, McClelland and Steward Ltd., 1975), p. 46.
50 G. Baureiss, "The Chinese Community in Calgary," *Alberta Historical Review* (Vol. 22, No. 2, Spring 1974), p. 3.
51 Betty L. Sung, *Mountain of Gold: The Story of the Chinese in America* (New York: Macmillan, 1967), p. 133.
52 *Ibid.* On the persecution of Chinese in the United States in this period read Chapter 5 of the above work.
53 On this topic see Paul C.P. Siu, "The Sojourner," *American Journal of Sociology* (Vol. VIII, July 1952), pp. 32–44.

54 Calgary *Herald*, January 28, 1956.
55 *Ibid*. Mr. Underwood provided the building at his own expense and for over 20 years he was president of the Chinese Mission and presided over the board of directors.
56 Calgary *Albertan*, January 25, 1922.
57 *Henderson's Directory*, 1911.
58 Calgary *Albertan*, July 8, 1910. The proposed route did not come into being because of public pressure but Chinatown had by that time been relocated.
59 Calgary *Albertan*, October 4, 1910.
60 Calgary *Albertan*, October 6, 1910.
61 Calgary *Herald*, October 10, 1910.
62 Calgary *Albertan*, October 11, 1910.
63 Calgary *Herald*, October 13, 1910.
64 Calgary *Albertan*, October 14, 1910.
65 Calgary *Albertan*, October 14, 1910. The proposed by-law was apparently not enacted.
66 Calgary *Albertan*, October 14, 1910.
67 Calgary *Herald*, October 11, 1910.
68 Calgary *Albertan*, October 14, 1910.
69 Calgary *Herald*, October 7, 1910.
70 *Ibid*.
71 Calgary *Albertan*, October 15, 1910.
72 Calgary *Herald*, October 14, 1910.
73 Calgary *Herald*, October 13, 1910.

Calgary: The Private Schools, 1900–1916
Douglas Coats

1 Canada Census figures, from *Canada Year Book, 1932*, Dominion Bureau of Statistics, Ottawa, King's Printer, p. 103.
2 F.G. Roe, "Remittance Men," *Alberta Historical Review*, Vol. 2, No. 1, January 1954.
3 Sheilagh Jameson, "Era of the Big Ranches," *Alberta Historical Review*, Vol. 18, No. 1, Winter 1970.
4 L.G. Thomas, "The Rancher and the City: Calgary and the Cattlemen, 1883–1914," *Transactions of the Royal Society of Canada*, Vol. VI, Series IV, June 1968, p. 213.
5 Calgary *Eye Opener*, February 4, 1905.
6 Calgary *Herald*, December, 1, 1898.
7 Calgary *Herald*, May 26, 1911.
8 *Calgary, Alberta: The Land of Plenty*, City Council and Board of Trade pamphlet, 1907, p. 42.
9 See L.G. Thomas, *op. cit.*
10 *Tregillus-Thompson Directory of Greater Calgary, 1913*, pp. 143–147.
11 Calgary *Herald*, April 22, 1903.
12 *Tregillus-Thompson Directory*, *op. cit.*, p. 148.
13 *Ibid*.
14 Phyllis E. Weston, "The History of Education in Calgary," un-

published M.A. Thesis, University of Alberta, 1951, p. 48.

15 *The Albertan*, November 6, 1965.

16 *Tregillus-Thompson Directory, op. cit.*, p. 147.

17 *Ibid.*

18 *Ibid.*

19 Advertisement from the *Medicine Hat News*, April 14, 1910.

20 Mrs. Wallace Cockeram, quoted in *The Albertan*, November 6, 1965.

21 *Ibid.*

22 Calgary *Herald*, November 5, 1965.

23 *Tregillus-Thompson Directory, op. cit.*, p. 146.

24 *Ibid.*, p. 147.

25 *Ibid.*, p. 147.

26 1905 list of shareholders, Glenbow Library and Archives.

27 *Tregillus-Thompson Directory, op. cit.*, p. 146.

28 Calgary *Herald*, August 28, 1958.

29 *The Albertan*, January 6, 1912.

30 Calgary *Herald*, August 12, 1958.

31 Calgary *Herald*, August 25, 1910.

32 Weston, *op. cit.*, p. 54.

33 List of Old Boys who served in the Great War, Glenbow Archives.

34 Calgary *Herald*, August 28, 1958.

35 Leroi Allister Daniels, "The History of Education in Calgary," Unpublished M.A. Thesis, University of Washington, 1954, p. 205.

36 Weston, *op. cit.*, p. 56.

37 *The Albertan*, June 3, 1911.

38 A.D. Winspear, "Bishop Pinkham College, Calgary's First [?]," *Golden West* March-April 1966, p. 31. A former student's reminiscences.

39 *Henderson's Calgary Directory*, 1915, p. 206.

40 *Tregillus-Thompson Directory, op. cit.*, p. 143.

41 *Ibid.*

42 *Ibid.*

43 Weston, *op. cit.*, p. 57.

44 Winspear, *op. cit.*, p. 32.

45 *Ibid.*

46 Weston, *op. cit.*, p. 57.

47 *Tregillus-Thompson Directory, op. cit.*, p. 145.

48 *Ibid.*

49 *Ibid.*

50 *Calgary, Alberta: Merchants and Manufacturers' Record* (Calgary: Jennings Publishing Company, 1911), p. 31. Promotional pamphlet.

51 *Tregillus-Thompson Directory, op. cit.*, p. 146.

52 Daniels, *op. cit.*, p. 206.

53 Norman L. McLeod, "Calgary College 1912–1915: A Study of an Attempt to Establish a Privately Financed University in Alberta," Doctoral Thesis, The University of Calgary, 1970.

54 *Henderson's Directory*, 1915, *op. cit.*, p. 206.

55 *Canadian Annual Review, 1914*, p. 668.

56 *Ibid.*

57 McLeod, *op. cit.*, p. 179.

58 *Ibid.*

59 Closely related to this Westernization, and undoubtedly occurring simultaneously, was a Canadianization of immigrants and a general weakening of the old Imperial spirit. This trend is discussed by Arthur Lower in his *Colony to Nation* (Toronto: Longmans, Green & Co., 1946) pp. 425, 431–32.

60 C.A. Dawson and Eva R. Younge, *Pioneering in the Prairie Provinces*, Canadian Frontiers of Settlement Series, edited by W.A. Mackintosh and W.L.G. Joerg (Toronto: Macmillan, 1940), pp. 13–14.

61 *Canada Year Book, 1932*, p. 91.

62 *Ibid.*

63 Calgary Herald, December 1, 1928.

64 *Canadian Annual Review, 1923*, p. 749.

The Response To Urban Growth: The Bureaucratization Of Public Education In Calgary, 1884–1914   *Robert M. Stamp*

1 The author wishes to thank Maurice Careless of the University of Toronto and Henry Klassen of the University of Calgary for their helpful comments on an earlier draft of this paper.

2 Maurice Careless, "Aspects of Urban Life in the West," in Anthony Rasporich and Henry Klassen, eds., *Prairie Perspectives 2: Selected Papers of the Western Canada Studies Conferences, 1970, 1971* (Toronto: Holt, Rinehart and Winston, 1973), p. 38.

3 See Calgary Board of Education Archives, *Minutes*, 1885–1914.

4 W.B. Fraser, *Calgary* (Toronto: Holt, Rinehart and Winston, 1967), pp. 59–60.

5 Max Foran, "Urban Calgary, 1884–1895," *histoire sociale—Social History*, V (9), April 1972, pp. 71–72.

6 Calgary *Herald*, February 13, 1884.

7 Most accounts locate the school in the old Boynton Hall, on the north side of Stephen (later Eighth) Avenue, east of Second Street E., the site later occupied by the Variety Theatre, although there is one mention of a site further east, between Eighth and Ninth Avenues, east of Fourth Street E.

8 Costello later transferred his allegiance to the Calgary Separate School Board, first as secretary-treasurer, then trustee, and finally school inspector.

9 Calgary *Herald*, April 23, 1884.

10 *Ibid.*

11 The word "Protestant" was not dropped from the official title until 1914. Today Calgary Public School District No. 19 is referred to as the Calgary Board of Education.

12 Burns and Elliot, eds., *Calgary, Alberta: Her Industries and Resources* (Calgary: Burns and Elliott, 1885), p. 84.

13 For a discussion of the rivalry between the two sections of early Calgary, see Max Foran, "The Birth and Expansion of Calgary, 1875–1895," a paper presented to the Urban History Conference, University of Winnipeg, October 1974, p. 2.

14 Four schools have included the word "Central" in their name at various times in the history of the Calgary Board of Education— "Old Central School on Fifth Avenue S.W.; "New" Central School, built in 1904 on the same block; Central High School, originally opened in 1908 as Calgary Collegiate Institute; and Central Memorial High School, constructed in the late 1960's.

15 Calgary Public School Board, *Minutes*, November 6, 1886.

16 Careless, "Aspects of Urban Life in the West," pp. 31–32.

17 Calgary *Herald*, December 23, 1891.

18 South Ward School is the oldest school building standing in Calgary in 1975; its datestone incorrectly reads "1892."

19 CPSB *Minutes*, August 15, 1894.

20 Calgary *Herald*, May 12, 1893.

21 CPSB *Minutes*, March 9, 1893 and January 23, 1896.

22 *Morning Albertan*, April 24, 1903.

23 Calgary *Herald*, December 9, 1903.

24 *Ibid.*, April 22, 1903.

25 *Ibid.*, April 23, 1903. Italics added.

26 Interview with Carrie Trotter Ross, Calgary, September 1974.

27 *Morning Albertan*, August 13, 1902.

28 Calgary *Herald*, May 25, 1904.

29 *Morning Albertan*, April 10, 1906.

30 Paul Rutherford, "Tomorrow's Metropolis: The Urban Reform Movement in Canada, 1880–1920," Canadian Historical Association, *Historical Papers, 1971*, p. 214.

31 CPSB *Minutes*, Superintendent's Report for September 1911.

32 *Ibid.*, Superintendent's Report for April 1913.

33 *Ibid.*, Superintendent's Report for January 1915.

34 Calgary *Herald*, February 28, 1913.

35 CPSB *Minutes*, Superintendent's Report for November 1912.

36 *Ibid*, August 8, 1911.

37 Seventeen of these thirty-four buildings were four to twelve-room imposing sandstone struc-
tures, so representative of pre-1914 Calgary. The remaining seventeen were temporary two-room "cottage" schools, hastily erected during the 1910–1912 boom years.

38 Calgary's decision to use the schools as the major vehicles for accomplishing the aims of the public health movement is coincident with similar steps in eastern urban centres. See Neil Sutherland, "To Create a Strong and Healthy Race: School Children in the Public health Movement, 1880–1914," *History of Education Quarterly*, XII (3), Fall 1972, pp. 304–333.

39 Careless, "Aspects of Urban Life in the West," p. 26.

40 See Michael Katz, "Class, Bureaucracy and Schools," in Douglas Myers, ed., *The Failure of Educational Reform in Canada* (Toronto: McClelland and Stewart, 1973), p. 18.

The Early History Of The Catholic Church In Calgary *M.B. Byrne*

1 Rodney William, *Kootenai Brown* (Sidney, B.C.: Grey's Publishing Co., 1969), p. 109.

2 Alberta Provincial Archives, Oblate Papers, Doucet's Journals.

3 J. Chevaliier, O.M.I., Origine et Premier Developpements de Calgary, Calgary, 1935, p. 18.

4 L.V. Kelly, *The Range Men* (Toronto: William Briggs, 1913), p. 94.

5 Alberta Provincial Archives, Oblate papers, Doucet Memoirs.

6 *Ibid.*

7 Alexander Morris, *The Treaties of Canada with the Indians* (Toronto: Belfords, Clarke & Co., 1880), pp. 247–50.

8 Alberta Provincial Archives, Oblate Papers, Father Scollen's letter to the Superior of the Missions, Fr. Leduc.

9 Katherine Hughes, *Father Lacombe* (New York: Moffat, Yard & Company, 1911), pp. 282–283.

10 Glenbow-Alberta Institute, Plunkett Papers, pp. 10–11.

11 Glenbow-Alberta Institute, C.P.R. Transfer Book, 1882–1901, p. 68.

12 Glenbow-Alberta Institute, Plunkett Papers, p. 16.

13 Calgary Diocesan Archives, Benedictines.

Central Methodist Church Before World War One
J. Fraser Perry

1 Author's note: This paper has not been footnoted in the conventional way because it was drawn from a textual draft which had been written without footnotes. Even if footnotes had been provided, however, many of them would have been very general. The statement that Calgary Methodist Church was concerned early in its life with poverty, for example, would be supported by a reference to minutes of the Quarterly Official Board for the period 1884 to 1905.

At least eighty per cent of the content of the paper relies basically on such church records as the QOB minutes and on contemporary newspaper accounts. As to the balance, the chief sources are private correspondence, reminiscences obtained for the purposes of a church history, and the published work of other authors.

Calgary's Early Anglicans
The Very Rev'd David J. Carter

1 David J. Carter, *Where The Wind Blows, A History of the Anglican Diocese of Calgary 1888–1968* (Calgary: Kyle Printers Ltd., 1968), p. 3ff.

2 Jean D'Artigue, *Six Years in the Canadian North-West*, Toronto, 1881.

3 David J. Carter, *Samuel Trivett, Missionary with the Blood Indians* (Calgary: Kyle Printers Ltd., 1974), p. 27ff.

4 David J. Carter, *Calgary's Anglican Cathedral* (Calgary: Kyle Printers Ltd., 1973), p. 15ff.

5 J.W. Tims, "A History of the Early Years of the Diocese of Calgary, 1880–1901" (unpublished MS), Calgary Diocesan Archives.

6 The Right Reverend William Cyprian Pinkham, Autobiography (unpublished), Calgary Diocesan Archives.

7 Mrs. W.C. Pinkham, Autobiography (unpublished), Calgary Diocesan Archives.

Land Speculation And Urban Development: Calgary 1884–1912   Max Foran

1 There were 3845 building permits issued in 1912; this figure was not reached again till 1950. *Municipal Manual*, 1969, p. 147.

2 Dominion Census: 11,967; Unofficial Census: 17,000.

3 Given as 10,000 in 1904. The *Herald* gave the population as 9,175 in February 1905 and 15,000 in October of the same year.

Herald, Feb. 6, Oct. 14, 1905.

4 Victoria Park was added in 1901 and the north-east quarter of Section 11 in 1903.

5 Some of these residences belonged to D.W. Marsh, R.J. Hutchings, J.J. Young, H.G. Mackid, W.H. Cushing, H.D. Sanson, W.H. Lee, H.S. Macleod, T. Underwood, J.C. Linton, W. Robertson.

6 Some of these buildings included the Bank of Montreal ($22,000), the Alberta Hotel ($36,000), Alexander Block ($16,000) and the Courthouse ($40,000).

7 Glenbow Historical Library & Archives (hereafter quoted as Glenbow), Wesley Orr papers, Orr to Mary Schreiber, March 20, 1892.

8 University of Alberta William Pearce Papers. Pearce to Dewdney, Feb. 6, 1892.

9 Orr Papers. Orr to Mary Schreiber, March 20, 1892.

10 *Herald*, May 21, 1908.

11 *Tribune*, Aug. 17, 1892.

12 The name Breweryville was not held in high repute. It was reported in 1909 that residents considered East Calgary a much better name than Breweryville. It was held and only partly facetiously that the motor bus system had failed because it termed its eastern terminus Breweryville. The *Herald* also reported that "one city firm is said to have learned discretion when it lost a $400 order by addressing a letter to Brewery Flats." *Herald*, May 21, 1909.

13 See *Tribune*, Sept. 23, Nov. 18, 1899. Also *Albertan*, Dec. 29, 1899.

14 Glenbow, *Gronlunds Guide and Map of Calgary* (n.d.). Probably 1902.

15 *Herald*, Sept. 22, 1909.

16 Specifically referred to as Block 69 or 10th Ave. between Centre and 1st St. W. Lots in this block were selling at $200 each in 1884. By 1895 the price had dropped to $25 per lot. Abstracted from the Canadian North-West Land Company Records, vol. 56.

17 *Tribune*, July 15, 1887.

18 Canadian Sessional Papers, No. 15 of 1893. Annual Report of the Commission of the N.W.M.P.

19 Abstracted from City of Calgary Voters' List 1894. (In possession of author.)

20 Glenbow. Walker, J.H. Calgary and District Observations 1889–91 (on microfilm).

21 *Tribune*, Dec. 11, 1889.

22 *Tribune*, Dec. 24, 1886.

23 A good example of which was *Dominion Illustrated*, 1890.

24 Canadian North-West Land Company Records, Vol. 56.

25 *Ibid.*

26 *Tribune*, June 8, 1892.

27 *Tribune*, July 7, 1894.

28 *Herald*, Aug. 8, 1891.

29 William Pearce Papers, ff10 6–22. Pearce to Dewdney, March 6, 1892.

30 *Tribune*, December 3, 1886; *Calgary Council Minutes*, May 1887.

31 *Herald*, Nov. 17, 1888; July 17, 1889.

32 Orr Papers. Orr to M. Schreiber, March 20, 1892.

33 *Tribune*, Sept. 10, 1890.

34 *Calgary Council Minutes*, Nov. 16, 1894.

35 *Herald*, Oct. 14, 1905.

36 *Herald*, April 9, 1906.

37 *Herald*, July 4, 1907.

38 *Herald*, Aug. 10, 1907.

39 Specifically lower deposits with more time to pay balance. *Herald*, May 1, 1909.

40 *News Telegram*, March 27, 1912.

41 *Herald*, May 12, 1911. Lowes is a fascinating figure. His rise from

obscurity to wealth—worth $7½ million in 1912—to fall in 1916 is certainly one of Calgary's most spectacular business careers.

42 For example: Bronx (½ mile north of Parkdale) $300 per acre, 1910; Alexander subdivision (Shaganappi) 5.10 acre plots $100–$150, 1909; 20 acres west of Mission Bridge $1500, 1907; north of Hillhurst $70 per acre, 1906; 5.10 acre plots near reservoir in S.W. Calgary $140–$200 per acre, 1909; lots in Glengarry $100 each, 1910; Kitsilano lots 2 miles N.E. from P.O. $30, 1910.

43 Glenbow City of Calgary Papers #19 ff127.

44 City of Calgary Papers #19 ff127.

45 *Herald*, March 15, 1910.

46 *Herald*, April 25, 1910.

47 See *Herald*, Aug. 13, 19, 1909; Sept. 13, 1910; City of Calgary Papers #22 ff182.

48 *Herald*, May 15, 1906.

49 *Herald*, July 3, 1909.

50 *Herald*, March 18, 1910.

51 These were Globe Elevator Co. Ltd. (12 men employed); P. Burns Co. (150 men); Calgary Brewery (100 men); W.H. Cushing Ltd. (130–140 men); Western Milling-Rising Sun Flour (18 men); Boackman Kerr Milling (15–20 men); Alberta Portland Cement Co. (300 men); Royal Crown Soap (50 men); Great West Saddlery Co. (12–15 men); *Herald*, March 28, 1910.

52 *Herald*, April 17, 1907.

53 *Herald*, May 4, 1909.

54 *Herald*, April 13, May 8, 1909. Lots could be had for $10 down in that year.

55 *Herald*, April 1, 9, Aug. 10, 1907.

56 *Herald*, July 31, 1909. See also Herald, July 24, 1909.

57 *Herald*, May 16, 1908.

58 *News Telegram*, March 27, 1912.

59 *Herald*, April 9, April 11, May 3, 1910; *News Telegram*, March 21, 1912; City of Calgary Papers #18 ff116.

60 *News Telegram*, April 24, 1912.

61 *Herald*, April 12, 1909.

62 *Herald*, March 24, 1910.

63 *Herald*, Jan. 30, 1912.

64 *News Telegram*, Jan. 2, 1912.

65 *News Telegram*, Oct. 24, 1911.

66 *News Telegram*, April 4, 1912. Specifically Section 13.

67 *Ibid.*

68 *Herald*, April 1, 1910.

69 *Herald*, April 24, 1912.

70 *News Telegram*, March 19, 1912.

71 *Herald*, May 27, 1911.

72 *Albertan*, May 16, 1911.

73 *Herald*, May 27, 1911.

74 *News Telegram*, April 4, 1912.

75 *News Telegram*, Aug. 2, 1912.

76 *Herald*, April 3, 1906,

77 *Herald*, Aug. 27, 1905.

78 *Herald*, Jan. 9, 1905.

79 *Herald*, April 24, 1909.

80 *News Telegram*, March 21, 1912.

81 *News Telegram*, June 24, 1912.

82 City of Calgary Papers. Evidence given before the Board of Railway Commissioners for Canada, July, 1907. #19 ff120.

83 *Ibid.*

84 *Ibid.*

85 *Ibid.*

86 *Ibid.*

87 *Herald*, June 10, 1909.

88 *Herald*, March 24, 29, 1910.

89 See *Herald*, June 4, 7, 8, 29, 1907.

90 *News Telegram*, March 25, 1912.

91 *News Telegram*, March 29, 1912.

92 *Ibid.*

93 *Ibid.*

94 For further information on this controversy see City of Calgary Papers, evidence given before Board of Railway Commissioners for Canada, 1907, #19 ff120.

95 See City of Calgary Papers #17 ff99.

96 *Ibid.*

97 *Herald*, April 18, 1910.
98 As in the instance concerning the erection of the first Centre Street Bridge.
99 *Herald*, May 13, 1908. Plebiscite involving 4 sites was held.
100 *Herald*, May 2, 1906.
101 *Herald*, April 9, 1908.
102 City of Calgary Papers # 22 ff181.
103 *Ibid.*

In Search of Wealth And Status: An Economic And Social Study Of Entrepreneurs In Early Calgary   *Paul Voisey*

1 *The Western Stockman*, March 26, 1932.
2 *The Calgary Brewing and Malting Company* (Calgary Brewing and Malting Co.: undated pamphlet, Glenbow-Alberta Archives).
3 Census manuscript 1901, Calgary Brewing and Malting Company Papers, Glenbow-Alberta Archives.
4 During prohibition (1915–1924) Cross was able to buy 50 hotels at bargain rates, Catherine Philip, "The Crosses of Alberta," Part Three, *Chatelaine Magazine* (Aug., 1965), pp.61–2.
5 *The Albertan*, Feb. 25, 1937.
6 Albert Frederick Sproule, "The Role of Patrick Burns in the Development of Western Canada" (Unpublished M.A. Thesis, University of Alberta, 1962), p. 74.
7 C.I. Ritchie, "Nation Builder," *Canadian Cattlemen*, Vol. 3, No. 3 (Dec., 1940), p. 484.
8 Grant MacEwan, *Blazing the Old Cattle Trail* (Saskatoon: Modern Press, 1962), pp. 181–5.
9 *The Albertan*, *The 100,000 Manufacturing, Building, and Wholesale Book Edition of the Morning Albertan* (Calgary: *The Albertan*, 1914), p. 36.
10 Theodore Strom, "With the Eau Claire in Calgary," *Alberta Historical Review*, Vol. 12, No. 3 (Summer, 1964), p. 4.
11 All figures from *Census of Canada 1911*, Vol. 3, Table 11; *Census of Manufacturing 1916*, Table 11.
12 *The Albertan*, *100,000*, p. 36.
13 Archibald Oswald MacRae, *History of the Province of Alberta*, Vol. 2 (Calgary: Western Canada History Co., 1912), p. 621.
14 *Calgary Daily Herald*, *Why Go to Canada* (Calgary: *Calgary Daily Herald*, 1910), p. 15.
15 Henry James Morgan, ed., *The Canadian Men and Women of the Time* (Second ed.; Toronto: William Briggs, 1912), p. 175. Sproule, *Burns*, p. 188.
16 Ritchie, "Nation Builder," p. 488.
17 Vancouver (1907), Edmonton (1912), Prince Albert (1918), Regina (1918), Winnipeg (1926), Seattle.
18 All figures from Sproule, "Nation Builder," p. 138; *The Albertan*, Feb. 25, 1937.
19 MacRae, *Albertan*, Vol. 2, p. 871.
20 *Ibid.*, p. 814.
21 *The Albertan*, *100,000*, p. 61.
22 MacRae, *Alberta*, Vol. 2, p. 864.
23 *The Albertan*, *100,000*, p. 36.
24 E.L. Richardson, *Calgary, Alberta*,

Commercial Metropolis of Western Canada (Calgary: Hundred Thousand Club pamphlet, 1907), p. 14; and Board of Trade, *Calgary, Alberta, The Manufacturing, Jobbing, and Commercial Centre of the Canadian West* (Calgary: Jennings Publishers pamphlet, 1911), p. 18.

25 *Henderson's Calgary City Directory* (1914).

26 *Calgary Daily Herald, Why Go*, p. 78.

27 *The Albertan, 100,000*, p. 69.

28 *Henderson's Calgary City Directory* (1914), p. 129.

29 *Calgary, Alberta, The Manufacturing*, p. 198.

30 Richard Cunniffe, *Calgary in Sandstone* (Calgary: Historical Society of Alberta, 1969), p. 6.

31 *Calgary Herald*, Nov. 15, 1913.

32 Ernest Watkins, *R.B. Bennett: A Biography* (Toronto: Kingswood House, 1963), p. 74.

33 *Census of Canada 1931*, Vol. 2, Table 1.

34 Of the forty businessmen listed in Table One, the most successful arrived in Calgary early; twenty-five arrived before 1900, fourteen before 1890.

35 In 1886 for a railway in Maine. Ritchie, "Nation Builder," p. 464.

36 *R.C.M.P. Quarterly*, Vol. 4, No. 1 (July, 1936), p. 70.

37 Initial capitalization was $3 million. Memorandum of Aggreement and Stock Book, Calgary Power Papers, Glenbow-Alberta Archives. In 1911 the Horseshoe Falls Plant was completed with a transmission line to Calgary. In 1912 a new reservoir was built at Lake Minnewanka with a second transmission line to Calgary. In 1914 the Kananaskis Plant went into operation. *Some Facts* (Calgary: Calgary Power Ltd., 1967).

38 See Lord Beaverbrook (Max Aitken), *Friends: Sixty Years of Intimate Personal Relations with Richard Bedford Bennett* (Toronto: William Heinemann, 1959).

39 E. Watkins, *Bennett*, p. 78.

40 Isaac F. Marcosson, "The New Voice of Empire," *The Saturday Evening Post*

41 *The City of Calgary Yearbook* (1919), p. 123.

42 In relation to their total population in the city in 1916, Englishmen and Americans were neither over-represented nor under-represented in the entrepreneurial elite.

43 MacRae, *Alberta*, Vol. 2, pp. 980–1.

44 John Clay, "A Cattleman's Views of Our Future," *Farm and Ranch Review*, Vol. 13, No. 8 (Sept., 1907), p. 11.

45 See T.W. Acheson, "The Social Origins of the Canadian Industrial Elite, 1880–1885," in *Canadian Business History*, ed. by David S. Macmillan (Toronto: McClelland and Stewart, 1972), p. 165.

46 Sproule, *Burns*, pp. 5–6.

47 For the United States see by Ray Allen Billington, in particular *America's Frontier Heritage* (N.Y.: 1966). This principle even applies to central European peasants. Usually only the better-off made it to the western frontier.

48 Mabel Grasley, "The First Time I Saw Pat Burns," *Calgary Herald*, Sept. 18, 1937; and Sproule, *Burns*.

49 See Tony MacUre, "R.B., Calgary's Forgotten Great," *Golden West*, Vol. 2 (Jan.-Feb., 1967); and Beaverbrook, *Friends*. Anecdote from Marcosson, "New Voice", p. 53.

50 Sproule, *Burns*, p. 110.

51 See in particular *Calgary News*

Telegram, Mar. 19, 1912; and Clay, "Cattleman's Views,"

52 He was found not guilty, Sproule, *Burns*, pp. 126–9.

53 Strom, "Eau Claire," p. 7.

54 *Census of Canada 1931*, Vol. 5, Table 13.

55 Strom, "Eau Claire," p. 7.

56 For detail on these and other employer-labour relations see Elizabeth Taraska, "Calgary Craft Union Movement, 1900–1920," (Unpublished M.A. Thesis, University of Calgary, 1975).

57 A 1907 muckraker novel about the Chicago packing plants. For comparison with P. Burns Co. see F.S. Jacobs, "Between Producer and Consumer of Meat," *Farm and Ranch Review*, Vol. 10, No. 21 (Nov. 5, 1914).

58 Only eight of the forty leading entrepreneurs were elected to city council. See also J.M.S. Careless, "Aspects of Urban Life in the West, 1870–1914," *Prairie Perspectives 2*, ed. by A.W. Rasporich and H.C. Klassen (Toronto: Holt, Rinehard and Winston, 1973), p. 34.

59 *City of Calgary Yearbook* (1919), p. 99.

60 *Land of Plenty*, p. 15; *Canadian Annual Review* (1908), p. 147.

61 Excerpts from *Land of Plenty*, pp. 37 and 24; Richardson, *Calgary*, pp. 1–2; *Calgary, The City Phenomenal* (Calgary: Geddes U. Sheffied, 1912), p. 10.

62 *Canadian Annual Review* (1906), p. 268.

63 *City of Calgary Yearbook* (1919), pp. 99–100.

64 Census Manuscript 1901, Brewery Papers, Glenbow-Alberta Archives.

65 *Calgary, Alberta, The Manufacturing*, p. 18.

66 *The Albertan, 100,000*, p. 36.

67 *By-Laws of the City of Calgary from the Date of Incorporation in 1884 to 5th May, 1913 Inclusive* (Calgary: City of Calgary, 1913), by-law no. 1486.

68 Richardson, *Calgary*, back cover.

69 *City of Calgary Yearbook* (1919), pp. 99–100.

70 MacRae, *Alberta*, Vol. 2, p. 623. For other examples see John Blue, *Alberta Past and Present: Historical and Biographical*, Vol. 1–3 (Chicago: Pioneer Historical Publishing, 1924).

71 *The Ranchmen's Club: A Slight Historical Sketch, 1891–1952* (Calgary: Ranchmen's Club, 1953), p. 8.

72 *Officers, Members, Constitution and Rules of the Ranchmen's Club* (Calgary: Ranchmen's Club, 1913), pp. 24–7.

73 Ranchmen's Club: *A Slight Historical Sketch*, p. 13.

74 C.W. Parker, *Who's Who in Western Canada*, Vol. 1 (Vancouver: Canada Press Association, 1911), pp. 107, 150, 215; MacRae, *Alberta*, Vol. 1, p. 515; Sproule, *Burns*, p. 22.

75 Henry C. Klassen, "Life in Frontier Calgary," in *Western Canada Past and Present*, ed. by A.W. Rasporich (Calgary: McClelland and Stewart West, 1975), p. 49. See Klassen for detail on cultural life in Calgary generally.

76 MacUre, "R.B.," p. 15. Watkins, *Bennett*, p. 38.

77 Elizabeth Motherwell, "Past Glories Forgotten," *Calgary Herald*, May 1, 1956; *Calgary Daily Herald*, Mar. 11, 1937.

78 *The Albertan*, May 18, 1911.

79 Mabel E. Jordan, "City of Sandstone. . ." *Calgary Herald*, Mar. 8, 1958.

80 MacRae, *Alberta*, Vol. 1, p. 582. *Calgary Herald*, Aug. 31, 1968.

81 It featured fifteen rooms, a billiard hall, indoor plumbing and running water, hardwood floors

and panels, black walnut pillars, three fireplaces, steam heat, natural gas, irrigated gardens, servants' quarters, two-foot thick walls, brick partitions, a wine cellar, two pantries.

82 *The Albertan*, May 18, 1911.

83 For more detail on the influence of English ranchers see L.G. Thomas, "The Rancher and the City: Calgary and the Cattlemen, 1883–1914," *Transactions of the Royal Society of Canada*, Vol. 6, Series 4 (June, 1968).

84 *Passim*, Brewery Papers, Glenbow-Alberta Archives.

85 Sproule, "Burns," pp. 25–6.

86 Grant MacEwan, *Eye Opener Bob* (Edmonton: Institute of Applied Art, 1957), p. 142.

87 *The Calgary Eye Opener*, Nov. 24, 1906.

88 MacRae, *Alberta*, Vol. 1, p. 566.

89 Sproule, "Burns," p. 123.

The *Bond Of Brotherhood*
And Calgary Workingmen   *Henry C. Klassen*

I am grateful to the Canada Council for grants to support my research.

1 *Alberta Labour News, September 3, 1921*. On the contemporary labor movement, see H.A. Logan, *Trade Unions in Canada* (Toronto, 1948), pp. 48–86, 297–344; Elizabeth Ann Taraska "The Calgary Craft Union Movement, 1900–1920" (Unpublished M.A. Thesis, University of Calgary, 1975); Robert H. Babcock, *Gompers in Canada; A Study in American Continentalism before the First World War* Toronto, 1974).

2 *Albertan*, September 4, 1901.

3 For accounts of these strikes, see Canada, Department of Labour, Sessional Paper No. 36, *Report of the Department of Labour* for the year ending June 30, 1904, pp. 37–41; Canada, *Labour Gazette*, August, 1903, pp. 140–143.

4 *Bond of Brotherhood*, July 17, 1903.

5 *Bond of Brotherhood*, June 26, 1903; July 3, 1903; Ivan Avakumovic, *The Communist Party in Canada*, (Toronto, 1975), pp. 1–21.

6 See *Bond of Brotherhood*, July 3, 1903; September 29, 1902.

7 *Calgary Herald*, December 6, 1902.

8 *Calgary Herald*, December 7, 12, 13, 1903; *Bond of Brotherhood*, December 5, 19, 1903.

9 *Calgary Herald*, December 13, 1904.

10 *Bond of Brotherhood*, January 2, 1904.

11 *Ibid.*, April 30, May 7, 1904.

12 *Ibid.*, June 5, September 12, 1903; *Albertan*, September 4, 1901; *Calgary Herald*, September 2, 1902; September 8, 1903; September 6, 1904.

SELECT BIBLIOGRAPHY

Baine, Richard P.,
  Calgary: An Urban Study (Toronto, 1973).
Barrass, Georgeen,
  "Calgary Jails and Police Force," (Unpublished manuscript, Glenbow-Alberta Institute Archives, 1966).
Baureiss, Gunter A.,
  "The City and the Subcommunity: The Chinese of Calgary," (unpublished M.A. Thesis, University of Calgary, 1971).
Baureiss, Gunter A.,
  "The Chinese Community in Calgary," *Alberta Historical Review*, Vol. 22, no. 2 (Spring 1974), 1–8.
Braden, Thomas B.,
  "When the *Herald* Came to Calgary," *Alberta Historical Review*, Vol. 9, no. 3, (Summer, 1961), 1–4.
Breen, D.H.,
  "The Canadian West and the Ranching Frontier, 1875–1922," (unpublished Ph.D. Thesis, University of Alberta, 1972.
Burns & Elliott,
  Calgary, Alberta: Her Industries and Resources (Calgary, 1974).
Bussard, L.H.,
  "Early History of Calgary," (unpublished M.A. Thesis, University of Alberta, 1935).
Bussard, L.H.,
  "The Establishment of Fort Calgary," *Alberta Historical Review*, Vol. 3, No. 1, (Winter, 1955), 34–41.
Byrne, M.B. Venini,
  From the Buffalo to the Cross (Calgary, 1973).
Careless, J.M.S.,
  "Aspects of Urban Life in the West, 1870–1914," in Anthony W. Rasporich and Henry C. Klassen, eds., *Prairie Perspectives II* (Toronto, 1973).
Carter, David J.,
  Calgary's Anglican Cathedral (Calgary, 1973).
Carter, David J.,
  Where the Wind Blows: A History of the Anglican Diocese of Calgary (Calgary, 1968).

Coppock, K.,
   "Calgary and the Company," *Beaver*, 271, (March, 1941), 42–47.
Cunniffe, Richard,
   Calgary in Sandstone (Calgary, 1969).
Dempsey, Hugh A.,
   "Calgary's First Stampede," *Alberta Historical Review*, Vol. 3, No. 3, (Summer, 1955), 3–13.
Dempsey, H.A.,
   "Calgary-Edmonton Trail," *Alberta Historical Review*, Vol. 7, no. 4, (Autumn, 1959), 16–21.
Dempsey, Hugh A., ed.,
   Men in Scarlet (Calgary, 1974).
Foran, M.L.,
   "The Calgary Town Council, 1884–1895: A Study of Local Government in a Frontier Environment," (unpublished M.A. Thesis, University of Calgary, 1970).
Foran, Max
   "Bob Edwards and Social Reform," *Alberta Historical Review*, Vol. 21, No. 3, (Summer, 1973), 13–17.
Foran, Max,
   "The Travis Affair," *Alberta Historical Review*, Vol. 19, no. 4, (Autumn, 1971), 1–7.
Foran, M.L.,
   "Urban Calgary, 1884–1895," *Social History*, Vol. 5, No. 9, (April, 1972), 61–76.
Fraser, William B.,
   Calgary (Toronto, 1967).
Houghton, J.R.,
   "The Calgary Public School System, 1939–1969: A History of Growth and Development," (unpublished M.Ed. Thesis, University of Calgary, 1971).
Jameson, Sheilagh S.,
   "A Visit to Calgary's New Museum," *Alberta Historical Review*, vol. 13, no. 2, (Spring, 1965), 19–22.
Jameson, Sheilagh S.,
   "The Era of the Big Ranches," *Alberta Historical Review*, vol. 18, no. 1, (Winter, 1970), 1–9.
Kennedy, Fred,
   Calgary Stampede (Calgary, 1964).
Kennedy, N.J.,
   "The Growth and Development of Music in Calgary,

1875–1920," (unpublished M.A. Thesis, University of Alberta, 1952).

Klassen, Henry C.,
"Life in Frontier Calgary," in A.W. Rasporich, ed.,*Western Canada Past and Present* (Calgary, 1975).

Klassen, Henry C.,
"Social Troubles in Calgary in the Mid–1890's," *Urban History Review*, No. 3–74, (February, 1975), 8–16.

Longstreth, T.M.,
The Calgary Challengers (Toronto, 1962).

MacEwan, Grant,
Calgary Cavalcade: From Fort to Fortune (Edmonton, 1958).

MacEwan, Grant,
Eye Opener Bob (Edmonton, 1957).

May, Ernest G. (Mrs.),
"A British Bride-to-be Comes to Calgary," *Alberta Historical Review*, Vol. 6, No. 1, (Winter, 1958), 19–24.

McLeod, N.L.,
"Calgary College 1912–1915: A Study of an Attempt to Establish a Privately Financed University in Alberta." (Unpublished Ph.D. Thesis, University of Calgary, 1970).

McNeill, Leishman,
Tales of the Old Town (Calgary, 1966).

Newinger, Scott,
"The Street Cars of Calgary," *Alberta Historical Review*, Vol. 22, no. 3, (Summer, 1974), 8–12.

Peach, J.S.,
"Calgary—The Foothills City," *Canadian Geographical Journal*, Vol. 53, (November, 1956), 168–181.

Petrigo, Walter,
Petrigo's Calgary (Calgary, 1975).

Rasporich, A.W., ed.,
Western Canada Past and Present, (Calgary, 1975).

Shiels, Bob,
Calgary: A Not Too Solemn Look at Calgary's First 100 Years (Calgary, 1974).

Smith, P.J.,
"Calgary: A Study in Urban Patterns," *Economic Geography*, Vol. 38, (October, 1962), 315–329.

Smith, P.J.,
"Change in a Youthful City: The Case of Calgary, Alberta," *Geography*, Vol. 56, (January, 1971), 1–14.

Stamp, Robert M.,
   School Days A Century of Memories (Calgary, 1975).
Stanley, George F.G.,
   "The Naming of Calgary," *Alberta History*, Vol. 23, no. 3, (Summer, 1975), 7–9.
Stead, R.J.C.,
   "Calgary—City of the Foothills," *Canadian Geographical Journal*, Vol. 36, (April, 1948), 154–170.
Strom, Theodore,
   "With the Eau Claire in Calgary," *Alberta Historical Review*, Vol. 12, No. 3, (Summer, 1964), 1–11.
Taraska, Elizabeth Ann,
   "The Calgary Craft Union Movement, 1900–1920", (unpublished M.A. Thesis, University of Calgary, 1975).
Thomas, L.G.,
   "The Rancher and the City: Calgary and the Cattlemen, 1883–1914," *Transactions of the Royal Society of Canada, VI*, Series IV, Section II, (June, 1968), 203–215.
Trouth, N.S.,
   "Land Development in Calgary," *Habitat*, 5, (May-June, 1962), 14–23.
Ward, Tom,
   Cowtown (Calgary, 1975).
Weadick, Guy,
   "Origin of the Calgary Stampede," *Alberta Historical Review*, Vol. 14, no. 4, (Autumn, 1966), 20–24.
Weston, P.E.,
   "A University for Calgary," *Alberta Historical Review*, vol. 11, no. 3, (Summer, 1963), 1–11.
Weston, P.E.,
   "History of Education in Calgary," (unpublished M.A. Thesis, University of Alberta, 1951).
Wilson, M.,
   "Fossils Bison and Artifacts from the Mona Lisa Site, Calgary, Alberta," Part I: Geology and Artifacts. *Plains Anthropologist*, 19 (63), 1974, 34–45.

Grant MacEwan / J. P. Dickin McGinnis / B.O. K. Reeves / Hugh A. Demps
Simon Evans / Sheilagh Jameson / Ermeline Ference / George F. G. Stanl
T. Thorner / Catherine Philip / Paul Voisey / John Jennings / M. B. Byr
Douglas Coats / Alison Jackson / J. Fraser Perry / David J. Carter / Max For
Robert M. Stamp / J. Brian Dawson